MOVE

MOVE

An American Religion

RICHARD KENT EVANS

OXFORD
UNIVERSITY PRESS

Oxford University Press is a department of the University of Oxford. It furthers the University's objective of excellence in research, scholarship, and education by publishing worldwide. Oxford is a registered trade mark of Oxford University Press in the UK and certain other countries.

Published in the United States of America by Oxford University Press
198 Madison Avenue, New York, NY 10016, United States of America.

© Oxford University Press 2020

All rights reserved. No part of this publication may be reproduced, stored in a retrieval system, or transmitted, in any form or by any means, without the prior permission in writing of Oxford University Press, or as expressly permitted by law, by license, or under terms agreed with the appropriate reproduction rights organization. Inquiries concerning reproduction outside the scope of the above should be sent to the Rights Department, Oxford University Press, at the address above.

You must not circulate this work in any other form and you must impose this same condition on any acquirer.

Library of Congress Control Number: 2019047206
ISBN 978-0-19-005877-7

3 5 7 9 8 6 4 2

Printed by Integrated Books International, United States of America

To those who died.

Contents

Preface — ix
Acknowledgments — xiii
A Note on Sources — xv
A Note on Labels and Names — xvii

   Introduction: Religion Unrecognized — 1

1. Conversions — 15
2. Belief and Practice — 37
3. Progress — 57
4. Pastoral Power — 89
5. Policing Religion — 123
6. Religion on Trial — 153
7. Building a Cult — 175
8. Innocence — 201
9. Unthinkable — 235

   Conclusion: John Africa's Body — 255

Works Cited — 263
Index — 269

Preface

John Africa's body is buried in an unmarked grave beneath an oak tree on the outskirts of a cemetery about thirty miles outside of Philadelphia. Next to him lie the remains of Frank Africa, his biological nephew and spiritual son. An oak tree grows out of Frank's grave as well. The trees are quite old. They were there long before John Africa and Frank Africa's bodies were laid to rest. To MOVE people, the trees contain the life force that John and Frank Africa's bodies once contained. Their carbon, long disintegrated, now permeates those trees. The cemetery is mostly a large open field of well-manicured grass, enclosed by a densely wooded area. I visited in the middle of winter, when the trees were barren and the grass a brownish-gray. The place must have looked beautiful in any other season. Most of the gravestones were in the grassy area, out in the sun, adorned by plastic carnations and stuffed animals. Small American flags lined the pathways that weave through the grounds. John Africa's body is not buried with the rest. His remains lie on the periphery of the cemetery, where the surrounding forest begins to reclaim the open field. John Africa's body is not quite in the cemetery, but not out of it, either.

I drove to the main office and walked inside. One of the staff members had just sold a plot to a couple and was about to show them where it was. The other staff member, Karen, asked if she could help me. I told her I was looking for two graves that I knew were somewhere in the cemetery, but that I didn't know where to look. She asked if I was family. I told her I was not. I told Karen that I was looking for the graves of two men who might be listed under one of a few different names. She asked me the names, and, for a second, I hesitated. I was hoping the other people in the office would leave before I had to say the name out loud. To invoke the name John Africa in Philadelphia is to conjure a ghost.

Karen had heard rumors that John Africa was buried there, but she had never known for sure. There was no record in her computer under any of the possible names. It took a few minutes of digging through the cemetery's antiquated filing system, but, to her surprise, she found the graves. She told me that there are several African Americans of some historical import buried there, and she was accustomed to showing their graves to high school or college students during Black History Month field trips. But, Karen told me, very few people have ever visited John Africa's grave. As far as she knew, no one had ever visited his grave before. She warned me that there wasn't much to see there—it's just a patch of grass. Somewhat embarrassed, I confessed that I still wanted to view the gravesite. I told Karen and the other staff members that I was a historian and that I was writing a book on MOVE. This seemed to ease their confusion a bit. Karen got in her car and asked me to follow her in mine. We drove for no more than a half a mile before she pulled to the side of the road and walked me to the base of the two oak trees. Somewhat apologetically, she told me that this was the final resting place of John Africa and his nephew Frank.

After she showed me the burial site, Karen suggested I talk to a member of the groundskeeping crew who had worked there for decades. We returned to our cars and circled the cemetery until we came upon his truck. The groundskeeper seemed to be taking a break. Karen introduced me as someone who wanted to talk about MOVE. I told the groundskeeper I was a historian, and I asked him to tell me what he remembered about the day of the funeral. He remembered standing several yards away, out of respect, the way the groundskeeping crew would in any funeral service. But most of all, he remembered the service being very small. Only a few dozen people showed to commemorate John and Frank. Many of them were reporters. It was his impression that the more famous mourners in attendance were there primarily to get their pictures in the paper. It seemed strange to him that after such a long and tumultuous history—after all the man had wrought—he would be laid to rest so unceremoniously. He wasn't really sure what else to say. His recollections of John Africa's funeral were not particularly helpful. They were not particularly accurate either. Like many people who lived this history, he didn't know quite how to talk about it.

During our conversation, the groundskeeper had a slight smirk on his face. It was an expression of incredulity; as if the whole MOVE mess—including my desire to visit John Africa's grave—was rather silly. It is a face I have come to recognize when I speak to people about MOVE—especially when I speak to other white people about MOVE. It's the kind of face that seems to be imploring me to offer up how crazy MOVE was so that we can both agree. It's a face that asks for an invitation—so that we can talk about how there's a right way to go about things and a wrong way; about how they were saying some things that were right, but the way they said it was wrong; about how MOVE people were crazy and got what was coming to them. I don't know if this is how the groundskeeper felt—I got the sense I should not ask—but these kinds of sentiments are not uncommon.

People who lived in Philadelphia in the 1970s and 1980s have a sense that they are both narrator and participant in this history. Some people feel that they were victimized by MOVE. They may recall a time when they were harangued on a street corner by MOVE people, or how they knew someone in the Philadelphia Police Department whose life was put at risk because of MOVE. Often, they place themselves in the position of MOVE's neighbors. They imagine how awful it must have been to live near the MOVE house and wonder what could have motivated those people to terrorize their neighbors like that. To be sure, many people maintain a more favorable memory of MOVE, and their numbers are growing. They remember MOVE as a besieged counterculture group that just wanted to be left alone. They tend to blame city officials, whom they imagine as bumbling old men, for the MOVE Bombing. Still others I have spoken to about MOVE feel that the world would be a better place if MOVE, and the MOVE Bombing, were simply forgotten. Almost everyone agrees that the story of MOVE is a tragedy—but tragic for whom?

Because MOVE's history is still so controversial—still so alive—people have often implored me to offer a history of MOVE "from both sides." I understand this request. There are people who believe that John Africa does not deserve to be made into a martyr, that MOVE people are not heroes, and that this story does not deserve to become history. It is a call to keep in mind those who were hurt by MOVE: the neighbors who felt unsafe in their homes, the ex-MOVE people whose experience with the group left them deeply hurt, and, above all, Officer James Ramp, a Philadelphia police officer who died in a shootout with MOVE. There is pain beneath the call to present both sides of this story. I want to acknowledge this pain.

But the story I am going to tell about MOVE is not a story of conflict. This is not a story of heroes and villains. My goal is to understand my subject within its time and place. I privileged MOVE-produced sources, whenever possible, to write this book. I supplemented archival materials with oral history interviews I conducted with MOVE people. When MOVE's account of an event conflicted with other accounts produced by the police, journalists, or MOVE's critics, I assumed, within reason and while maintaining the historian's skepticism, that MOVE was telling the truth. This produced a very different account of MOVE than has yet been written. I set out to write a history that portrayed MOVE in a way that MOVE people would recognize. This is not an attempt to downplay the pain many people feel about MOVE. I did not set out to write a history of MOVE that makes them out to be the good guys. But I also did not set out to write a history of MOVE that makes them out to be the bad guys. This is not a hagiography or a polemic, but a work of history. My goal is to understand a religion, not a conflict. I realize not everyone can approach this story the same way.

This is the story of a man named John Africa who founded a religion called MOVE. It is the story of the people who converted to MOVE and found in the Teachings of John Africa a transformative faith. It is the story of a group of people—most of them Black—who fought, and failed, to gain recognition for their religion. And it is about the people they hurt along the way. This is the story of how John Africa's body got to that gravesite, beneath that oak tree. It is a history that is still very much present. It is a story that still haunts.

Acknowledgments

This story is not mine to share. It has been entrusted to me by the people who lived it, and to them I am profoundly grateful. I especially want to thank Carlos Africa, Debbie Africa, Kareem Howard, Mike Africa, Sr., Mike Africa, Jr., Pam Africa, Ramona Africa, Sue Africa, and Louise Leaphart James. For the last several years, MOVE people have welcomed me with kindness and generosity. I have found them to be a remarkably resilient, warm, dedicated, and—in the face of it all—happy group of people. I hope that MOVE people recognize themselves in this book. Thank you for allowing me to share your story.

A number of colleagues, teachers, and friends have taken the time to shape this project through discussions, reading portions of this manuscript, and helping me think through these ideas. I especially want to thank Rebecca Alpert, Clifford Ando, Talal Asad, Minju Bae, Stephen Bentel, Jason Bivins, James Cook-Thajudeen, Jesse Curtis, Sam Davis, Amy Defibaugh, Anthony Fiscella, Holly Genovese, Philip Hamburger, Stephen Hausmann, Elizabeth Hayes-Alvarez, Melissa Heller, David Hollinger, Andrew Koppelman, Laura Levitt, Vincent Lloyd, Timothy Lombardo, Charles McCrary, Mona Oraby, Terry Rey, Ali Straub, Barry Sullivan, Winnifred Sullivan, Ben Talton, and Heather Ann Thompson. David Watt saw the potential of this project long before I did, and taught me how to be a better scholar and person. Let it be known that he did, in fact, teach someone something.

This project has been made better by the insightful comments I received while presenting this research before audiences at the American Academy of Religion, the Center for the Humanities at Temple University, the Institute for Critical Social Inquiry, the Law and Society Association, and the Yale Debating Law and Religion Conference.

I have had the honor of working with a number of brilliant archivists, without whom this book would not have been possible. Thanks to Don Davis of the American Friends Service Committee Archive, Chris Densmore of the Swarthmore Quaker Library, Lisa Jacobson of the Presbyterian Historical Society, as well as Msgr. Gerard Mesure and Shawn Weldon of the Philadelphia Archdiocesan Historical Research Center. I want to thank the entire staff of the Special Collections Research Center at Temple University, especially John Pettit and Margery Sly.

This project would not have been possible without generous funding from the Philadelphia Foundation, the Institute for Critical Social Inquiry, the Center for the Humanities at Temple University, and the College of Liberal Arts at Temple University.

Above all, I want to thank Bethany Michelle Evans for supporting me, in a thousand ways, through the process of writing this book. She has been my most insightful reader. She accompanied me as I did my fieldwork. She even built the desk on which most of this book was written. I cannot imagine a more supportive partner. Nor can I imagine a better human being.

A Note on Sources

The most important source from which this book draws is *The Guidelines of John Africa*, a document that very few people outside of MOVE have ever seen. For the first few years of MOVE's history, MOVE people tried to share *The Guidelines* as widely as they could. John Africa made plans to publish the manuscript. Around 1976, for reasons that we will explore in this book, MOVE people stopped sharing *The Guidelines* with people outside the group. This posed an obvious problem for me, a historian working in religious studies. To write the kind of book I wanted to write—the kind of book on MOVE that I believe we need—would require a close critical reading of the group's sacred text. I brought these concerns to MOVE people early on in this project. I argued that *The Guidelines of John Africa* are an important document in American religious history, and for the sake of scholarship (my own and that of others) the document should be published or, at the very least, be deposited in an archive.

To write the dissertation upon which this book is based, MOVE people allowed me to read *The Guidelines of John Africa*. This was an imperfect compromise, as the strictures of scholarship forbid me from quoting or citing a source that only I have seen. I relied instead on citing portions of *The Guidelines of John Africa* that were published before the document was closed to outsiders. By my rough estimate, about 20 percent of the manuscript is published elsewhere. For a time, MOVE people ran regular columns featuring the manuscript in *The Philadelphia Tribune*. Other sections of *The Guidelines* were reproduced in a 2013 self-published memoir written by Louise Leaphart-James, a former MOVE person who is still on good terms with MOVE.

As I was revising my dissertation into a book manuscript, I received an email from the National Archives and Records Administration (NARA). When I started this project, I submitted requests through the Freedom of Information Act for any MOVE files created by the Federal Bureau of Investigation, the Bureau of Alcohol, Tobacco and Firearms, the Pennsylvania State Police, and the Philadelphia Police Department. None of these requests was directly successful. However, I came across, quite by chance, a listing in the NARA records of a classified MOVE file that had been created by the FBI and that was stored at the NARA facility in College Park, Maryland. I filed a new request, this time through the NARA. This request was successful. In the summer of 2018, I drove to College Park to retrieve three large PDF files containing a portion of the FBI's MOVE file.

The FBI files shed a great deal of light on the Bureau's role in the MOVE Bombing, which we will get to in due time. The files also contained a stolen manuscript of *The Guidelines of John Africa*. The manuscript was smuggled out of MOVE headquarters by an undercover informant whom the FBI had planted in MOVE, who then made a photocopy and returned the original manuscript. This manuscript is now technically in the public record, although it is nearly impossible to access. From a strictly scholarly standpoint, this manuscript is fascinating. It was stolen, I would estimate, around 1975. This manuscript of *The Guidelines* is under construction. Parts are hand edited, and the organization of the text is still in flux. There were many sections that I had never read before.

There are obvious ethical concerns related to my use of this manuscript. It is a stolen artifact. It should never have left MOVE's provenance. Here's what I—in conversation with MOVE people—have decided to do: on the whole, when I quote passages from *The Guidelines*, the sections I am quoting are already published elsewhere. When I rely on the FBI manuscript of *The Guidelines*, I refrain (as much as possible) from quoting directly, relying instead on generalizations. I make explicit in my endnotes when I use the FBI manuscript, and in all other cases, I cite the published material. I have also shared the FBI manuscript with two scholars who are currently writing on MOVE, and have given a copy of the files to MOVE. I am not sure that I have done the right thing. I still think *The Guidelines of John Africa* should be published, and perhaps they will one day. But, of course, I have no say in that. Out of respect for the wishes of MOVE people, and the wishes of the original author of the document, I have kept direct quotations from the stolen text to a minimum.

A Note on Labels and Names

In this book, I use the phrase "MOVE people" to refer to people who followed the Teachings of John Africa. This is, admittedly, a clunky phrase, especially compared to the more conventional and alliterative "MOVE members." I use "MOVE people" for three reasons. First, it is MOVE's preferred designation, and it has been since the early 1970s. As MOVE and I use the phrase, "MOVE people" refers to followers of the Teachings of John Africa who may or may not be MOVE members. In other words, every MOVE member is a MOVE person, but not every MOVE person is a MOVE member. Second, when MOVE people use the phrase "MOVE members," they do so in a very particular way: it is used to contrast with MOVE supporters, who are people who may or may not follow the Teachings of John Africa but who are generally in accord with MOVE's political or activist aims. In some cases, MOVE supporters are people who follow the Teachings of John Africa, but not at the expense of other religious commitments. Third, people outside of MOVE have, at times throughout MOVE's history, used the phrase "MOVE member" to articulate a claim about MOVE's classification. The use of descriptive labels is data for this project, so for that reason I have adopted what I believe to be a more neutral label.

Writing about groups who share surnames proves difficult. For this book, I have followed a pattern used by scholars of microhistory as well as by scholars of groups, such as the Nation of Islam, who run into similar difficulties. Academic convention calls for naming someone using only the surname on second mention. This presents obvious difficulties when writing about groups that share a last name. For the most part, I use full names on first mention and only first names on subsequent mentions. The exception to this is John Africa, who has never, as best as I can tell, been referred to in MOVE sources as simply "John."

Introduction

Religion Unrecognized

Get up. Birdie Africa awoke on the morning of May 13, 1985, to the rumble of diesel engines outside. It was pitch dark—the sun had not yet begun to rise and there was no electricity—but Birdie could tell that there was already a tense bustle of activity in the house. Birdie's mother, Rhonda Africa, and the other grown-ups hurried about, waking the children, telling them it was time. There was an urgency in her voice. The grown-ups were afraid, but were pretending they weren't. Birdie lay on the floor a moment trying to decide if this was another dream. For the past few weeks, Birdie had been having nightmares where he was being attacked by demons. He was thirteen—too old to still be scared of dreams. But these dreams seemed different. More real. When he asked John Africa what they meant, John Africa said the demons represented the System which was coming to kill them all. Birdie heard the sound of a bullhorn cracking on outside. The voice of Philadelphia Police Commissioner Gregore Sambor said, "Attention, MOVE. This is America. You have fifteen minutes...."[1]

Get up. Birdie had rehearsed this. Pulse racing, he jumped to his feet and joined the other children who had been sleeping next to him. One by one, they grabbed sopping blankets out of buckets where they had been soaking in water. They knew what was going to happen. John Africa had told them days earlier that the System was coming to kill them, just as in their dreams, with bullets, bombs, and fire. Their dreams were real, premonitions, prophecies. Though they were not blood relatives, the other children were, for all intents and purposes, Birdie's siblings. They were the only other children with whom Birdie had ever had sustained interactions.[2]

Still in darkness, Birdie groped toward the stairway leading from the street level to the basement and quickly but carefully descended. The blankets were heavy, and water dripped onto the creaking wooden stairway, making it slippery. He could still hear Sambor's droning outside. Once in the basement, Birdie waited as Conrad Africa helped the other children, one by one, through a hole the grownups had spent the past few weeks laboriously excavating. The hole passed through a fire wall that separated the basement—which faced the street and the System outside—and the garage, which could open into the back alley. If the children were to escape with their lives, out the back alley was the only possibility. In the garage, his eyes beginning to adjust, Birdie looked around at the faces of his MOVE brothers and sisters. There was nine-year-old Tomaso, sisters Zanetta and Tree, thirteen and fourteen, ten-year-old Phil, and twelve-year-old Delisha. They huddled, naked, underneath the blankets, beneath railroad ties that the grownups had brought in to fortify the garage. Birdie was crying. He looked at the other kids. They were crying, too. By the end of the day, they would be dead.

Birdie listened from the garage as Sambor finally finished his announcement. Ramona Africa used a bullhorn to respond. MOVE would not be surrendering. Not long after that, the shooting started. It was the loudest sound Birdie had ever heard. There were three hundred police officers outside, but the guns they were using were not designed for police work. These were M-16s, Uzi submachine guns, Thompson machine guns, sniper rifles—weapons of war. The children, a story below ground, listened to the roar. Bullets whirred overhead, and .50 caliber rounds embedded with a thud into the side of the house. The shooting lasted for ninety minutes. They fired ten thousand rounds into the MOVE house. By the time the shooting was over, the sun was up.[3]

The next several hours felt like an eternity. The fire department pumped thousands of gallons of water into the house, and slowly and steadily, the puddles in the garage began to rise. Birdie was not accustomed to marking the passage of time with numbers, but he did realize he hadn't eaten all day. His stomach hurt. There would be no breakfast. At 10:30 in the morning—about an hour after the shooting stopped—the children in the basement heard a loud explosion at the front of the house. It was a bomb which the police had thrown at the front porch. It succeeded in damaging the porch, but little else. A few minutes later, another explosion—this one much louder, again at the front of the house. This explosion let the light in. Birdie couldn't see, but this bomb had blown the front wall clean off the house. As the smoke cleared, the police who had thrown the bomb saw what it had accomplished: John Africa, the mysterious man who had brought all this trouble upon the people in that house, lay decapitated in the ruins of his makeshift temple.[4]

For the next seven hours, nothing happened. There was no sound from the grown-ups upstairs. The three MOVE men who had been shooting at police—John Africa, Raymond Africa, and Frank Africa, the man Birdie believed to be his father—were dead. The police were still there. Birdie could hear police officers jackhammering the firewalls separating the garage from the neighboring houses. They were opening up a hold to pump tear gas into the garage. The police officers next door could hear the children crying through the wall.

At 5:30 in the afternoon, Birdie heard the sound of a helicopter buzzing closely overhead. Another explosion, this one much stronger. The house shook to its foundation. For a moment Birdie couldn't hear himself crying. His ears didn't work. The grown-ups in the garage—Ramona Africa, Conrad Africa, and Rhonda Africa, Birdie's mother—tried their best to put on a brave face, but Birdie could tell they were as terrified as he was. Even Conrad—the bravest man Birdie ever met—looked scared. That was the scariest part.

After the explosion, the garage began to grow hot. There already wasn't enough air to breathe, even before the tear gas. The water was now up to the children's thighs, and it was hot. It felt like Birdie was boiling. Conrad lit a match. The haze in the air was no longer tear gas, but smoke. The house was on fire. Birdie listened to the grown-ups talk about surrendering to the police outside the back door. They didn't want to, but there was no choice. Conrad decided it was time. He opened the rear garage door with a monkey wrench. When he stuck his head out, the police shot at him. They missed, and Conrad ducked back inside. Maybe they didn't hear him. He opened the latch again and told the police not to shoot, that the children were coming out. They shot at him again. Birdie watched as it dawned on Conrad's face that they were not going to leave the house alive. Maybe if the police saw one of the children, they would hold their fire. Conrad grabbed Tomaso. He was the best choice. His skin was white. Conrad and Tomaso shimmied through the rear door. Conrad carried Tomaso in his arms, and took a few cautious steps toward the police. They shot them. Conrad ran back to the house and threw Tomaso into the garage. Tomaso was screaming. He had a bunch of little holes in his chest. Shotgun pellets. Conrad was bleeding, too. Birdie watched Theresa Africa rock Tomaso back and forth as he screamed into her chest.[5]

The heat was excruciating as the flames roared overhead. Birdie saw Phil's skin start to melt. The adults screamed at each other about what to do next. Finally, Ramona decided that it was better to die in the street than to endure one more minute of burning alive. She threw open the back door and stepped out into the rear alley with her hands up. Nothing happened. She stood there for what felt like an eternity, waiting to be shot. After a few moments, Ramona realized it was finally safe to evacuate. She yelled back at Conrad in the garage to send the children out. One by one, the children ran out of the burning garage. Tree ran first, then Phil. They reached Ramona unharmed, and she helped them climb onto an elevated walkway the grown-ups had constructed in the rear alley. Birdie watched as they ran toward the police to surrender. Then it was Birdie's turn. He bolted toward Ramona, but couldn't make it up on the walkway without a boost. Ramona helped him up, but it took every last bit of strength she had. She crumbled to the ground and fell unconscious. Her skin had melted. Birdie began to cross the walkway, but he lost his balance and fell. He hit his head on the concrete below and fell unconscious too. The fire grew out of control, and by the early morning, the entire block had been destroyed, sixty-four homes in all. The pictures of the burned-out block look like Dresden after the war—spires of ghostly brick chimneys rise out of a bed of smoldering ash.[6]

MOVE formed in 1972 when a small group of people began meeting to discuss the teachings recorded in a manuscript titled *The Guidelines of John Africa*. The author of that document was, until around 1968, known as Vincent Leaphart, a forty-one-year-old, divorced Army veteran. After 1968, Leaphart underwent a transformation. He became John Africa, a prophet, a divinity; someone who is more in touch with God than others. Over the next five years, John Africa built up a following of devoted MOVE people, many of whom lived with him, studied his teachings, both written and embodied, and sought to build an alternative cosmos—one free from the systems of evil that imprison humanity. MOVE was in constant conflict for a variety of reasons—some deserved, some not—that we will explore in this book. One of these conflicts, in 1976, resulted in the death of a MOVE infant, Life Africa. Another conflict, in 1978, resulted in the death of a police officer, Officer James Ramp. These earlier conflicts—and there were many more— were preludes to the MOVE Bombing.

In the months following the MOVE Bombing, a group of law enforcement officials, religious leaders, and community figures called the Philadelphia Special Investigation Commission tried to determine how the MOVE Bombing could have happened. A chapter of this book is devoted to thinking about the questions the MOVE Commission asked, and the story that it told about the MOVE Bombing. For now, suffice it to say that the MOVE Commission collected twenty-nine linear feet of empirical information about the MOVE Bombing, and wrote a report that laid out, in unflinching detail, the story of the MOVE Bombing. But the MOVE Commission did not try to answer the big question—*how could this have happened?* It was not that they deflected from answering this question; the question itself was, at the time, too big.

In the years since, the question has grown pressing, and more rhetorical. A few books have been written on the MOVE Bombing, all of which seek, to some degree or another, to explain how the MOVE Bombing could have happened. Some are quite good, but none, I found, answered the question to my satisfaction. Every May 13th, there is a flurry of media coverage marking another anniversary of the MOVE Bombing. In recent years, these stories increasingly wonder why no one, especially outside of Philadelphia but increasingly in Philadelphia as well, has heard this story. I worry that as the MOVE Bombing slips into history, the urgency of this story will be lost, and the events of May 13, 1985, will be relegated to a tragic, inexplicable episode in our nation's racist past. What is it about this group—which never numbered more than a few dozen—that inspired the US government, at all three levels, to spend hundreds of thousands of man hours, and millions of dollars, working toward its destruction? What was it about this man's teachings—the Teachings of John Africa—that would inspire people to such awe-inspiring, life-destroying levels of devotion? What is it about this group of people that holds them together today in the face of an unrelenting history of oppression? Above all, I wondered still, *how could this have happened?*

The answer to this question that I find the most persuasive was not delivered before the MOVE Commission. Nor has it made its way into any of the books. But it comes from someone who would know—Laverne Sims. Laverne Sims had once gone by the name Laverne Africa. She had been in MOVE since the very beginning. Though she had grown apart from the group in the years preceding the MOVE Bombing, her heart was still with them. John Africa was her brother. All five of her children were MOVE people, at one time or another, though none died in the bombing. Three of them had left the group in recent years. The other two were spared because they were serving thirty to one hundred years in prison, along with four other MOVE people, for the murder of a police officer seven years earlier. MOVE was—literally and figuratively—her family. Her answer to this question—*how could this have happened*—was one of the first I came across as I began to try to answer this question for myself. Her answer surprised me. If she was right, the entire history of the MOVE Bombing would have to be rewritten. According to Laverne Sims, MOVE had been killed because they were a religion.

I discovered Laverne Sims's explanation for why the MOVE Bombing happened on one of my first days researching this story. I had decided to try to answer these questions for myself, first by digging through the archives the MOVE Commission left behind, then through other archives around the country that held bits and pieces of evidence. In the archive built by the MOVE Commission there is a letter from Laverne Sims to the MOVE Commission. The letter was, she wrote, a statement she planned to deliver during her public testimony but was unable to. It is a remarkable text, filled with excerpts from *The Guidelines of John Africa*, prophecies of divine retribution, and lamentations for all she had lost—for all that had been taken from her.

In the letter, Laverne recounts, in excruciating detail, twelve years of "religious persecution"—all of which, she wrote, was because MOVE was "unfamiliar, misunderstood . . . branded unjustly." For their entire history, Laverne wrote, MOVE people were "called lunatics, cults, radicals, and crazy. Called dirty, nasty, filthy, and insane." Laverne wanted the MOVE Commission to know, as human beings, the people who had been killed in the MOVE Bombing. She wanted them to know that MOVE people had been "faithful and just. Lawful, Righteous and Godly, without exception, without allowance." She wanted them to know that MOVE people would never "sell out their God" or "abandon their belief, their Religion." In the letter, Laverne explained that the city dropped the bomb because MOVE followed "the law of God rather than Man." Because MOVE people paid ultimate allegiance to their religious beliefs and not the government, she argued, "their lives were snuffed out." To her, MOVE was destroyed because they were a religion unrecognized.[7]

Laverne Sims was not the only MOVE person to suggest that MOVE was a religion. The more I began to dig through the MOVE archive, the more it became clear that MOVE people believed, from the very early days of the group, that their leader, John Africa, was a prophet, that his teachings, both written and embodied, had miraculous effects, and that the shared beliefs and practices that constituted MOVE were religious in nature. To MOVE people, John Africa was capable of performing miracles, healing the sick and injured, and communicating on behalf of the divine. John Africa inspired a remarkable level of devotion in his followers, who called themselves his "disciples." He was, according to one MOVE person who was interviewed after she left the group, "like a messiah." When asked to compare John Africa to Jesus, another MOVE person scoffed, "Jesus Christ—who is he? We're talking about John Africa, a person who is a supreme being, who will never die and will live on forever." MOVE people, to this day, proclaim John Africa as "a religious symbol and a person who is better than anyone else in the world and better than anyone who has ever lived up to the present time." The Teachings of John Africa were the exclusive truth, the path to redemption, and the ultimate reality. MOVE, to those inside the group, was a religion.[8]

To many people outside the group—including the police, the court system, MOVE's neighbors, and other religious groups—MOVE was anything but a religion. A Quaker group classified MOVE as "a street gang with a thin veneer of politico-religious philosophy." A group of MOVE's neighbors who were hostile toward MOVE's presence in the neighborhood considered MOVE an "armed terrorist" organization. A lawyer representing Birdie Africa rejected the premise that his client was a former "MOVE member" on the basis that the label presupposes that a child can belong to a political group. In the lawyer's estimation, Birdie "was no more a member of MOVE than a child of Republican or Democratic parents would be styled by a particular party label." A judge asked to decide whether MOVE was a religion concluded that MOVE was "independent of religion and with separate and distinct purposes." Even liberal religious groups sympathetic to MOVE preferred to understand MOVE in political terms, calling them a "revolutionary organization that advocates a return to nature and spurns all social conventions." At almost every turn, MOVE, a group that was desperate to be recognized as a religion, found themselves categorized as secular. As one MOVE person put it, "they just spit all over our religion like our religion didn't count."[9]

At first blush, MOVE's classification—the question of whether or not MOVE was a religion—seems trivial in light of what befell the group on May 13, 1985. My task in this book is to prove that it was not. It is commonplace to think about religion as something that exists in the world. It is commonplace, that is, to think that some groups, beliefs, practices, texts, and experiences are, because of their characteristics, "religious." If this were true—if "religion" were something that existed in the world—MOVE would have fit the bill. It has a sacred text and a prophetic leader. It is both a sophisticated belief system and a set of practices. It deals with ultimate matters of life, death, evil, and the divine. I have yet to come across a definition of religion—sophisticated or simplistic, old or new—that MOVE does not positively match.

Why, if MOVE seemed to be a religion, did people outside of MOVE decide that it was not? The problem with defining religion is that the category—however we might define it—has no stable meaning. For these reasons, critical scholars of religion have begun looking beyond beliefs and practices, focusing instead on the power structures and discursive formations that allow those of us who live in the modern West to imagine that *religion* is a discreet realm of social life. *Religion*, we now know, is not something out there in the real world. It is not, one might say, an observable reality. Instead, religion is a category of social life, unique to the modern West, that is inseparable from the power that constitutes it. The central question in the academic study of religion is not *what makes this religious?* or *what is the nature of religion?* Instead, in the words of Talal Asad, the central question facing the academic study of religion is "*how does power create religion?*"[10] Asking this question through the history of MOVE tells us a great deal about MOVE, about what happened to MOVE on May 13, 1985, and about the category of religion in the modern United States.[11]

This book seeks to accomplish two things. On one hand, this book is a religious history of MOVE. The first three chapters of this book narrate the history of MOVE from the group's emergence in the late 1960s through 1976. Using the methodologies of religious studies, including ethnographic research, textual criticism, and religious history, I offer a systematic study of MOVE's beliefs and practices, past and present. Readers looking for answers to the questions *what was MOVE?* and *what do MOVE people believe?* will find them in these first three chapters.

On the other hand, this book is also—even *mainly*—a book about power. Religion, as MOVE's story illustrates with devastating clarity, is not something that exists in the world as a matter of fact. Religion is a category of social life carved out from the rest and set aside. It is a legal category that bestows certain privileges (and protections) from the state. And religion is a category that, in MOVE's case, has very little to do with a group's characteristics. Even though MOVE had all the recognizable hallmarks shared by groups typically classified as religions—a sacred text, a set of beliefs about ultimate things, a set of practices that they described as religious, even a prophetic leader—and even though MOVE people, themselves, were certain that MOVE was a religion, MOVE people still found themselves classified as secular. MOVE is a religion that cannot be fully understood apart from debates over their classification. That MOVE people believed themselves to be a religion simply did not matter to those with the power to define lived experience as religious or secular. So, Chapters 4 through 9 of this book are a study of power; an observation of the mechanisms of religion in the modern United States. Though MOVE remains the focus of the book, these chapters are also about the social actors—in MOVE's case, judges, police officers, journalists, neighbors, and religious leaders—who decided, at different times, at different places, and for different ends, that MOVE was not a religion.[12]

Chapter 4, "Pastoral Power," highlights the role that representatives of religious authority played in determining MOVE's classification. From 1977 to 1978, the Philadelphia Police Department established a blockade around the MOVE house. Eventually, this blockade became a starvation blockade, when the mayor, Frank Rizzo, determined the best way to end the standoff was to starve MOVE people into surrendering. During this standoff, respected religious leaders representing various faith traditions negotiated between MOVE and the city. These religious leaders initially came to MOVE's defense. Some of them believed that MOVE was a religion, and that the city's actions threatened religious freedom in the city. As the negotiations wore on, however, MOVE lost their initial support. The religious leaders who previously defended MOVE decided that MOVE was not, in fact, a religion and sided with the city. In doing so, these religious leaders articulated a series of claims about the nature of "true religion" to explain why MOVE was not, in their view, a religion.

Chapter 5, "Policing Religion," focuses on the role that policing plays in classifying groups, beliefs, and practices as either religious or secular. Almost from the very beginning of the group, MOVE was under surveillance from the city police's extensive intelligence apparatus. By the early 1980s, the Bureau of Alcohol, Tobacco, and Firearms (ATF), the Federal Bureau of Investigation (FBI), the Pennsylvania State Police, and the Secret Service had all targeted MOVE for surveillance, infiltration, or prosecution. To be sure, MOVE brought much of this attention on themselves. But their claims to religious legitimacy were met, early on, with the presumption of criminality. One reason MOVE was not allowed to be a religion was because MOVE never existed apart from government policing and surveillance.

Chapter 6, "Religion on Trial," highlights the social actors who have perhaps the most outsized influence on religious classification in the modern United States: judges. In 1981, MOVE's claims to religious legitimacy received their day in court. A MOVE person, Frank Africa, who was then incarcerated in a Pennsylvania state prison, requested from the prison a religious accommodation for his MOVE diet. The prison denied his request, and Frank appealed to the Third Circuit Court of Appeals. Before the court could decide on Frank's request, the judges had to first determine whether or not MOVE was a religion.

Chapter 7, "Building a Cult," studies how and why Americans in the 1960s, 1970s, and 1980s came to believe that some religions were "cults," and interrogates the assumptions that underlay that category. After 1981, many people outside the group began to suspect that MOVE was a cult. This belief had less to do with transformations within MOVE, I argue, than it did with transformations in American culture. Americans began to think of MOVE as a cult because scholars, journalists, and their government taught them to.

Finally, Chapter 8, "Innocence," tells the story of the MOVE Bombing. In the thirty-five years since the MOVE Bombing, writers, artists, and filmmakers have struggled to make sense of what happened on May 13, 1985. Overall, they have failed to do so. I do not expect I will succeed. My main contribution to our understanding of the MOVE Bombing is this: it is not exceptional and it is not inexplicable. Such acts of state violence have happened many times before, and there is no reason to suspect that they will not happen again. Rather than looking at the MOVE Bombing as an inexplicable event, we should look at it as a perfectly normal behavior of the secular state. The MOVE Bombing, I argue, makes sense only when we see it as the logical extension of secularism; as the secular state preempting "illegitimate" religious violence with "legitimate" state violence.

In Chapter 9, "Unthinkable," I trace the process by which the MOVE Bombing evolved from event to history to memory. As in the construction of any historical narrative, the asking of some questions precluded the asking of others. And those with the power to shape the process of historical construction ensured that some stories were highlighted and others suppressed. For many, the MOVE Bombing is unthinkable, and for this reason, many of the story's details—and often the story itself—have been forgotten.

This book is a study of how religion is manufactured, policed, imagined, and defended in the modern United States. It traces the history of one group, MOVE, from its inception in the late 1960s to the present in order to illustrate how the category of religion functions in the modern United States. Reconstructing MOVE's relationship to the category of religion confirms what scholars of religion have long maintained—religion is constructed. But the history of MOVE shows us that we must not mistake religion's constructedness—and at times its capriciousness—for meaninglessness. MOVE people struggled from the group's beginning to achieve religious legitimacy. They fought unsparingly for over a decade to prove that they had a religion and that what was happening to them was religious persecution. They lost that fight. We cannot know how their history would have played out had they won. I cannot claim that the MOVE Bombing would not have happened if everyone had agreed that MOVE was a religion. There are, after all, plenty of examples of state violence against groups deemed religious. But I will argue that the category of religion mattered a great deal to MOVE people, and that they believed that being recognized as a religion was essential to their survival. This is, ultimately, the most important lesson MOVE's history has to teach us: religion is a category of privilege, the ramifications of which, in MOVE's case, were literally life and death.

Who decides what is—and what is not—a religion? The answer to this question is power; the power of the state, the power of those already within established religious traditions, and the power of our shared cultural assumptions about what constitutes true religion. The history of MOVE demonstrates with unusual clarity the mechanisms—the human agency—through which the category of religion is created, reinforced, and policed in the modern United States. To ask whether MOVE was a religion is to miss the point. The better question to ask is why they were not. And the answer to that question tells us a great deal about what we imagine religion to be.[13]

* * *

Birdie Africa awoke late in the evening after the MOVE Bombing in a hospital bed. He was burned over much of his body, and it hurt. He breathed through a respirator. The police were there to ask him questions. Birdie learned that night that only he and Ramona had survived. There had been thirteen people in that house. Eleven were dead. John Africa had died. So had Frank Africa, the man Birdie thought was his father. Birdie's mother, Rhonda Africa, was dead. Conrad and Raymond Africa were dead. All the other kids were dead. Even though Birdie saw Phil and Tomaso running for safety, their burned remains were found in what was left of the garage, a discrepancy that remains one of the enduring mysteries of the MOVE Bombing. Zanetta, Tree, and Delisha Africa died there as well.[14]

It has been thirty-five years since May 13, 1985—the day of the MOVE Bombing. Thirteen people died. They were all surnamed Africa, and they belonged to a religion called MOVE. *How could this have happened?*

Notes

1. Video of Testimony of Michael Ward, Philadelphia Special Investigation Commission, Series 1, Special Collections Research Center, Temple University Libraries, Philadelphia.

2. Transcript of Testimony of Michael Ward, Box 20, Folder 1, Philadelphia Special Investigation Commission, Series 1, Special Collections Research Center, Temple University Libraries, Philadelphia, PA.
3. Philadelphia Police Department Homicide Division, Investigation Interview Record, May 14, 1985, Box 63, Folder 9, PSIC; Philadelphia Police Department Homicide Division, Investigation Review Record, May 18, 1985, Box 63, Folder 9, PSIC; Ralph Teti to William Lyton, July 9, 1985, Box 63, Folder 7, PSIC [enclosure]; Philadelphia Police Department Civil Affairs Unit, Confidential Police Report, May 15, 1985, Box 63, Folder 9, PSIC; Philadelphia Police Department Juvenile Aid Division, Interview of Birdie Africa, undated, Box 63, Folder 9, PSIC.
4. Philadelphia Special Investigation Commission, The Findings, Conclusions, and Recommendations of the Philadelphia Special Investigation Commission, PSIC.
5. Michael Ward Testimony; Philadelphia Police Department Homicide Division, Investigation Interview Record, May 14, 1985, Box 63, Folder 9, PSIC; Philadelphia Police Department Homicide Division, Investigation Review Record, May 18, 1985, Box 63, Folder 9, PSIC; Ralph Teti to William Lyton, July 9, 1985, Box 63, Folder 7, PSIC [enclosure]; Philadelphia Police Department Civil Affairs Unit, Confidential Police Report, May 15, 1985, Box 63, Folder 9, PSIC; Philadelphia Police Department Juvenile Aid Division, Interview of Birdie Africa, undated, Box 63, Folder 9, PSIC.
6. Ibid.
7. Laverne Sims to William H. Brown III, November 9, 1985, Box 7, Folder 20, PSIC; Testimony of Laverne Sims, Ex-MOVE Member," Box 19, Philadelphia Special Investigation (MOVE) Commission Records, Special Collections Research Center, Temple University, Philadelphia, PA; Laverne Sims to William H. Brown III, November 9, 1985, Box 7, Folder 20, PSIC.
8. Interview with Gerald Africa, Box 8, Folder 1, PSIC.
9. "Proposal for Project to Facilitate Work against Police Abuse in Philadelphia," July 1977, Box: General Admin, 1978, Information Services Dept., Folder 3436, American Friends Service Committee Archives, Philadelphia, PA; "Statement by David Shrager on Behalf of Michael Moses Ward," Box 7, Folder 5, PSIC; "Laverne Sims to William H. Brown III," November 9, 1985, PSIC.
10. Talal Asad, *Geneologies of Religion: Discipline and Reasons of Power in Christianity and Islam* (Baltimore, MD: Johns Hopkins University Press, 1993), 15–24. Emphasis added.
11. Within the field of American Religion, the move away from religious as a *sui generis* phenomenon has been, in my view, not as complete as we'd like to think. For an illuminating entrée into this debate, see William E. Arnal and Russell T. McCutcheon, *The Sacred Is the Profane: The Political Nature of "Religion"* (New York: Oxford University Press, 2013). My frequent invocation of "true religion" throughout this book draws from Robert A. Orsi, *Between Heaven and Earth: The Religious Worlds People Make and the Scholars Who Study Them* (Princeton, NJ: Princeton University Press, 2005), 188 and John Lardas Modern, *Secularism in Antebellum America: With Reference to Ghosts, Protestant Subcultures, Machines, and Their Metaphors; Featuring Discussions of Mass Media, Moby-Dick, Spirituality, Phrenology, Anthropology, Sing*

Sing State Penitentiary, and Sex with the New Motive Power (Chicago: University of Chicago Press, 2011), 7–12.

12. Jonathan Z. Smith, *Relating Religion: Essays in the Study of Religions* (Chicago: University of Chicago Press, 2004), 179–196 and 375–390; Tisa Wenger, *Religious Freedom: The Contested History of an American Ideal* (Chapel Hill: University of North Carolina Press, 2017); Tisa Wenger, *We Have a Religion: The 1920s Pueblo Indian Dance Controversy and American Religious Freedom* (Chapel Hill: The University of North Carolina Press, 2009);

13. Saba Mahmood, *Religious Difference in a Secular Age: A Minority Report* (Princeton, NJ: Princeton University Press, 2016), 1–28; Isaac Weiner, *Religion Out Loud: Religious Sound, Public Space, and American Pluralism* (New York: New York University Press, 2014), 5–9.

14. Philadelphia Police Department Homicide Division, Investigation Interview Record, May 14, 1985, Box 63, Folder 9, PSIC; Philadelphia Police Department Homicide Division, Investigation Review Record, May 18, 1985, Box 63, Folder 9, PSIC; Ralph Teti to William Lyton, July 9, 1985, Box 63, Folder 7, PSIC [enclosure]; Philadelphia Police Department Civil Affairs Unit, Confidential Police Report, May 15, 1985, Box 63, Folder 9, PSIC; Philadelphia Police Department Juvenile Aid Division, Interview of Birdie Africa, undated, Box 63, Folder 9, PSIC.

1
Conversions

In the fall of 1968, thirty-seven-year-old Vincent Leaphart watched mournfully from his apartment in West Philadelphia as the world burned around him. His sparse studio, which he had rented after his divorce two years earlier, had become his refuge from the world. He culled his possessions, including the slick tailored suits that had once reflected his jovial gregariousness. Increasingly, it seemed as if those suits had been worn by another man who had lived another life. Vincent was in the process of putting that life behind him. Vincent Leaphart had lived a working-class life. He had dropped out of school at a young age, worked hard, served his country in Korea, gotten married, gotten divorced. When he ascended the stairs to that apartment, he escaped a world that had become disordered. Vincent Leaphart was becoming a new man, a special man, a man who could point humankind out of its chaos.

Vincent Leaphart was certainly not the only American beginning to suspect that the social order that had existed since World War II was collapsing. Across the nation—from Newark to Berkeley, Philadelphia to the Pentagon, Kent State to Watts—Americans took to the streets, stormed government buildings, and blockaded college campuses, furious that their lives seemed to matter so little and that no one in positions of power seemed to care. Vietnam was at its bloodiest; the Tet Offensive, in January, disabused Americans of their notion that the enemy in Vietnam was "on the run," as the government insisted. In April, Martin Luther King, Jr., was killed, sparking more riots across the nation. In June, John F. Kennedy's brother, Robert, was assassinated, and with him the hope for a new politics that promised a way out of "the terrible alienation of the best and bravest of our young." By "young," Kennedy meant the half-million young men President Lyndon Johnson sent to Vietnam, including Vincent's brother Fonnie. Johnson, who had just been elected in a landslide victory four years earlier, was crumbling under the weight of the war. Some in his own party questioned his sanity. In August, the Democratic National Convention in Chicago descended into chaos as tanks rolled through the streets. This generation was promised a Great Society. It seemed, to Vincent Leaphart, that society was broken.[1]

When he finally emerged from his apartment in late 1968, it wasn't as Vincent Leaphart anymore. He was now a prophet named John Africa. He brought with him a text, incomplete but growing—his ongoing revelation. John Africa's solution to the world's disorder was not salvation. He did not promise heaven. He offered no escape from a fallen world, only a promise that the world wasn't supposed to be this way. The people who found their way to MOVE were people who had given up on finding solutions to the world's problems. They found in the Teachings of John Africa an alternative reality and a reordered cosmos. They found themselves created anew. MOVE provided them a way of embodying the sacred in the here and now, and it allowed them to live ultimate truths by defying the ways of the world. The men and women who converted to MOVE found in the Teachings of John Africa a way of opting out of an irredeemably evil society without living an apathetic life. MOVE was a religion of redemption.

Vincent Lopez Leaphart was born in West Philadelphia on July 26, 1931. Vincent's parents, Frederick Eugene Leaphart and Lennie Mae Leaphart, had only recently arrived in Philadelphia. In the late 1920s, Vincent's parents and much of their extended families had moved from Georgia to Philadelphia. In doing so, the Leapharts joined an exodus of one and a half million African Americans who moved from the Deep South to the industrial cities of the North in the interwar years—a demographic shift that historians call the Great Migration. There were many reasons for the Leaphart family to make the move. The prolonged stagnation of the Southern agrarian economy and restricted immigration from Asia and Europe meant a steady supply of high-paying jobs in the industrial economies of the North. But many African Americans who participated in the Great Migration moved North to escape the resurgence of state-sanctioned racial violence in the Deep South. Jim Crow laws had restricted the civil liberties and political rights of African Americans in the Deep South since the end of Reconstruction. And of course, racial violence had always been a hallmark of the African American experience. But in the interwar period, racial violence became more public, more institutionalized, and more prevalent than any time since the defeat of the Confederacy. This was particularly true in the Leaphart family's home state of Georgia. The second Ku Klux Klan formed in Atlanta in 1915, receiving an official charter from the state of Georgia, and became in the 1920s one of the most powerful political organizations in the United States. The Klan was but one symptom of a much deeper disease. The Deep South in the interwar years was an apartheid state, and many Southern governments were founded upon a commitment to white supremacy, enforced by endemic extralegal violence. From 1910 to 1919, the state of Georgia alone averaged more than one lynching per month.[2]

The promise of economic prosperity in the North turned out to be illusory for the Leapharts, as it did for many African Americans. In 1930, the year before Vincent's birth, Fred and Lennie Leaphart lived in a cavernous, wooden-frame house in the Mantua section of West Philadelphia. Fred and Lennie shared the house with seventeen other people, including their firstborn son, Fred Jr., their two daughters, Lillian and Louise, extended family, and the occasional boarder. Eventually, the extended family members moved out of the home, leaving it to Fred, Lennie, and their growing family. The house was drafty, built more like a barn than a home. Winters were especially harsh. The windows were poorly insulated, so the Leaphart children stuffed newspapers into the cracks to keep out the cold. The house was heated by a coal furnace in the basement, but it worked poorly and coal was expensive. More often, the family heated the house by burning paper and scrap wood in the pot-belly stove in the kitchen. It was a terribly noisy house. It was less than a block from the busy railroad junction connecting the east-west Pennsylvania Railroad with the north-south New York rail line. The zoo was less than a quarter of a mile away, and on quiet nights, the Leaphart children drifted off to sleep to the sound of lions roaring.[3]

Vincent was the fourth of Lennie and Fred's children, and they would go on to have six more through the 1930s. Each new mouth to feed made it harder to make ends meet. The Great Depression hit African Americans the hardest, and the Leapharts were no exception. Fred worked hard to support his growing family. He worked in construction for a time and then found a stable living as a paperhanger. The pay was modest but the work was stable, and Fred took great pride in mastering the craft. As Vincent got older, Fred took him and his brother Fonnie along to learn the trade. All the children pitched in. The older daughters helped Lennie with the cooking, ironing, cleaning, and child care. Some of the older boys worked with their father hanging wallpaper. Vincent and Fonnie made a little money on the side shining shoes.[4]

Like many African American families in the 1930s, the Leapharts found spiritual belonging, material assistance, and community in the Black Church. The Great Migration transformed African American religion in the industrial cities of the North. Many Southern migrants belonged to Baptist, Pentecostal, and charismatic denominations. They brought these Southern religious folkways with them, but some Southern migrants found established congregations in the North unwelcoming. As a result, many migrants recreated their Southern congregations as "storefront churches." As small businesses failed during the Great Depression, Southern migrants, and some Northerners, rented out former storefronts to house their reconstructed congregations. When Vincent was a young child, his family joined one of these upstart storefront congregations, led by an itinerant revivalist named Rev. John H. Williams. The church, which became Fifty Ninth Street Baptist Church, was made up of recent migrants and retained its Southern character throughout the first half of the twentieth century.[5]

Though Vincent's childhood was undeniably shaped by his upbringing in the Black Church, the Philadelphia he grew up in was rich with religious diversity. Joining Southerners in their exodus north were millions of migrants from the Caribbean and South America, many of whom brought their own religious traditions, notably Roman Catholicism and various forms of African-derived religions such as Santería, Vodoun, and Candomblé. The religious milieu of the Great Migration also gave rise to inventive religious traditions in Philadelphia—some within the confines of Afro-Protestantism and some without. In 1924, an African American woman named Ida B. Robinson, who had recently relocated to Philadelphia from Florida, founded a pathbreaking holiness-Pentecostal denomination built around the ordination of women called Mount Sinai Holy Church of America. The Nation of Islam and other Black Muslim groups were prominent in Philadelphia. Father Divine, leader of the Peace Mission Movement who taught that he was God in the flesh, headquartered his movement in Philadelphia in 1942, when Vincent was eleven years old. Although there is no direct connection between the Leaphart family and the Peace Mission Movement, there are connections between Father Divine's teachings and those of John Africa. As Judith Weisenfeld has argued, Father Divine's followers "understood themselves as liberated altogether from what he taught was the negative construct of race"—a theology that John Africa would adopt in the late 1960s.[6]

Vincent's childhood was marked with tragedy. In 1942, Vincent's older brother, Frederick Jr., was killed in a gang shooting. Frederick Jr., whom the family called Fe, was only sixteen when he died. It is unclear whether Fe was in a gang. His family contended that the shooter mistook him for another boy. Lennie and Frederick Leaphart sunk into a deep depression at the loss of their firstborn, from which Lennie never recovered. She died in 1951, when she was only forty-three.[7]

Vincent, like his siblings, attended the local public school. After completing the fifth grade, Leaphart was diagnosed with a learning disability and was transferred to a school that educated "orthogenically backward" students. His siblings and his friends knew what it meant to be sent to the "O.B. Class." They joked that O.B. stood for "odd ball." Whenever Vincent got into a tiff with one of his siblings, they knew just how to cut him down: *"you in the OB class."* The term "orthogenically backward" refers to the pseudoscientific theory of orthogenesis, a strain of thought within evolutionary biology that wielded considerable influence from the 1880s to the 1930s. Proponents of the theory of orthogenesis argued that some force—God, or an ideal master race—guided evolution, not natural selection. Within the context of education, orthogenetic theories suggested that students like Vincent had not fully evolved.[8]

Vincent's disability was a source of great shame for him. His siblings were embarrassed that the neighborhood children knew Vincent went to the O.B. school. According to Vincent's sister, Louise Leaphart James, "nobody wanted a member of their family going" to the school "where 'dumb' kids were sent."[9] Though he performed very poorly on IQ tests as a child, it seems unlikely that those tests were accurate measurements of his intelligence. Those who grew up with Vincent remembered him being just as smart as anyone else—and anyone who has read his writings can attest to his high intelligence. He struggled, however, to read and write throughout his life. As an adult, Vincent received informal tutoring to develop his reading and writing skills, and probably developed a rudimentary ability. He preferred, however, to let others read to him and write for him. If Vincent had received a diagnosis today, he might have been diagnosed with a learning disability, rather than an intellectual disability. As it was, he dropped out of school when he turned sixteen, having completed only the fifth grade.[10]

For Americans of Vincent Leaphart's generation who came of age at midcentury, war was a constant presence. Vincent was eleven years old when the Japanese air force attacked Pearl Harbor, and he had just turned fourteen when the United States dropped atomic bombs on Hiroshima and Nagasaki. His brothers Wayne, Marv, Fonnie, and Dennis served in the military. Dennis Leaphart was seriously wounded in Vietnam. In 1952, when he was twenty, Vincent Leaphart was drafted into the United States Army and sent to fight in Korea. He was an infantryman and served on the frontlines in the last year of the war. Vincent received an honorable release from active duty in October 1954, having served his full two-year commitment.[11]

Vincent Leaphart's tour of duty in Korea was, in light of his later prophetic career, one of the most formative experiences of his life. By the time Vincent was drafted, the war had become almost incomprehensibly brutal, even by the standards of twentieth-century warfare. As American forces pushed across the Yalu River to take the fighting to North Korea, they were met with a devastating offensive from the Korean People's Army and their Chinese allies. Sino-Korean forces pinned down General Douglas MacArthur's marines, stopping their advance. In return, MacArthur ordered a massive airstrike targeting every "installation, factory, city, and village" in his path. The airstrikes decimated thousands of square miles. Men, women, and children—entire villages—were wiped off the face of the earth. A war correspondent for the *New York Times* toured the remains of one of the villages in MacArthur's path and saw its former residents in the "exact postures they held when the napalm struck—a man about to get on his bicycle, fifty boys and girls playing in an orphanage, a housewife strangely unmarked, holding in her hand a page torn from a Sears-Roebuck catalogue."[12]

When Vincent Leaphart landed in Korea, the war had become a stalemate. Truman had threatened to use the new hydrogen bomb should the Chinese or the Soviets exacerbate the conflict. This was enough to force all parties to the negotiation table. For two years, negotiations progressed in fits and starts while coalition troops held an uneasy front across the 38th parallel. As the diplomats talked, the aerial assaults on North Korea continued. By August 1951, one observer remarked that there were "no more cities in North Korea."[13] This was a bit of an exaggeration, but only slightly so. By the end of the war, the United States–led coalition had destroyed between 40 and 90 percent of all towns and cities in North Korea. It is quite likely that Vincent Leaphart witnessed the destruction of the war firsthand. It would have been nearly impossible for an infantryman to spend a year in Korea without witnessing civilians maimed by napalm, forests reduced to ash, and bodies piled in mass graves. When John Africa wrote about the senselessness of war, he likely had in mind what Vincent Leaphart had witnessed in Korea. The Korean War was a war of ideas—of abstractions, political theories, and grand strategies—ideas which the men on the ground didn't fully understand or particularly care about. The Korean War was a performance for an audience in Moscow and Beijing. It was a war meant to project American power over the postwar order and to halt the march of Communism in Asia. It was, from the American perspective, about anything other than Korea and Koreans.[14]

After his discharge from the Army, Vincent spent the next decade splitting his time between Philadelphia, Atlantic City, and New York—wherever he could find work. In 1961, Vincent Leaphart was living in Atlantic City, and he met and married a woman named Dorothy Clark. Vincent and Dorothy's marriage was rocky and, at times, violent. They could not have children, which was a great disappointment to them both. The couple moved back to Philadelphia in the mid-1960s, around the same time Dorothy began following the teachings of a religious movement called the Kingdom of Yahweh.

The Kingdom of Yahweh was founded by Reverend Joseph Jeffers in 1935. Jeffers's movement initially departed from his Baptist upbringing by combining the Seventh-Day Adventist belief that Saturday, not Sunday, was the proper Sabbath. To this, Jeffers added British Israelism, the belief that the Anglo-Saxon race was descended from one of the twelve tribes of Israel. By the time Dorothy converted to the Kingdom of Yahweh in the mid-1960s, Jeffers was teaching an esoteric, syncretic faith that combined new-age spirituality and Sacred Name theology (the belief that God's proper name was Yahweh and that God must be addressed as such). Through subscribing to the group's periodicals, Dorothy, who was Black, would have been taught that Jesus was not God in the flesh but God's representative, that he was actually named Joseph, that he was not a Jew but an Anglo-Saxon, and that he was not crucified but escaped persecution. Dorothy was taught that reincarnation was real, and that extra-sensory perception was a path toward enlightenment. Vincent wanted nothing to do with his wife's new faith. Dorothy's conversion to the Kingdom of Yahweh, and the couple's trouble conceiving a child, caused a rift between the two. A year after she began following the Kingdom of Yahweh, Dorothy filed assault charges against Vincent. Before prosecution could commence, she withdrew her complaint, telling police that the domestic violence "only happened twice." Shortly thereafter, Vincent took a job in New York City and the couple separated permanently. Years later, Dorothy Clark downplayed the domestic violence and told a reporter that her split with Vincent was the product of two people moving in very different spiritual directions. Dorothy told the reporter, "I had made up my mind that I had to make a new life for myself, and I gave him the same freedom."[15]

Around 1967, after the end of his marriage, Vincent Leaphart began to transform into John Africa. Vincent's friends and family noticed that he had grown withdrawn, contemplative, and aloof. He wasn't his normal self. Back when he was Vincent, he was gregarious, a snazzy dresser, a jokester. He had a large group of friends who were always in and out of the apartment he shared with Dorothy. Their door was always unlocked. Vincent spent a lot of time with his brothers and sisters. But around this time, Vincent became something of an ascetic. He started dressing more simply, got rid of most of his possessions, and ended most of his relationships. He spent almost all his time holed up in his apartment in Powelton Village.[16]

In early 1969—the same time John Africa was developing his teachings—Delbert Orr, one of John Africa's first converts, was flirting with a young woman at a party on the south side of Chicago. She rebuffed him rather quickly, though. She only dated Black Panthers. Delbert had spent the last four years as an airman in Vietnam, so he had not heard of the Panthers, the revolutionary Black Power group founded three years earlier in Oakland, California. By the late 1960s, the Panthers had spread to other major cities in the United States, and by December 1968, the Illinois chapter of the Panthers had coalesced under the leadership of Bobby Rush and Fred Hampton. Delbert joined the Panthers and quickly worked his way through the ranks of party leadership. Delbert was well read on Marxist-Socialist philosophy. Party members were required to read twelve books: six were on Mao and the other six were written by Party leaders.[17]

The meteoric rise of the Black Panthers in Chicago drew the attention of the FBI, which was already at work combating the group in Oakland and other cities. J. Edgar Hoover believed that the Black Panther Party represented the "greatest threat to internal security" facing the United States. Hoover's ally in the fight against the Panthers was the Chicago Police Department's Red Squad, an elite unit formed in the 1950s to combat communists and labor organizers. The Red Squad worked in concert with the FBI to infiltrate the Chicago Panthers. They spied on the group's meetings, filled the party's ranks with counterintelligence agents meant to disrupt the party's organization, and coordinated assassinations of party leadership. On December 4, 1969, the Chicago Police Department, working in concert with the FBI, raided party leader Fred Hampton's apartment. The police shot Hampton and deputy defense minister Mark Clark as they slept. After the party leaders' assassinations, the Chicago Police Department and the FBI put out warrants for the arrests of other known party members, including Delbert Orr.[18]

Delbert Orr and two other party members spent the fall and winter of 1969–1970 as fugitives in Canada. They were cut off from financial support from the Chicago Panthers, which was in disarray after multiple raids and arrests over the summer. To make ends meet, Delbert and his fellow fugitives committed armed robberies. Risking capture, Delbert periodically crossed the border and drove from Canada to Chicago to check in with family and friends and to reconnect with what was left of the Panthers there. In October 1969, on his way back to Canada after one of these trips, Delbert was in a serious car crash. Two passengers in the car, one of them Delbert's cousin, were killed. Delbert survived, but with serious injuries that required a three-month hospital stay. Doctors told him that he would have difficulty walking and would likely never return to full mobility. Local police began investigating the car crash upon discovering that the car Delbert was in had been stolen. Soon they learned of Delbert's warrants and contacted the FBI. Agents interviewed Delbert in his hospital bed, but, to Delbert's surprise, did not arrest him.[19]

In March 1970, shortly after he was released from the hospital, Delbert and his two fugitive comrades decided to try their luck in Philadelphia. One of his Panther friends was originally from Philadelphia and had some contacts there, so the three men found an apartment in Powelton Village that was cheap enough, and that would allow Delbert to continue his rehabilitation. Delbert went about the long, painful process of adjusting to life with limited mobility. It was a monumental undertaking to walk around the block. He had a brace on his back and one leg was still immobile. On one of these walks, he ran into some people set up on a street corner talking about revolution. They were speaking his language. He listened for a while and agreed with what they had to say. The young Panther pressed them on their revolutionary bona fides. Had they read Mao? What was their position on democratic socialism? They shut him down. These MOVE people were talking about a very different kind of revolution.[20]

A few weeks later, Delbert's Panther roommates learned that the charges against them had been dropped, and they returned to Chicago. Delbert, however, suspected that it was a trap and stayed in Philadelphia. No matter; it would give him a chance to learn more about MOVE. Delbert—crutches, braces, and all—continued to make the trek down the block to hear them talk. It was "uplifting." It seemed like every time he went, he felt a little less pain, moved a little bit better, and got a little bit stronger. It was as if the Teachings, themselves, were healing him. Healing is a recurring motif in MOVE conversion narratives. For Delbert, the more he heard the Teachings of John Africa, the stronger he got—physically and spiritually. He shed the braces and crutches and was soon walking and running just as fast as he had before the car accident, despite the doctors' pessimistic prognosis.[21]

Conversions are stories that can only be told with the aid of memory. They always happen twice: in the present, as they are happening, conversions are incremental processes. Every time Delbert hobbled around the block to hear MOVE people speak, he was growing a little closer to the Teachings of John Africa and a little further from Delbert Orr. In memory, after the fact, conversions "crystallize" into binary forms. It is only through the process of remembering that a long, gradual process is rendered as a dramatic road-to-Damascus conversion. In its crystallized form, conversions involve two people: the person before and the person after. The transformation sometimes warrants a new name. For MOVE people, the surname Africa marks the singular, ruptured moment in time in which a new life begins. Delbert, in his own account of his conversion, tells both stories. There is the long story: he was in Philadelphia for several months, listened to MOVE people speak about the Teachings of John Africa, and gradually accepted what they had to say. But there is also the crystalline structure, which, for Delbert, coincided with his physical healing: "some information I had gotten from MOVE Law just put me on my feet . . . I have been here ever since. That is an oversimplification, but that's just what happened."[22] In this binary form, Delbert's conversion is a story of "break and a rupture through which the new is separated from the old and the old is consigned to the past."[23]

The new Delbert Africa renounced the Black Panthers. He considered his former interests in Black Power and Marxism to be "theoretical scientific nonsense." John Africa gave his new convert a title borrowed directly from the Panthers. He made Delbert MOVE's "Minister of Confrontation and Security." John Africa didn't want to change Delbert's past. He wanted him to *understand* it. John Africa taught Delbert that he had benefited from two miracles within a matter of days: he survived a fatal car accident and he managed to elude the FBI. These were no mere strokes of luck. What happened to Delbert—the injustice of the FBI's treatment of the Panthers, living as a fugitive, having to steal to survive, even the car crash—was of cosmic significance.[24]

John Africa believed that his revelation had the power to change the world. In July 1972, John Africa and Delbert Africa boarded a plane bound for Miami, the site of that year's Democratic National Convention. They carried with them a copy of *The Guidelines of John Africa*. By the end of the four-day convention, the Democratic Party would nominate George McGovern, an anti-war, liberal senator from South Dakota, to run against the popular incumbent Richard Nixon. McGovern was not the only man hoping for an ascension to power that week. As John Africa understood it, this trip was his opportunity to stake his claim as the leader of the Black freedom struggle. He had meetings set up with Ralph Abernathy, Corretta Scott King, Dick Gregory, and several other leading figures of the civil rights movement. He was going to tell them about the sacredness of Life, about *The Guidelines*, and about the Law of Mama. He was going to convince them that they could never improve the world by operating within its fallen "System." He was going to show them that African Americans could only be free if they knew what freedom really was. This was John Africa's opportunity to launch a spiritual revolution on a global scale. All it required was leadership. Martin Luther King had been dead for four years and no one had filled his void. King was a man of God—a prophet. The world needed a prophet.[25]

John Africa's journey into the nexus of American political and religious power began several weeks earlier when John Africa and Delbert Africa approached Dick Gregory, the civil rights leader, political activist, and comedian, after a speaking engagement at West Chester College in suburban Philadelphia. John and Delbert talked to Gregory about their views on diet and lifestyle. Gregory was intrigued, and he invited them to meet with him and a few other comedians at a house owned by Bill Cosby's mother. Gregory read a few pages of *The Guidelines*. Inspired by what he read, Gregory invited John and Delbert to meet him at his speaking engagement at another local college the following night. They did, and Gregory again invited the MOVE people back to his hotel room to learn more about the Teachings of John Africa. According to MOVE, Dick Gregory spent two hours reading through *The Guidelines*, after which he "jumped up, clenching the manuscript and waving it wildly in the air." They quote Gregory as saying, "This is it, this is the truth I have been searching for."[26] However, in MOVE's record of the event, Dick Gregory's "ego mania" prevented his conversion. He was not willing to surrender his celebrity, his wealth, or his standing to follow John Africa. Gregory "became very nervous" and started "pacing up and down his motel room." He asked them to leave the manuscript with him so he could think it over. They refused. *The Guidelines* were for MOVE people only. John Africa must have been surprised when, weeks later, Dick Gregory called and asked if the two men could meet while Gregory was in Miami for the Democratic National Convention. Gregory offered to introduce John Africa to the highest echelon of Black religious and political leadership.[27]

The trip was a disaster. MOVE struggled to raise the money to get John Africa and Delbert Africa to Miami. After a thirty-hour train ride, they arrived in Miami with little sleep, no place to stay, and no money to afford a hotel. All they had were a few photocopies of *The Guidelines* and Dick Gregory's phone number. According to MOVE, every time they tried to call, though, Gregory was unavailable. His assistants offered one excuse after another: he's on the beach, he's in a meeting, he's getting an enema. Finally, John Africa managed to reach Dick Gregory, only to find the activist evasive. He had no time to meet after all. John Africa talked Gregory into meeting with him at the opulent Fontainebleau Hotel the next day, but Gregory never showed. John Africa called him from the hotel, and Gregory told him to meet him at the Convention Center. John Africa walked two miles down the beach to the Convention Center, but he didn't have a pass to get in. John Africa sat outside and waited. Two hours passed, but Dick Gregory never showed.[28]

Finally, Dick Gregory and his throng of admirers and media members passed by. Gregory stopped at the door of the convention center to smile for pictures, sign autographs, and shake the hands of his fans before going inside. But, according to MOVE, Dick Gregory wouldn't shake John Africa's hand. He wouldn't even look at him. As MOVE people understood it, the "System" clearly had a hold on Dick Gregory. Undeterred, John Africa followed the crowd inside. He tried repeatedly to get Dick Gregory's attention, but the celebrity activist was "ego tripping." John Africa became frustrated. "Just what do you intend to do? Do you intend to speak with me or do you expect me to stand around and wait until you are finished with all this nonsense?" That got Dick Gregory's attention. "Listen man, if you want to get an attitude, I don't have to help you," he snapped. Help John Africa? John Africa was here to help *him*. MOVE people believed that John Africa was owed "more respect than he, Dick Gregory, could ever give." What's worse, Dick Gregory knew this. He had read most of *The Guidelines*. He had been exposed to the truth. He knew that John Africa was an "authority on life" and he was still thumbing his nose. So, John Africa decided to assert his religious authority right there in the convention center lobby. He began to preach—in front of Gregory's fans, passing delegates, and media members—to his reluctant disciple about the danger of those enemas he was so fond of. Dick Gregory was mortified. Gregory, MOVE later wrote, tried "his damnedest to insult, embarrass, make small this black man who was there at his invitation."[29] Security guards stepped in, and John Africa was removed from the building. He left Miami feeling betrayed. Politics was no place for a prophet.

When John Africa and Delbert Africa returned to Philadelphia from the Democratic National Convention, they went about building a more modest organization, from the grassroots up. One of John Africa's early followers was a white man whom John Africa knew as Donald Grossman. Grossman was an adjunct professor of sociology at the Community College of Philadelphia, and he decided to teach his students *The Guidelines of John Africa*, which he interpreted as a particularly astute social analysis. John Africa was very proud to learn that Grossman planned to teach his writings to college students. It was vindication. The man who had once been told he was "orthogenically backward" had written a book that people were taking seriously.

Many of MOVE's founding generation of converts found their way to the group through Grossman's community college course. John Africa phoned his sister, Louise, with whom he had become estranged, to tell her the exciting news, and to invite Louise and their sisters Laverne Sims and Muriel Austin to participate in the course. What little information we have about the early classroom meetings comes from a memoir Louise Leaphart James wrote in 2013. Her memories of Grossman's classroom—and especially of Grossman himself—have been vitiated by her belief that Grossman betrayed MOVE and John Africa. This is a common belief among MOVE people to this day, and it is one that is not without justification. Louise remembers the class meetings to be frustrating. Grossman was unprepared to answer the sisters' questions, and had not studied *The Guidelines* deeply enough to defend it against their critiques. After several weeks, if only to defend against the sisters' seemingly limitless skepticism, Grossman began taking his classroom preparation more seriously. He began spending more time under John Africa's tutelage and studied *The Guidelines* more carefully. As the semester wore on, according to Louise James, some of the students in the class became convinced that *The Guidelines of John Africa* contained the answers they had been looking for.

When the semester ended in December 1972, Louise, Laverne, Muriel, Donald Grossman, and a handful of Grossman's former students continued meeting to discuss *The Guidelines*. Many of these meetings took place in Grossman's apartment. Some took place in John Africa's apartment at 3207 Pearl Street. John Africa's sisters brought their families with them to the meetings. Laverne Sims brought her five children with her: sixteen-year-old Debbie, fourteen-year-old Gail, twelve-year-old Chuckie, and her two youngest, Sharon and Dennis. Laverne and all five of her children would eventually convert to MOVE, and build their lives in the religion. Louise

James attended those early meetings with her only son, thirteen-year-old Frank James. One of Grossman's former students, Jerry Ford, soon converted to MOVE and became Jerry Africa. Before MOVE, Jerry played college football at Maryland State College, and belonged to a fraternity. He was a mountain of a man, and struck people as jovial and laid back. Jerry joined Delbert, Laverne, Louise, Muriel, Don Grossman, and John Africa's seven nieces and nephews to form the earliest core of MOVE.[30]

Within a few months, John Africa's growing congregation had outgrown their meeting spaces. On May 13, 1973, MOVE people pooled their money and bought 309 North 33rd Street, one half of a dilapidated Victorian twin in Powelton Village, for $7,500 under Donald Grossman's legal name, Donald Glassey. The adjacent house, 307, was sold in 1968 to one of the many real estate companies hoping to buy up cheap property and profit from the city's redevelopment plans. Like many houses in Powelton in the late 1960s and early 1970s, 307 was left abandoned. The companies that purchased these properties had little interest in maintaining them or renting them out, as they expected the houses to be demolished. Within a few weeks of purchasing 309, MOVE people began squatting in 307.[31]

In the early 1970s, Powelton Village was a hotbed of New Left radicalism. The neighborhood bordered both the University of Pennsylvania and Drexel University. Though it had once been a predominately middle-class African American neighborhood, it was gentrifying. By the time MOVE purchased their house, Powelton had become a neighborhood for radical students and professors. Undercover FBI agents, a constant presence in the neighborhood, often failed comically to fit in with the hip radicals who lived there. It was not uncommon for the neighborhood to throw block parties welcoming the new crop of undercover agents—all bellbottoms and crewcuts, tie-dye and loafers—to the neighborhood. The Powelton Village that MOVE called home was white but integrated, fiercely left-wing, and well-educated. The working-class Black neighborhood Vincent Leaphart had grown up in, though just a few blocks over, was a world away.[32]

MOVE transformed the houses into a sacred domestic space for the religion. Some lived in the house. Others slept elsewhere but spent most of their time with their MOVE family. MOVE's large and growing population of dogs, which probably numbered two to three dozen, lived in one half of the duplex. MOVE lived, worked, and worshiped in the other. Upon purchasing the house, MOVE nailed a sign on the front porch that read, "This is the House that John Africa Built. Long live John Africa." The sign signaled the end of the public sphere and the beginning of the sacred domestic space inside.

The MOVE house was, to MOVE people, a sacred space—set apart from the corruptions of the world outside. The ground floor was reserved for studying *The Guidelines* and hosting public meetings. A small room off the entryway contained two desks and a chair, with few exceptions the only furniture in the building. A copy of *The Guidelines* was stored in a file cabinet. In the unfinished, cement basement of the main house were two long wooden tables where MOVE people ate their meals together. The basement was lit by two chandeliers with candles. Upstairs, where MOVE people often slept, was almost empty as well. MOVE people stored their clothes there, though they rarely owned more than one or two outfits. John Africa taught his disciples the virtues of an ascetic lifestyle, and MOVE's domestic space reflected their sincerity to those teachings.[33]

MOVE people owned very few possessions. Aside from the desk chair downstairs and the dining tables in the basement, there was nowhere to sit. MOVE people did not own beds or couches; they slept on the floor. The domestic space MOVE people shared was designed to force constant motion, which John Africa taught was essential to human flourishing. There was always work to do: stripping the wallpaper off the walls, pulling the electrical wires out of the walls, or digging up the sidewalk in front of the house. By rejecting most technology, MOVE kept the System away. MOVE built a high wooden fence around the house. The fence kept people out and dogs in. But it also provided a barrier separating the sacred from the profane. Behind the large wooden fence, MOVE carved out a quarter-acre in the universe that was immune from the System. MOVE was determined to keep their domestic space sacred—removed from the System, unpolluted.[34]

MOVE invited the public into the Powelton house and actively recruited new converts. Throughout the early 1970s, MOVE's teenagers (mostly John Africa's nieces and nephews) would routinely go throughout the Powelton neighborhood ringing doorbells in an effort to recruit young people to MOVE. On Monday and Wednesday nights, MOVE held gatherings at the Powelton house that were open to the public. MOVE people read from *The Guidelines*, shared food with their guests, and talked about current events. MOVE billed these meetings as lectures on various topics, including childbirth and natural diet. They offered the Teachings of John Africa freely, twice a week, to anyone who was interested.[35]

It was at one of those public meetings that Janet Hollaway found the home she had always been searching for. Janet's mother was the oldest daughter in a family of twenty children living in Newark, New Jersey. It was a busy, expensive household. Janet's mother—a child herself—was busy raising her younger siblings when she got pregnant. She knew she couldn't raise Janet "in the cold streets of Newark," so Janet's mother sent her to live with an older aunt in the suburbs. Janet lived a privileged childhood—as privileged as a Black girl could be growing up in the suburbs of Newark in the 1950s. She took ballet lessons, played youth sports, went to school dances—she got everything she wanted. When Janet was eleven, her mother had established herself well enough to support her daughter. Janet spent the rest of her youth going back and forth between her aunt and her mother, each one trying to vie for her affection with lavish gifts and new clothes. Her mother bought her a new car the day she got her driver's license. Despite her material comforts, Janet was spiritually lost. As she entered adulthood, Janet couldn't shake the suspicion that there was "something missing" in her life. "Inside of me," she wrote in her account of her conversion, "there was always this empty feeling even when I was with people I was close to. I still, deep down inside felt like I was alone, that I didn't really fit and I didn't understand it . . . I just went through the motions." After her conversion, with the aid of memory, she realized that she was looking to feel "satisfied, secure." She was looking for home.[36]

In 1970, Janet moved to Philadelphia, found a job, met a man, got married, and had a baby daughter. The feelings didn't go away. One night, as she rocked her baby girl to sleep, she experienced a spiritual crisis. She remembers "feeling the same way my mother felt, wanting something better for my daughter, wanting her to be safe, happy, free of the hurt, pain, disappointment and disillusion." After her conversion, she realized that she wanted her daughter to be free from the "cold, cruel, prejudice System." But she wasn't like her mother. She wasn't a child busy caring for nineteen siblings. She wasn't poor, one missed paycheck away from living in the streets of Newark. She was married, employed, stable; not rich by any means, but not poor either. Still, she felt crippled, in need of "guidance, direction," something to give her daughter a good life. Janet did the only thing she could think of: she prayed. She tried religion, but realized that the "people calling themselves vessels of God, people who were supposed to be channeling me to righteousness" were hypocrites. They "claimed to be moral," but were as "ungodly" and "unclean" as the behavior they railed against. She was about to give up on religion when she heard, through word of mouth, about MOVE. An acquaintance asked her to attend one of MOVE's biweekly gatherings. There, she heard *The Guidelines of John Africa* read aloud. The MOVE gathering that night was Janet's singular moment in time; the rupture in her life that marked the emergence of a new person: Janet Africa. The Teachings were "so clear, analytical and absolute it took me out." MOVE was what she was looking for her whole life. Finally, she felt "familiar and connected." That night, the night she said "changed my life forever," Janet found home.[37]

In her memory, Janet's conversion from Janet Hollaway to Janet Africa took place in a singular moment. But in her narrative of her conversion, it also had been taking place all along. She always felt the weight of the System, first as a child in the Newark suburbs, then as an unfulfilled wife and mother. She planned to carry the burden herself, but couldn't ask her daughter to do the same. Her conversion, like Delbert's, followed a narrative sequence of crisis, climax, and resolution. Delbert's crisis had been physical, the near destruction of his body; Janet's, the emotional distress of a lifetime feeling disconnected. For both, the climax of meeting MOVE served as a rupture point, demarcating the divide between a past life and the present/future one. In MOVE, they found the resolution to these crises. And they also found each other. Janet and Delbert became romantic partners and raised a family together in MOVE.

Some of MOVE's early converts found the House that John Africa built to be a refuge from a life of street violence. West Philadelphia in the early 1970s was notorious for endemic gang wars. In 1972, the year before MOVE people established the House that John Africa Built, thirty-nine young people—mostly Black boys—were killed in gang violence in West Philadelphia. The average age of both shooter and victim was only sixteen. Street violence, for many young Black men in West Philadelphia, was inescapable. It seemed that way for Charles "Chuckie" Sims and his brother Dennis Sims. Their mother, Laverne Sims, was Vincent Leaphart's sister and one of John Africa's earliest converts. To the Sims brothers, gang affiliation provided "identity." Possession of their gang turf gave them a "place they could have that was theirs."[38]

In 1973, the Sims brothers, thirteen and fourteen years old, threw a brick through a window of a house owned by a member of a rival gang. They drew the ire, instead, of a woman who lived in the house. The woman charged into the Sims family home looking for a fight. She pushed Sharon Sims—Laverne's daughter and Chuckie and Dennis's sister—into Sharon's one-year-old son. This enraged Sharon and her sister Debbie. Soon all four Sims siblings were fighting the woman. The police arrived and arrested Sharon, who was released on bail. With Sharon's court date looming, John Africa attempted mediation. He explained to both warring families that their dispute was only a reaction to the confusion caused by life within the System. The mediation worked, and the charges were dropped. The Sims siblings joined their mother in MOVE, and began following the Teachings of John Africa. Debbie Sims's husband, Michael Davis, was a Marine deployed in Vietnam. When his tour of duty ended in 1973 he found his wife, now named Debbie Africa, at MOVE headquarters. Mike, as he is called, "felt the family vibe" and soon joined his wife in MOVE, becoming Mike Africa. When the time came for Mike to return to active duty, he went AWOL.[39]

Several people who converted to MOVE did so because they believed the MOVE diet had miraculous effects on the body. Lee Sing Africa found MOVE through Don Grossman, with whom she had a romantic relationship. Lee Sing was named Sharon Penn. When she first met MOVE, MOVE people found Lee Sing to be "depressed and withdrawn," and "very bitter and disturbed." Lee Sing told them she had dropped out of college, fallen out with her family, and been told by her doctors that she was unable to have a child. Like many college-aged youth of her generation, she found the trappings of white, upper-middle-class American life to be drowning in inauthenticity. She was looking for something *real*. Lee Sing was not immediately welcomed into MOVE. She lived with Don in his apartment and not in the MOVE house. It took time for her to gain MOVE's trust. Eventually, however, she was granted permission to read *The Guidelines* and to learn from John Africa himself. John Africa taught Lee Sing that her "alleged sterilization" was not a biological fact, but an illusion—the consequence "of all that she had been taught."[40]

So Lee Sing began to unlearn. MOVE people showed her how to exercise, work, and eat healthy. They oriented her body away from the System. After six months, Lee Sing became pregnant, but experienced a miscarriage. John Africa warned her this would happen; "her body was still not at the level of motherhood." After her miscarriage, Lee Sing pored over *The Guidelines* night and day, hoping that her devotion could produce a child. John told her she needed to stop looking for fault in his teachings and simply trust it. As Lee Sing reported to her MOVE family, John Africa "told me through *The Guidelines* I could have a baby, it was a statement, and therefore left no room for question." In August 1975, Lee Sing gave birth to her first child, a boy named Israel, unassisted and naturally, in the apartment she shared with Don. She, like everyone else in MOVE, interpreted Israel's birth as the "magnificence of the crystallization of the principle of JOHN AFRICA." Israel was John Africa's first miracle, made flesh.[41]

By 1974, there were around two dozen MOVE people, most with the surname Africa. Many, though not all, were Black. Many were biological relatives. They spent their days working on the house, tending the animals, and cooking communal meals. A reporter visited the Powelton house in these early days and asked what kind of organization this was. A MOVE person told the reporter that MOVE was an acronym that stood for Movement for Vocation and Education. Others suggested that MOVE was a shortened form of American Christian Movement for Life. MOVE people were not quite sure in these early days what, exactly, MOVE was going to be. What united these early MOVE people was a shared identity, a sense of family under the headship of John Africa, and a veneration of a sacred text. It is that text—*The Guidelines of John Africa*—to which we now turn.

Notes

1. Todd Gitlin, *The Sixties: Years of Hope, Days of Rage* (New York: Bantam Books, 1987), 305–318; David Farber, *The Age of Great Dreams: America in the 1960s* (New York: Hill and Wang, 1994); Rick Perlstein, *Nixonland: The Rise of a President and the Fracturing of America* (New York: Scribner, 2008), 220.
2. Kelly J. Baker, *The Gospel According to the Klan: The KKK's Appeal to Protestant America, 1915–1930* (Lawrence: University of Kansas Press, 2011), 4–5; James N. Gregory, *Southern Diaspora: How the Great Migrations of Black and White Southerners Transformed America* (Chapel Hill: University of North Carolina Press, 2005), 29; The figure citing the prevalence of lynching in Georgia was calculated using the data set gathered as a part of a recent update to the qualitative data in Stewart E. Tolnay and E. M. Beck, *A Festival of Violence: An Analysis of Southern Lynchings, 1882–1930* (Urbana-Champagne: University of Illinois Press, 1995).
3. 1930 US census, Philadelphia County, Pennsylvania, population schedule, Philadelphia, p. 33, dwelling 109, family 115, household of Charlie Mitchell; Louise Leaphart James, *John Africa . . . Childhood Untold until Today* (self-published, 2013), 2–5.
4. James, *John Africa*, 11–14.
5. Wallace D. Best, *Passionately Human, No Less Divine: Religion and Culture in Black Chicago* (Princeton, NJ: Princeton University Press, 2005), 35–93; "Our History," Fifty Ninth Street Baptist Church, http://www.59sbc.org/about-us/our-history/.
6. The definitive treatment of African American religion during and after the Great Migration is Judith Weisenfeld, *New World A-Coming: Black Religion and Racial*

Identity during the Great Migration (New York: New York University Press, 2017); Terry Rey, *The Priest and the Prophetess: Abbé Ouvière, Romaine Rivière, and the Revolutionary Atlantic World* (New York: Oxford University Press, 2017); Terry Rey and Ariella Werden-Greenfield, "African Spirits in the Holy Experiment: Philadelphia's Botanicas and the Odunde Festival," in *Religion in Philadelphia,* edited by Elizabeth Hayes Alvarez (Philadelphia: Temple University Press, 2017), 271–278; Leonard Norman Primiano, "When 'God in a Body' Lived in Philadelphia," in *Religion in Philadelphia,* edited by Elizabeth Hayes Alvarez (Philadelphia: Temple University Press, 2017), 247–253; on Father Divine's understanding of the category of race, see Weisenfeld, *New World A-Coming,* 79.
7. "Youths Involved in Fatal Gang War," *Baltimore Afro-American,* December 12, 1942; "Deaths of the Week," *Philadelphia Tribune,* October 13, 1951; James, *John Africa,* 23.
8. Orthogenesis, though discredited by the 1940s, was widely influential in the hard sciences and the social sciences. E. B. Tylor, an important early figure in the scientific study of religion, borrowed liberally from theorists of orthogenesis to formulate his theories of religion. Mark A. Ulett, "Making the Case for Orthogenesis: The Popularization of Definitively Directed Evolution, 1890–1926," *Studies in History and Philosophy of Biological and Biomedical Sciences* 45 (2014): 124–132; Peter J. Bowler, *The Eclipse of Darwin: Anti-Darwinian Evolution Theories in the Decades around 1900* (Baltimore, MD: Johns Hopkins University Press, 1992).
9. James, *John Africa,* 18.
10. James, *John Africa,* 18–20.
11. Ibid., 30.
12. Ibid., 21–29, 30.
13. Bruce Cummings, *The Korean War: A History* (New York: Modern Library Chronicles, 2010), 29.
14. Ibid., 149–161.
15. Craig R. McCoy, "Who Was John Africa?" *Philadelphia Inquirer.* Jeffers began his career as a fundamentalist Baptist preacher. He studied at Howard College in Birmingham, Alabama (now Samford University), received a degree from Baylor University, and was ordained at Southwest Baptist Theological Seminary in Fort Worth. Ralph Lord Roy, *Apostles of Discord: A Study of Organized Bigotry and Disruption on the Fringes of Protestantism* (Boston: Beacon Press, 1953), 101–106; J. Gordon Melton, *The Encyclopedia of American Religions,* Vol. II (Wilmington, NC: McGrath, 1978), 215–216.
16. Louise James, *John Africa,* 43–44.
17. Murray Dubin and Andrew Wallece, "The MOVE Surrender," *Philadelphia Inquirer,* May 7, 1978.
18. Jakobi Williams, *From the Bullet to the Ballot: The Illinois Chapter of the Black Panther Party and Racial Coalition Politics in Chicago* (Chapel Hill: University of North Carolina Press, 2013) 167–190.
19. MOVE Organization, "Delbert Africa," On a MOVE: Website of the MOVE Organization, http://onamove.com/move-9/delbert-africa/ (accessed October 27, 2017).

20. Ibid.
21. Ibid.
22. Ibid.
23. Matthew Scherer, *Beyond Church and State: Democracy, Secularism, and Conversion* (New York: Cambridge University Press, 2013), 32.
24. MOVE Organization, "Delbert Africa."
25. MOVE, untitled document, undated [estimated between June 25, 1974, and July 24, 1974] Box 91a, Folder 1, Philadelphia Yearly Meeting of the Religious Society of Friends, Friends Peace Committee, Friendly Presence Papers, Friends Historical Library, Swarthmore College, Swarthmore, PA, 2.
26. Ibid.
27. Ibid.
28. Ibid.
29. Ibid.
30. Philadelphia Special Investigation Commission, Interview with Fareed Ahmed aka Eugene Hearn, Director of the Southwest Center City Civic Association, Box 8, Folder 2, PSIC.
31. Deed of sale of 309 N. 33rd Street from Rita Slotter to University City Association, September 14, 1987, City of Philadelphia, Pennsylvania, Records of Mortgages and Deeds, City of Philadelphia Archives; Deed of sale of 309 N. 33rd Street from Philadelphia County Sheriff's Office to Rita Slotter, July 2, 1984, City of Philadelphia, Pennsylvania, Records of Mortgages and Deeds, City of Philadelphia Archives; Deed of sale of 309 N. 33rd Street from Donald Glassey to Rita Slotter, July 2, 1984, City of Philadelphia, Pennsylvania, Records of Mortgages and Deeds, City of Philadelphia Archives; Deed of sale of 3207 Pearl Street from Thomas E. and Mary Ellen McDyer to Community Housing, Incorporated/Penna. Corporation, October 27, 1971, City of Philadelphia, Pennsylvania, Records of Mortgages and Deeds, City of Philadelphia Archives; Deed of sale of 3207 Pearl Street from Community Housing, Incorporated to John Dodson, June 27, 1974, City of Philadelphia, Pennsylvania, Records of Mortgages and Deeds, City of Philadelphia Archives; Mortgage agreement between John Dodson and Community Housing, Incorporated, June 27, 1974, City of Philadelphia, Pennsylvania, Records of Mortgages and Deeds, City of Philadelphia Archives. It is worth noting that both Donald Glassey and the Philadelphia County Sheriff sold the same property, 309 N. 33rd Street, to the same buyer, Rita Slotter, on the same day.
32. Susan Rappaport, "From Block Party to Blockade," *University City News* (April 1978).
33. Charles Layton, "Body of Baby Seen at MOVE Commune," *Philadelphia Inquirer*, April 10, 1976.
34. Ibid.
35. MOVE, untitled document, undated [estimated between June 25, 1974, and July 24, 1974] Box 91a, Folder 1, Philadelphia Yearly Meeting of the Religious Society of Friends, Friends Peace Committee, Friendly Presence Papers, Friends Historical Library, Swarthmore College, Swarthmore, PA, 13.

36. MOVE Organization, "Janet Africa," On a MOVE: Website of the MOVE Organization, http://onamove.com/move-9/janet-africa/ (accessed October 27, 2017).
37. Ibid.
38. Wayne King, "In West Philadelphia, Gang Wars Are a Way of Death," *New York Times*, June 11, 1973.
39. Mike Africa, Jr., transcript of an oral history conducted May 17, 2016, by Richard Kent Evans, MOVE Oral History Project, Special Collections and Urban Archives, Temple University, Philadelphia, PA; Debbie Africa, transcript of an oral history conducted by Richard Kent Evans, MOVE Oral History Project, Special Collections and Urban Archives, Temple University, Philadelphia, PA.
40. Louise Africa, "On the MOVE," *Philadephia Tribune*, September 2, 1975.
41. Ibid.

2
Belief and Practice

Like many religious geniuses, John Africa was a man of contradictions. He possessed a powerful, rigid intellect, but little formal education. Though he was a remarkably creative thinker, he had no tolerance for nuance. He wielded logic, not as a tool of reason, but as a weapon useful for its destruction. He was wholly convinced that his teachings were absolutely true, and that any other system of thought—religious, political, philosophical, or otherwise—had collapsed under the power of his revelation. Yet, behind the self-righteousness and the domineering intellect was a kind, gentle man. When MOVE people speak about John Africa, they speak of someone fully present, fully alive. He is someone who means the world to MOVE people; a man who wanted nothing more than for humanity to "rest peacefully in the . . . magnitude of his words [and] the dimensions of his teachings." To understand John Africa's religion—and what became of it—we must first understand his revelation, his contribution to American religious thought: *The Guidelines of John Africa*.[1]

John Africa dictated *The Guidelines* over a span of six years. Several different people helped him create the manuscript. They describe the process similarly. John Africa would sit in a chair or on the floor and begin speaking. A second person, first family members and, later, disciples, would type his words into a typewriter, struggling to keep up with his stream of revelation. John Africa instructed his assistants to type in all capital letters and not to use any periods. Occasionally he would pause, not to gather himself or to think about what to say next, but to give the typist a moment to catch up. Then he simply picked up right where he left off.

At some point in the late 1970s, the manuscript was broken into sections and arranged topically. The oldest sections, those drafted as early as the fall of 1967, are on economics, gang prevention, and John Africa's view of government. Over time, *The Guidelines* grew to include sections on a host of topics, including gender, sex, diet, death, entertainment, animal welfare, marriage, divorce, childrearing, and abortion. By early 1974, *The Guidelines* had become a typewritten, printed manuscript that MOVE people revered as a sacred scripture. MOVE people often referred to the text as "MOVE's bible" and believed that it had the supernatural ability to affect the "body chemistry" of those who heard it spoken. It is a large and complex text, but there is throughout the manuscript an underlying theme: the world as we experience it is not as God intended. It is being held captive by an evil force called the System.[2]

The Guidelines of John Africa are an explanation for, and solution to, the problem of evil. John Africa called these forces of evil the "reformed world system," or, more frequently, "the System," borrowing a phrase that New Left radicals made popular in the 1960s to describe capitalism, political corruption, and the emerging neoliberal order. John Africa had these things in mind when he wrote about the System, but he meant much more than that. To John Africa, the System was fundamental to the cognitive process. Humans, unlike any other animal, have the ability to think critically about themselves and to view themselves abstractly. This ability to think abstractly made humankind dissatisfied with the natural order of Life. Animals do not feel this dissatisfaction with the world. They act on instinct, fulfilling their natural impulses. And this, according to John Africa, is what puts animals in touch with the divine. Humans grew proud of their minds and their abilities to comprehend and influence their surroundings. But consciousness backfired. Humans created concepts, ideas, systems, order, logic, numbers—all categories of thought that further abstracted them from the natural order of life. These second-order concepts, all born out of the mind of humankind, alienate us from what John Africa called the "common expression of [the] absolute." The uniquely human experience of living in alienation from Life is what John Africa meant by the System.[3]

In John Africa's religious thought, the System was an active, kinetic force. It had to be counteracted. It held the world captive, but it could be escaped. And once MOVE people were outside of the System, they could work to bring it down. In practice, MOVE people sought to counteract the damage the System had wrought. What this practice looked like changed over time, but in the group's first few years, MOVE believed that pointing out the contradictions and hypocrisies inherent in the System would open people's eyes to the evils of the world and force the System to implode—an idea John Africa borrowed, in a roundabout way, from Hegel and Marx.

MOVE's first attempt to expose the hypocrisy of the System ended in failure. In the summer of 1973, an elderly Jewish man named Ken Lubitz approached MOVE, asking for help. Lubitz told MOVE that he had recently been released after a prolonged stint in the hospital and had been looking for a place to stay. A social worker employed by the hospital referred Lubitz to a boarding home network run by Rev. Edward Courtney, the associate minister of an African American Pentecostal denomination in West Philadelphia. Lubitz moved into 217 West Manheim Street, one of Courtney's four boarding homes, but found it in appalling condition. He told MOVE that around twenty-five people, most of them elderly or ill and on public assistance, shared the five-bedroom home. Many slept on couches in the basement or on the floor, yet everyone paid Courtney thirty dollars a month in rent. MOVE agreed to help Lubitz expose what they viewed as an exploitative racket between Courtney and the social workers at the hospital. MOVE helped Lubitz, who was calling himself a MOVE member, find new housing, and on June 18, several MOVE people demonstrated outside one of Courtney's boarding homes. Delbert Africa recorded interviews with residents and took photos of their living conditions, which he sent to the three major daily newspapers. The residents told Delbert that there were no healthcare workers employed by Rev. Courtney, despite the fact that many of the boarders required regular medical care. Some boarders described laying in their own waste for days before another boarder provided the care they needed. Residents were also responsible for distributing their own medication, which was prescribed by a doctor who visited infrequently. Most of the boarders said they, like Lubitz, were referred to Rev. Courtney by the same social worker at the same hospital.[4]

Delbert Africa learned that none of Courtney's boarding homes was licensed. He also learned that the Department of Welfare did not list any of Rev. Courtney's properties on their list of recommended homes, but that at least seventeen welfare recipients listed one of Courtney's boarding houses as their address. Delbert turned to Philadelphia's Department of Licenses and Inspections for help, but Courtney, in anticipation of the inspector's visit, hid the evidence. He moved several of his boarders to another home, cleaned up the building, and placed bowls of fresh fruit on the table. The city's inspector found no code violations.

A few months later, the furnace in the basement of the boarding house on Manheim Street caught fire. The house burned down, killing two residents and critically injuring a third. It could have been worse. The house caught fire during the day, when some residents were gone and fewer were in the basement. The fire drew the attention of reporters from the *Philadelphia Tribune*, the city's African American daily, who dusted off the information Delbert

Africa had sent them months earlier. But it was too late, and Rev. Courtney was too well connected. He stormed into the *Tribune* offices and set the record straight, as he saw it. Courtney told the paper that "Kenny Lubitz was a troublemaker," and that he was insane. The Department of Welfare, the press, the Bureau of Licenses and Inspections had all investigated the Manheim Street location and found everything "in order." And the violations found at other properties were the landlord's responsibility. Rev. Courtney told the *Tribune* that he shared the house with his boarders and treated them like family. He mourned the deaths more than anyone. That was enough to convince the *Tribune*, and the Department of Welfare and the Department of Licenses and Inspections had more pressing matters to worry about than shutting down Courtney's other unlicensed boarding homes. MOVE's first attempt at exposing the System did not work. But MOVE did not disparage. Nor were they surprised. They knew exactly what this was. Taking advantage of people too weak to defend themselves, powers that be looking the other way, using religion to profit on the misfortunes of others, the rampant hypocrisy, the callous disinterest in human life—this was the System at work.[5]

John Africa's theodicy of the System has obvious parallels with the Christian theodicy of the Fall. John Africa was raised in the Black Church, so he would have been most familiar with some variation of Augustinian theodicy. In this reading of the Book of Genesis, humankind was created to commune with God and live in perfect harmony with the natural world. But humans rebelled, trading this perfect existence for the knowledge of good and evil. The consequences of this rebellion include death, shame, and sin. John Africa carried the Eden narrative to its logical extreme. Adam and Eve learned something they should not have learned, so if forbidden knowledge led to humankind's fall from an Edenic existence, the wholesale rejection of systems of human comprehension would return humankind to paradise. Like some readings of the Fall, the story of the origin of the System is one that does not exist in time. It is both primordial and ever present: past, present, and future. The System emerged when humankind first began cooking food. It emerged when humankind sought to replicate the flight of birds through aircraft. And it continues to emerge when scientists genetically modify food. The System, in MOVE belief, is constantly evolving, constantly being reinvented, and is self-perpetuating.[6]

Although the System was, in many ways, a repackaging of the Fall, the way John Africa articulated his theodicy and his offer of redemption was firmly rooted in the religious and political currents of the late 1960s. The construction of the System was, for humankind, a self-imposed exile from the natural world because the second-order constructs that humans developed to comprehend the world "alienated" humankind from the natural order of life. Alienation was in the air when John Africa developed this theodicy in the late 1960s and early 1970s. Some in the baby boomer generation—the generation from which MOVE's core emerged—developed a "post-scarcity" radicalism. This was a politics that focused on cultural, social, and political alienation rather than on issues of economic inequality that had concerned previous generations. Across the country, in organizations ranging from the YMCA to the Student Nonviolent Coordinating Committee, from the Students for a Democratic Society to the Black Panthers, the generation that came of age in the 1960s developed a religious and political radicalism based upon the language of Christian existentialists such at Kierkegaard, Tillich, and Bonhoeffer. To them, the key to escaping alienation was to live lives of "authenticity." Certainly John Africa was not reading in Christian existentialism, but he was undoubtedly engaging with these ideas in other forms. Christian existentialism was in the zeitgeist of late 1960s. Indeed, as John Africa's neighborhood in West Philadelphia transformed into a hotbed of New Left radicalism with the expansion of the nearby universities, existentialism *was* the zeitgeist, even if the concepts were presented in secular forms. It should come as no surprise, then, that authenticity was precisely what the Teachings of John Africa offered. John Africa called MOVE "the most organized body to ever wear the title of human with total comprehension."[7]

Although the System was the product of humankind, it had agency apart from the actions of humans. It was a supernatural force as well as a human one. In John Africa's thought, because people are naturally opposed to the System (perfect in essence), they are "allergic" to it. In a section of *The Guidelines* written in May 1967, John Africa explained that "everybody's allergic to violation and when you violate you can expect to suffer, when you got a pain in your head you got an allergy, when you got a pain in your chest you got an allergy . . . anytime your own heart attacks you, you know you ain't doing right . . . ain't nothing common 'bout a cold, a virus ain't nothin' but a term devised by science to describe unfamiliar ailments they ain't got around to so-called accurately describin' yet." Humans' allergy to the System manifests as illness, injury, and addiction. The allergies could be overcome, John Africa taught, by dietary and exercise adjustments and by understanding the illusory nature of illness. He wrote, "you ain't allergic to eatin', you ain't allergic to sleepin' or drinkin', you are allergic to the attempted application of this reformed System that ain't nobody been able to digest, accept, engage with. . . ."[8] The idea that sickness is an illusion caused by an evil entity has a long history in American religion. For example, Mary Baker Eddy, founder of Christian Science, taught that "disease is an error, and has no character nor type, except what mortal mind assigns to it." John Africa taught that addictions arose from the alienation people intuitively felt within the System. Addictions, like illnesses, could be overcome once the sufferers realize that their affliction is only an illusion caused by a supernatural, evil force. It was this realization that helped Delbert Africa recover from the car crash: his injuries weren't real.[9]

The System, powerful though it was, is not the only force at work in John Africa's cosmos. John Africa's universe was dualistic; a site of conflict that pitted forces of good against forces of evil. The force of good went by many names: the Law of Mama, the Law of Nature, God, Natural Law, and most frequently, Life. Natural processes, according to MOVE, are "coordinated" by this active force. When we experience thirst, that is Life telling us to drink water. When we experience tiredness, that is Life telling us to sleep. This, to MOVE, is God. The life God desires for human beings—indeed, for all living things—could not be more apparent. God wants nothing more than for humans to eat, sleep, reproduce, and die. As John Africa wrote in *The Guidelines*, ". . . the total application of this principle should be crystal clear, you must eat, you must sleep, you must drink, this is the common expression of life, the instinctual Law of Mama that all must adhere to. . . ." The degree to which people live their lives in accordance to this natural state—the Law of Mama—is the degree to which they live a fulfilling life according to God's will. Indeed, living in perfect accord with Natural Law—something that is possible and has been performed by at least two human beings—is the degree to which we *are* God.[10]

According to *The Guidelines*, there was one other person besides John Africa who lived in total harmony with Natural Law: Jesus of Nazareth. John Africa had deep respect for Jesus and saw him as a forerunner for his own message. John Africa called Jesus "the god of self, lord of reality, omniscient of wisdom." "Look at this man," *The Guidelines* state, "and see the god, truth that he is, the god that you must be if you too are to become a Christ." "In looking at god, at Jesus, at self you need look no further, for you are seeing the truth, the comprehensiveness of reality, the cultural manifestation of self, the life and breath of nature, of god, of all." To John Africa, Jesus can rightfully be called God, not because he is a supernatural being, but because he was a man who lived life in perfect accord with Nature. Christians are to blame for "intermixing Jesus with their mythical god, making it appear that they are one and the same." Jesus is not God because he was all powerful. Jesus is God because he lived a human life in total conformity with the Law of Mama.[11]

The Guidelines of John Africa posit a God that is both transcendent—existing apart from matter—and thoroughly immanent in creation. John Africa's God is not a personal being. The God of *The Guidelines* is a creative, omnipresent, feminine ("only a woman can give birth, produce life") force. John Africa taught that "man has for so long been crippled with the idea of god as a separate force, a separate power, something that is supernatural, not of this world." *The Guidelines* teach that the world's religions erred in imagining God as a superhuman person deity that exists apart from the created world—a mistake John Africa called the "synthetic god" of human imagination.[12]

John Africa presented a conception of the divine that could be, for the sake of comparison, classified as a kind of panentheism. Whereas pantheism is a conception of the divine (often associated with Ancient Greece) that God exists in the natural world as an "animistic force," panentheism posits that God is both immanent and transcendent. To John Africa, the natural world was not God, but it was God's revelation. The immanent and the transcendent are effectively the same. God was the "animinstic force" blowing the wind, churning the tides, and germinating the seeds, but God was also separate from the created world. God could intervene in natural forces if she wished, she could speak through her prophets, and she could exact justice and revenge. This is why the passage speaks of God's "power" as being "common as dirt," but also speaks of a road that leads to God. The dirt—the natural world—is the medium through which God manifests her agency. But the passage also makes clear that God is immanent in matter: "Don't tell me my Momma ain't just in Her wisdom." Of course, no theology is static, and MOVE's conception of God evolved over time. From the early 1980s through his death in 1985, John Africa became a divinity, himself. But MOVE consistently disavowed a conception of the divine that was exclusively transcendent and spirit.[13]

John Africa's conception of God grows from a broader rejection of what he called "the folly of mythology." Like many African American and African-derived religions, MOVE rejects some aspects of supernaturalism. John Africa argued against the belief that spirit, God, and the soul are "some kind of supernatural, transparent mass of nothingness floating around in space."

The Guidelines insist that otherworldliness of other religions is a misreading of the Bible and a sacrilege toward the natural world. Though there are deep connections between John Africa's theology and the humanist tradition within African American religious thought, MOVE's theology does not neatly fit the category. *The Guidelines of John Africa* do not present a wholesale rejection of supernaturalism, but, rather, an elevation of the natural to the sacred.[14]

In the fall of 1973, MOVE people attended a meeting of the Theosophical Society, a Western esoteric religion based on the teachings of late nineteenth-century occultist Helena Blavatsky. Theosophy, like its predecessor Spiritualism, was a broad, flexible system of spiritual communication built around the belief that the Masters—a class of guiding spirits including Jesus, the Buddha, and various other sages—have guided and (especially during Theosophy's more spiritualist decades) continue to guide humanity toward enlightenment. Theosophy was undergoing a revival in the 1970s, thanks in part to a renewed interest in Eastern spirituality in the West. When MOVE people visited, they were pleased to learn that the Theosophical Society "claimed they were studying god," but, when they pressed the Theosophists' "spiritual leader" on their conception of the divine, MOVE people were disappointed to learn that the Theosophists' god was understood to be wholly separate from nature. Their god was a spirit. MOVE explained to the Theosophists that thinking about God in the abstract—as "that which cannot be substantiated in fact, life"—was causing the Theosophists to drift "further away from the meaning of clarity, perceptivity, true education, GOD." MOVE people interpreted the Theosophist leader's claim that God was a spirit as an admission "that his god didn't exist."[15]

MOVE people found the Buddhists disappointing as well. In the summer of 1973, MOVE people confronted a group they referred to as "the main Buddhist group in Philadelphia." As MOVE understood it, this group believed "that if you chant to their particular Buddha, anything that you wanted would be granted," and that if all the world converted to Buddhism, "there would be peace and love throughout the world." After listening to a presentation by the leader of the Buddhist group, MOVE people objected. They complained that the Buddhists were too materialistic. As MOVE understood it, this Buddhist group chanted to their "particular Buddha" in order to acquire cars and money—things that, John Africa taught, would only impose on life and obstruct peace. The MOVE people in attendance were also bothered by the Buddhists' chanting, which MOVE people said placed them "out of touch with themselves, life." MOVE people told the Buddhists that "if their religion, their god, required them to chant in order to be in touch with life, then their religion was a violation, and their god a prefabrication of man, a concept."[16]

A few weeks after confronting the Buddhist group, MOVE attended a public lecture given by the Maharishi Mahesh Yogi, who was by 1973 a world-famous spiritual leader known for popularizing the Science of Creative Intelligence and Transcendental Meditation. MOVE interpreted the Maharishi's message as an incorporation of "scientific theories with Eastern philosophy and the practice of meditating, presenting this package as a vehicle to a higher level of consciousness." It was precisely this "higher level of consciousness" that bothered MOVE people. By positning that enlightenment can be found in a transcendent plane of existence, the Maharishi had, according to the Teachings of John Africa, rejected the sacredness of the immanent. To MOVE people in the audience, the Maharishi's habit of picking and wearing flowers in his hair was evidence that the guru had deeply confused the sacred and the profane. Confronting the guru after his presentation, MOVE people argued that "picking, re-arranging, and prostitution of flowers" was the result of a his deeply flawed assumption about the nature of the universe: "that man is on a higher level than the rest of life."[17]

To complete their foray into the American metaphysical revival, in December 1973, MOVE people attended a lecture offered by Dr. John Turner, a former psychiatrist who served as "eastern coordinator of covens" for a neo-Pagan group called the International Druidic Society (IDS). In his presentation, Turner said that the IDS believed in "the existence of a God or Supreme Force," but they believed that discovery of that divine nature comes "from within a person," not from an externalized religious structure. As druids, Turner and his co-religionists practiced magic and clairvoyance, believed in reincarnation, developed extrasensory perception, and issued prophecies. After listening to his lecture, the MOVE people who were in the audience challenged Turner's conception of the divine. MOVE people objected to Turner's use of the concept "natural law."[18]

Interestingly, the group with which MOVE imagined they had the most in common—and with whom they had the most prolonged interreligious dialogue—was the Quakers. It was the Quakers' mysticism, commitment to social activism, and transcendentalist heritage that attracted MOVE's interest. MOVE people understood the Quakers as a group that, like MOVE, stood "against the System that has historically exploited all life." In January

1974, the Frankford Meeting of the Society of Friends invited any interested organizations to attend an open forum at their meetinghouse. MOVE people attended the forum and spoke for an hour and a half about MOVE's activities and beliefs. The Quakers were interested in learning more about MOVE and invited them to their monthly Adult Discussion Group. At that meeting, MOVE people discussed their anti-drug program and gang intervention activities. They concluded their discussion by reading a passage from *The Guidelines* explaining that human law was an usurpation of divine law. The Quakers were impressed with MOVE. They donated thirty dollars to them and agreed to raise another five hundred toward MOVE's legal defense.[19]

Through their connections with the Frankford Quakers, MOVE people gained a slot speaking at the annual meeting of the broader Philadelphia Yearly Meeting, which was held at the Arch Street Meetinghouse in March 1974. The Philadelphia Yearly Meeting in 1974 was preoccupied with Vietnam, efforts toward world peace and abolishing the death penalty. So Delbert spoke their language. In front of over two hundred Quakers, Delbert spent forty-five minutes reading from *The Guidelines of John Africa*. MOVE sources record a favorable reaction from their Quaker audience. Some Quakers seemed deeply moved by *The Guidelines*. After Delbert's reading, several Quakers approached MOVE people "with emotion in their eyes" and "silently shook [their] hands." The Quakers, MOVE people believed, were "favorably impressed" with the Teachings of John Africa. The minutes of the Philadelphia Yearly Meeting record Delbert speaking about how many governments were essentially oppressive and violent, and that true peace would only come about through "total revolution": a revolution of the individual, both mind and body, so that the individual would not need government to thrive. Though many of the Quakers there might not have voiced this sentiment in quite the same way, Delbert's understanding of the essentially violent nature of government was not beyond the pale for many Quakers. After his speech, Delbert requested and received additional time to address the Philadelphia Yearly Meeting again later in the evening.[20]

The Philadelphia Yearly Meeting reconvened at 6:30 that evening, and Delbert began reading the section on prayer from *The Guidelines of John Africa*. The Frankford Friends assumed that Delbert wanted additional time to speak about MOVE's gang program, their drug interventions, and the success of their alternative lifestyle—the kind of things MOVE people had spoken about with them before. Instead, Delbert launched into an assault on the legitimacy of prayer, arguing that supplications to a sky god abstract religious practice to the realm of "hallucination" and "obscure the meaning of life." He read a passage from *The Guidelines* that questioned the motives of "cosmetic religion"—belief systems that are more concerned with supernatural than with the natural, more other-worldly than this-worldly. MOVE thought Delbert received a mixed reaction. But when the Philadelphia Yearly Meeting published its account of the proceedings, they described Delbert's speech as "an unexpected visit from MOVE, a black organization in the city." The report recognized the "agony and frustration and even despair" underlying MOVE's message. The Quakers thanked MOVE for "trusting us enough to speak to us rather than turn away from us." However, the Teachings of John Africa were too much for the Quakers to accept. The report admitted that "as Friends," the Philadelphia Yearly Meeting could not "work from the philosophy that they enunciated." The Frankford Quakers rescinded their offer to contribute five hundred dollars to MOVE's legal defense fund.[21]

MOVE people were frustrated with the Quakers' lack of enthusiasm for the Teachings of John Africa. Six months after the Philadelphia Yearly Meeting, MOVE wrote a letter to James Laird, a member of the Frankford Meeting that had denied MOVE the five hundred dollars. The letter recognizes that the Quakers, like MOVE, "claim to be against the system that has historically exploited all life." But it insists that the writings of John Africa are "the only information that can validate this claim." "You can attempt to pretend to yourself that the writing of JOHN AFRICA is of no significance, rhetorical, ordinary, something you've heard before," MOVE wrote, "yet how can you explain the fact that your body chemistry reacts to it like nothing you've ever heard anywhere. How can you explain the fact that you've never heard words used in the way they are used by JOHN AFRICA. THE MOVE ORGANIZATION knows that this is because you've never heard power until confronted by this writing, never heard truth until hearing the words of JOHN AFRICA." MOVE's message to the Quakers was this: one cannot remain a Quaker after having heard the Teachings of John Africa. One cannot be a Quaker and a follower of the Teachings of John Africa. MOVE was a religion, and John Africa was God's prophet. The Quakers had missed the point.[22]

MOVE's early interactions with other religious groups show a group experimenting with its theology—devising ways to critique the System from the outside. But, as MOVE people were painfully aware, their efforts were ineffectual. As John Africa's religion continued to grow, he learned that the System was more pervasive, and more pernicious, than he realized. People liked the System. They struggled to see the incompleteness of their religions. If MOVE people were to confront the System to any effect, they had to issue deeper, more fundamental critiques. John Africa warned his followers not to expect to find another religion that offered teachings similar to his own. According to *The Guidelines*, religions were the "common denominator between technology and insanity." John Africa believed, not unlike Clifford Geertz, that religion depended upon the power of the symbolic for its ability to, in Geertz's phrasing, "establish moods and motivations" in people. But John Africa taught that the "so-called symbol" was nothing more than a "philosophical abstraction, a distortion" which could never represent that which it was meant to symbolize. The fatal flaw of religions, according to John Africa, was that they relied on the symbolic to explain the divine and humankind's relationship to it, creating an illusory separation between God and the natural world. The Buddhists, Quakers, Theosophists, and the Druids all purported to be searching for God, but their complex theologies amounted to little more than "cosmetic religions" that offered no concrete arrangement of religious practices that might bring people closer to God. Even if these other religions made their followers aware that they were trapped in the System, they provided no answers to the central question facing humankind: how do we escape?[23]

The Guidelines of John Africa can be fairly called pessimistic. The book is a lamentation; a mournful meditation on the evil that rules the world. But MOVE was not a pessimistic religion. *The Guidelines* are pessimistic because they are but one half of the Teachings of John Africa. The heart of John Africa's message was that there was a way out of the System. It could be escaped and, eventually, would be defeated. As important as *The Guidelines* were, the Teachings of John Africa were also embodied, imparted on the believers through the day-to-day interaction with John Africa himself. This is why living under the same roof was so important to MOVE people. Both textual and lived, the Teachings of John Africa gave MOVE people a way of understanding themselves as embodied believers, as members of a religious family, as caretakers of the natural world, and as warriors in a cosmic conflict against forces of evil. By living with John Africa, MOVE people participated in an ongoing process of revelation. They modeled their lives on John Africa. He was, to MOVE people, "the man in whose footsteps we all walk."[24]

Escaping the System was possible through MOVE's system of religious practices: both those found in *The Guidelines of John Africa* and in those modeled by John Africa himself. To John Africa, in order to escape the

System one must first learn how to unlearn; that is, one must first ground abstracted theoretical concepts into everyday, lived reality. A useful tool for this process of unlearning was the body. To John Africa, the body was the crucial site at which abstract, intangible theological concepts translated into the mundane and the site at which the cosmic conflict between good and evil was fought. John Africa wrote:

> our religion is our body, it is our eyes, our ears, our feelings, our union, our lungs, our limbs our blood rich with life, of family, of firmly engaging commitment, all things thats [sic] immediate and cannot be argued, cannot be amended, conceded or promised, or auctioned or swapped or given away, for as the body is the lung, limb, the eye, the vein to engagement, it is the heart-beat to pump the blood of connection, and as there is no fiber of the body that is not of the body, there is nothing for MOVE to concede or negotiate without giving away the necessity of life, an arm, a leg, an eye, a lung, all things of completion when you are together, the love of true family, the peace that trust brings, the freedom that only exists when you're faithful, the body that MOVE is committed to be, without hesitation, for this is our breath, as certainty is the real strength of true law, the order that powers the way of together.[25]

The Teachings of John Africa map the intangible: "commitment," "all things immediate," the "necessity of life," "love of true family," and "peace" onto the body, making the invisible visible. The body became a tool of translation for MOVE people; a way of rendering second-order concepts into first-order realities.[26]

To free his followers from the effects of the System, John Africa made the body a site of discipline. To John Africa, the body was, in its natural and unpolluted form, perfect. But like everything held victim to the System, the body was polluted—even the bodies of MOVE people. MOVE people strove for perfection, for total purity of their material selves, but they knew they could never achieve it. What was important, to John Africa, was that MOVE people believed they could perfect their bodies and pursued perfection in principle. In *The Guidelines*, he wrote, ". . . until you learn to believe in perfection, accept the meanin' of totality, realize the common expression of absolute, you will be hungry for truth, for justice, sufferin' from shortness of breath, cryin' for the only liquid of perfection what will quench the historical thirst of reformed inadequacy. . . ." MOVE people believed in perfection and pursued it. Only John Africa, who was supernaturally gifted, and the MOVE children, who were born outside of the System and thus exempt from its domination, were capable of living a life in perfect accord with Mama. The rest could not reach perfection, but they were expected to try through strict bodily discipline.[27]

Living a life in perfect harmony with Mama could be pursued through a restrictive religious diet. MOVE people followed what today might be called a raw, whole-foods diet. Usually, they ate vegetables, grains, nuts, fruits, roots, raw eggs, and, rarely, raw poultry and meats. By necessity, MOVE people cooked some foods, including rice, beans, and other foods that are inedible raw. Ideally, all foods should be wild, organic, uncut, unpeeled, and unprocessed in any way. According to MOVE belief, God provided food in the form that it should be eaten. If a food could be chewed and swallowed raw, God intended it to be eaten raw. It is humankind, in all of its vanity, that decided food should be cooked. Food and water which is unpolluted and unadulterated is most like God. Consuming this kind of food—and only this kind of food—placed MOVE people in communion with the divine.[28]

The second way the Teachings of John Africa disciplined the body was through work. To MOVE people, hard work was a sacrament. To work hard was to be fully human, in touch with the divine. On a typical day, MOVE people woke before dawn, boarded a school bus they owned, and drove to Clark Park, a large open field ten minutes from the Powelton house. There, MOVE men, women, and children ran around the park for an hour or more. After the morning run, MOVE people returned home to walk their dogs. MOVE cared for dozens of dogs at any given time. Because their theology forbade them from having their dogs spayed or neutered, new litters were constant. After walking the dogs, MOVE sat down for breakfast. Then the day's work began. MOVE supported themselves through handyman services and by pooling their welfare checks. They also ran a carwash in front of the MOVE house, consisting of a garden hose and some buckets and sponges. On busy days, the car wash could bring in $300–$400 in donations. Much of the work was divided by gender, though this was less of an ideological prescription as it was a practical necessity. The men picked up odd jobs around the neighborhood and manned the car wash. The women were responsible for the unending work of preparing meals for the growing congregation. They bought fresh fruits and vegetables from the market daily. Because there was no electricity or gas much of the time, most of the meals were cooked outside over a barrel fire.[29]

The Teachings of John Africa taught MOVE people to guard against anything that alters the body's natural chemistry. MOVE people were expected not to smoke or drink. Drugs of all kinds—including marijuana, prescription medication, and over-the-counter medicines—were strictly forbidden. John Africa called these "violations of the body." One of the most effective means of escaping the grips of the System was to eliminate all violations. In MOVE, violations included eating too much food, drinking too much water, and not sleeping enough. John Africa did not punish violations of the body; violations were not transgressions against him, but against Life. Life punishes violations. When someone drinks too much water, for example, they are punished with an urgent, painful need to urinate. When they drink too much, they suffer from hangovers. When they overeat, they suffer from intestinal discomfort. John Africa taught MOVE people to interpret some of their bodies' signals—especially pain—as divine punishment for violating their bodies. John Africa understood that, while striving toward perfection was necessary, MOVE people would inevitably fail. In MOVE, he instituted what he called "distortion days." These were special occasions when MOVE people were encouraged to engage in some of the violations they were striving to rid themselves of. Of course, many violations were unthinkable: there was no drug use or alcohol or promiscuous sex on distortion days. Instead, MOVE people might gorge on junk food and candy, watch television, or skip their daily exercise regimen. It was not as much of a day of licentiousness as it was a dieter's cheat day.[30]

The process of disciplining religious bodies alters religious bodies. The altered body, like the regulated body, is a way for religions to set boundaries, to include and exclude, and to claim the body of the believer for the religion. MOVE people looked like MOVE people, dressed like MOVE people, and smelled like MOVE people. All MOVE people wore their hair naturally, uncombed and uncut, a style that was controversial in the early 1970s, especially among middle-class and upwardly mobile African Americans, for whom respectability was the most promising way toward racial advancement. MOVE people dressed unfashionably. Both men and women wore unwashed sweatshirts, blue jeans, and work boots. Most alarming to MOVE's critics, MOVE people did not take baths, except for the occasional dip in the creek. They did not use soap or personal hygiene products. Instead, they occasionally rubbed their bodies with a mash of garlic and herbs. The smell, too, was a way for MOVE people to mark themselves as a separate people and to reclaim their bodies from the System.

For MOVE people, reclaiming the body from the System was empowering and salvific. This was doubly true for the Black people in MOVE. Reclaiming their body for nature and rescuing it from the System was a radically agentive act given that the Black body was more closely watched and tightly regulated. Ramona Africa, who joined MOVE in the late 1970s, found the Teachings of John Africa to be profoundly empowering. On one particularly beautiful day, John Africa encouraged MOVE people to take a break from their work and go outside to get some sun. Everyone happily obliged except for Ramona, who stayed behind. John Africa asked Ramona why she rarely went outside. It hadn't occurred to Ramona that she spent most of her time inside, but John Africa began rattling off examples of times Ramona had avoided going out in the sun. John Africa's probing questions led Ramona to realize that, as a child, she had internalized the idea that Black skin was ugly. Subconsciously, she had been avoiding the sun because she was afraid of getting darker. The System taught people to feel ashamed of their bodies. John Africa taught her to see her body as beautiful, perfectible, and exempt from the System.[31]

The Teachings of John Africa oriented the body away from the System and toward the divine. MOVE people's clothing, hygiene, and grooming choices were a way of setting themselves apart as a religious community. But opting in to MOVE was, in effect, opting out of the System. The lifestyle the System demanded—working a job, dating non-MOVE people, even driving a car—was rendered much more difficult after the physical changes MOVE people underwent. But MOVE people found orienting their bodies toward nature to be transformative, physically and spiritually. The Teachings of John Africa gave MOVE people a way of understanding their bodies in relation to the divine, of mapping the communal onto the corporeal, and of establishing the boundaries of their peoplehood. MOVE people's bodies became religiously formed bodies, positioned in relation to the Teachings of John Africa. Positioning the body allowed MOVE people to locate themselves within the wider sphere in which their religion dwelled: the home.[32]

MOVE people embraced, even sacralized, marriage, family, and parenting. In MOVE, family was both a description of the corporate kinship the Teachings of John Africa inspired and a model social institution. John Africa believed traditional, nuclear family structures were ideal. MOVE people were expected to couple, marry (unofficially, of course), and produce children. Children knew their parents. Nuclear families shared domestic space together. John Africa taught MOVE people to parent using two principles, which he called the Principle of Caring and the Principle of Sharing. He believed that children in the System suffered from the "pain of separation" caused by absent or disengaged fathers or by being left with caregivers while parents "partied" or worked. John Africa taught parents in MOVE to be with their children all the time. Ideally, the child should always be within reach. If a child requests attention, the parent should prioritize child care over everything else. This philosophy of childrearing offended some judges, who considered it inappropriate for children to attend court dates or were offended by MOVE women breastfeeding in the gallery.[33]

John Africa instituted a family-based sense of home in MOVE through his relatively conservative teachings on sex and reproduction. Sex in MOVE was strictly monogamous and heterosexual. John Africa encouraged MOVE people to couple with other MOVE people, and to bear as many children as Mama intended. MOVE people did not use birth control in any form, which they regarded as antithetical to the proliferation of Life. John Africa taught that homosexuality was "perverted" and "distorted." John Africa disdained the "punishment" of abortion. He taught that abortion was murder, arguing that "to murder is to exploit, kill off, abort." Marriage in MOVE was for life. John Africa hated divorce and mentioned it frequently in *The Guidelines*. Divorce, John Africa wrote, existed only in the System "because there was never any marriage, any harmony, there is only the illusion of wedlock." Undoubtedly, John Africa's teachings on divorce drew from Vincent Leaphart's marriage with Dorothy Clark.[34]

John Africa taught that people living within the System should pursue relationships only with those of the same race. John Africa viewed race as a fixed biological reality. God created humans as different races because each race was meant to inhabit a different part of the world: Africans in Africa, Europeans in Europe, Asians in Asia, and so on. Racism—and a whole host of other problems, including war, famine, and the need for external government—resulted from the fact "one race cannot relate rationally to another." "Mixing of the races," John Africa wrote, "is a distortion of Nature's intentions"—both on the world-historical level and on the personal level. For this reason, interracial relationships should be strictly avoided. *The Guidelines* state that people who are mixed race "must, indeed, will be corrected" by being "absorbed into the dominant races." John Africa, aware that some people may find this teaching hurtful, assures people of mixed race that they "need not feel . . . <u>especially</u> perverted, as this violation is merely physical in character, and no worse than any other."[35]

But race, and the problems it caused, afflicted those still trapped in the System. Although people outside the System were instructed to find partners from within their own races, people inside MOVE frequently partnered with people of different races. Most children born in MOVE were of mixed race. For MOVE people, race had been eradicated. MOVE people used the surname "Africa" to both mark conversions and signify the construction of a new "racio-religious identity" based on a shared commitment to following the Teachings of John Africa. The name Africa did not, as many have assumed, signal a commitment to afrocentrism. Rather, John Africa adopted the name because he believed the continent of Africa is where all life originated. The "Africa" that John Africa's name evokes is the Edenic, primordial place and time when Life was not yet victim to the System. It did not refer to a geopolitical entity. Nowhere in his thought did John Africa suggest that Africans in diaspora should return to Africa. Nor did he revere the geopolitical Africa as a symbolic ideal. In fact, John Africa held a very pessimistic view of Africa. In *The Guidelines*, John Africa wrote that "the Africans invested their lives in government and the relics and ruins of that civilization still remain." The name "Africa" rooted MOVE people in the primordial past. By evoking a place/time that existed apart from the System, "Africa" bestowed upon those that took the name the status of outsider, set apart from the ravages of the System.[36]

Most prophets contend their revelation is sui generis, and most historians will argue that is rarely the case. John Africa's thought derived from many sources: the Black Church, the American metaphysical tradition, the Black natural law tradition, Hegelian metaphysics, Marxism, Black Power, and others. It is an eclectic belief system, but it is an intelligible one. It is no less sophisticated than many of the traditions that constitute American religious history. It is a religious system that few outside of MOVE understand—MOVE people prefer it that way—and this secretiveness has played no small role in how difficult their history has been. The Teachings of John Africa have inspired MOVE people to remarkable levels of piety and self-discipline. They have both fulfilled and destroyed MOVE people's lives. They have inspired peace and violence. MOVE is a system of beliefs and practices that, like its creator, is full of contradictions.

Notes

1. Robert Africa, "On the MOVE," *Philadelphia Tribune*, August 5, 1975, n.p.
2. Louise James, *John Africa . . . Childhood Untold until Today* (self-published, 2013), 53–54; Table of Contents to The Book or The Guidelines of John Africa, PSIC.
3. Excerpts from John Africa, *The Guidelines of John Africa*, published in "On the MOVE," *Philadelphia Tribune*, July 26 and 29, 1975.
4. MOVE, untitled document, 9–10.
5. Harry Amana, "Nursing Home Head Called 'Inhumane,'" *Philadelphia Tribune*, February 12, 1974; MOVE, untitled document, 11.
6. Excerpts from John Africa, *The Guidelines of John Africa*, published in "On the MOVE," *Philadelphia Inquirer*, June 28, 1975, July 1, 1975, and July 4, 1975.
7. Doug Rossinow, *The Politics of Authenticity: Liberalism, Christianity, and the New Left in America* (New York: Columbia University Press, 1998), 1–22; "On the MOVE," *Philadelphia Tribune*, June 28, 1975, 17.
8. "On the MOVE," *Philadelphia Tribune*, July 29, 1975, 2.
9. Mary Baker Eddy, *Science and Health with Key to the Scriptures* (Boston: Allison V. Stewart, 1913), preface, 107–162; Amanda Porterfield, *Healing in the History of Christianity* (New York: Oxford University Press, 2005).
10. John Africa, *The Guidelines of John Africa*, as quoted in "On The MOVE: From the Writings of John Africa," *Philadelphia Tribune*, July 29, 1975.
11. John Africa, *The Guidelines of John Africa*, FBI manuscript.
12. Ibid.
13. John Africa, "God is as Common as Dirt," excerpt from *The Guidelines of John Africa*, reproduced in Louise Leaphart James, *John Africa . . . Childhood Untold until Today* (self published, 2013), 180–182; Loriliai Biernacki, "Panentheism Outside the Box," in *Panentheism across the World's Traditions*, edited by Loriliai Biernacki and Philip Clayton (New York: Oxford University Press, 2014): 1–17.
14. MOVE, untitled document, 11. On the rejection of supernaturalism in Black religion, see Anthony B. Pinn, "Religion, Race, and Humanism," in *The Oxford Handbook of Religion and Race in American History*, edited by Kathryn Gin Lum and Paul Harvey (New York: Oxford University Press, 2018). J. M. Floyd-Thomas, "The Burning of Rebellious Thoughts: MOVE as Revolutionary Black Humanism," *The Black Scholar* 32, no. 1 (2002): 11–21.
15. MOVE, untitled document, 11; Leigh Eric Schmidt, *Restless Souls: The Making of American Spirituality from Emerson to Oprah* (San Francisco: HarperCollins, 2005), 158–161; Bruce F. Campbell, *Ancient Wisdom Revived: A History of the Theosophical Movement* (Berkeley: University of California Press, 1980), 147–204; Catherine L. Albanese, *A Republic of Mind and Spirit: A Cultural History of American Metaphysical Religion* (New Haven, CT: Yale University Press, 2008), 257–283.
16. MOVE, untitled document, 11.
17. Ibid.
18. Ibid., 10.

19. Ibid., 11–12.
20. Proceedings of the Philadelphia Yearly Meeting of the Religious Society of Friends, 1974, Friends Historical Library, Swarthmore College, Swarthmore, PA, 34.
21. *Proceedings of the Philadelphia Yearly Meeting*, 4.
22. MOVE to James Laird, September 11, 1974, Box 91a, Philadelphia Yearly Meeting of the Religious Society of Friends, 1974, Friends Historical Library, Swarthmore College, Swarthmore, PA.
23. Clifford Geertz, "Religion as a Cultural Symbol," in *The Interpretation of Cultures: Selected Essays* (Waukegan, IL: Fontana Press, 1993), 125; John Africa, "On Religion," from *The Guidelines of John Africa*, reproduced in "MOVE History," Box 8, Folder 5, Philadelphia Special Investigation (MOVE) Commission Records, Urban Archives, Temple University, Philadelphia, PA; MOVE, "An Open Letter to City and State Officials," March 7, 1978, Cardinal's Commission on Human Relations, MOVE Folder, Philadelphia Archdiocesan Historical Research Center, Wynnewood, PA.
24. Louise Africa, "On the MOVE," *Philadelphia Tribune*, December 6, 1975.
25. John Africa, *The Guidelines of John Africa*, unpublished manuscript.
26. Thomas A. Tweed, *Crossing and Dwelling: A Theory of Religion* (Cambridge, MA: Harvard University Press, 2006), 98.
27. Excerpts from John Africa, *The Guidelines of John Africa*, in "On the MOVE," *Philadelphia Tribune*, June 28, 1975.
28. *Frank Africa v. The State of Pennsylvania, et al.*, 520 F. Supp. 967 (United States District Court, E. D. Pennsylvania, 1981).
29. Louise Africa, "On the MOVE," *Philadelphia Tribune*, October 21, 1975; Larry Eichel, "MOVE Members Speak Out—Loudly and Often," *Philadelphia Inquirer*, April 21, 1975; Federal Bureau of Investigation, Philadelphia Field Office, Memo, Agent Turner to Special Agent in Charge, May 13, 1975.
30. Louise Africa, "On the MOVE," *Philadelphia Tribune*, November 29, 1975.
31. Ramona Africa, transcript of an oral history conducted in 2016 by Richard Kent Evans, MOVE Oral History Project, Special Collections and Urban Archives, Temple University, Philadelphia, PA.
32. Tweed, *Crossing and Dwelling*, 83.
33. Louise Africa, "On the MOVE," December 6, 1975, and December 9, 1975.
34. John Africa, *The Guidelines of John Africa*, as quoted in "On The MOVE: From the Writings of John Africa," *Philadelphia Tribune*, July 12, 1975.
35. *Guidelines*, 49.
36. Judith Weisenfeld, *New World A-Coming: Black Religion and Racial Identity during the Great Migration* (New York: New York University Press, 2016), 13–15; Excerpts from John Africa, *The Guidelines of John Africa*, in "On the MOVE," *Philadelphia Tribune*, June 28, 1975, 17.

3
Progress

In September 1974, the city of Philadelphia hosted a re-enactment of the 1774 Continental Congress. It was the first official event of the city's upcoming bicentennial celebrations. Governors from eleven of the original colonies attended the event, and President Gerald Ford delivered the keynote address to a crowd gathered on Independence Mall. For these politicians, the Continental Congress was an opportunity to reaffirm their "belief in America's basic principles" and a chance to debate the most pressing public policy issues facing the new administration. But most of all, it was a celebration of progress. At the concluding dinner inside Independence Hall, President Ford spoke about how far America had come in its first two centuries. At the time of the first Continental Congress, there were only around 2.5 million people living in the thirteen colonies. Now, he said, "our people number more than 211 million." In just two hundred years, Americans had conquered the entire continent, spreading into fifty states as far flung as Hawaii and Alaska. The Founders' belief that they controlled their own destinies—that they could bring about a better future through their own agency—"remain[ed] a lesson as to what a few, a very few, dedicated people can do," the president said. The bicentennial offered Americans in the 1970s the opportunity to reflect on what a commitment to progress had wrought. And President Ford was confident that the progress America had achieved proved that the past two hundred years had been "the greatest experiment in the history of man governing himself."[1]

To the MOVE people demonstrating outside, the progress being celebrated in Independence Hall was nothing but a false god. From their perspective, the re-enactment of the Continental Congress exposed the hypocrisy of American politics. The politicians inside venerated free speech as demonstrators outside were confined behind police barricades. They praised the brilliance of the Constitution (one politician called it a "perfect document") just weeks after Nixon resigned for his role in the Watergate scandal. They gave thanks for peace and prosperity at home after a decade of assassinations and urban rebellions. They enjoyed safety and comfort while sowing death and destruction abroad. For MOVE, the Continental Congress presented the perfect opportunity to lay bare the hypocrisy of the System—to expose the false god of progress as nothing more than cruel irony. To expose a false god, they reasoned, one must profane it. So, from 1974 to 1976, MOVE people did just this. They profaned the god of progress by demonstrating against politicians, religious leaders, entertainment figures, and political movements. They used profane language, situationally inappropriate attire, and disrespectful behavior to draw attention to the sacredness with which American society imbued organized religion, political advancement, and formal education. They refused to genuflect before the power of the state in order to expose, they believed, the false trust Americans had placed in government. John Africa taught that by merely forcing Americans to confront the hypocrisy inherent in their false religion of progress, the System would crumble. But to do that, MOVE people had to profane what American society held sacred, and to venerate the sacredness of Life that American society had forgotten. Progress—the idea that we can make the world a better place, that technology can relieve our suffering, that we control our own destinies—*this* was America's golden calf. And it was up to MOVE to smash it.

Progress is a commitment—a faith, really—that entered the world around the turn of the eighteenth century. The historical ruptures of that time, including the American and French Revolutions, assured Enlightened moderns that they controlled the course of their own lives, and that they might create for themselves a radically different and better world. Progress, in the words of political philosopher Peter Wagner, depends on a certain conception of the human being "as capable of autonomy and as endowed with reason." Reason allowed human beings to comprehend the problems they faced and to develop solutions to those problems. Progress lives in the temporal horizon between human experience and anticipated human futures. It was (and is) an inherently optimistic idea that relies on certain fundamental assumptions about the human condition: that with the coming of modernity, human beings are entering an age in which rationalism has supplanted supernaturalism, and forms of formal domination are beginning to fade away, when human beings could expect the accumulation of knowledge (institutionalized in the rise of modern universities) to yield intergenerational, permanent accumulation of knowledge, and in which technological advancement might create a more just and peaceful future.[2]

To John Africa, progress was a false god. The theology he developed could be understood as not only a rejection of the optimism inherent in the

Enlightenment concept of progress, but also its conception of the human as ideally rational and autonomous. According to *The Guidelines*, humankind, in its arrogance, was not satisfied with the perfect, natural order of Life. Humans put their faith in themselves, their autonomy, their technology, and in their rationality. Human beings rejected the sacredness in the everyday—the existence of life, water, air, food—the very presence of which evinced the immanence of the divine. These things, the basic elements of life, these were what humankind should hold sacred. The earth, food, water, and air were the medium through which God creates and sustains Life. The world was God's unfolding revelation: the manifestation of the sacred, perfect in essence. Whereas earth, food, water, and air produced the sacredness of Life, humankind's false god of progress produced death, disease, violence, and exploitation. Within the System, people kill one another, poison the water, and pollute the air—all in the name of progress. In doing so, they profane the sacred. Many people who have written about MOVE have noticed the group's "anti-technology" stance. Indeed, MOVE people rejected most modern conveniences. They did not use electricity or heat. They cooked with fire. They used automobiles only when necessary. They drank and bathed with rainwater. But MOVE's spurning of most technologies was just one manifestation of a much more deeply seated theology: humankind had placed their trust in the false god of progress.[3]

John Africa explained this theology in a section of *The Guidelines* titled "On Progress":

THE WHEEL WAS INTRODUCED AS AN ATTEMPTED REPLACEMENT OF THE LEGS AND FAILED, GAS WAS TAKEN FROM THE ASSURED ARTERIES OF GAS VEINS AND PUMPED THROUGH THE FAILING PIPES OF ASPHYXIATED DECEPTION, THE AUTOMOBILE WAS INTRODUCED AS A REPLACEMENT FOR NATURAL MOBILITY, AND IMMOBILIZED YOUR LEGS, CRAMMED YOUR LUNGS WITH POISON, RETARDED YOUR BREATHING RHYTHM AND CAUSED THE ACTIVITY OF YOUR HEART TO FAIL, ELECTRICITY HAS BEEN PROSTITUTED FROM THE SECURE ORIGIN OF ENERGY, ADMINISTRATOR OF SAFETY, DISTRIBUTOR OF ASSURED EQUILITY [sic], NATURAL DISPENSATION OF SUBSTANCE AND HAS STRUNG OUT THE BLAZING FIRES OF ACCIDENT THROUGHOUT THE FAILING HISTORY OF PROSTITUTION, THE AIRPLANE WAS SUPPOSED TO BE THE PERSONIFICATION OF TRANSPORT, THE EPIC CONCLUSION OF TRAVEL, SPACE AGE DUPLICATION OF THE BIRD, AND THE TRAGEDY, THE ACCIDENT RATE, INSURANCE PREMIUM OF THIS

> CONTEMPTIBLE DEMON OF NOSE-DIVING DECEPTION IS STILL GOING UP, THE ELECTRIC LIGHT BULB IS NOTHING MORE THAN A FAILING EXPRESSION OF THE SUN THAT IS CONSTANTLY BLOWING OUT, BEING REPLACED, FAILING AGAIN AND BEING HALED AS NECESSARY, YET IF THE SUN WERE TO FAIL JUST ONCE WHO OF US WOULD BE AROUND TO ARGUE THE NECESSITY OF THIS DISASTER, FOR THE PURPOSE OF NECESSITY IS THE ABSENCE OF FAILURE.[4]

Throughout *The Guidelines*, John Africa uses technology both literally and figuratively, to refer to the ways humans use progress to interrupt the natural order of Life. Humans create technology to replicate that which God has provided. Literal technology—the product of human invention—is a simulacrum of the sacred, a graven image. When John Africa writes that the "natural dispensation of substance has strung out the blazing fire of accident," he is suggesting that we can read divine agency into "accidents" of technology. Plane crashes, car accidents, even blown light bulbs are evidence of "duplication," that the energies of the divine have "been prostituted from the secure origin of energy." To place one's faith in progress was not only to tempt divine retribution (the "blazing fires of accident"), it was to reject God.[5]

If John Africa was right—if Americans worshipped a false god of progress—then Buckminster Fuller was their high priest. Few people embodied the faith that Americans had in progress in the mid-1970s quite like Fuller. The self-described "comprehensive anticipatory design scientist" was globally famous for his futuristic inventions and idealistic plans for world peace. Some of his most notable inventions—an eleven-seat automobile with three wheels and a mass-produced circular house that could be airlifted and assembled in a day—withered on the vine. Others, most notably the geodesic dome—proved wildly successful. It was this success that transformed Fuller from an obscure eccentric into, as the *Philadelphia Inquirer* put it, a "hero of American culture."[6]

To be sure, Buckmister Fuller wanted to be known as a prophet of progress. He relished his larger-than-life reputation and carefully cultivated a mystical persona. Over the course of his career, Fuller developed a myth surrounding his early life that is not unlike the kinds of stories prophets tell about their lives. Indeed, the story Fuller told about the launch of his career was not unlike the story John Africa told about his. According to his lore, Fuller lived the first thirty-two years of his life as a failure. He had a wife and newborn daughter, but no job to support them. Despondent, Fuller walked along the shoreline of Lake Michigan calculating how long he'd have to swim before he died from hypothermia. He had to make his suicide look like an accident so that his wife and daughter would benefit from his life insurance policy. Just as he was about to jump in the water, however, Buckminster Fuller heard a voice in his head which told him, "You do not have the right to eliminate yourself. You belong to the universe." Suddenly, Fuller discovered his life's calling. He would share his genius with the world. He would no longer have to work: he felt assured that as long as he worked for the betterment of mankind, his family would never know want. So, the story goes, Buckminster Fuller left the shores of Lake Michigan a new man. He told his wife that he would not have to work anymore, and then retreated into solitude for two years. Over those two years, Fuller, entranced, created five thousand pages of drawings, writings, and blueprints for technology that would lead mankind, he believed, toward the future. The story Fuller told about his life as a young man is surely familiar to students of American religious history. The dramatic conversion experience, the years of solitude, and the trance-like production of knowledge can be found throughout the American metaphysical tradition, especially in figures like Andrew Jackson Davis, Joseph Smith, and Mary Baker Eddy. To his most astute biographers, Fuller's origin story seems to contain far more fiction than fact. But it tells us a great deal about the man's faith in progress—the kind of faith John Africa set out to profane.[7]

In 1972, Buckminster Fuller accepted the post of World Fellow in Residence at the University of Pennsylvania. He lived in Philadelphia through 1975 and frequently gave public lectures. It was at one of these lectures, probably in the fall of 1974, that MOVE first confronted the scientist-philosopher. MOVE people in the audience challenged the faith that Fuller placed in progress. According to MOVE sources, Fuller was intrigued by what the MOVE people had to say, and invited them to speak with him privately afterward. MOVE people most often confronted groups and thinkers they imagined as most similar to themselves, and Buckminster Fuller was no different. John Africa had much in common with Fuller. Both men had undergone a dramatic conversion experience. Both men believed that Nature was perfect in essence—so much so that both insisted upon capitalizing the word. Fuller saw perfection in Nature and wanted to replicate it through technology. He hoped this would prove humankind's salvation. John Africa saw perfection in Nature, but believed that humankind's attempts to replicate it had been a mistake. It was as if both men had received the same revelation, but had taken that revelation in opposite directions.[8]

MOVE people and Buckminster Fuller spoke for over four hours. According to MOVE sources, Fuller was deeply impressed by the MOVE people's wisdom and admired their understanding of the nature of the universe. He concluded that their prophet, John Africa, was not unlike himself. He asked for a copy of *The Guidelines*, and the MOVE people explained that, although they could not leave a copy with him, they would gladly meet with him again to discuss the Teachings of John Africa in depth. Fuller agreed and met with MOVE a second time. MOVE people read a passage from *The Guidelines* which, they believed, "completely analyzed and disqualified the concept of time." In the passage, John Africa teaches that time is an illusion, "a pointless, preoccupation that serves only to separate, divide the . . . unbroken activity of Life's movement." As MOVE people remembered it, Fuller agreed with the essence of John Africa's teachings, and explained how his own philosophy accorded with the illusory nature of time. Fuller thought he was recognizing the genius of MOVE's prophet, but the MOVE people there thought he was missing the point. They explained to Fuller that if he truly agreed that time was an illusion, he was wasting his life. Science, they argued, was at its core an attempt to reform the universe. Fuller's life pursuit had been a "perpetual question, a problematical maze of blind theories, reckless guesses that have . . . no relation to the factual reality of the universe." In Fuller's philosophy and in John Africa's theology, humankind lived in a disordered state within an ordered universe. But to MOVE people, Fuller's attempts to reform humankind's disordered state only led to more disorder. Fuller's faith in progress had blinded him to what MOVE people believed was an ultimate truth: human progress is predicated on a false division between humankind and the natural world. According to MOVE's recollection of the meeting, Buckminster Fuller grew very nervous. MOVE people believed they forced Fuller to admit that he did not fully comprehend the meaning of the universe and to admit that his life's work—even his geodesic dome—was nothing more than an illusion. Finally, he asked MOVE to leave him be. MOVE people interpreted Fuller's behavior as an admission that his genius was no match for that of John Africa. It is far more likely that Fuller was realizing that MOVE people did not intend to have a dialogue with him at all.[9]

MOVE's disagreement with Buckminster Fuller was over the nature of time. Progress is, according to Peter Wagner, a way of conceiving time as a "linear path that leads from the limited past experiences to an even better future." Human history, according to this way of thinking, is an ongoing program of improvement. John Africa taught that a linear, progressive conception of time was a "pointless preoccupation"—an artificial reality that the System imposed onto Life. He conceived of "time" as cyclical, not linear or progressive. Human agency did not lead *toward* perfection, but away from it. To MOVE people, that human agency led away from perfection was self-evident. "We are often reminded of the age of so-called progress in which we live," Louise Africa wrote. "How is it possible to see ourselves as living in an age of so called progress when the very world in which we are so called progressing is steadily going DOWN HILL." When MOVE people looked at human history, they did not see progress, but deterioration. Technological progress, the kind Buckminster Fuller was famous for, led not to more prosperity and peace, but to "destruction" and "starvation." Computers made millions of people's jobs obsolete. More "advanced" bombs were capable of destroying civilization itself. To MOVE people, progress was a dangerous illusion, a fundamental misperception of the nature of time.[10]

MOVE people confronted Fuller several more times during public forums and lectures, but the scientist did not again show an interest in the Teachings of John Africa. In December 1974, MOVE people attended a symposium at the University of Pennsylvania on world peace. Buckminster Fuller had inaugurated the three-year symposium a year earlier with the goal of bringing the world's brightest minds to Philadelphia to take part in a series of lectures and workshops. Fuller believed that the imbalance between the means of production and distribution—which he believed had made war necessary throughout human history—was on its way toward equilibrium, and that "permanent world peace" was attainable by the year 1985. MOVE people visited a public symposium which featured the United States ambassador to the United Nations, Charles Woodruff Yost, Joseph Clark, a former United States senator and mayor of Philadelphia, and Buckminster Fuller. MOVE people sat quietly in the audience during the presentations. As the question-and-answer period began, a MOVE person stood up and asked the panel members to "explain what peace is." The panel was unsure how to go about answering the question. After a long pause, one of the panelists answered that peace was "an environment in which people can work at solving their problems" without resorting to violence. This answer—that peace was the absence of violent conflict—was unsatisfying to the MOVE people in the audience. To MOVE people, the faith these world leaders had in their false god of progress—in their belief that the world could be made a better and more peaceful place through human efforts—was hopelessly misguided. These thought leaders were working through a framework of progress: they used their rational minds to comprehend the problems they faced (war, famine, conflict) and then used their agency to devise solutions to those problems. To John Africa, "as long as such things as problems, another word for conflict, exist, there can be no peace." Conflict was not a natural phenomenon, but the product of human agency—the logical outcome of human beings trying to impose order on an already perfectly ordered universe. Peace was not the absence of conflict. Peace was the absence of progress.[11]

John Africa's teachings on the need to profane Americans' faith in progress explains why MOVE appeared to outsiders as surprisingly hostile to the political left. Today, MOVE's politics have shifted decidedly to the left, but in the 1970s, MOVE people viewed political liberalism as the manifestation of humankind's misguided sacralization of progress. On February 27, 1974, MOVE people confronted Tom Hayden and Jane Fonda at a speaking engagement in Philadelphia (the two had married a year earlier). MOVE objected to the activists' self-description as "revolutionaries." How, MOVE asked, could they claim to be revolutionaries if they did not understand the true meaning of revolution? According to MOVE sources, Jane Fonda left the stage almost as soon as MOVE people began to speak. Tom Hayden chose to engage the MOVE people in the audience, and they discussed John Africa's definition of "revolution" for about an hour. A similar exchange took place that same month between MOVE and Daniel Ellsberg, the former Rand Corporation military analyst who leaked the Pentagon Papers. Ellsberg chose to end his question-and-answer period after a particularly confrontational question from a MOVE person in the audience. After a public speech, Walter Mondale—then a senator from Minnesota—had security guards bar MOVE from the question-and-answer session.[12]

Because New Left activism depended on progress, MOVE people believed it was doomed from the beginning. In April 1974, MOVE people received permission to address an audience who had gathered to hear a speech by Russell Means, the national director of the American Indian Movement who had led the group's occupation at Wounded Knee a year earlier. MOVE people who attended Means's speech understood him to be arguing that "Indian people wanted to be left alone, that they didn't want to overthrow the government, but wanted the treaties enforced." As MOVE people explained to the dwindling audience after Means's speech, Means's demands amounted to asking for the "crumbs doled out by the same people who stole the cake." Several passages in *The Guidelines* refer to the Law of Equal Distribution.

According to this law, God had given all people groups a natural habitat, and deviation from this natural order led to violence, exploitation, and racism. Native Americans played a key role in this theology. God had placed Native Americans on the North American continent. It belonged to them. All other races currently living in the United States were violating divine law. Thus, the MOVE people during their speech accused Means—whom they called a "schizophrenic traitor"—of "endors[ing] the thieving, gang raping policy that was responsible for the genocide perpetuated on the Indians in the first place."[13]

The Law of Equal Distribution motivated MOVE people to confront Cesar Chavez, leader of the United Farm Workers and civil rights activist, in May 1974. Unlike Russell Means, whom MOVE people believed was not going far enough in his advocacy on behalf of Native Americans, Cesar Chavez was going too far. MOVE people, again addressing the audience after Chavez had left the stage, argued that Chavez was "doing nothing but misleading the Chicanos when advocating unionizing tactics to gain rights." In fact, MOVE people argued, Chicanos deserved no rights while in the United States, which, according to the Law of Equal Distribution, did not belong to them. "In asking for a fair share of a country which belongs to neither his people, nor those who rule," MOVE people said of Chavez, "he is putting his people in the boomerang position of the victim asking for part of the crime."[14]

MOVE's critique of progress led them to confront the women's movement as well. John Africa taught his followers that gender, like race, was "philosophical nonsense" created to "alienate [and] create inferiority." In a state of nature, men and women are "harmoniously . . . accepted as inseparable, equal." It is only because people in the System accept the idea of gender that women remain subjugated. In February 1974, four MOVE women attended an International Women's Day celebration. After an opening tribute to Susan B. Anthony, the conference organizers aired a film honoring Vietnamese women who took up arms to defend their villages. A member of the United Farm Workers' union then spoke out on the need for better working conditions for women in agriculture. A lesbian activist spoke on, as MOVE put it, "new avenues of love for women." Finally, a women's liberation activist spoke on the need for a feminist revolution. When the speakers had finished, the four MOVE women approached the dais and requested five minutes of the conference's time to "communicate valid and important information." MOVE believed that the International Women's Day celebration exemplified the misplaced faith the women's liberation movement had placed in progress. The participants believed they were leading a feminist revolution, but in fact, by accepting gender as a valid categorization, the women's activists gained only "the opportunity to hold hands with the slave master." The MOVE women objected to the idea that a Vietnamese woman taking up arms represented a feminist ideal, and rejected the conference's acceptance of same-sex relationships. As they explained to the women at the conference, women had not made progress "towards a better way of life, but had merely exchanged problems, swapped chaos with the alleged superior sex, man."[15]

MOVE's criticism of the left was not that they disagreed with particular policies. It was much more fundamental than that. Their critique was of the foundational assumption undergirding liberal and leftist politics: that humankind can make the world a better place through their own agency. Progress—what Means, Chavez, Mondale, Ellsberg, Hayden, Fonda, and the women behind the Women's Day celebration were working for—"will never work, as you cannot solve a problem by perpetuating the problem." MOVE people agreed that the world was disordered and unjust. But faith in the false god of progress was only making it worse.[16]

To John Africa, humankind's misguided sacralization of progress originated in the belief that humans were superior to other life forms with which we shared the planet. Humans' treatment of animals was especially emblematic of humankind's propensity to imprison, manipulate, and exploit supposedly lesser forms of life. A passage in *The Guidelines* on animals offers both practical advice for caring for pets (he instructs his readers how to train a puppy to walk safely with and without the use of a leash) and broader teachings about humankind's distorted practice of altering the bodies of animals. *The Guidelines of John Africa* warns against the "mantality [sic] that kills meaninglessly, murders, butchers, burns and skins animals, fleecing them of their coats, [and] selling them at a profit." There is a long passage denouncing pet stores and the elevation of certain dog breeds above mutts. John Africa supported people caring for dogs as pets in their homes. He recommends adopting dogs from the A.S.P.C.A. The book teaches that recreational hunting, fishing, and even camping inflict "all manner of pain, feeding the germ of extinction, distortion, and mutation." Shoeing horses, spaying and neutering household pets, docking their ears and tails, and whipping and spurring animals are also decried. Elsewhere in that section of *The Guidelines*, John Africa writes that circuses, zoos, and other forms of human recreation involving the captivity of animals exist only to "feed some perverted ego."[17]

MOVE people put John Africa's teachings about animals into practice with a series of public demonstrations in the summer of 1973. A typical MOVE demonstration (MOVE sources nearly always use the word "demonstration" instead of "protest") involved several MOVE people holding signs with quotes from *The Guidelines*. Often, a MOVE person would read aloud relevant sections from the manuscript. John Africa occasionally attended these demonstrations but never participated directly, choosing instead to observe from a distance. In the summer of 1973, MOVE people presented the Teachings of John Africa during demonstrations against the Barnum and Bailey Circus, the Philadelphia Zoo, the Bronx Zoo, and a Philadelphia area horse-racing track. During these demonstrations, MOVE people tried to explain to passersby that MOVE was not singling out that particular zoo, circus, or racetrack, but that they were using them as illustrations to make a larger point "against the System that thinks in terms of imbalance [and] exploitation." To MOVE people, forms of recreation requiring animal captivity were but one symptom of a much larger problem. They explained during these demonstrations that the same broader system of evil that imprisoned animals for fun was that which "will continue to create Watergates, exploit Vietnams, invade Cambodias . . . corrupt the meaning of common, inflame the morals of people, [and] provoke disruption." As they tried to explain to the public, the same System that imprisons animals threatens to imprison us all.[18]

In August 1973, MOVE spent five days demonstrating at the meeting of the American Veterinary Medical Association. As veterinarians traversed the blocks outside the convention center, MOVE told them that they were "sadistic scalpel-wielding perverts." As MOVE explained it, the System taught these veterinarians that they were doing God's work. They believed, falsely, that they were "dedicated to helping, caring for, and healing animal life." But veterinary science, like medical science and any other form of specialized knowledge, was "an outgrowth of distortion, a perverted offspring of this degenerating style of life." According to John Africa, veterinary science was "trying to play God." Any attempt to alter the "body chemistry" of any species of life will inevitably backfire, and that "any violation of this fixed principle by an external influence will cause the animal or any species of life, to become unfixed, sick, degenerate."[19]

It was this same belief in the false elevation of humankind over other forms of life that inspired MOVE people to storm the stage at a taping of the Mike Douglas Show, a nationally syndicated daytime television talk show.

Weeks earlier, a trained chimpanzee named Marvin the Magnificent, who often appeared on television and in movies, had been a guest on the show. During the taping of the segment, a spoof of Planet of the Apes, Marvin stormed toward the camera crew, bit his trainer, and smashed equipment. Marvin was subdued hours later by a tranquilizer delivered via blow dart from a zookeeper. Several national papers ran a photo of Marvin, unconscious and in police handcuffs, being stretchered out of the studio into an awaiting ambulance. Marvin's rampage through the television studios did not air live—the television show was taped—but it did make national news. This news caught the attention of MOVE people who viewed the picture of the unconscious and restrained chimpanzee as especially symbolic of humankind's crass exploitation of nonhuman forms of life. At the next taping, MOVE people in the audience stormed the stage and placed Mike Douglas in handcuffs in front of his studio audience. MOVE people explained that they had made the host into a prisoner, just as he had done to Marvin the chimpanzee.[20]

MOVE's performance on the Mike Douglas Show was simultaneously a brazen attempt to gain media attention and an exercise in what MOVE people viewed as righteous profanity. In a section of *The Guidelines* titled "On Profanity," John Africa explained that MOVE people used profane language, wore situationally inappropriate attire, and flouted social conventions because they were trying to bring attention to those aspects of social life in which Americans had placed too much faith:

> What kind of an insane lifestyle would show you a film of the attempted massacre by Hitler of an entire race of people, and preoccupy itself with editing out a single four letter word? Feeling that it will incense, inflame, upset, corrupt the morals of people, allowing this to take priority over what you are immediately witnessing. How can any word, four letters or otherwise, inflame, incense or corrupt a person, any more than the criminal, insane acts of Hitler, and all the rest of your dressed up gangsters? Showing your corruption, profanity, and senselessness, and preoccupy yourself with editing out a four letter word. Showing the profane, cruel, debased acts of a madman, and attempting to edit out profanity.
>
> Seeing the raping, plundering, murdering and enslaving of an entire black nation, and getting upset when sighting a four letter world.
>
> Protecting your son against profanity, and sending him off to Vietnam. Screening out profanity on television, and showing the massacre of Indians,

the invasion of tanks and guns into Czechoslovakia. Editing our profanity and watching black Africans shooting down other black Africans, East Indians massacreing Pakistanians, blood baths in the middle east, as you sit back and get concerned about a four letter word.[21]

In the religious thought of John Africa, society's convention of policing small profanities—the ultimately capricious regulation of language—masked what was truly profane: wars, genocide, and racism. Americans, especially, reacted with more disgust to profane words than profane deeds. This confusion over the nature of the profane was, to John Africa, rooted in a confusion over the nature of the sacred, represented most fully in humankind's faith in progress.[22]

Even though progress is fundamental to the way humans understand their own species, according to the Teachings of John Africa, humankind is not naturally born believing in progress. Faith in the false idol of progress had to be learned and taught. A fundamental assumption of progress is that the accumulation of knowledge can lead to a better world. But MOVE people rejected this idea. Robert Africa explained John Africa's teachings on education this way: "children, when born into this lifestyle, are innocent of these violations. It is not until the imposition of scientific education that they are taught the superficial categorizations, alienating divisiveness that causes war. Taking the formed, complete state of life and dividing, separating, this is white, this is red, this is China, this is Germany, this is the United States. It is not until the child starts saying 'this is my turf, this is your turf'. . . that people start getting upset."[23]

Education, to MOVE people, instilled a belief in the false god of progress. According to the Teachings of John Africa, humans are born "naturally educated," instinctually equipped with all the knowledge necessary to live in accordance with the will of God. Formal education taught children that the present was inadequate, that the natural world had to be subdued, and that time was linear. Still, MOVE held out hope that education could be redeemed from its enslavement to the System. The System was taught, so the System could be untaught. "Every time we demonstrate," Louise Africa explained in the *Tribune*, "we are truly educating people." To MOVE people, nothing could be gained from formal education; everything that could be known (and that *should* be known) was instinctive. Education only abstracted from that original knowledge. This, to MOVE people was "true education;" the only kind that led to God.[24]

In order to bring to light humanity's mistaken sacralization of the accumulation of knowledge, MOVE people spent the spring of 1974 demonstrating at meetings of the Philadelphia School Board and the New York City Board of Education. Their first effort to profane Americans' commitment to education came on February 25, 1974, when Delbert and Ted Africa cued in line to speak at the Philadelphia School Board meeting. Delbert began his speech by asking the School Board to withhold judgment of MOVE based on their appearance, tone of voice, and humble social standing. He informed the School Board that MOVE people had some important information to share and then turned the microphone over to Ted Africa, who began to read a passage from *The Guidelines* on education. As MOVE people understood it, the members of the School Board grew enraged because their power, and the sacredness with which they imbued education, had been profaned. They ordered the microphones and the television cameras cut off and abruptly adjourned the meeting. Delbert Africa tried again a few weeks later. He met with the School Board president prior to the public meeting and the two men worked out an agreement. Delbert would be allowed to speak, but only as long as he spoke on a topic relevant to the issues facing the board. Delbert agreed to speak on the problem of gangs in the public schools. However, when Delbert's allotted time arrived, the board again abruptly adjourned the meeting. The president of the School Board announced afterward that he could not allow the meetings of the School Board to become "a platform for anybody's social views."[25]

On April 8, 1974, MOVE submitted a list to the School Board prior to the meeting of seventeen MOVE people who intended to speak on issues relevant to education. The evening before the meeting, the School Board telephoned MOVE headquarters and invited Delbert and Ted Africa to meet with the School Board president prior to that evening's public meeting. According to MOVE sources, the School Board president "refused to have a two-way conversation" and instead began "raining down his arrogance, heaving his tyrannical schism all over us." At the School Board meeting later that evening, all seventeen MOVE people listed on the docket were allowed to speak. Taking turns reading from *The Guidelines*, they told the School Board that "their educational system was not working, had never worked, and would never work." For thirty minutes, MOVE people profaned all that American society held sacred about education. They called the accumulation of knowledge "useless masturbation" that can only "deform" the already "perfect form of Life." MOVE people accused the School Board of "criminally prostituting" themselves and Philadelphia's schoolchildren. After all, it was educated men who invented the cannon, the switchblade, and the atomic bomb. When they finished, Ted Africa asked the School Board if they had anything to say in their defense. They did not. They asked MOVE for a copy of *The Guidelines*, and MOVE refused. The meeting was adjourned.[26]

Over the next several weeks, MOVE people tried three more times to present John Africa's teachings on education before the school boards in Philadelphia and New York. Each time, they were informed that they would not be allowed to speak. MOVE people interpreted their ban from the school boards as religious persecution. Using an allusion to the persecution of early Christians, MOVE people wrote that their ban from the school boards was further confirmation that the Teachings of John Africa were "indicting information, healthful, life-sustaining solutions." "Truth," MOVE people wrote, "has always been banned, locked behind prison cells, stoned, crucified, silenced."[27]

MOVE's growing suspicion that they were being silenced for their religious beliefs gained credence when police officers served them with an injunction while demonstrating outside a police station. The injunction barred MOVE people from protesting in front of any municipal building (including police stations and the Board of Education building) unless they followed four stipulations: no more than five MOVE people could protest, they had to stay at least twenty-five yards away from the building, they could not use loudspeakers, and they could not "verbalize any obscenities or have them written on signs." Violating any of those four stipulations, the injunction stated, made MOVE's protests illegal and all MOVE participants subject to arrest. Furious at the injunction, MOVE people protested the next day in front of the offices of the Fraternal Order of Police (FOP; cleverly, not a municipal building), whom MOVE people suspected were behind the injunction. Within minutes, they received an amended injunction that added the FOP building to the list.[28]

Despite the new injunction against them, MOVE people continued their crusade against Americans' misguided sacralization of education. Their plan to get around their ban was to use Don Grossman, the white college instructor, to infiltrate the meetings. Because Grossman was a clean-cut white man, he would not be suspected of being a MOVE person. Grossman fell within a category often referred to in MOVE sources as a "MOVE supporter." He read *The Guidelines*. He believed in and followed the Teachings of John Africa. But as a MOVE supporter, he was not expected to believe in them exclusively. Grossman did not live in the MOVE house, though he frequented it. Like other MOVE supporters, he kept his day job and his last name. John Africa relished counting a white college professor among his adherents. And, MOVE people learned, having a well-educated, white male face representing your organization carried considerable weight.[29]

On May 20, 1974, MOVE succeeded in their plan to circumvent the injunction. As chance would have it, MOVE was the topic *de jure* for the other speakers on the docket. One of the first speakers that evening, a white man with no association with MOVE, excoriated the School Board for its prejudicial treatment of MOVE in prior weeks. He also complained about the heavy police presence that had become a staple of School Board meetings since MOVE's first appearance months earlier. Another speaker, a Black man who was also not associated with MOVE, demanded to know why MOVE had been blacklisted from the meetings. The School Board president replied that they had listened to MOVE's speech on April 8 and had been left completely baffled. He also told the speaker that the Board could not allow MOVE to speak because of their profanity. Finally, it was Donald Grossman's turn to speak. He began by listing his academic credentials. Then he announced that he was a member of MOVE. Grossman accused the School Board of lying when it said earlier that it did not understand MOVE's speech on April 8. They understood full well the scope of MOVE's charge but had no reply, Grossman alleged. The School Board again adjourned the meeting, and Donald Grossman was escorted out of the building by police. According to MOVE sources, the police began beating Grossman, kneeing him in the back and kicking him in the groin. Importantly, MOVE sources say that Grossman began screaming for the undercover Civil Affairs Unit still inside the building to come to his rescue.[30]

As MOVE people were beginning to learn, profaning the god of progress comes with a price. Several MOVE people, including Donald Grossman, were arrested that night for defying the injunction that barred them from the proceedings of the Philadelphia School Board. Those arrests were just the beginning. In the fall of 1974 the Philadelphia Police Department began arresting MOVE people in far greater numbers than they had before. Because of the injunction, the police could arrest MOVE people almost whenever they decided to. And they decided to with unusual frequency. Police arrested all the MOVE people present at the Continental Congress demonstration. Two of the MOVE people arrested were minors. When they appeared before the Municipal Court to account for their crime, Judge Jerome O'Neill accused them of being "brainwashed" by MOVE and ordered them to spend twelve days in a Youth Study Center. The sentence was later lowered to one day. Incensed by the judge's sentencing of the MOVE children, on September 27, 1974, eight MOVE adults demonstrated outside Judge O'Neill's home. This earned them an arrest for attempting to intimidate an elected official. They showed up to their court date thirty minutes late, and the judge found them guilty of contempt of court. Each MOVE defendant was sentenced to ninety days in jail, in lieu of a $300 fine, which MOVE people could not afford. Delbert Africa, who was spectating in the courtroom, angrily objected to the contempt convictions. He too earned 120 days in jail.[31]

MOVE's legal troubles should be understood from the perspective of MOVE's theology. According to the Teachings of John Africa, the most egregious—indeed the most *sacrilegious*—aspect of humankind's false worship of progress was the creation of law. To MOVE people, belonging to MOVE meant rejecting human law as a sacrilege of divine law, the Law of Mama. As Louise Africa explained, "Lest the impression be given that we have no respect for the LAW, we'd like to make clear that we know the LAW, and we have the most profound respect for IT. LAW is the very basis of our Organization, it is our Doctrine, it is our—Religion—and when you know what LAW is—you know what 'law' ain't."[32] As Vincent W. Lloyd has shown, appeals to natural law have a long history in African American religious and political thought. And John Africa was certainly engaging with this tradition as he formulated his own Law of Mama. John Africa's conception of natural law was an extreme rendering of the tradition Lloyd describes. Whereas Black natural law posited that human laws which conflicted with natural law (or God's law) were unjust and thus not worthy of obedience, to John Africa, *all* human law conflicted with natural law because no law was necessary beyond the natural. To put this another way, natural law was the only law required for human flourishing. To place one's faith in human institutions of law was to reject the law of God. All forms of human law conflicted ipso facto with natural law and were therefore evil.[33]

As the arrests began to mount and the convictions began to multiply, MOVE people were forced to put their belief in John Africa's teachings on natural law into practice in the courtroom. MOVE people on trial refused to stand as the judge entered the courtroom so as not to concede the legitimacy of human law. MOVE people who were spectators of these trials often ate food, breastfed babies, and slept during the proceedings, partly for the same reason. One courtroom incident, which took place in November

1975, is representative of the kind of chaos MOVE people introduced into the proceedings of the courts. Delbert, Conrad, and Jerry Africa were on trial for violating the injunction against interrupting the School Board meeting. The judge asked them to sign a subpoena, which they refused to do on the grounds that by signing the document they would be conceding the legitimacy of human law and violating their religious principles. Delbert explained to the court why MOVE people would not sign the subpoena. As he spoke, the judge gave all three MOVE defendants six months in jail for contempt of court. The MOVE men on trial erupted in anger at the judge's pronouncement and were escorted out. As they left, Eddie and Sam Africa entered the courtroom for their own hearings. When they saw Delbert, Conrad, and Jerry being forcibly removed, they objected as well and received contempt convictions of their own. The judge ordered the courtroom cleared. All five men were brought into the hallway, where they found two more MOVE people, Steve and Chuckie Africa, awaiting their hearings. As the MOVE people continued to object to the events in the courtroom, an "army of cops" stormed down the hall. They arrested the MOVE men in a manner that struck MOVE people as brutal.[34]

Because of the restrictive injunction against MOVE's public demonstration, arrests of MOVE people grew exponentially. From MOVE's first arrests at the Continental Congress re-enactment through the spring of 1975, MOVE people were arrested at a rate of nearly one per day. By the summer of 1976, MOVE people figured they had been arrested four hundred times. Nearly every arrest begat a series of demonstrations, resulting in more arrests arising from MOVE's use of profanity in public. Because MOVE people refused to concede the legitimacy of human law, those arrests led to courtroom appearances, which often led to the arrest of both defendants and spectators on contempt of court charges. MOVE people interpreted their multiplying arrests as the consequences of trying to draw attention to the System's worship of progress. They believed that the injunction, the endless arrests, and the beatings were the result of systematic police persecution. And they became convinced that they were being persecuted for their religious beliefs.[35]

On March 31, 1975, six MOVE women held at the House of Corrections—Laverne, Gail, Sue, Consuella, Fox (Sharon Cox, Laverne's daughter), and Sharon Penn Africa—initiated a hunger strike to draw attention to their religious persecution by government authorities. Four of them, Sue, Consuella, Fox, and Sharon Penn Africa, were pregnant when they began the strike.

Both Sue and Fox were in their third trimester. Three days into the MOVE women's hunger strike, four MOVE men—Edward, Jerry, Delbert, and Conrad Africa—began their own hunger strike from the men's wing of the House of Corrections. In a letter to prison officials, Edward, Jerry, Delbert, and Conrad Africa explained that they, and the MOVE women, had begun a hunger strike "so that our religion may be recognized." The sole purpose of the hunger strike, they wrote, was to "protest the many violations of our religious belief" which they had suffered at the House of Corrections. They wrote that their religion forbade them from receiving medical treatment of any kind, including medications and intravenous feeding, and that the hunger strike would not end until MOVE people received a "full and complete recognition of our full religious and legal competence." They demanded that certain non-incarcerated MOVE people be allowed the privileges the House of Corrections afforded ministers of other faiths. They also called for the firing of abusive corrections officers, their removal from solitary confinement, and the release of all currently incarcerated MOVE people, including those at the youth detention center.[36]

Four days into the hunger strike, prison officials decided to take action to prevent the public relations fallout that would result from a medical emergency involving one of the pregnant MOVE women. The prison superintendent went to court to request that Sue Africa be released from her sentence early for medical reasons. Sue Africa, who was white and seven months pregnant, refused to leave the House of Corrections unless the five other incarcerated MOVE women left with her. The following evening, prison guards forcibly removed Sue Africa from her jail cell. According to Sue, she fought her removal and kicked the warden. She said that guards handcuffed and shackled her and drove her to the hospital, where she refused treatment. According to the prison superintendent, the prison officials' growing concerns over Sue Africa's health and her baby's survival outweighed "her religious beliefs of not accepting medical aid." The superintendent also denied that a physical struggle had taken place. Regardless, after Sue Africa declined medical attention, she received her discharge papers. Her sentence was over.

The other nine MOVE people still in the House of Corrections continued their hunger strike. And, as the police crackdown on MOVE continued, their ranks swelled. Four MOVE people were arrested in the House of Corrections visitors' room after they refused to leave once visiting hours were over. Three days after leaving the hospital, Sue Africa attended the trial of six other MOVE people who were facing assault, disorderly conduct, and riot charges stemming from a prior demonstration. During the proceedings, Sue Africa stood up in the gallery and announced that the judge was a "schizophrenic maniac" and a "goddamned fool." She demanded that the sheriffs drag her out of the courtroom. They complied. Sue received a sentence of nine months in the House of Corrections for contempt of court. Robert Africa, Sue's husband, told the press that Sue expected to join her MOVE family in the House of Corrections. He admitted that he worried for his wife and unborn child, but that "we still have to hold fast to our beliefs."[37]

As the hunger strike began its third week, lawyers representing the MOVE women grew concerned that their clients—and their clients' unborn babies—would not survive the hunger strike. They wrote a letter to the sentencing judge asking him to meet at least some of MOVE's demands. The lawyers met with their clients on April 14 and found them to be in very poor health. Sue Africa had been suffering from severe hemorrhaging for the past three days, and the lawyers worried that she was going to miscarry. Fox Africa had lost all complexion in her skin. Sharon Africa could no longer move and required a wheelchair in and out of her cell. Even worse, the lawyers reported, the MOVE women had recently decided to stop taking water as well. They warned the judge that a fetus could not survive dehydration long. Several religious leaders, including Fathers David Gracie and Paul Washington, both Episcopal rectors and prominent civil rights leaders, signed on to the lawyers' letter. The prison superintendent, Louise Aytch, also signed.[38]

Despite the pleas of MOVE's lawyers, religious leaders, and the prison superintendent, the judge refused to negotiate, and the hunger strike continued. On April 17, Robert Africa and Clarence Farmer, the executive director of Philadelphia's Commission on Human Relations, visited Sue Africa at the House of Corrections. Though a journalist accompanied them, prison officials refused to allow the journalist inside. Robert Africa and Clarence Farmer found Sue in poor health. Though she had been able to break her hunger fast for the three days she was out of jail, Sue was nonetheless very weak. Prison officials did not allow Robert Africa and Clarence Farmer to visit the other MOVE women, who had been fasting for eighteen days.

On April 18, prison officials again released Sue Africa, temporarily this time, so that she could give birth at MOVE headquarters. According to Sue, she was again forcibly removed from the House of Corrections against her will.[39] Sharon Penn, a white woman who was seven months pregnant, and Fox Africa, a Black woman who was eight months pregnant, were also released early. Consuella, the only remaining MOVE woman in the House of Corrections, ended her fast. She had not eaten for nineteen days. On April 23, an independent doctor examined the four MOVE men in the House of Corrections. The doctor determined that Conrad and Edward Africa, though dehydrated, were in fair condition. Delbert and Jerry Africa, on the other hand, were in very poor health and needed "to resume their diets immediately." Prison officials, reacting to the doctor's dire warning, received a court order on April 29 which allowed them to admit Conrad, Delbert, and Jerry Africa to the hospital, where they were force-fed intravenously. Once they were fed, Conrad and Delbert were released on parole. They had refused food for nineteen days. Ted Africa was transferred to a prison in neighboring Delaware County, Pennsylvania, where he continued his fast.

The hunger strikes received a considerable amount of media attention, much of it centering on the drama surrounding Sue Africa. Much of the coverage suggested that MOVE people were on hunger strike for religious reasons. Even so, these reporters classified MOVE as a "revolutionary group," that "espouse[d] a non-violent return to nature," and as "a radical organization." One journalist writing for the *Daily News* visited the Powelton House and wrote one of the first profiles of MOVE to appear in the mainstream press. Robert Africa, speaking on behalf of MOVE, told the reporter that MOVE's recent legal troubles were because "people don't like to hear the truth." People within the System "don't like to be confronted with their inconsistencies." He tried to explain the basics of MOVE's theology. He told the reporter that "you can't improve on something that's already perfect. You can't improve on Life."[40]

A few journalists decided to look into MOVE's claims that they were victims of systematic harassment from law enforcement. They found that the mounting arrests of MOVE people, and the multiplying court cases that inevitably ensued, struck several city officials as excessive. The Philadelphia Sheriff disagreed that MOVE was being targeted for their religious beliefs. Their legal troubles, he said, were because MOVE people were "mentally sick" and had "horrible body odor." Lawyers with the ACLU, however, thought there might be something to MOVE's claims. ACLU director Spencer Cox pointed out that the injunction preventing MOVE from protesting in front of municipal buildings, which effectively barred them from the proceedings of the School Board, was patently unconstitutional. Court of Common Pleas Judge Judith Jamison, who just six months earlier had convicted several MOVE people of contempt of court, told the reporters that the police crackdown on MOVE was a waste of time. MOVE people, she said, were "childish" and "annoying," "but not really dangerous." She thought that there were likely "more important things for the police to be doing" than tying up the court system by arresting MOVE people for cursing in public.[41]

The police enforcement of the injunction intensified, despite the growing sense among some in the judiciary that it was unnecessary and possibly unconstitutional. On May 8, 1975, Civil Affairs officers arrested thirteen MOVE people in front of a city building downtown. They were there to protest a judge's decision to force-feed Jerry Africa intravenously in prison. The judge had condemned his colleagues' decision to let the other MOVE people who were on hunger strike out of prison. He was quoted in the press as saying "it would be a very bad precedent if someone could get out of jail by not eating." Civil Affairs officers determined that the MOVE people who had gathered to protest the judge's decision were in violation of the injunction.[42]

Sheriff's deputies arrested more MOVE people on June 7 after they formed a human chain in an effort to prevent a MOVE supporter, Davita Thomas, and her two children from being evicted from their home. Thomas's landlord alleged that she had not paid her eighty-five dollar a month rent for "about two months." MOVE people, speaking on Thomas's behalf, said Thomas was withholding rent because the landlord refused to keep the apartment in adequate condition. They suspected that the real reason the landlord sought to evict Thomas was because of her connection to MOVE. It was "religious persecution." When sheriff's deputies arrived to evict Thomas, they found twenty-five MOVE people preventing access to the home. When they moved toward the house anyway, MOVE people fought back. Delbert Africa pushed one police officer down the stairs, bruising him. Another police officer suffered a head injury. When the dust cleared, seventeen MOVE people had been arrested.[43]

Ten days later, dozens of MOVE people gathered in front of a police station to protest what they understood as systematic religious persecution at the hands of police officers. The only relatively impartial account of the events of June 17 comes from a reporter for the *Philadelphia Inquirer*. He had been assigned to cover MOVE's protest at the police station. It was a rather boring assignment. MOVE people cursed. People passed by. Civil Affairs officers, wearing street clothes, watched calmly from beneath a shady tree. He stayed for three hours and left without much to report on. When the reporter returned to the *Inquirer* building, however, he received a phone call from a MOVE person who told him that, as soon as he left the scene, the Civil Affairs unit arrested the MOVE people quite violently. The MOVE person said that a Civil Affairs officer threw Rhonda Africa into a metal-reinforced window pane at the rear entrance to the police station, causing her to bleed from the head. The MOVE person on the phone worried that Rhonda needed medical attention, even though it was against MOVE's religion, but said that doctors refused to care for her at the police station. When the reporter returned to the police station, the MOVE people from before had indeed been arrested. He observed a shattered glass window with an indention roughly the size of a human head. The police officers he interviewed denied that any struggle had taken place.[44]

According to MOVE sources, later that evening corrections officers dragged Alberta Africa out of her cell, pinned her down, and repeatedly kicked her in the stomach and between her legs. MOVE people claim that Alberta Africa suffered a miscarriage as a result of this beating. It is impossible to say definitively what is true when relying on MOVE's accounts of the violence they suffered at the hands of police. To state the obvious, MOVE people had much to gain by exaggerating. But the Philadelphia Police Department, as I will show in Chapter 5, indeed exhibited a pattern of excessive violence during these years. And they also had an interest in misrepresenting the amount of violence they inflicted upon MOVE people. If indeed Alberta lost a child, the father was presumably John Africa.[45]

The familiar pattern continued. The arrests of MOVE people led to contentious and sometimes violent courtroom appearances. These led to convictions for contempt of court, which, of course, led to more contentious courtroom appearances. MOVE people were in jail nearly as often as they were not. On August 4, Sue Africa gave birth to a baby boy, Tomaso Africa, in a holding cell in the 33rd Street Police Headquarters. On May 8, 1975, eight MOVE women fought corrections officers who were trying to remove two babies from a basement cell the MOVE women shared at Police Headquarters. On July 3, seven MOVE people were arrested for demonstrating in front of the home of the prison superintendent. They were charged with attempting to intimidate a public official. A week later Debbie, Valerie, Rhonda, and Gail Africa were arrested in front of that same house on the same charge. In September, Delbert Africa was convicted in absentia to two years in jail for assaulting a police officer. Steve Africa, a white man, received one to three years for a similar charge. Raymond Africa received a sentence of three to ten days in jail, and Merle Africa a sentence of ten days, for harassing neighbors. On October 3, Jerry Africa was sentenced to three years' probation for threatening a neighbor and his wife back in the summer of 1974. On October 6, twenty-four MOVE people were found guilty of violating the injunction in a single case. Because they refused to acknowledge the legitimacy of human law, only three of them received their sentences before the courtroom had to be cleared.[46]

This impasse might have gone on forever if not for a Supreme Court of Pennsylvania case called *Commonwealth of Pennsylvania v. Africa*. To MOVE people, *Commonwealth v. Africa* was validation that the Law of Mama would, in the end, prevail over the laws of humankind which sought to silence it. On October 24, 1974, Civil Affairs detectives arrested seven MOVE people—Merle, Laverne, Africa, Jerry, Ted, Conrad, and Don Africa—on charges of disorderly conduct, failure to disperse, and criminal conspiracy for violating the protest injunction during one of MOVE's public demonstrations. The MOVE defendants, as usual, chose to represent themselves. They began their defense by filing a motion asking the judge to recuse himself. The judge dismissed their motion and asked the defendants to enter their pleas. The first defendant refused to enter a plea on the grounds that the judge was vindictive and prejudiced against them. She chose instead to challenge the judge's authority to decide the guilt or innocence of those who answer to a higher law. When it was clear that MOVE did not intend to enter pleas, the judge allowed them to stand silently while pleas of not guilty were entered on their behalf.[47]

Because MOVE wanted to expose the hypocrisy of the System's understanding of profanity, they pursued a line of defense in which they attempted to challenge the arresting officers' understandings of what constituted the profane. After a Civil Affairs officer testified that he heard MOVE using profane language at the protest, Ted Africa asked whether the officer found war, bombs, science, and rape as profane. If the word "motherfucker" was profane enough to offend the arresting officer, why, Ted asked, shouldn't the officer arrest war-makers at the Pentagon? Surely those men had profaned the sacred much more than he had. The Court would not entertain Ted's line of reasoning. The lawyers for the Commonwealth objected repeatedly to Ted's arguments and the Court sustained. When this line of defense proved ineffective, MOVE built a case that they were the victims of systemic, targeted police harassment. By late 1974, MOVE had begun to worry, publicly and privately, that the police were engaged in "a long-term policy to silence and exterminate them." MOVE suspected that the media participated in this as well by writing "slanted articles" that had discredited MOVE in public opinion. This conspiracy, which was not altogether false, manifested, MOVE argued, in frequent episodes of police brutality. Conrad Africa told the court that he had been violently attacked by sheriff's deputies and police officers, often during court appearances. He wondered why, if this court was indeed committed to justice, these officers had yet to be charged.[48]

Conrad's refusal to concede the legitimacy of human law proved the last straw for the judge. He ordered Conrad to return to his seat and announced that if he refused, Conrad would be "bound and gagged." This left Conrad stunned. "What do you mean 'bound and gagged'? I have a right to freedom of speech." His protest was ignored. The judge ordered bailiffs to bind and gag Conrad and warned that "anybody else that makes one move is going to be bound and gagged" as well.[49] As the bailiffs surrounded Conrad, the other MOVE defendants erupted in protest. Donald Grossman, sensing an opportunity to force the Court to confront its own hypocrisy, demanded that all MOVE people in the courtroom be bound and gagged along with Conrad, because "if one is bound and gagged, we will all be bound and gagged . . . we will always be united." Don got his wish. The judge ordered all of the defendants to be silenced and restrained. As the bailiffs did their work, Jerry Africa continued to protest. He accused the judge of granting Conrad permission to make a statement only to cut him off and punish him for speaking. To Jerry, this was both a blatant violation of MOVE's freedom of speech and a "disruptive tactic" meant to prevent the Teachings of John Africa from being heard in public. As the bailiffs restrained the defendants, the MOVE supporters in the gallery could not be brought to order. The judge lost control of the courtroom. He exited the bench and declared a recess for lunch. The bailiffs brought Conrad, Jerry, Don, Africa, Merle, Laverne, and Teddy Africa to a holding cell. Once the restraints were removed, the defendants met with City Councilman Lucien Blackwell, who was brought in to mediate between the court and MOVE. Blackwell urged the MOVE defendants to make their point without disrupting the proceedings of the court.[50]

When the trial resumed after the extended lunch recess, the MOVE defendants heeded Blackwell's advice and behaved respectfully. At the advice of their court-appointed lawyers, who were serving as backup counsel, MOVE requested a mistrial on the grounds that the court had demonstrated its prejudice against them during the morning session. The court declined to grant the mistrial, and MOVE people proceeded with their defense "without incident." Conrad Africa examined the prosecution's star witness: Inspector George Fencl, head of the Civil Disobedience Squad which had monitored MOVE's demonstration on October 24, 1974. Fencl testified that he had heard MOVE use profane language. And he could prove it: he made an audio recording of MOVE's tirade, which he brought home to play for his wife so that she could get a taste of this most unusual group. In his cross-examination, Conrad took issue with Fencl's recording. If Fencl was so offended by MOVE's use of profanity, Conrad wondered, why bring it home and share it with your wife? Conrad had Fencl on the ropes, but pushed his point too far. "I am saying," he asked Fencl, "since you feel these words are profane, why would you take them home to your wife and play them on tapes to your wife unless your wife was a motherfucker like you?" The judge answered this outburst with another order to bind and gag the defendants. As the bailiffs again brought out the restraints, the MOVE people on trial emptied their arsenal of insults, profanities, and accusations on the court. Frustrated, the judge recessed the court for the day and ordered the bailiffs to carry the defendants out of the courtroom and to bind and gag them once they were in the holding cell.[51]

The municipal court judge had played right into John Africa's hands. Indeed, John Africa had meticulously orchestrated the MOVE defendants' behavior in the courtroom. MOVE people often rehearsed their courtroom tactics with mock trials held at the MOVE house. One MOVE person would play the role of the judge, and another would play the role of the prosecutor. The others would anticipate lines of attack, and John Africa would point out ways to subvert the prosecution's logic. John Africa's courtroom strategy grew out of his larger teachings that the System had inverted the sacred and the profane. By forcing a courtroom—the epitome of American culture's displaced faith in man's law instead of God's—to confront its own hypocrisies and contradictions, the entire System might collapse. By binding and gagging the MOVE defendants, the municipal court judge had come awfully close to proving John Africa's point. How could a court, which professes the sacredness of a fair trial, free speech, and the right to a defense, bind and gag defendants who are acting as their own lawyers? How could "profane" words merit imprisonment in a world so rife with unpunished evil? Forced to confront his own hypocrisy, MOVE people believed, the judge had removed all pretense of justice, fairness, and equality. The System had no interest in upholding the law, only in silencing the Teachings of John Africa.

The trial resumed the next morning, but before proceedings could begin, the judge declared a mistrial. He then summarily convicted all of the MOVE defendants of contempt of court. The judge sentenced Debbie Africa and Conrad Africa to ninety days in prison. As the judge announced the convictions and sentences, Don Grossman hurled himself to the floor and demanded to be bound and gagged once again. Instead, he was also sentenced to ninety days in prison. Jerry, Merle, Laverne, and Teddy Africa received sentences of thirty days in prison. Everyone in the courtroom was stunned. The state prosecutors were so taken aback by the judge's actions that they filed a motion to drop all original charges against the MOVE defendants.[52]

The judge's behavior drew the attention of the Pennsylvania Supreme Court, which assumed jurisdiction over the MOVE cases on February 19, 1975. Upon taking the case, the Supreme Court ordered the release of the MOVE defendants on bail, and consolidated the cases under the name *Commonwealth v. Africa*. Eight days later, the prosecutors dropped the original charges against the MOVE defendants stemming from the protest. On March 17, 1976, the Court ruled in a four-to-three decision in favor of MOVE. Writing for the Court, Justice Samuel Roberts recognized that "special problems seem to be presented when people who believe that the 'system' ought to be on trial are themselves on trial for violations of the law." He also understood that MOVE people had no interest in cooperating with the enforcement of laws they recognized as being fundamentally unjust. Still, Roberts wrote, the municipal court had erred in its decision to bind and gag the MOVE defendants. If the MOVE defendants refused to conduct themselves with the appropriate decorum, the judge ought to have revoked their right to represent themselves and remove them from the courtroom. He certainly should not have bound and gagged them, an action that, the Court wrote, "can do nothing to ease tensions" in an already fraught courtroom. They vacated the sentences MOVE people had received in the municipal court, discharged Merle Africa, Laverne Africa, and Ted Africa, and granted the four other defendants a new trial.[53]

MOVE's victory in *Commonwealth v. Africa* was more than a legal victory. It was, to MOVE people, the triumph of John Africa's conception of the sacred over Americans' misguided faith in progress. It was the victory of God's law—the Law of Mama—over the law of the land. And it was, to MOVE people, proof that even the courts had to acknowledge John Africa's miraculous ability. From 1972 through 1974, MOVE people confronted what they viewed to be the misguided faith Americans had placed in progress, and they did so by profaning it. They used profane language to draw attention to the apathy with which Americans viewed violence, racism, war, and genocide: that which was actually profane. They refused to follow social decorum to draw attention to the faith Americans had in their technology, and their education, and their politics. They refused to follow the law because they viewed it as human usurpation of God's law. And, for a while, it worked. MOVE had beaten the injunction, won the support of the highest court in the state, and the media were now paying attention to MOVE's complaints of police harassment.

But, as was often the case in MOVE's history, this victory would be short-lived. In the predawn hours of March 28, 1976, the newly released MOVE people boarded a bus and rode to the MOVE house in Powelton. When the bus arrived, MOVE people inside the house poured out into the front yard to welcome them home. As MOVE people described it, they were "loudly greeting our sisters and brothers—hugging them, kissing them, weeping, crying, glad to have them home." Almost as soon as everyone was off the bus, a police squad cruiser drove up. The police officer, who frequently interacted with MOVE people, explained that he had received a complaint that MOVE was disturbing the peace. Chuckie Africa—Laverne's fifteen-year-old son—explained that the MOVE people on the bus had just gotten out of jail and that they were just happy to have them home. More police officers arrived on the scene, and Chuckie grew aggravated. To Chuckie, the rapid police response was further evidence that the police were systematically targeting MOVE for their religious beliefs. "Y'all must think MOVE people are stupid," he said. "Ain't no way you can tell us they had to send all these cars to answer some damn complaint about disturbing the peace."[54]

According to MOVE's account of events, Chuckie's insolence earned him a billy club to the head. Several police officers surrounded Jerry Africa, jumped him from behind, and restrained him. Jerry—a very large man who once played collegiate football—worked his way free from the police and began fighting the police officer who struck Chuckie. By now, around a dozen police cars had responded, and the melee was getting out of hand. Chuckie, dazed from the initial blow, lay on the ground as police officers continued to hit him in the back with batons. Greg Africa was kicked in the face, and blood poured from the back of his head. Delbert Africa and Conrad Africa sustained minor injuries fighting police. A police baton was broken over Robert's head. The police eventually apprehended six MOVE men: Delbert, Jerry, Robert, Chuckie, Phil, and Greg Africa. All of the men faced charges of resisting arrest, conspiracy, aggravated assault, riot, and recklessly endangering the lives of others. As the paddy wagons drove away, the MOVE people who had not been arrested realized that Janine Africa was missing. They soon found her sobbing in the basement. She was holding her newborn son, Life Africa, in her hands. His skull was caved in. She had been holding him as she tried to stop a police officer from striking her husband, Phil Africa. The police officer hit her instead, knocking her down.

Life Africa had been crushed to death.[55]

Notes

1. Gerald R. Ford: "Remarks at a Dinner Concluding the Reconvening of the First Continental Congress in Philadelphia, Pennsylvania.," September 6, 1974. Online by Gerhard Peters and John T. Woolley, *The American Presidency Project*, http://www.presidency.ucsb.edu/ws/? pid=4692; James T. Wooten, "1774 Convention Reconvened in Philadelphia," *New York Times*, September 6, 1974; "'Continental Congress' Alive after 200 Years," *Los Angeles Times*, September 6, 1974.
2. Peter Wagner, *Progress: A Reconstruction* (Cambridge: Polity Press, 2016), 7.
3. John Africa, "Depression, Economics, and Government" from *The Guidelines*, reproduced in "On the MOVE," *Philadelphia Tribune*, July 5, 1975. See also "On the MOVE," *Philadelphia Tribune*, June 28, 1975, and July 1, 1975.
4. John Africa, "On Progress," reproduced in Robert Africa, "On the MOVE," *Philadelphia Tribune*, August 5, 1975, 3.
5. See, for example, Louise Africa, "On the MOVE," *Philadelphia Tribune*, January 10, 1976; Louise Africa, "On the MOVE," *Philadelphia Tribune*, January 13, 1976.
6. Michael Kernan, "Buckminster Fuller, The Magnetic Presence: Magnetic Genius," *Washington Post*, February 11, 1976; *Philadelphia Inquirer* obituary quoted in Jonathan Keats, *You Belong to the Universe: Buckminster Fuller and the Future* (New York: Oxford University Press, 2016), 18.
7. Keats, *You Belong to the Universe*, 1–23.
8. Hugh Kenner, "Bucky Fuller and the Final Exam: To Be against Technology Is to Be against the Universe and Smart Radishes," *New York Times Magazine*, July 6, 1975; "About Fuller," Buckminster Fuller Institute, accessed March 8, 2017, https://www.bfi.org/about-fuller/biography/timeline.
9. MOVE, untitled document, undated [estimated between June 25, 1974, and July 24, 1974], Box 91a, Folder 1, Philadelphia Yearly Meeting of the Religious Society of Friends, Friends Peace Committee, Friendly Presence Papers, Friends Historical Library, Swarthmore College, Swarthmore, PA.
10. Wagner, *Progress*, 6; Louise Africa, "On the MOVE," *Philadelphia Tribune*, January 13, 1976, 10.
11. MOVE, untitled document, 29; Wayne King, "Symposium Envisions a Lasting Peace: 'We Have an Option' Cites Hopelessness Planned Aggression," *New York Times*, November 14, 1973.
12. MOVE, untitled document, 22.
13. Ibid., 24.
14. Ibid., 26.

15. Ibid., 22–23.
16. Ibid.
17. John Africa, "On Animals," reproduced in Louise Leaphart James, *John Africa . . . Childhood Untold until Today* (self-published, 2013), 70–74.
18. MOVE, untitled document, 4–7; MOVE, Press Release of Liberty Bell Race Track Demonstration, undated (before August 4, 1973), Box 91a, Philadelphia Yearly Meeting of the Religious Society of Friends, Friends Peace Committee, Friendly Presence Papers, Friends Historical Library, Swarthmore College, Swarthmore, PA; MOVE, Notice of Demonstration against Bronx Zoo, Box 91a, Philadelphia Yearly Meeting of the Religious Society of Friends, Friends Peace Committee, Friendly Presence Papers, Friends Historical Library, Swarthmore College, Swarthmore, PA.
19. John Africa, "On Animals," *The Guidelines*, reproduced in James, *John Africa* (2013), 70–74.
20. "But, Mike . . . He's Only 11," *Chicago Tribune*, September 5, 1974; "Marvin the Chimp KO'd after a Costly Rampage on TV Show," *Los Angeles Times*, September 5, 1974; "Chimp Goes Wild, Chases News Staff," *Atlanta Daily World*, September 10, 1974.
21. John Africa, "On So-Called Profanity," *The Guidelines*, reprinted in James, *John Africa*, 64–65. *Sic* throughout.
22. Louise Africa wrote a six-part series based on John Africa's teachings on profanity in her "On the MOVE" column. See Louise Africa, "On the MOVE," *Philadelphia Tribune*, July 27, 1976; Louise Africa, "On the MOVE," *Philadelphia Tribune*, July 31, 1976; Louise Africa, "On the MOVE," *Philadelphia Tribune*, August 3, 1976; Louise Africa, "On the MOVE," *Philadelphia Tribune*, August 7, 1976; Louise Africa, "On the MOVE," *Philadelphia Tribune*, August 14, 1976; Louise Africa, "On the MOVE," *Philadelphia Tribune*, August 17, 1976.
23. Robert Africa, "On the MOVE," *Philadelphia Tribune*, August 5, 1975; James, *John Africa*, 18; Louise Africa, "On the MOVE," *Philadelphia Tribune*, March 27, 1976; Louise Africa, "On the MOVE," *Philadelphia Tribune*, March 30, 1976.
24. Louise Africa, "On the MOVE," *Philadelphia Inquirer*, June 15, 1976, 23.
25. MOVE, untitled document, 16–18; "School Board Ousts 2," *Philadelphia Daily News*, March 12, 1974; Richard Deasy, "School Proxy Ends Session to Silence Man," *Philadelphia Daily News*, March 26, 1974; Paul Taylor, "Uproar Ends School Meeting," *Philadelphia Inquirer*, March 26, 1974.
26. MOVE, untitled document, 16–17.
27. Ibid., 18.
28. Ibid., 34–35.
29. Ibid., 18–19.
30. Ibid.
31. Harry Amana, "MOVE Members Say Police Are Out to Exterminate Them," *Philadelphia Tribune*, November 30, 1974; "8 from MOVE Get Late Fines," *Philadelphia Daily News*, February 19, 1975.
32. Louise Africa, "On the MOVE," *Philadelphia Tribune*, August 30, 1975, 5.
33. Vincent W. Lloyd, *Black Natural Law* (New York: Oxford University Press, 2016).
34. Louise Africa, "On the MOVE," November 18, 1975.

35. MOVE, "Disruption," undated, Box 91a, Philadelphia Yearly Meeting of the Religious Society of Friends, Friends Peace Committee, Friendly Presence Papers, Friends Historical Library, Swarthmore College, Swarthmore, PA; "8 from MOVE Get Late Fines," *Philadelphia Daily News*, February 19, 1975; MOVE to Gov. Shapp, reproduced in Louise James, "On the MOVE," *Philadelphia Tribune*, May 8, 1976.
36. Edward Africa, Jerry Africa, Delbert Africa, and Conrad Africa, "Press Release and Formal Statement," Box 91a, Philadelphia Yearly Meeting of the Religious Society of Friends, Friends Peace Committee, Friendly Presence Papers, Friends Historical Library, Swarthmore College, Swarthmore, PA.
37. Larry Eichel, "Woman Anxious to Stay in Jail Gets a Year," *Philadelphia Inquirer*, April 8, 1975.
38. Gregory Paulson and Stephen F. Fitner to The Honorable Alex Bonavitacola, April 15, 1975, Box 91a, Philadelphia Yearly Meeting of the Religious Society of Friends, Friends Peace Committee, Friendly Presence Papers, Friends Historical Library, Swarthmore College, Swarthmore, PA.
39. Matthew J. Countryman, *Up South: Civil Rights and Black Power in Philadelphia* (Philadelphia: University of Pennsylvania Press, 2005), 262–264.
40. Chuck Stone, "There WAS a Baby and Now He's Gone," *Philadelphia Daily News*, April 9, 1976, 1.
41. Larry Eichel, "MOVE Members Speak Out—Loudly and Often," *Philadelphia Inquirer*, April 21, 1975.
42. "Hurt in Scuffle," *Philadelphia Inquirer*, May 9, 1975.
43. "Wouldn't MOVE, 2 Cops Are Hurt," *Daily News*, June 7, 1975; "Seventeen Held in MOVE Eviction Fracas," *Philadelphia Inquirer*, June 7, 1975.
44. Bob Lancaster, "MOVE Rally Moves Few," *Philadelphia Inquirer*, June 18, 1975.
45. MOVE, *25 Years on the MOVE*, (self-published, 1996), 11.
46. MOVE, *25 Years on the MOVE*, 11; "Hurt in Scuffle," *Philadelphia Inquirer*, May 9, 1975; "MOVE Members Held after Protest," *Philadelphia Inquirer*, July 11, 1975; Mike Leary, "4 Ejected from Court, Convicted in Absentia," *Philadelphia Inquirer*, September 24, 1975.
47. *Commonwealth v. Africa*, 353 A. 2d 855 (Supreme Court of Pennsylvania 1975).
48. *Commonwealth v. Africa*; Harry Amana, "MOVE Members Say Police Are Out to Exterminate Them," *Philadephia Tribune*, November 30, 1974.
49. Ibid.; *Commonwealth v. Africa*.
50. *Commonwealth v. Africa*; Dave Racher, "Contempt of Court Ordered for Riotous Defendants in State," *Philadelphia Daily News*, March 22, 1976.
51. *Commonwealth v. Africa*.
52. Ibid.
53. *Commonwealth v. Africa*, 466 Pa. 603 (1976); Dave Racher, "Contempt of Court Ordered for Riotous Defendants in State." *Philadelphia Daily News*, March 22, 1976. Justice Nix filed a dissent arguing that the MOVE defendants should have received a new trial in the Court of Common Pleas.
54. Louise Africa, "On the MOVE," *Philadelphia Tribune*, April 9, 1976.
55. Louise Africa, "On the MOVE," *Philadelphia Tribune*, April 10, 1976; Linn Washington, "MOVE Says Mth.-Old Baby Killed in Clash with Police."

4
Pastoral Power

On the afternoon of March 28, 1976, Janine Africa and Phil Africa buried their son in accordance with the Teachings of John Africa. They took Life Africa's body to "the resting grounds," a serene, out of the way location in a nearby park which MOVE people describe as a "sacred space." They wrapped Life's body in a blanket and placed him in a shallow grave, which they lightly covered with dirt and brush. The act of burial, to MOVE people, is the returning of the body to the earth. No one really dies, according to the Teachings of John Africa. They "cycle." Like a seed produces a plant, the human body produces life—either through reproduction or through returning the body to the carbon cycle. Death does not mean that one ceases to exist. Death means that one has been reincorporated into Life.[1]

Reporters had been gathering at the MOVE house in Powelton since that morning, and MOVE people told them about the death of Life Africa. Sue Africa assured reporters that Life "was taken care of. He didn't have no fancy clothes. He didn't have no embalming. He was taken out in the country, put in a blanket and left." Janine and Phil Africa spent several hours mourning the death of their son, then returned to the MOVE house late that evening. Reporters investigating the death of Life Africa watched Janine, across the street from the MOVE house, lying in the dirt, sobbing uncontrollably.[2]

MOVE was a different religion after the death of Life Africa. John Africa became more apocalyptic. The group grew more insular and paranoid for reasons that were not entirely mistaken. MOVE people began to fantasize about an end to the evil reign of the System and wondered what part they might play in its downfall. The System was no longer a theological construct. It was not simply a religious symbol, it was an active, evil force set out to destroy MOVE. Bringing hypocrisy to light—forcing Americans to confront the inconsistencies inherent in the System—was no longer enough. For three years, MOVE had tried to spark a spiritual revolution by speaking truth to power, by offering their bodies as a sacrifice to the System. They had hoped that "if people followed our example, this whole System would collapse." They had hoped the System would cave in on itself, that more people would join their countercultural crusade against the modern world. But all they had to show for it were scars, broken bones, rap sheets, and now a dead baby. If the System were to be overthrown, like John Africa said it would be, MOVE would have to do the overthrowing.[3]

The death of Life Africa was also a turning point in MOVE's history, setting into motion a chain of events that led, ultimately, to the MOVE Bombing. Convinced that the System was actively trying to destroy the group to suppress the Teachings of John Africa, MOVE abandoned their commitment to nonviolent resistance and embraced a doctrine of armed self-defense. They announced this change publicly on May 20, 1977, with a symbolic show of force. This event, which the press dubbed the Guns on the Porch standoff, announced MOVE's new doctrine concerning self-defense. It also led to a blockade of MOVE's headquarters, which lasted over a year, eventuating in the death of a police officer named James Ramp.

The death of Life Africa was also a turning point in MOVE's claim to religious legitimacy. For a few months, MOVE had the attention of the religious community, politicians, and the news media. They had, for a time, the benefit of the doubt. Recognized, respected leaders in the religious community—the American Friends Service Committee; Rev. Paul Washington, an Episcopal priest and a towering figure in Philadelphia's civil rights movement; a powerful priest from the Archdiocese of Philadelphia with inside connections to the city's political establishment; and an influential Lutheran minister who headed a social concerns group representing much of Philadelphia's Protestant community—came to MOVE's aid after the death of Life Africa and through the ensuing blockade. These religious leaders negotiated between MOVE and the city, lending MOVE the weight of their religious authority in what they viewed as a conflict between Church and State.

There was, however, a disconnect between how MOVE viewed their conflict with the city of Philadelphia and how their allies in the religious community defended them. MOVE complained to these religious leaders that the United States government was violating their religious rights. These leaders of the religious community, however, chose to defend MOVE not on the grounds of their *religious* rights, but because of MOVE's *human* rights. While MOVE argued that the police blockade was further evidence that they were the targets of religious persecution, their allies in the religious community argued that the blockade should end because it represented an assault on the human rights afforded to all people, religious or not. This small shift in discourse, from religious liberty to human rights—from a collective form of rights toward an essentially individual form—allowed these representatives of established, state-recognized, and politically influential religious groups to defend MOVE without defending MOVE *as a religion*.

MOVE gained powerful allies after the death of Life Africa, partly because it seemed as if the police had tried to cover up the incident. The police account of the events of March 28, 1976—the day Life Africa died—differed substantially from MOVE's account. In their telling, police officers responded to the MOVE house at around four that morning because MOVE people were fighting one another in the front yard. As they arrived on the scene, police say, MOVE people began throwing bricks at them. One officer reported that he arrived at the MOVE house and "observed a large group of male and female people" in the front yard. He "observed officer Palermo go down," after being hit with a brick. Then, MOVE people "started yelling in a most fanatical way." The officer observed "white girls screaming at the top of her lungs, holding a black naked baby," and heard someone shout "get a shotgun." The police officer said that he and his fellow officers were "outnumbered four or five to one," and that "bricks were flying—cinderblocks—a brick hit me." According to official accounts, officers responded to the threat with reasonable force, including batons. The police initially denied that Life Africa existed. Officers testified that no children had been involved in the arrests, that Janine had not been holding a baby, and that MOVE had fabricated Life's death—indeed the baby's existence—to gain sympathy in the media. As the ranking detective told reporters, police were "very skeptical" of MOVE's story.[4]

When reporters began investigating the events of March 28th, the police account began to fall apart. Louise Africa filled two of her "On the MOVE" columns with her neighbors' testimony, which mostly corroborated MOVE's telling. Journalists from the major dailies interviewed witnesses as well. No one had seen flying bricks or cinderblocks as the police alleged. They *had* seen Life Africa, the infant the police said never existed. One neighbor was sitting in her home when she heard screams. She ran outside and saw two MOVE people being held up by police officers so that other officers could punch them. Another neighbor (the *Inquirer* provided a picture of the witness and was careful to point out that she was a white woman) said that the police response was "the worst thing I ever saw." She thought that the police had been provoked by MOVE's rude demeanor and general disrespect, but not bricks. In her opinion, the police had overreacted. She told a reporter that she had "never seen such brutality." All of the neighbors interviewed reported having seen Life Africa. After Life Africa had been born, Janine took him around the neighborhood to introduce her son to his new neighbors.[5]

As news of Life Africa's death spread, politicians began calling for investigations into the police officers' behavior. Pennsylvania Supreme Court Justice Robert Nix ordered the Philadelphia district attorney's office to launch an investigation into the infant's death. The district attorney's office was willing, but investigators faced a roadblock. They could not investigate the death of Life Africa without having access to the infant's body. The district attorney set up two appointments with MOVE people at his offices downtown to discuss the issue, but no one showed. When a reporter asked Robert Africa why MOVE seemed to be stonewalling the investigation, he told the *Inquirer* that MOVE did not plan to attend any appointments or let anyone inspect the body. MOVE would, however, "do whatever's necessary to bring down the mentality that perpetrates the beating and killing of children." Weeks passed, and pressure to investigate the death of Life Africa grew more vociferous. Two city councilmen, Lucien Blackwell and Joseph Coleman, introduced a resolution that would formally ask the state of Pennsylvania, the City of Philadelphia, and the federal government to investigate. Both MOVE and the district attorney's office were in a tight spot. The district attorney wanted to launch an investigation, but did not have the cooperation of MOVE people. MOVE wanted justice for Life Africa, but did not want to disturb his final resting place. John Africa's preoccupation with the sacred and the profane was turned on its head. In order to bring justice for Life Africa, MOVE had to profane his sacred burial site.[6]

On April 2, 1976, Robert Africa invited two city councilmen, a Baptist minister who was a member of the city's Human Relations Commission, and two journalists from the *Inquirer* to a dinner at MOVE headquarters. Robert refused to tell his guests why they were being asked to the house. He only said that there would be an important announcement. The six dinner guests (the wife of one of the councilmen attended as well) waited outside the MOVE house in the cold rain for nearly an hour, wondering among themselves why they had been invited. As they waited, they saw one side of the duplex filled with dozens of dogs, excitedly pressing their noses against the windows at the dinner guests outside. When they finally were allowed inside MOVE headquarters, it was, according to one of the reporters, "like entering another world." There was no lighting or heat, except for candles. They saw several small children wearing what seemed to be too few clothes, given the cold. The adults wore blue jeans and sweatshirts.[7]

Twenty MOVE people and their six dinner guests descended to the basement, which was lit by two large chandeliers filled with candles over two long wooden tables, which had been set up, the reporter thought, "as though someone had studied the place-setting section of the Ladies Home Journal." MOVE wanted to make a good impression on their dinner guests. Both tables overflowed with mounds of corn on the cob, potato salad, rice, and spinach. For the guests, MOVE served fried chicken. For the children, they served raw chicken legs, arranged so symmetrically the reporter thought it almost looked appetizing. The dinner struck some of the guests as unusually "formal, almost ritualistic." They were wary of the food. They cautiously served themselves and smelled the food before taking small, careful bites. At the other table, the MOVE children and adults interacted as if the dinner was not all that unusual. Robert made small talk with MOVE's guests as they ate. He explained that MOVE people were quite comfortable in their home. Despite not having electricity or heat, or much furniture, Robert said, "We have all the comforts we need." When everyone had finished the meal, MOVE people served watermelon slices for dessert.[8]

After the meal, Robert Africa retrieved a spiral notebook and wrote in it. He passed the notebook around to MOVE's dinner guests. It read, "The baby is here. You'll see it after dinner." Robert explained that MOVE people had to take such precautions because they suspected the house was bugged by the police. When all of the dinner guests had read the note, Robert rose from the table and walked upstairs. The dinner guests followed. Robert led them to the front room of the house, which was very dimly lit by three candles in the corner of the room. The room smelled of rot. There was not much furniture in the room; only two small desks and a chair which some of the dinner guests bumped into because it was so dark. Robert pointed to a cardboard box on the floor. The box was lined with some dirt, grass, seashells, and some fruit, upon which lay the body of Life Africa.[9]

MOVE's dinner guests were stunned into a long silence which was broken only by the shutter of the camera of one of the reporters. The other reporter looked at the body long enough to be sure of what she had seen, and then retreated from the smell. She felt "numb, and sickened," by the scene. The whole night "seemed so bizarre, so mystical, and those flickering candles—it seemed so ritualistic." One by one, the dinner guests approached the box to get a good look. After they had all seen the body, Robert said, "let all here be satisfied once and for all that the baby does exist." Jerry Africa removed the box from the room, but the smell remained. Another MOVE person asked the reporters, councilmen, and the minister, and the councilman's wife to not reveal what they had seen that night. They all agreed, and left the MOVE house. When the story leaked to the press a week later that two councilmen, the wife of a councilman, two reporters, and a minister had seen the body, the police again requested access to the body of Life Africa so that they could conduct an investigation into his death. MOVE refused. Writing in her "On The MOVE" column, Louise Africa wrote that the police "have repeatedly violated our Religion and we're calling a halt to it—they will not violate it in this instance." Life Africa had been laid to rest for the last time.[10]

The fall of 1976 was a frustrating time for MOVE. It was clear there would be no investigation into the death of Life Africa. MOVE people continued to circulate in and out of jail on various charges that continued to accumulate exponentially. Years later, the man whom MOVE people knew as Don Africa testified in court that MOVE spent these months planting suspicious-looking ignition switches in various hotels around the country and in various cities in Europe. The goal, Don Glassey alleged, was to make it seem as if MOVE had a large, global underground of supporters that would commit acts of terrorist violence if MOVE's demands were not met. As outlined in the next chapter, there is considerable doubt as to whether any of this took place. What we can say for sure is that the fall of 1976 through the summer of 1977 was a period of mourning for MOVE. Louise stopped writing her "On the MOVE" column in August 1976. The group stopped actively proselytizing—a policy that remains in place today—though a few new converts would trickle in over the years anyway.

During this time, John Africa revised his earlier teachings on nonviolence, embracing instead a doctrine of armed self-defense. In earlier years, John Africa taught that guns, as objects of death, were anathema to Life. And MOVE people took this teaching seriously: until May 1977, no one from the Civil Affairs Unit had ever seen a MOVE person with a gun. After the death of Life Africa, however, John Africa began to teach that nonresistance in the face of police violence was itself an act of violence. Not fighting back, in other words, allowed violence to occur. If anyone attacked MOVE, they would be met in kind. John Africa became convinced that the System would not rest until MOVE had been exterminated. He prophesied that there would be a violent confrontation between MOVE and the United States government. He instructed Don Africa to purchase firearms from local sporting goods stores so that MOVE people would be prepared for this confrontation, and gave

Delbert Africa the title Minister of Confrontation—a title evoking the Black Panthers.

MOVE publicly announced their new doctrine on armed self-defense with a symbolic show of force. Shortly after dawn on May 20, 1977, Civil Affairs Officers arrested Chuckie Africa, who had been walking some of the dogs around the block while carrying one of the rifles Don Africa had purchased using a fake driver's license. When the other people in the MOVE house learned of Chuckie's arrest, they grew incensed. They donned military-style fatigues, armed themselves with baseball bats, lumber, and holstered pistols, and paraded menacingly across the front porch. The Civil Affairs officers who had arrested Chuckie called for backup, and within minutes, two hundred police officers armed with heavy weaponry, body armor, and sniper rifles had amassed outside the MOVE house.

As they paraded across the porch, MOVE people hurled epithets at the police officers, Mayor Frank Rizzo, and President Jimmy Carter. MOVE people were upset that Chuckie had been arrested and feared for his safety in police custody. They were also fed up with the constant police surveillance, wiretapping, and harassment they had endured for years. Most importantly, however, MOVE people were angry about the way they were being classified. As the standoff wore into the late afternoon, MOVE sent a letter to the head of the Civil Affairs Unit, George Fencl, explaining that they wanted the police, their supporters, their critics, and the neighbors that had gathered to watch the ruckus to understand that MOVE was "not a bunch of frustrated, middle-class college students, irrational radicals or confused terrorists." Instead, MOVE was a "deeply religious organization totally committed to the principle of our belief as taught to us by our founder, John Africa."[11]

Rev. Paul Washington, rector of the Episcopal Church of the Advocate in North Philadelphia, had just settled down to dinner with his wife when he received a phone call from one of MOVE's neighbors. The police presence around the MOVE house had drawn a crowd of around three hundred onlookers. Tensions between the city's Black residents and the Philadelphia Police Department were high, and West Philadelphians had seen more than their fair share of abuse at the hands of law enforcement. The *Philadelphia Inquirer* had begun publishing a series of reports detailing rampant police abuse and a culture of corruption throughout the Philadelphia Police Department. Though the Philadelphia Police Department and Mayor Frank Rizzo enjoyed high levels of support from the city's white population, tensions with the city's communities of color—which disproportionately felt the brunt of police violence and corruption—ran high. While certainly not all of the residents of Powelton Village enjoyed having MOVE as a neighbor, it was clear that MOVE was preferable to a large police presence. The caller urged Rev. Washington to drive to the MOVE house right away and see what he could do to resolve the situation, but offered a final warning before hanging up. "There's going to be violence."[12]

Paul Washington had maintained a cordial relationship with MOVE since 1974. In March of that year, Washington's wife, Christine Washington, was watching the local public television station as it broadcast the meeting of the Philadelphia School Board, and she heard Delbert Africa share John Africa's teachings on education. Delbert had argued that education "was the training of slaves" and that it taught human beings to disregard Natural Law in favor of distorted, man-made ideas. As MOVE understood it, "true education [was] GOD." Christine Washington found Delbert's speech convincing and she urged her husband to reach out to MOVE.[13]

Paul Washington phoned Delbert and invited him to his office at the Church of the Advocate in North Philadelphia. Delbert brought with him ten other MOVE people. Washington and MOVE discussed John Africa's teachings on education, social justice, food, the need to keep children free from literal and metaphorical contamination, the hypocrisy of modern society, and animal rights. Only on this last point did Washington and MOVE disagree. John Africa taught that animals should be afforded the same dignity as humans while Washington did not. Washington was deeply impressed by MOVE and he decided that day to "stay in touch with them." Washington frequently accompanied MOVE people to court appearances, visited incarcerated MOVE people, and wrote letters defending MOVE's free speech to organizations, including the School Board, that sought to silence them. Washington was, and would remain until his death in 2002, one of MOVE's "closest clergy sympathizers."[14]

When Washington arrived on the scene outside MOVE headquarters, he found a line of hundreds of policemen and wooden barricades separating MOVE from the several hundred onlookers. He approached Police Commissioner Joseph O'Neill who apprised him of the situation. MOVE was angry because the police had lawfully arrested Chuckie Africa earlier that morning. The MOVE people on the porch and in the house were in possession of firearms that were suspected to be illegal and must be surrendered to the police. Washington expressed to O'Neill his desire to speak to MOVE, so the commissioner allowed him to pass through the police line.

Washington approached Delbert Africa, who took a break from parading to speak with him. Washington told Delbert that the police wanted MOVE to surrender their guns. Delbert responded that MOVE would turn over their weapons if the police returned Chuckie to the MOVE house, temporarily, so that everyone who had gathered could see whether or not Chuckie had been subjected to physical abuse while in police custody. Washington delivered MOVE's demand to Commissioner O'Neill, who agreed to bring Chuckie from his cell to MOVE headquarters to prove that he was in good health. Washington again crossed the police line to tell Delbert that an agreement had been reached. Delbert informed him that MOVE's demands had changed; they now wanted Chuckie released and his charges dropped. Washington "felt like a fool" as he crossed the police line once again to deliver the news to Commissioner O'Neill. The Commissioner was not surprised, "You see, Reverend, you don't know these people."[15]

Delbert's unwillingness to negotiate with Commissioner O'Neill in good faith was a turning point in Rev. Paul Washington's relationship with MOVE. Before this, Washington identified with MOVE. He believed that John Africa could have been a "prophetic voice in society" but, because his group did not behave like authentic religious groups should, his message would fall on deaf ears. As Washington saw it, "true prophets may scold, chide, warn, and pronounce judgment on the people but they do it out of love, concern and compassion." John Africa's message would be lost to a society that needed to hear it because MOVE was not behaving like true religion should. When he passed back and forth through the police barricades he was negotiating as an established, politically powerful religious authority defending an upstart, socially aware religious group from a potentially violent confrontation with the police. From this point on, he acted as a religious authority preventing MOVE from attaining religious legitimacy.[16]

Washington remained behind the police line with the gathered crowd into the evening. At 11:30 p.m., the crowd, which had swelled to nearly a thousand, pushed its way past the police, linked arms, and formed a blockade of their own between the police and the MOVE house. Having clearly lost control of the situation and hoping to avoid worsening the confrontation, Commissioner O'Neill ordered his uniformed officers to pack up and leave. As the police retreated, the crowd began to sing hymns. The plainclothes officers from the Civil Affairs Unit remained behind, taking careful notes on which MOVE people and which community activists were "inciting riot." Once the police left, the crowd dispersed and MOVE people returned inside their home. Although MOVE and their community supporters had won the day, the war was just beginning.[17]

From May 20, 1977, on, the Philadelphia Police Department stationed an around-the-clock observation squad, ranging between twenty and fifty officers, outside MOVE headquarters. They had orders to arrest any MOVE person caught leaving the house. Detectives from the Civil Affairs Unit reviewed their photographs and determined that eleven MOVE people had committed weapons violations and incited a riot during the standoff. (In point of fact, only Chuckie Africa had committed a firearms violation that day. In 1985, Officer Cresci of the Civil Affairs Unit testified that the other MOVE people seen bearing weapons were within their rights to do so.) For the next nine months, the observation squad, which consisted of detectives from Civil Affairs as well as officers from the Stakeout Unit, blockaded the MOVE house with barricades. Eventually, the perimeter grew to a six-block section of Powelton Village. Police officers kept meticulous files on everyone who frequented the area, checked identification of those coming and going, and harassed people who attempted to visit the MOVE house.[18]

The Observation Squad prompted a deluge of complaints from the left-leaning inhabitants of Powelton Village. The American Friends Service Committee (AFSC), who petitioned the city on behalf of MOVE's besieged neighbors, described the police Observation Squad as "an army of occupation covering a three or four block area." The Observation Squad routinely videotaped and photographed residents as they went about their days, which the AFSC claimed had an "intimidating effect on passersby." The Observation Squad arrested one Powelton Village woman for circulating petitions asking the police to leave the neighborhood. She claimed, during an NAACP hearing on police abuse, that she was violently interrogated at Police Headquarters and threatened that "if she knew what was good for her" she would "keep her nose out of the whole business between the police and MOVE." To the AFSC, the heavy police presence in Powelton Village had the potential for violating citizens' human rights.[19]

The MOVE blockade coincided with what scholar Samuel Moyn has termed "the breakthrough year for human rights." The discourse of human rights rose to the forefront of the American lexicon on January 20, 1977, when newly elected President Jimmy Carter proposed a new morality to guide American foreign policy. Carter linked American freedoms with the need to ensure freedoms around the world and suggested that this "commitment to human rights must be absolute." Prior to Carter's appropriation of the concept, leftist revolutionaries in Latin America used human rights to rally against right-wing dictatorships. Throughout the Soviet Bloc, dissenters frequently invoked the concept of human rights to similarly criticize oppressive regimes. Even after Carter appropriated the term, it was not at all clear what human rights were. Critics on the right conflated human rights with anticommunism, while leftists such as Noam Chomsky accused human rights discourse of being "a device to be manipulated by propagandists to gain popular support for counter-revolutionary intervention." Human Rights as understood today—a supranational commitment to certain freedoms, including freedom of religion, speech, and freedom from certain forms of state violence—was not a coherent concept in the late 1970s.[20]

The incoherence of human rights in the late 1970s was evident in the ways MOVE's critics employed human rights discourse to advocate starving MOVE people out of their home. The idea to starve MOVE out of the house was the creation of the Powelton Emergency Human Rights Coalition (PEHRC), a neighborhood group representing Powelton residents most adamantly opposed to MOVE's presence in the city. Though they did not represent a majority of Powelton residents, this group had the mayor's attention. PEHRC represented Powelton's angry, disaffected middle-class whites. The typical PEHRC constituent looked askance at the counterculture and blamed breakdowns in the structure of society for their own social and economic ills. It was the very same constituency that had propelled Rizzo from police commissioner to mayor. Rizzo met with PEHRC on July 11, 1977. PEHRC was already in the process of getting federal court approval of a plan to starve MOVE out of the house. In the view of PEHRC, a starvation blockade was a "gruesome suggestion," but it was "far better to cut off their sustenance than to wait around for diseases to break out in our neighborhood."[21]

In a petition directed at Mayor Rizzo and District Attorney Ed Rendell, PEHRC argued that the city of Philadelphia could have arrested MOVE people years ago in response to the numerous "acts of physical assault, death threats, terrorist threats to do bodily harm and destroy homes." However, despite the numerous criminal acts, health and sanitation, parking code, and child welfare violations, the city had pursued a strategy of appeasement. On behalf of their own human rights, PEHRC demanded that Rizzo and Rendell "take immediate nonviolent action to remove MOVE." They proposed expanding the police line into a full-scale blockade. They suggested shutting off all utilities, including water, electricity, and gas, to MOVE headquarters. They also suggested that no food or water be allowed to pass between the police line. They believed that these actions would rescue the children living inside the house from malnutrition and unsanitary living conditions. The petition carried seven hundred signatures.[22]

While the city mulled over PEHRC's blockade proposal, the round-the-clock observation unit was beginning to work. On June 17, 1977, Sue Africa became the first MOVE person to be arrested as a result of the May 20 standoff. Sue tried to elude the police blockade by climbing through a basement window wearing a wig and sunglasses. She snuck through neighboring yards and hailed a cab. The police promptly pulled the taxi over and Sue took off on foot, throwing a canister of mace at police officers as she ran. Like all the adults in the MOVE house on May 20, she was wanted on charges of conspiracy to riot and inciting a riot. She gained an additional felony charge for throwing the mace can at the officers. Her bail was set at $95,000, which she was unable to pay.[23]

When Sue Africa appeared before Judge McDermott, he questioned her mental competency to stand trial. Sue was jailed at Pennsylvania State Hospital for one month to allow state psychiatrists to determine whether she was insane. When the state psychiatrists determined Sue fit to stand trial, the judge rejected their recommendation and ordered Sue to Dyerberry Hospital for a second evaluation. The psychiatrists at Dyerberry determined Sue unfit to stand trial on the basis that she did not recognize the supremacy of the law of the United States. The psychiatric team asked Sue if she could take orders from Judge McDermott and cooperate with the judicial proceedings. Sue replied that she will submit only to "true law" as taught by John Africa and that any other system of law is "invalid and unjust." The psychiatric team determined that this answer suggested that Sue was not competent to represent herself at trial. In court, one of the psychiatrists testified that he believed Sue Africa was a "paranoid schizophrenic."[24]

After six months of detainment in hospitals and jails, Sue Africa wrote a letter to United Nations Ambassador Andrew Young, claiming that the government of the United States was violating her religious liberties. As she understood it, "All these intimidation deprivations have been heaped on my person because of my commitment to my religious beliefs, the teachings of JOHN AFRICA. Yet the 'free' United States of America is heralded across the world as the country that guarantees it's [sic] citizens religious freedom." Sue argued that Judge McDermott had sentenced her to medical evaluation because he knew medical treatment of any kind was against the teachings of John Africa as recorded in "MOVE's Bible." She explained that being a follower of John Africa forbade her from allowing another person to represent her in court. Her religious beliefs backed her into a corner: she was accused of being mentally incompetent, in part, because she desired to act as her own representative in court. She could not represent herself, however, because she was declared "mentally unfit." Because she believed the government of the United States had no interest in defending her religious liberties, her only recourse, as she lay in a confinement cell at a mental hospital, was to ask the United Nations to defend her human rights.[25]

Two other MOVE people arrested shortly after Sue did not fare much better in the criminal justice system. Conrad Africa and Robert Africa were arrested later in the summer of 1977, also on conspiracy to riot and firearms charges stemming from the Guns on the Porch standoff. While in the city's detention facility awaiting arraignment, Conrad and Robert became involved in a scuffle with a prison guard. They had asked the guard if they were allowed to take fresh fruit and vegetables from the dining facility to their cells in order to accommodate their religious diet. When the guard refused, the situation escalated to the point that Conrad and Robert received medical attention. At the conclusion of the investigation into the conflict, Deputy District Attorney Bernard Siegel determined that the prison guard was at fault and urged District Attorney Ed Rendell to drop the charges against Conrad and Robert in hopes that they would not press charges against the guards.[26]

MOVE people viewed the blockade as the latest episode in a long history of religious persecution. During the blockade, MOVE people released a four-page letter—a kind of extended press release—in which they offered their interpretation of the blockade, asserted the validity of their religious beliefs, and offered a solution to their impasse with the city. MOVE worried that people whose only knowledge of MOVE was gleaned from news reports might underestimate the seriousness with which MOVE people took their religion. "John Africa gave us everything we have, all that we need, nothing to want." MOVE people wrote in the letter that they "devoutly pursue our belief" despite the obvious persecution that belief wrought. They pointed to a long history of "beatings, the illegal jailings, the slaughter of our children, the outrageously excessive bails and fines imposed on our family" as evidence of the sincerity of their belief. MOVE people assumed that some people could not "tolerate the uncompromising approach of our belief, [and] our unwavering loyalty to the teaching of our founder, John Africa."[27]

The letter also pointed toward a way out of MOVE's impasse with the city of Philadelphia. The letter claimed that the "dictates of our religious belief" required MOVE to eventually relocate to a "rural environment." The letter stated that MOVE wanted to acquire a tract of land of "at least twenty acres." On this land, MOVE people would either build a large farmhouse to accommodate MOVE people or renovate an existing structure. A second farmhouse would provide lodgings and host programs for visitors. Animals would graze in the pastures, and MOVE people would farm the soil. Visitors would come and go, learning the Teachings of John Africa while working alongside MOVE people. Some would convert and stay, others would bring the Teachings of John Africa back to their communities. The letter states that a move to the countryside was the natural evolution for the group: "Just as the teaching of our founder, the principle of Natural Law, is disseminated in the urban setting of Philadelphia, so would this belief be communicated within the rural environment."[28]

On February 21, 1978, eight months after the standoff began, the City of Philadelphia offered MOVE an eight-point conditional surrender. The proposal required MOVE to vacate the house in Powelton and relocate at least two miles away. The sixty dogs and cats living in the MOVE house would be turned over to the Society for the Prevention of Cruelty to Animals, who would provide shelter for the animals until MOVE settled into a new location. All MOVE people with outstanding warrants would be arrested, booked, arraigned, and immediately released without bail all while under observation of a third party of their choosing to ensure their safety. The city floated this agreement because they assumed that MOVE was working toward the purchase of a new home in a rural area outside of the city. MOVE had one week to respond.[29]

One day before the deadline to accept or decline the city's proposal, MOVE rejected it. They cited a newspaper report, published in the *Daily News*, in which a journalist overheard a group of policemen discussing plans to attack the MOVE house. The planned siege was to take place before the deadline to accept or reject the city's offer. MOVE people interpreted the leak to mean that the city was not offering the proposal in good faith. MOVE also said that the altercation involving Conrad and Robert called into question the impartiality of the city's criminal justice system. Minutes after MOVE rejected the proposal, an incensed Frank Rizzo held an impromptu conference and announced that the starvation blockade would begin the next morning at 9 a.m. He pledged to expand the blockade, to increase the police presence, and to construct more barricades to ensure that "even a fly won't be able to get in." When pressed about the morality of starving a group of people known to include several small children, Rizzo responded that "maybe they can live off their own fat for a couple of days."[30]

Rizzo's police officers took a more lenient stance than their famously cantankerous boss. Officers patrolling the barricades on the afternoon before the starvation blockade was set to begin looked the other way as vehicle after vehicle brought boxes of canned food and water to the MOVE house. MOVE's supporters knew that MOVE would not easily accede to the mayor's demands of unconditional surrender. As the press began to assemble outside the barricades, Delbert Africa took the opportunity to frame the starvation blockade as an assault on MOVE's religious liberty. Rizzo, he said, had "made plans for murder" and was "denying us our due process of law." All the while, undercover detectives from Civil Affairs took note of everyone who passed food through the blockade.[31]

Sue, Conrad, and Robert Africa eventually found themselves in front of Judge DiBona on February 28, 1978. In the courtroom that day were two clergymen: Dr. Rufus Cornelsen and Msgr. Charles Devlin. Cornelsen was a Lutheran minister who headed the Metropolitan Christian Council, a confederation of churches and ministries committed to social justice. Devlin was a Catholic priest who led the Cardinal's Commission for Human Relations of the Philadelphia Archdiocese. Cornelsen had phoned his colleague Devlin earlier that morning to invite him to the hearing. This was the first Devlin had heard of MOVE. Cornelsen informed Devlin that they were "some type of back to nature group who had barricaded themselves in a house and wanted to exercise their beliefs without regard to civil jurisdiction and health and sanitary regulations." Devlin was reluctant to get involved with such a contentious issue, but agreed with Cornelsen that their religious authority was needed "in the interest of human rights."[32]

Judge DiBona of Philadelphia's Court of Common Pleas noticed the two clergymen in the gallery and invited them to his chambers before the hearing began. DiBona asked Cornelsen and Devlin if they would be interested in acting as third-party negotiators between the Philadelphia Police Department and MOVE. The clergymen agreed to try to talk some sense into MOVE, but only because of their commitment to human rights. DiBona, Cornelsen, and Devlin returned to the courtroom to announce the new arrangement. DiBona instructed the MOVE people present at the hearing to "consider communicating" with Devlin and Cornelsen "and to pay attention to what help [they] could give." He then found Robert, Sue, and Conrad guilty of inciting a riot.[33]

Msgr. Devlin forged a remarkably amicable relationship with MOVE people, particularly Phil, Delbert, and Ishongo. He and Cornelsen visited the MOVE house nearly every day. To pass through the police blockade, they had to first report to a mobile command vehicle to be patted down. Once cleared, they walked through the police line, all the while being watched through snipers' scopes. Devlin took the lead in the conversations. For reasons he was never aware of, MOVE people seemed to like him. Phil Africa, in particular, liked to tease the priest about his smoking habit. Neither Devlin nor Cornelsen went inside the MOVE house. Instead, they spoke with whomever was "on watch" on the porch. Usually, Devlin and Cornelsen inquired about the health of the people inside, especially the children. MOVE, as usual, framed the standoff as a religious liberty issue and assured the priest that everyone inside was healthy and happy. Over time, the priest developed what he called a "semi-trust" relationship with MOVE to the point that Police Commissioner O'Neill began wryly referring to him as "Monsignor Africa."[34]

Throughout the negotiations, Devlin understood his role as a representative of religious authority in a collaborative effort between Church and State. Devlin had no discomfort about his role, arguing that "we often express so much concern about the separation of Church and State that we fail to realize how often the Church and State cooperate and collaborate for the betterment of society." He believed that the MOVE negotiations were an opportunity for Church and State to work together to protect a besieged neighborhood from a problematic, yet sympathetic countercultural group. The priest was a close friend to Mayor Frank Rizzo, Police Commissioner O'Neill, and Judge DiBona. Devlin said these friendships "perdured and resulted in a period of close cooperation during the first MOVE confrontation—a confrontation which brought together the best resources of the State and the Church."[35]

Devlin believed that MOVE was a group that had chosen to "select a way of life which differed from the common cultural standards of the day." This was not an unfamiliar concept to Devlin. The early Christians, after all, made a habit of living outside of "common cultural standards," and this cultural dissonance was a key to the religion's growth. To Devlin, however, MOVE's cultural dissonance was not the religious kind. MOVE buried their feces and garbage in the yard and refused to exterminate the rats and cockroaches living in the house. As Devlin understood it, *this* kind of cultural dissonance could not be tolerated, because, after all, "there were health and sanitary laws to be observed." MOVE buried their feces and garbage (which, as a result of their lifestyle, consisted almost exclusively of food waste) in the yard because they believed that all once-living things must complete the "cycle" of life and death and be returned to the earth. Though MOVE made him aware of this, Devlin did not entertain the idea that MOVE's unusual practices reflected authentic religious beliefs and instead sought to protect the religious right of deviating from cultural standards from any association with MOVE.[36]

Devlin, Cornelsen, and Washington were not the only representatives of established religion to intervene in the MOVE standoff. The AFSC, an international Quaker peace and social justice advocacy organization based in Philadelphia, was drawn to the situation by the mayor's threats to starve MOVE out of the house. The AFSC saw the MOVE Blockade as another chapter in a much longer history of police brutality in the city. Partly in response to Rizzo's press conference, the AFSC launched the Philadelphia Police Abuse Project, an umbrella coalition that was designed to centralize the many neighborhood groups and churches working on police violence and to provide coordination between smaller groups and the American Civil Liberties Union (ACLU). The link between the Quakers of the AFSC and the Philadelphia ACLU was quite strong in the 1970s. Spencer Coxe, the head of the Philadelphia ACLU, was a Quaker who maintained a close relationship with the AFSC. Ali Shabazz, the lead field worker on the AFSC's Philadelphia Police Abuse Project, was also a member of the Citywide Black Coalition for Human Rights, an interfaith advocacy group that brought together African American religious leaders, including Rev. Paul Washington, to protest the MOVE blockade.[37]

In addition to the Philadelphia Police Abuse Project, the AFSC coordinated with a group called the Friendly Presence. The Philadelphia Yearly Meeting, the umbrella group that organizes the region's Quaker congregations, created Friendly Presence to provide nonviolent conflict resolution to the contentious Black Panther Party Convention held in Philadelphia in 1970. The group reformed in 1978 in hopes of offering the same kind of conflict resolution to the city's standoff with MOVE. From the time the blockade began, Friendly Presence maintained a religious vigil outside the MOVE house. They also instituted around-the-clock surveillance of the nearby National Guard Armory that was serving as the Civil Affairs Unit's command center to ensure that Powelton residents' human rights were not violated by the Philadelphia Police Department. Friendly Presence reported numerous human rights violations around the blockade, mostly caused by overzealous police officers. Those who expressed interest in checking on MOVE were routinely harassed, had their identification confiscated without cause, had their photographs taken, and were warned not to return.[38]

Though the AFSC and Friendly Presence were perhaps MOVE's most fervent defenders, like Washington, Devlin, and Cornelsen, these Quaker groups did not consider MOVE to be a religion. Rather, they categorized MOVE as a "revolutionary group . . . that advocates a return to nature and spurns all social conventions." Through the vigil, the Quakers of Friendly Presence transformed MOVE into a vehicle for their own religious practice. For John Hughes, a Quaker who was involved with the AFSC's response to the city's blockade, the vigil was "absolutely a religious experience." Hughes manned the vigil every day from midnight to six in the morning. Even during the overnight hours, Hughes and his co-religionists provided a warm cup of coffee to passersby, religious seekers, and those who came to see the blockade for themselves. Almost everyone who visited Hughes at the barricades expressed disbelief that a city would attempt to starve its own citizens out of a house. MOVE was the kind of group that could be pitied and sympathized with. But they were not a religion. The Quaker vigil and the observation of the police compound were not designed to endorse MOVE's complaints regarding their religious rights, but rather were designed to protect MOVE's human rights from violation at the hand of the state. The Quakers of Friendly Presence and the AFSC imagined the vigil as providing a dose of religious authority to an otherwise secular confrontation.[39]

Father Paul Washington, frustrated by his inability to influence MOVE to surrender to police, hoped to revive the community support that had broken through the police lines a year earlier to force a peaceful resolution to the Guns on the Porch standoff. On April 4, 1978, his group, the Citywide Black Coalition for Human Rights (CWBCHR), led a march on City Hall to protest the city's violations of MOVE's human rights. Washington's CWBCHR was an interfaith social activism group that featured African American religious and political leaders representing a variety of faith traditions. The march, which was funded by the Quakers of the AFSC, culminated with over one thousand demonstrators linking arms to form a circle around city hall to symbolically blockade Rizzo inside. Sister Falakah Fattah, the leader of an African American Muslim group and the spokesperson for the CWBCHR, told reporters that the blockade was a "massive protest against the human rights violations certainly apparent in Powelton Village."[40]

While MOVE's religious supporters were decrying violations of human rights, MOVE launched a media initiative to argue for their religious liberties. Through weekly press releases, Delbert Africa made the case to the public that MOVE was a religion of peace. He argued that continuous police harassment had forced MOVE to buy guns, but that merely being in possession of weapons was a violation of MOVE's "religious principles." Still, he reminded the media that MOVE owning guns was "in keeping with their constitutional rights to defend their property." Louise and Laverne Africa spoke with reporters as often as possible to call for an end to "religious persecution" of MOVE and an apology from President Jimmy Carter and Mayor Frank Rizzo. In an open letter to Rizzo and the people of Philadelphia, MOVE suggested that Rizzo meet Delbert Africa in a public debate. MOVE suggested that, after the debate, the public would be polled to decide whether they supported MOVE or their mayor. If the mayor won, MOVE promised an unconditional surrender. John Africa framed the standoff as an issue of religious liberty, stating, "Our position is not negotiable, it ain't a concession, a thing to be traded and altered and gambled, for our position is our religion."[41]

On the evening before the starvation blockade was to go into effect, the Quaker leadership of the AFSC was in a closed-chambers meeting with Chief Justice of the Pennsylvania Supreme Court Robert Nix, arguing on behalf of MOVE's human rights. The AFSC leadership informed Nix of their role in the blockade. Jeanette Knighton of Concerned Citizens to Insure Justice had contacted them on behalf of MOVE and asked the AFSC to monitor police behavior when the blockade was first established. When the various community groups formed in response to the blockade, the AFSC met with each one and attempted to find common ground between the groups that wanted MOVE out of the neighborhood at any cost and those who wanted MOVE recognized as a legitimate religious group. Most importantly, the AFSC argued to Chief Justice Nix that Judge DiBona was on a crusade to destroy MOVE and that his bias provided grounds for the Supreme Court to stop the starvation blockade before it began.[42]

The closed-door meeting between the Quakers and Chief Justice Nix proved successful in delaying the starvation blockade. Late in the evening on the night before the starvation blockade was set to commence, the Pennsylvania Supreme Court issued an emergency injunction invalidating DiBona's judicial approval of the starvation blockade. According to Nix, Judge DiBona's ruling in favor of Rizzo's blockade was invalid because MOVE was not present during the hearings. DiBona scheduled a hearing a week later and ordered MOVE to appear. MOVE, in a letter given to

Msgr. Devlin, refused to appear and suggested that DiBona invite the three MOVE people already in his custody to represent the MOVE family in court. DiBona, to appease Nix, held a second hearing on March 7 as Sue, Conrad, and Robert Africa sat in chains at the defendant's table. DiBona again ruled that the starvation blockade was legal but also issued a temporary injunction on the ruling pending Supreme Court review. When Chief Justice Nix was again faced with determining the legality of DiBona's decision, he was forced to allow the starvation blockade to go into effect. He did, however, make it clear in his concurring opinion that the court's decision should not "be construed as an approval" of Rizzo's starvation blockade.[43]

At dawn on March 16, 1978, the starvation blockade went into effect. Canned and processed foods were against the teachings of John Africa, but these were desperate times. There were eighteen people inside the house, including several young children. MOVE had managed to stockpile a few months' worth of food, but even more worrisome than the limited food supply was the city's plan to shut off the utilities to the house. MOVE did not use electricity and rarely used the gas heat, but the absence of running water would create a dangerous situation well before MOVE ran low on food. Devlin and Cornelsen continued to visit with MOVE nearly every day. Devlin justified his intervention to the police on the grounds that the basic philosophy of MOVE was nonviolence. Their troublesome practices and beliefs, including the rat infestation and the recycling of human feces, were premised on something fundamentally good: the "principles of nonviolence and respect for life."[44]

The deluge of national media attention caused by the escalation of the blockade forced city officials to consider a more humanitarian approach. In April 1978, community groups opposed to the blockade began a campaign to convince the city to allow food and water to the children inside the MOVE house. These groups considered the MOVE children to be hostages to their parents' ideology. Initially, the city refused to consider feeding the children because MOVE might consider it as "an act of weakness." Nevertheless, community groups and Washington's CWBCHR continued to offer proposals to feed the children in the name of human rights.[45]

As the MOVE blockade began to attract the attention of the national media, the debate over MOVE's classification spilled into community gatherings and town hall meetings. All the while, Msgr. Devlin, Father Paul Washington, and the Quakers of the AFSC were there to guide the conversation away from religious liberty and toward human rights. At one such meeting, called by Washington and held at an Episcopal Church in Powelton, Washington, Devlin, and Cornelsen assured worried neighbors that they were doing their best to prevent the standoff from turning violent. At the meeting, a fervent MOVE supporter announced his plans to hold "basic training" to prepare for a violent confrontation with police. He vowed to "do whatever is necessary" to remove what he believed was an illegal siege of the Powelton neighborhood by the police. Meanwhile, Rev. Rufus Cornelsen, the Lutheran minister who led the Metropolitan Christian Council of Philadelphia, assured Pedro and Elva Perez that their son Carlos Africa was healthy and happy inside the MOVE house. He told the worried couple that he had shaken hands with Carlos just days ago and that "he is well, healthy—relaxed—but I know he is worried about you." Not everyone at the meeting looked upon MOVE so glowingly. Many Powelton residents complained to the clergymen that MOVE, not the police, were the ones terrorizing the neighborhood. They complained about MOVE's penchant for harassment and violent threats. One woman complained through tears that she and her husband were beaten up by MOVE people for complaining about the rat infestation caused by MOVE's recycling practices.[46]

One month after the starvation blockade began, Father Washington informed the Philadelphia Police Department and Mayor Rizzo that his CWBCHR was going to defy the blockade to deliver food to everyone inside the MOVE house. Washington hoped that he and the eleven other religious leaders in the CWBCHR would be arrested for breaking the blockade, leading to a judicial review of the starvation blockade itself. Washington viewed the blockade as a challenge to his own religious liberty. He believed the blockade was designed to "prevent the church from fulfilling its divine mandate to feed the hungry, give water to the thirsty and minister to the oppressed." On April 16, about fifty demonstrators with the CWBCHR met outside the police barricades with food, water, and medical supplies. Demonstrators cleared a path through the chain-link fencing and police barricades, and a few began to walk toward the MOVE house. Police officers wrestled them to the ground and arrested them. Using police horses to disperse the crowd, other officers ordered the dozens of onlookers back to their homes.[47]

Inside the house, MOVE people began to run out of water. With twenty-three people inside the house, as well as dozens of dogs, the water they had collected before the starvation blockade went into effect quickly ran out. John Africa assured the MOVE people in the house not to worry; God was on their side. On the day that MOVE people used their last drop, it began to rain, and

MOVE people filled their buckets with rainwater. To MOVE people, the rain was one of John Africa's most important miracles.

The longer the starvation blockade wore on, the more pressure Mayor Rizzo faced to offer food and water to the women and children inside the MOVE house. Rizzo, wanting the food to come from the city and not Washington's CWBCHR, ordered Judge DiBona to coordinate a food delivery from the city. Judge DiBona phoned Devlin and asked the priest to meet him at his home in South Philadelphia. DiBona told Devlin that the city wanted to make an offer of food and water to the children trapped inside the MOVE house. Devlin was skeptical of the idea. He thought MOVE would use the city's food delivery as an opportunity to win sympathy through the media and doubted that the food would ever make it to the children. He agreed, however, that in the interest of human rights, the city had to make the offer. DiBona put Devlin in charge of buying and delivering the food.[48]

On the afternoon of April 22, 1978, Devlin walked through the blockade with a box full of food. Dozens of reporters and a crowd of bystanders looked on. Undercover, plainclothes police snipers watched the priest approach the MOVE house through their riflescopes. Devlin placed the food on MOVE's front porch. He announced to MOVE people inside the house that the city had offered the food for the hungry children and nursing mothers. He then retreated behind the barricades. As video cameras rolled, a MOVE person inside the house shouted, "We are one. Either all of us eat or none of us will!" Delbert Africa emerged from the house, picked up the food, and dumped it in the street halfway between the porch and the barricades. The next day, newspapers ran photographs of the rejected box of food, overturned, and covered in rats. Public sympathy for MOVE—what was left of it—evaporated.[49]

Reports that MOVE had rejected the city's offer of food forced Father Washington and Msgr. Devlin to defend their roles in the standoff to their respective religious communities. Washington had enjoyed little success in earning MOVE's trust since the May 20th standoff. Due to his schedule, he visited the MOVE house irregularly. Each time, he found MOVE to be "rigid" and disrespectful. His support for MOVE put him in a difficult position with the Diocese and with his colleagues. Bishop Lyman Ogilby, head of the Episcopal Diocese of Pennsylvania, sent a letter to all the clergy stating that he had placed Washington in charge of their response to the MOVE blockade. According to Bishop Ogilby, the Diocese, through Washington, was becoming involved in the negotiations officially in order "to minister, to show love and compassion." As the blockade wore on, however, the Diocese began to waver in its support of Washington's intervention. After considerable pushback from constituents, Bishop Ogilby clarified his position on MOVE. He explained that Washington's involvement in the blockade did not represent the Diocese's endorsement of the group. Rather, the Diocese was intervening as a "gesture" toward "the ministry of reconciliation [that] has always been a part of the Church's mission and ministry." Bishop Ogilby assured callers that the Diocese would never support a group like MOVE that breaks laws and is a "destructive element" in society.[50]

Devlin, too, was drawing the ire of the religious community he represented over the food delivery. Some Philadelphia Catholics questioned Devlin's use of Archdiocesan funds during the negotiations, arguing that Devlin's intervention amounted to an endorsement of the group. A few parishioners began withholding tithes to their parishes to protest Devlin's involvement until the Archdiocese found more "worthy recipients" of their charity. Another critic of Devlin's involvement said, "I do not want my money (and it is partly my money) thrown away to rats." Devlin's critics did not agree that MOVE's trouble with the police was the result of a religious controversy. On the contrary, they believed that MOVE had "broken every rule of human decency and indeed probably every commandment" and did not warrant the Archdiocese's intervention.[51]

Devlin assured his critics that the Archdiocese was only acting on behalf of human rights and was not defending MOVE as a religion. In a memo sent to the staff of the Cardinal's Commission on Human Relations, Devlin instructed those answering the phone to tell angry callers that the food was purchased and offered by the city. Devlin and the Archdiocese were only involved in delivering the food in order to prevent the "loss of human life." Even those who previously supported Devlin's intervention in the MOVE standoff contacted the priest to offer sympathy, realizing it must have been difficult for Devlin "to show socially deviant brothers and sisters the loving face of Christ."[52]

Having lost public support, MOVE became more receptive to Devlin's pleas for surrender. On May 8, 1978, after spending a year confined to the MOVE house and two months behind a starvation blockade, MOVE agreed to a peace settlement with the city. According to the terms of the agreement, which was negotiated in a meeting between Devlin, Cornelsen, and District Attorney Ed Rendell, MOVE offered to relinquish all of the guns in the house if the city agreed to release three incarcerated MOVE people on bail pending trial. The city agreed and transported Jerry, Conrad, and Robert Africa to the Powelton house that afternoon. MOVE turned over their weapons and allowed police to inspect the house, where they found enough food to last MOVE people three more months. In the settlement, MOVE agreed to vacate the Powelton house and relocate to the countryside within ninety days. The city agreed to leave the house intact to serve as a sacred space for MOVE gatherings in the city. As MOVE people imagined it, the Powelton house would become more of a conventional religious facility—part shrine, part church. The SPCA would shelter the animals temporarily before returning them to MOVE's custody. MOVE people facing criminal charges agreed to turn themselves in to the police, who would drop all charges upon arraignment. This new peace settlement between MOVE and the city is an important, albeit ultimately inconsequential, footnote in MOVE's classification: agreeing to leave the MOVE house intact to serve as a temple was the first time that the city did not immediately dismiss MOVE's claims to religious legitimacy.[53]

John Hughes, the Quaker who manned the Friendly Presence vigil overnight, learned of the settlement as his shift ended. A man in a car drove up to the vigil and beckoned Hughes to the driver's side window. The man's nephew was a MOVE person living in the house. He thanked Hughes for saving his nephew's life. Hughes spent the morning celebrating with the other vigil participants. By 9 a.m., officers from the Philadelphia Police Department began removing the barricades, and Jerry, Robert, and Conrad were released from jail. The Philadelphia Archdiocese mailed out dozens of letters in which Devlin thanked the Archdiocese's allies for their support and congratulated the fact that the new agreement had "precluded the necessity for our active participation." Devlin believed that his religious authority, along with that of Washington, Cornelsen, and other religious mediators, had prevented a violent confrontation between the city and MOVE.[54]

Despite the breakthrough, the peace between MOVE and the city was short-lived. Two weeks in, the city began acting outside of the agreement. Police officers razed a large fence MOVE had constructed separating the MOVE house from a neighbor's house. For MOVE, the house was a sacred structure; destroying even a part of it was iconoclastic. When the SPCA arrived at the MOVE house for the dogs, they told MOVE that the city had ordered them to spay and neuter the animals. This, again, was a violation of the Teachings of John Africa that MOVE could not allow. Phil Africa and Sue Africa, who surrendered to police with the expectation that their charges would be dropped according to the agreement, found themselves instead before Judge DiBona. Phil and Sue caused a ruckus in the courtroom and called DiBona a liar for removing the fence and ordering the dogs to be spayed and neutered. In response, DiBona revoked Phil's bail and charged him and Sue with contempt of court. Oscar Gaskins, MOVE's court-appointed lawyer, objected to DiBona's actions, arguing that the judge had no right to interfere in the city's agreement with MOVE because it had been orchestrated by another judge. MOVE people were further perturbed a week later when they received subpoenas to appear in court to face charges that they believed had been dropped. Believing the subpoenas to be a clerical error, no MOVE people appeared on their court date, resulting in further contempt charges.[55]

Over the next ninety days, MOVE stayed in constant communication with John Africa, who was living at a second MOVE house in Rochester, New York. John Africa, along with a few other MOVE people, managed to escape Philadelphia for Rochester just days after the May 20th standoff. While in Rochester, John Africa began to develop a more eschatological theology. He believed that modern society would soon self-destruct as a result of its own technological excesses and that MOVE's conflict with the city of Philadelphia would ignite this apocalyptic scenario. John Africa instructed his followers not to leave the MOVE house by the August 1 deadline and to ignore a court hearing scheduled for that day.

On August 2, 1978, a day after the deadline for MOVE to vacate the house, Mayor Rizzo held another furious press conference on the steps of City Hall. This time, he vowed that there would be "no more barricades, no more conversations." The Philadelphia Police Department had spent $1.2 million, just on salaries and overtime, watching the MOVE house. The blockade had gone on long enough. Rizzo announced plans for the Philadelphia Police Department to raid the MOVE house and arrest everyone inside. He warned that if anyone resisted arrest, they would be "put down with legal force."[56]

The next day, Rizzo, Police Commissioner O'Neill, and Deputy Fire Chief William Richmond met to devise a plan to evacuate the MOVE house. The plan involved the fire department's "Giant Deluge Gun," which was capable of spraying 2,000 gallons of water per minute into the house from a distance of 300 feet. Fire Chief Richmond recommended placing the Giant Deluge Gun ninety feet from the MOVE house so that wooden slats on the windows would be easily blown away. Richmond warned that the water cannon should only be used intermittently because three minutes' worth of water could be enough to collapse the house. If the flooding did not force MOVE people out of the house, the police department would escalate to tear gas. The city leaders planned to evacuate and temporarily house hundreds of people living in the surrounding six blocks out of fears that the plan could provoke an armed response from MOVE.[57]

Msgr. Charles Devlin received a phone call at his home on the evening of August 7, 1978, from his "good friend" George Fencl, head of the Civil Affairs Unit. Fencl warned Devlin that the Philadelphia Police Department was going to raid the MOVE house at seven the following morning. That night, as he lay in bed, Devlin received a series of visions. He was overcome by a sense of evil and death. He saw a shootout that resulted in the death of a policeman. He saw himself fall to the ground to escape crossfire, splitting his pants. He saw grieving family members ask him to deliver the homily at the dead officer's funeral. He resolved to go to the MOVE house before the planned raid to try, one last time, to convince MOVE to surrender.[58]

When he arrived at the house at 5 a.m., Devlin met with Delbert, who was on watch. To Devlin's surprise, Delbert allowed him and Inspector Fencl to go inside the house. Though Devlin had visited the MOVE house hundreds of times, this was the first time he was allowed inside. The priest and the detective descended through a ground-level window into the dark basement, where they found sixteen MOVE people holed up. They knew that the raid was coming. Devlin and Fencl tried to assure MOVE people that they could have their day in court and that the police had no intentions of hurting anyone. Devlin reminded MOVE of their commitment to life and encouraged them to allow the women and children to leave the house before the assault. Fencl explained, moment by moment, what would happen in the next few hours if MOVE did not surrender—to no avail. Devlin and Fencl left the house and took up positions safely behind the barrier.[59]

The plan went off without a hitch. At 6:30 in the morning, bulldozers began destroying MOVE's reinforced porch to allow the water cannons to penetrate the house. The fire department began pumping water into the house at 7:56 a.m. After four minutes, the water was shut off to allow Devlin one last opportunity to convince MOVE to surrender. Devlin took the bullhorn and asked MOVE to think of the children. MOVE did not respond. Over the next fourteen minutes, the police department launched tear gas canisters into the house.[60]

Devlin had seen enough. Defeated, the priest turned to walk to his car when he heard a police officer shout, "they have guns." Before he could turn around, the scene erupted in gunfire. Just as he had envisioned, Devlin threw himself to the ground and split his pants. He looked up to see Officer James Ramp, a twenty-three-year veteran of the Philadelphia Police Department's Stakeout Unit, take a bullet to the head. The shooting lasted for fifteen minutes. By 8:30, eight MOVE people had surrendered to police. Over the next forty minutes, the remaining five adults and six naked children left the house as well. One of the last adults to leave the house was Delbert Africa, who had taken on the role of MOVE's spokesman throughout the blockade. Newspaper photographers and reporters watched as four Philadelphia police officers, upon recognizing MOVE's second-in-command, attacked Delbert as he lie prostrate on the ground surrendering. Photographs captured police officers beating Delbert in the head with the crown of a police helmet. MOVE alleged that all eleven adults were beaten once they were in police custody. All told, four police officers, one firefighter, and one MOVE person were treated for gunshot wounds.[61]

Devlin followed the ambulance to the hospital and gave Officer Ramp the Last Rites. Ramp was declared dead on arrival. He offered his condolences to Commissioner O'Neill and to the Ramp family before returning to the MOVE house. Despite the fact that the city had proposed to leave the MOVE house standing so that MOVE people could use it as a sacred space, by the time Devlin made it back to the house that afternoon, there was nothing left. Police Commissioner O'Neill received a court order from Judge DiBona granting him the power to raze the house so that it would not become a "cult symbol." A combination of thousands of rounds of ammunition and thousands of gallons of water caused the house to collapse, and city bulldozers razed what remained. The only thing that still stood was a hand painted sign that read, "Long Live the House that John Africa Built."[62]

Msgr. Devlin delivered the homily at Officer Ramp's funeral. He began by offering condolences on behalf "of the entire religious community: Catholic, Protestant, Jewish." Devlin positioned himself and Officer Ramp as warriors in "a battle between good and evil." In this instance, evil won. Groups like MOVE, he argued, were allowed to grow because American society absolves such groups from responsibility through an appeal to tolerance. MOVE had been "explained away by sociological, physiological, and psychological factors." In reality, American society was unable to call MOVE what it was: evil. By speaking on behalf of "the entire religious community," Devlin positioned himself between MOVE and the category of religion. During Ramp's homily, Devlin was not just a priest; he was the representative of true religion. Devlin seemed genuinely embarrassed over his role in the MOVE negotiations. He believed that MOVE had tricked him into being a "double agent." MOVE, Devlin thought, had no real intentions of negotiating a peaceful resolution with the city, but was using the religious community to worsen the conflict and further their propaganda. By positioning himself as the representative of religious authority—indeed as a representative of "the entire religious community"—Devlin disassociated MOVE from the religious legitimacy they desired.[63]

Nine of the twelve MOVE adults in the house on May 20th—Jeanine, Delbert, Michael, Eddie, Chuckie, Debbie, Janet, Phil, and Merle Africa—were charged, collectively, with the murder of Officer Ramp. The MOVE 9 defendants waived their right to a jury trial, leaving their fate in the hands of Judge Edwin Malmed, a veteran Common Pleas Court judge who had presided over numerous MOVE cases in the past. The prosecution showed video evidence of one or more unidentified MOVE people firing at least three shots out of the basement window toward police, and presented the testimony of dozens of police officers who witnessed the shootout. Within weeks, all MOVE defendants had been barred from the proceedings, leaving their defense to their court-appointed backup counsel. The defense argued that potentially exonerating forensics evidence had been destroyed when police razed the MOVE house, and that the prosecution was unable to establish who killed Officer James Ramp. Perhaps, the defense alleged, Ramp had been killed by friendly fire. They noted that the bullet that struck Officer Ramp had entered on a downward trajectory while MOVE allegedly fired upon police from below street level. The trajectory of the bullet, however, was consistent with the eyewitness testimony that someone in the MOVE house shot Officer Ramp shortly after he dove to the ground for cover.[64]

After the longest and most expensive criminal trial in state history, on May 8, 1980, Judge Malmed found the MOVE 9 guilty of the murder of Officer Ramp, the attempted murder of seven injured first responders, and of entering into a criminal conspiracy. On August 4, 1981, Judge Edwin Malmed sentenced each of the MOVE 9 to between thirty and one hundred years in prison. At their sentencing, the MOVE 9 warned Judge Malmed that by fighting John Africa's movement he was "fighting God." They prophesied that God would make Malmed's heart "jump right outta your chest" in retribution for the verdict and sentencing. (MOVE people believe this prophecy was fulfilled when Judge Malmed died in 2013.) Malmed defended his sentencing by telling reporters that "in my opinion, any thought of rehabilitation of these defendants would be absurd. They have persisted in setting their own bizarre codes of conduct without regard for the laws of the commonwealth or the rights of others, and I don't think their attitude will change." He said that he sentenced all MOVE 9 members equally, despite the lack of evidence, because "they have repeatedly shouted that they were a family . . . and I have treated them as a family with equal guilt shared." The FBI tested all twelve MOVE adults in the house on August 8 for firearms residue. Only three, Michael Africa, Chuckie Africa, and Phil Africa, tested positive for firearms residue.[65]

The three police officers caught on video beating Delbert Africa—Officers Charles Geist, Terrence Mulvihill, and Joseph Zagame—were charged with aggravated assault, simple assault, and official repression. For over a year, District Attorney Ed Rendell's office refused to release the names of the officers seen on video. They were not brought to trial until 1981. The prosecution aired the video recording from the local CBS affiliate that showed the three officers beating Delbert after he had surrendered. Before the jury could issue a verdict, however, Judge Stanley L. Kubacki issued a directed verdict of not guilty. Kubacki reasoned that, although "the entire world saw photographs of the three defendants striking Delbert Africa," the prosecution had failed to prove intent. "Any conviction returned by the jury would have been the product of speculation." Kubacki understood that his directed verdict could be interpreted as covering up police brutality, but was willing to be the "lightning rod for the great public controversy" that was likely to ensue.[66]

Much had changed since the death of Life Africa. For a while, after the death of Life Africa, MOVE was very close to attaining the religious legitimacy they so desired. Established religious leaders, politicians, and judges—people with power—took their complaints seriously. When the city of Philadelphia erected a blockade around MOVE's house, representatives of religious authority stepped in to negotiate a peaceful resolution, sometimes at MOVE's defense. From May 1977 to August 1978, the boundaries that define the study of religion—church and state, religious and secular, good religion and bad religion, the sacred and the profane—became real. For a time, that which separated MOVE people from the religious legitimacy they desired was built into barbed wire and police barricades. It was representatives of religious authority who moved back and forth across this boundary. When Rev. Paul Washington rejected MOVE's claim to religious legitimacy because "true prophets" do not behave the way John Africa did, when Msgr. Charles Devlin framed the conflict between the city and MOVE as one between "good and evil," and when MOVE's allies in the religious community defended their human rights, but not their religious liberties, these representatives of religious authority were making claims about what "true religion" was. They were policing the boundaries of what counts as religion. Ultimately, these men and women determined that MOVE was not, in fact, a religion—a conclusion that another group of social actors, the police, had already reached.

Notes

1. Mike Africa Jr., transcript of an oral history conducted in 2016 by Richard Kent Evans, MOVE Oral History Project, Special Collections and Urban Archives, Temple University, Philadelphia, PA.
2. Marc Schogol and Robert J. Terry, "Commune Members Clash with Police; Six Arrested," *Inquirer*, March 29, 1976; Murray Dubin, "MOVE Commune Mourns Death of Baby," *Philadelphia Inquirer*, March 30, 1976.
3. Chuck Stone, "MOVE Hangs in There, But It's Rough," *Philadelphia Daily News*, June 18, 1975.
4. Mike Leary, "6 MOVE members held for trial." *Philadelphia Inquirer*, April 14, 1976; John L. Dubois and Thomas J. Gibbins, Jr., "7 Policemen Injured in Clashes with MOVE Commune Members," *The Evening Bulletin*, March 29, 1976, 3.
5. Murray Dubin, "MOVE Commune Mourns Death of Baby," *Philadelphia Inquirer*, March 30, 1976; Linn Washington, "MOVE Says Mth.-Old Baby Killed in Clash with Police: Police Say Baby Did Not Exist," *Philadelphia Tribune*, March 30, 1976.
6. Dave Racher, "D.A. Ordered to Show if MOVE Baby Died in Clash," *Daily News*, March 30, 1976; "D.A.'s Office Is Probing Claim of Infant's Death," *Philadelphia Inquirer*, March 31, 1976; "D.A. Asks MOVE to Help with Probe," *Daily News*, April 14, 1976; untitled, *Inquirer*, April 23, 1976.
7. Charles Layton, "Body of Baby Seen at MOVE Commune," *Philadelphia Inquirer*, April 10, 1976.
8. Ibid.
9. Ibid.
10. Ibid.; Louise Africa, "On The MOVE," *Philadelphia Tribune*, April 27, 1976.
11. MOVE to Commissioner O'Neill, May 20, 1978, Box 8, Folder 1, Philadelphia Special Investigation (MOVE) Commission Records, Urban Archives, Temple University, Philadelphia, PA.
12. Paul Washington, "MOVE—Empathetically Viewed," Box 26, Folder 1, Father Paul Washington Papers, Charles L. Blockson Afro-American Collection, Temple University, Philadelphia, PA.
13. Father Paul M. Washington with David McInnes Gracie, *"Other Sheep I Have": The Autobiography of Father Paul M. Washington* (Philadelphia: Temple University Press,

1994), 176–177; "MOVE Organization Guidelines," Box 60, Folder 10, Philadelphia Special Investigation (MOVE) Commission Records, Urban Archives, Temple University, Philadelphia, PA. Emphasis in original.
14. Washington, *Other Sheep I Have*, 177.
15. Ibid., 178.
16. Ibid., 179.
17. Ibid.; Paul Washington, "MOVE—Empathetically Viewed;" Pamela Smith and James Davis, "MOVE!" *Philadelphia Tribune*, August 11, 1978.
18. Philadelphia Special Investigation Commission, Examination of Officers Cresse and Draper of Civil Affairs, October 8, 1985, Box 19, PSIC; Ali Shabazz, "Concerned Citizens to Insure Justice for MOVE," January 6, 1978, Box General Admin., Folder 3423, Philadelphia Police Abuse Project, Philadelphia Surveillance Program, American Friends Research Center, Philadelphia, PA.
19. American Friends Service Committee, "Proposal for Project to Facilitate Work against Police Abuse in Phila.," July 1977, Box General Admin., Folder 3436, Philadelphia Police Abuse Project, Philadelphia Surveillance Program, American Friends Research Center, Philadelphia, PA.
20. Samuel Moyn, *The Last Utopia: Human Rights in History* (Cambridge, MA: Harvard University Press, 2012), 118 and 120–158.
21. "City Agrees to Starve MOVE Out," *Philadelphia Daily News*, July 11, 1977.
22. Powelton Emergency Human Rights Committee, "Open Letter to Mayor Frank L. Rizzo," Box General Admin., Folder 3423, Philadelphia Police Abuse Project, Philadelphia Surveillance Program, American Friends Research Center, Philadelphia, PA.
23. "Police Arrest 2nd MOVEr," *Daily News*, June 18, 1977.
24. Sue Africa to Ambassador Andrew Young, December 9, 1977, Files of the Cardinal's Commission on Human Relations, Philadephia Archdiocesean Historical Research Center, Wynnewood, PA.
25. Ibid.
26. Cynthia Adcock, "MOVE-Blockade-Powelton," *The Philadelphia Phoenix*, April 1978; Bernard Siegel to Deputy District Attorney Ed Rendell, April 27, 1978, Box 8, PSIC.
27. MOVE, letter accompanying "Proposal for Funding of the MOVE Organization," July 10, 1978, PSIC.
28. Ibid.
29. "Proposal Made by City to MOVE February 21, 1978 Through Joel Todd and Rejected Point by Point by MOVE February 27, 1978," PAHRC.
30. Margaret Van Houten, Thelma Segal, Ali Shabazz, "Surveillance Project Role in MOVE-City Conflict," March 2, 1978, Box General Admin., Folder 3406, AFSC; Joe Davidson, "Members Brace for Siege," *Philadelphia Evening Bulletin*, March 1, 1978.
31. Davidson, "MOVE Members Brace for Seige"; Pamela Smith, "MOVE Thanks Public for Support during Confrontation," *Baltimore Sun*, July 4, 1978.
32. Msgr. Charles Devlin, *I Am Ready and Willing . . . With the Help of God: A Portrait of the Priesthood as Seen through Icons of Ministry and Service by a Priest—One Among Many*, unpublished manuscript, PAHRC, 84–85.

33. Ibid., 85–87.
34. A. W. Geiselman, "Three Clergy Bridge Armed Impasse between Police, Residents of House," *National Catholic Reporter*, April 21, 1978; Devlin, *I Am Ready*, 89.
35. Devlin, *I Am Ready*, 81.
36. Ibid.
37. Proposal for Project to Facilitate Work against Police Abuse in Philadelphia, July 1977, Box General Admin., Folder 3436, AFSC; Charles Walker, "Quakers Involved with MOVE," March 22, 1978, Box General Admin., Folder 3413, AFSC.
38. Philadelphia Yearly Meeting, Minutes of the Philadelphia Yearly Meeting, 16; Memorandum by John Hughes, May 18, 1978, Folder 3413, AFSC; John Sullivan and Ali Shabbaz, "Paragraph on Staff Work on MOVE for Lou Schneider's Report," April 5, 1978, Folder 3413, AFSC.
39. Proposal for Project to Facilitate Work against Police Abuse in Philadelphia," July 1977, Folder 3436, AFSC; Memorandum by John Hughes, May 18, 1978, Folder 3413, AFSC.
40. Paul Washington, "Draft," June 9, 1978, Box 26, Folder 1, Father Paul Washington Papers, Charles L. Blockson Afro-American Collection, Temple University, Philadelphia, PA.
41. "MOVE Makes 6 Demands," *Philadelphia Tribune*, March 7, 1978; "An Open Letter to City and State Officials," PAHRC.
42. Margaret Van Houten, Thelma Segal, and Ali Shabazz, "Surveillance Project Role in MOVE-City Conflict," March 2, 1978, Folder 3413, AFSC; John Sullivan and Ali Shabazz, "Paragraph on Staff Work on MOVE for Lou Schneider's Report," April 5, 1978, Folder 3413, AFSC.
43. *City of Philadelphia v. Donald Glassey*, 477 Pa. 456 (S.C. PA March 15, 1978).
44. Carol Wallace, "Mediator: MOVE Planned Violent Conflict," *Philadelphia Daily News*, August 9, 1978.
45. Christopher Phillip to The Honorable Judge Fred DiBona, April 5, 1978, PAHRC.
46. Cynthia Adcock, "MOVE-Blockade-Powelton," *The Philadelphia Phoenix*, April 1978.
47. Paul Washington, "Draft," June 9, 1978, Box 26, Folder 1, Washington Papers; Friendly Presence, "Friendly Presence Vigil," June 27, 1978, Box 91a, Philadelphia Yearly Meeting of the Religious Society of Friends, Friends Peace Committee, Friendly Presence Papers, Friends Historical Library, Swarthmore College, Swarthmore, PA.
48. Internal Memorandum, Cardinal's Commission for Human Rights, April 26, 1978, PAHRC.
49. Paul Washington, "Draft," June 9, 1978, Box 26, Folder 1, Washington Papers.
50. Rt. Rev. Lyman C. Ogilby to the Clergy of the Episcopal Diocese of Pennsylvania, April 19, 1978, Box 26, Folder 1, Washington Papers; Transcript of Code-A-Phone Message by Bishop Ogilby, April 14, 1978, Box 26, Folder 1, Washington Papers.
51. A. L. Ellerkamp to Right Reverend Msgr. Charles V. Devlin, May 22, 1978, PAHRC; Mrs. C. Callahan to Rt. Rev. Msgr. Devlin, April 28, 1978, PAHRC; Diana Sulpizio to Devlin, April 28, 1978, PAHRC.
52. Steve Hanrum to Msgr. Charles Devlin, May 6, 1978, PAHRC.

53. Statement of City Managing Director Hillel S. Levinson, March 1, 1978, PAHRC; Devlin to District Attorney Ed Rendell, March 29, 1978, PAHRC.
54. Memorandum by John Hughes, May 18, 1978, Folder 3413, AFSC; Untitled Form Letter by Charles Devlin, PAHRC.
55. Interview with Gerald Africa, Box 8, Folder 1, PSIC.
56. Jill Porter, "Rizzo Sets Deadline: MOVE It or Lose It," *Philadelphia Daily News*, March 1, 1978.
57. "MOVE Won't: Phila. Radicals Defy Court Order," *Baltimore Sun*, August 2, 1978; Action against Premises 307-309 North 33rd Street, May 3, 1978, Box 7, PSIC.
58. Devlin, *I Am Ready*, 93–94.
59. Ibid., 94; Carol Wallace, "Mediator: MOVE Planned Violent Conflict," *Philadelphia Daily News*, August 9, 1978.
60. Robert Strauss, "MOVE Aftermath: Sorting the Pieces," *Philadelphia Daily News*, August 9, 1978.
61. Devlin, *I Am Ready*, 94–95; Robert Strauss, "MOVE Aftermath: Sorting the Pieces," *Philadelphia Daily News*, August 9, 1978; "The Toll," *Philadelphia Daily News*, August 9, 1978.
62. Devlin, *I Am Ready*, 94; Joseph O'Neill, Testimony of Joseph O'Neill before the Philadelphia Special Investigation (MOVE) Commission, Box 9, Folder 20, PSIC; Dan Dunne to Bill Brown and Bill Lytton, "Memorandum," June 20, 1985, Box 9, Folder 18, PSIC.
63. Homily for the Funeral of Officer James Ramp by Charles Devlin, PAHRC.
64. "Videotape of Gunfight with Police Is Shown at Trial of 9 Radicals," *New York Times*, December 28, 1979; "Last of Nine Defendants Ousted in Philadelphia Trial of Radicals," *New York Times*, January 20, 1980; "Lawyers for a Philadelphia Group Ask Dismissal of Murder Charges," *New York Times*, March 26, 1980.
65. Joyce Gemperlein, "9 in MOVE Get 30 Years for Killing," *Philadelphia Inquirer*, August 5, 1981; Federal Bureau of Investigation, Lab Report, September 8, 1978, Box 8, Folder 5, PSIC.
66. *Commonwealth of Pennsylvania v. Geist, et al.*, 5 Phila. 210. Linn Washington, "MOVE: A Double Standard of Justice?" *Yale Journal of Law and Liberation* 1, no. 1 (1989): 72.

5
Policing Religion

In May 1973—back before the death of Officer James Ramp, before the death of Life Africa, before the court injunction against MOVE protest activity and *Commonwealth v. Africa*—MOVE amounted to little more than an unlicensed car washing operation. John Africa had returned from the Democratic National Convention just a few months earlier. MOVE people were settling into their new home in Powelton Village where they went to work stripping the walls bare of paint, removing all the carpet, and disconnecting the appliances. No one had been arrested for anything, nor had they begun to confront the System with any regularity. MOVE had only appeared in public twice: once to attend a lecture by nutritionist Adele Davis and once to harangue Dick Gregory after his lecture at a nearby university.[1]

And yet, if MOVE people had looked up from their buckets and hoses, they might have noticed a nondescript sedan parked at the end of the block. Inside, two men watched through binoculars as MOVE people washed cars. They were members of the Philadelphia Police Department's Civil Disobedience Unit. The two men kept track of everyone who came in and out of the house. They photographed MOVE people and their clients, recorded license plate numbers, pulled criminal records, and speculated on who was a "member," a "sympathizer," or "unaffiliated." The detectives of the Civil Disobedience Unit were trying to figure out what kind of group this was.[2]

Eleven months later, the Civil Disobedience Unit issued its first internal report on MOVE. After observing MOVE for nearly a year, the detectives determined that there were probably around two dozen "MOVE members" and dozens more sympathizers. They speculated that MOVE may, at one time, have been called the American Christian Movement for Life. The authors of the intelligence report struggled to classify MOVE. They noted that "a majority of MOVE's members are Black, although there are some white members." The Civil Affairs detectives cross-checked the names of MOVE members with the voluminous files they kept on religious and political groups in the city and discovered that "one white member," had "been through a Buddhist group and on a Jesus Freak trip" prior to joining

MOVE. Two MOVE people, the report alleged, had formerly belonged to the American Nazi Party, and a few once belonged to the Black Panthers. The detectives suggest that MOVE seemed not unlike a philosophical movement, but noted that MOVE people rejected that label because "philosophers are always searching," while MOVE people rested comfortably in the truth of John Africa. The report observed that MOVE people revered teachings recorded in "The Book," the manuscript that would later be called *The Guidelines of John Africa*, and noted that followers of John Africa from around the city gathered at 309 North 33rd Street on Monday and Wednesday nights to learn those teachings. Yet, the Civil Disobedience Squad did not conclude that MOVE was a religion. Instead, the authors of the classified report determined that MOVE "can only be identified as reactionary and potentially fascist."[3]

The Civil Disobedience Unit's 1974 intelligence report on MOVE—the culmination of a yearlong investigation—was just the beginning of a sustained campaign of intelligence gathering at the local, state, and federal level that is still ongoing.[4] Throughout the group's history, MOVE was subjected to constant surveillance, infiltration, and counterintelligence operations—all of which began almost from the very beginning of the group. Both local and federal police agencies planted informants in MOVE, tapped their telephone lines, intercepted their mail, conducted subterfuge operations, and embedded listening devices inside the MOVE house. In 1981, these investigations culminated in federal weapons charges against John Africa and most of his followers. These police investigations shaped MOVE's history and transformed its theology. Perhaps most importantly, the mere existence of sustained police investigations created a specter of criminality around MOVE that confirmed, in the minds of many inside and outside of law enforcement, that MOVE was not a religion.

MOVE's relationship with law enforcement was not unusual within the history of Black religion in the twentieth century. Law enforcement agencies have, at times throughout American history, exercised the power to define religion—to demarcate what is "true religion" from false, to conclude when someone's beliefs and practice are authentically religious and when they are mistaken, and to decide which groups should flourish and which should be suppressed. As the contributors to *The FBI and Religion* have shown, the Federal Bureau of Investigation was invented to "establish racial, ethnic, economic, and social order"—a task that frequently pitted them against mostly Black religious groups deemed threatening to this order.[5]

Though the FBI has been remarkably ecumenical in the religions they policed, surveilled, and subverted, American law enforcement, generally, has reserved special scrutiny for Black religions. Perhaps the clearest example of police classification of religious groups is African American Islam. The FBI concluded that the Moorish Science Temple was made up of African Americans who were "fanatic[s] on the subject of equality for all races" and that "reliable Negroes" would condemn the group as "crazy." As Sylvester A. Johnson has pointed out, the FBI dismissed the Moorish Science Temple's claim to be a religion, deciding instead that "the group was the result of mental imbalance and delusion." We would know very little about the formative years of the Nation of Islam if not for the assiduous note taking of undercover FBI agents posing as converts but actually gathering intelligence against the group. FBI agents categorized forms of African American Islam as "hate groups," "political extremists," an "anti-American and violent cult"—anything other than as a religion. MOVE is a part of this history. Beginning with the 1974 intelligence report, the Philadelphia Police Department and, later, various federal law enforcement agencies policed the boundaries of "religion" as they policed MOVE.[6]

In the early 1970s, around the time the Civil Disobedience Squad began its investigation into MOVE, the policing of religious groups was undergoing a transformation. For decades, the FBI ran a series of covert counterintelligence operations called COINTELPRO which targeted religious groups, political organizations, and social movements that, in FBI director J. Edgar Hoover's opinion, challenged the social order of American society. Though it began in the 1950s as a way of combating communism in American society, the program eventually targeted the civil rights movement, the anti–Vietnam War protests, celebrities, and elected officials. Hoover instructed his agents to "expose, disrupt, misdirect, discredit, neutralize or otherwise eliminate" groups he considered undesirable. His agents responded, in some cases, with false prosecutions, sabotage, and assassinations. COINTELPRO became public in 1971 only after a group of New Left activists broke into an FBI field office in suburban Philadelphia, stole troves of documents, and turned them over to the press. The resulting news reports detailing the FBI's sometimes-illegal operations attracted the attention of Congress, eventually leading to more oversight of the Bureau.[7]

Although COINTELPRO formally came to an end in April 1971, federal law enforcement's interest in policing Black religion did not. Increasing congressional oversight did little to end domestic surveillance.

COINTELPRO-style operations continued at the FBI (and continue to this day). If anything, increasing congressional oversight forced the FBI to decentralize its operations. Increasingly, the work of surveilling, infiltrating, and sabotaging Black religion was taken up by local police departments, often in the form of specialized red squads. Red squads, as the name suggests, were units within large urban police departments that emerged in the mid-twentieth century originally to combat communism, organized labor, and other political dissidents. Often, these specialized units were situated outside of department bureaucracies, answering only to police chiefs (if anyone). This relative independence allowed many red squads to collaborate with federal law enforcement. The FBI under Hoover, for example, worked quite closely with red squads across the country, a relationship that long predated COINTELPRO. It was Chicago's red squad, the Subversive Activities Unit, which, in coordination with the FBI, assassinated Black Panther Party leader Fred Hampton in 1969. In short, the religious surveillance and policing operations traditionally operated by the FBI fell to specialized units within local police departments that, not coincidentally, collaborated closely with the Bureau.[8]

Philadelphia's red squad was named the Civil Affairs Unit (CAU). Originally named the Civil Disobedience Squad, the CAU was founded in 1964 to surveil political dissidents and labor movements, monitor protests, and build files on thousands of religious or political organizations in the area. From its creation to his retirement in 1983, the CAU was headed by George Fencl, a former Marine who joined the Philadelphia Police Department in 1950. Fencl quickly worked his way into the good graces of department leadership. The police commissioner liked Fencl so much, in fact, that he made him his driver and personal assistant. He was everything Commissioner Thomas Gibbons wanted in a cop. Fencl was a towering man—intimidating enough to prevent most conflicts from escalating. But it was Fencl's ruddy face and quick smile, along with his intelligence and unusually agreeable personality, that made him such a successful detective. In 1956, Fencl was promoted again, this time to sergeant in charge of investigating racketeering in the city. In that role, Fencl learned the value of intelligence gathering and built upon a reputation as an officer with unimpeachable ethics. When the police department decided to create a new unit in charge of monitoring the growing civil unrest of the 1960s generation, they chose Fencl to lead it.[9]

There were rumors throughout City Hall that George Fencl was on the shortlist to become the next police commissioner. Instead, that job went to

Frank Rizzo, a brash, tough-nosed street cop who worked his way up from beat cop to commissioner in 1967. The two men, though polar opposites in temperament, built a formidable and mutually beneficial alliance. Rizzo found Fencl's unit invaluable. Rizzo used the intelligence Fencl's men had gathered to threaten his political enemies—a tactic that his role model, J. Edgar Hoover, had pioneered at the FBI. Rizzo used his alliance with Fencl to muscle his way to the mayorship in 1972. Fencl benefited from the relationship as well. The CAU expanded dramatically under Rizzo's administration. Fencl inherited a small operation—ten men, two cars, and a typewriter—but by 1979 the CAU had grown to one hundred officers. In 1973, Rizzo broke state civil-service regulations to promote Fencl to inspector, bypassing two ranks along the way. Fencl's new position, the requirements of which were tailored so that no one other than Fencl would qualify, paid him more than ten times what he had made as a highway patrolman.[10]

Together, Rizzo and Fencl kept a tight lid on dissent in Philadelphia. Rizzo's popularity, both as commissioner and later as mayor, was due to his bravado, his public displays of police violence, and his unashamed defense of white, middle-class values. To his critics, Rizzo was a jackbooted thug who ran his city like a mafia boss. This portrayal, though simplistic, was not wholly inaccurate. Rizzo cultivated an almost cartoonish personality. He preferred to be photographed in jackboots, and he rarely missed an opportunity to score political points with his white, blue-collar base who felt that Blacks, Vietnam War activists, and other dissenters needed a swift kick to the curb. It was not unusual for Rizzo to brag in front of reporters about the latest dissident he had personally beaten up. In one of his first acts as commissioner, in November 1967, Rizzo unleashed his men against a crowd of 3,500 Black schoolchildren who were advocating, peacefully, for a Black studies program at their high school. Once the police had surrounded the demonstrators, Rizzo instructed his men to "get their black asses!" Led by Rizzo, officers from the Philadelphia Police Department clubbed schoolchildren in what critics called a "police riot."[11]

To his supporters—who far outnumbered his critics, especially among white Philadelphians—Rizzo was just the man Philadelphia needed. As historian Timothy Lombardo argues, Rizzo's popularity through much of the 1970s and 1980s reflected deeper systemic political change. The white working class, increasingly alienated by globalizing economics and the rise of rights-based liberalism, saw in Rizzo an exemplar of their frustrations and a last gasp of their declining political and economic power. Many

Philadelphians saw Rizzo—a high-school dropout, son of an immigrant turned mayor of the fourth largest city in America—as an up-by-the-bootstraps embodiment of common-sense conservatism; an amalgam of Rocky Balboa and George Wallace. Rizzo's supporters, watching New York collapse into crime and disarray, were happy to trade some extra-legal police violence for safe streets.[12]

George Fencl, on the other hand, avoided the conspicuous pugnaciousness of his boss, opting instead to develop a rapport with the groups he was surveilling. He preferred to run his CAU with—in the words of the *Philadelphia Inquirer*—a "velvet glove stretched tightly over his iron fist." Fencl was suave, calm, and congenial, and his detectives preferred to operate in the shadows. Fencl hand-selected his own agents and trained them to mirror his own zen-like demeanor during tense confrontations. The CAU leader struck many of Philadelphia's radicals as someone so nice, you might not notice as he and his men trampled your civil liberties. But Fencl's niceness belied the fact that he and his detectives conducted extensive surveillance and infiltration operations against political and religious groups, often at the fringes of the law and sometimes beyond it. Though the files the CAU gathered were not subject to public inspection (local records were, at the time, exempt from sunshine laws) the existence of a large system of surveillance was not a secret. Rizzo and Fencl once appeared on a nationally televised NBC special and bragged about the far reaches of their intelligence operations. Rizzo boasted that his CAU had files on over six hundred organizations, including violent extremist groups such as the Ku Klux Klan and the Weathermen, and peacenik religious groups like the Quakers. And the CAU's intelligence operations did not end with record-keeping. Throughout the 1970s, the FBI and the Philadelphia Police Department conducted COINTELPRO-style counterintelligence, subversion, and surveillance operations against a wide variety of social groups.[13]

Fencl and Rizzo developed a highly effective scheme for ridding the city of undesirable ideologies. Their scheme often went like this: an informer would alert the CAU to the presence of explosives, a firearms cache, or inflammatory literature, prompting a raid where police would discover the alleged materials. Sensational media reports would follow, wherein Rizzo explained that the group was just one part of a much larger and more sinister plot, which his CAU had thwarted in the nick of time. These episodes were not uncommon in Rizzo's Philadelphia. Convictions, however, were far less frequent. Often prosecutions of these "bomb plots" could not go forward for lack of evidence, sometimes because the defendants pleaded to lesser charges or because the recovered explosives had been planted by the police.[14]

Rizzo and Fencl first put their bomb plot into action in August 1966 against the Student Nonviolent Coordinating Committee (SNCC). Hundreds of police officers raided four houses in North Philadelphia, where they recovered two sticks of dynamite. Nine SNCC leaders were arrested, and Rizzo informed the public that the "SNCC dynamite plot" was emblematic of a wider plot on behalf of violent civil rights organizations. Though the charges were eventually dropped, Rizzo had effectively put an end to the SNCC in the city. Rizzo and Fencl used the bomb plot tactic several more times during their tenure, often working hand in hand with the FBI's COINTELPRO program. In 1967, the CAU raided a house containing pamphlets and writings that purportedly proved the existence of a violent "Black Guard" within the Philadelphia Revolutionary Action Movement (RAM). Six RAM members were arrested on charges of disorderly conduct, breaching the peace, and conspiracy to incite a riot—charges that stemmed solely from the confiscated literature and which were soon dropped. Over the next year, Rizzo and Fencl continued to arrest RAM members because of their supposed relationship with the Black Guard, which may not have existed. Under growing pressure, RAM folded.[15]

The FBI worked closely with Philadelphia's CAU. The Bureau paid the CAU's informers, and the CAU shared the intelligence they gathered with the FBI. The CAU often recruited informers from within communities. Their favorite target was young, white men who had been caught committing serious crimes—crimes that could be forgiven if the young man agreed to become an informant for the CAU and the FBI—men like Don Africa.

Don Africa, the man whom MOVE people knew as Donald Grossman, was actually named Donald Glassey. Glassey was born in 1946. He graduated from Michigan State University in 1968 and moved to Philadelphia to enroll in the graduate program in sociology at the University of Pennsylvania. In January 1971, Glassey took a trip to Jamaica. There were two reasons for Glassey's trip. He had just finished his degree, and like many recent graduates, he needed a Caribbean getaway. But the more pressing matter for Glassey was that the United States was in the midst of a marijuana shortage due to Nixon's opening salvos in the War on Drugs. While in Jamaica, Glassey bought several pounds of marijuana and mailed it to his apartment back in Philadelphia. But when Glassey went to pick up his package, he found federal law enforcement agents waiting to arrest him. Glassey's marijuana had a street value of five thousand dollars. According to the sentencing guidelines at the time, Glassey faced up to fifteen years in federal prison and a fine of up to $25,000. Glassey did not face trial on charges of drug smuggling. Instead, his case was dismissed.[16]

After his brush with the law, Glassey returned to his life in Philadelphia. He took a position as an adjunct professor of sociology at the Community College of Pennsylvania and ingratiated himself with a number of West Philadelphia's New Left organizations, including the East Powelton Concerned Residents and the housing cooperative that owned John Africa's apartment—all groups that were targeted for surveillance by the CAU. When Donald Glassey met Vincent Leaphart in the Spring of 1972, he was calling himself Donald Grossman.[17]

Because the Philadelphia Police Department is reluctant to release its intelligence files on MOVE, it is difficult to reconstruct exactly what forms the CAU's operation against MOVE took. There are, however, some things we can say things for certain. First, the CAU began conducting surveillance on MOVE on May 13, 1973—the same day Don Africa purchased 309 North 33rd Street on behalf of MOVE. Over time, the CAU expanded their surveillance operation to include wiretapping, infiltration, and subterfuge. Investigation records show that the CAU had an informant inside MOVE as early as May 16, 1974—around the same time MOVE was confronting the Philadelphia and New York school boards. On May 20, 1974, Don Africa was arrested after he violated the court injunction against MOVE people entering the meetings of the Philadelphia School Board. As police officers roughly arrested him outside the meeting room, Glassey called on CAU detectives to protect him. Donald Glassey admitted, under oath, that he began working as an informant for federal law enforcement agencies in June 1977. The evidence suggests, but does not prove, that Glassey may have been the unnamed informant who had been providing the CAU with intelligence on MOVE since 1974.[18]

In March 1974, the FBI opened an investigation into MOVE. The investigation was run out of the FBI's Philadelphia field office and was organized under the Bureau's "extremist matters" files. The FBI maintained two informants for their MOVE investigation. The second source, labeled Source Two, seems to have had little direct access to MOVE's decision-making, and believed that MOVE posed little threat to anyone. The other source, Source One, had a far more dire assessment of the group. Source One believed that MOVE was a "quasi-militant group of rather articulate individuals" that "advocates nothing less than the total overthrow of the existing government." Source One believed that MOVE's avowed commitment to nonviolence was merely "noise" designed to gain attention and "adherence to their cause." On this characterization, the FBI began investigating whether anyone associated with MOVE was plotting a "rebellion or insurrection," or a "seditious conspiracy," against the United States.[19]

The FBI informants proved invaluable. On more than one occasion, an undercover FBI agent wore a wire during a public MOVE meeting, providing the Bureau with a transcript of MOVE's internal discussions. An undercover source smuggled out a copy of *The Guidelines of John Africa*, which the FBI photocopied and studied. FBI agents surveilled MOVE at public demonstrations. By March 1975, the Philadelphia Field Office of the FBI had expanded its MOVE investigation to individual investigations of five MOVE people: Merle, Consuella, Conrad, Louise, and Sue Africa.[20]

FBI Headquarters was suspicious of the Philadelphia Field Office's investigation from the onset. FBI Field Offices may begin an investigation without seeking approval from Headquarters, but they must submit their findings for approval within ninety days. The Philadelphia Field Office failed to provide Headquarters with a report outlining the legal basis for their investigation into MOVE until March 1975—one year after the investigation began. Still, FBI Headquarters authorized, if reluctantly, the Field Office's continued investigation. By the spring of 1975, however, FBI Headquarters had grown impatient with their Philadelphia Field Office. The Special Agent in Charge of the MOVE investigation, Carl Turner, refused to provide the Bureau with their MOVE files, and provided no legal basis for continuing the investigation outside of the warnings issued by Source One. On April 7, 1975, FBI Director Clarence Kelly wrote Special Agent Turner asking why he placed such faith in this source, given the unthreatening writings Source One had provided the Bureau. Source One had provided the FBI with a copy of *The Guidelines of John Africa*, but in the estimation of Director Kelly, "the writings and statements contain nothing which would lead one to believe there is a plot to destroy the government." Without further evidence of MOVE's dangerous nature, the FBI Director ordered the Field Office to suspend its MOVE investigation.[21]

Facing pressure from FBI Headquarters to end their investigation, the Philadelphia Field Office found further evidence of MOVE's potential to overthrow the United States government. One of the FBI's undercover sources (the FBI file is heavily redacted, so it is impossible to determine whether this is Source One or Source Two) told Special Agent Turner in April 1975 that MOVE had formed a Black Guard—a hard core of violent MOVE men including Beowolf, Delbert, and Hampton Africa—that "will act in reprisal for misdeeds done to MOVE members." The Black Guard was secretive—according to the undercover source, even the MOVE women did not know about its existence. And it was violent. The source told Special Agent Turner that "Black Guard persons are all trained in Kung Fu or some other variety of the martial arts." The source told Turner that the Black Guard was interested in appearing larger and more threatening that it really was. According to the undercover source, Beowulf Africa traveled by himself to Boston to telephone the Philadelphia Sheriff's Office and issue threats. Assuming the phone call would be traced, it would appear to the Sheriff's Office that the Black Guard was more extensive than MOVE itself. Special Agent Turner followed up with the Philadelphia Sheriff's Office weeks later. They did not receive a phone call from anyone claiming to represent the Black Guard. The same day that a source informed the FBI about the existence of a Black Guard, a separate source, embedded within the Black Panther Party, told Turner that "MOVE, due to its religiously held beliefs, is an extremely dangerous organization which is capable of causing a great deal of harm in the near future." These two investigation breakthroughs—the purported existence of a Black Guard and a second source stating MOVE's potential to commit acts of violence—provided the Philadelphia Field Office with the evidence Headquarter demanded: that MOVE was indeed capable of committing acts of violence (importantly, across state lines) worthy of a federal investigation.[22]

On June 3, 1975, the Philadelphia Field Office finally submitted its entire MOVE Report to Headquarters and requested approval for continuing its investigation. The report identified both undercover sources, and reiterated the dire warnings issued by Source One. The report mentions the threat of the Black Guard. Inspector George Fencl of Philadelphia Police Department's CAU features prominently in the report. Fencl told the FBI that "in and of themselves, MOVE members are not violent and would not attempt to cause problems." The Philadelphia Field Office conceded in the report that MOVE "will not attempt to overthrow the government," but insisted that the investigation continue because MOVE is "expected to continue their efforts to embarrass public officials" at the following year's bicentennial celebration in Philadelphia. FBI Headquarters was unimpressed. After a "careful review" of the Field Office's MOVE report, FBI Director Kelly determined that "there is no basis for a continued investigation of MOVE or of its members because of their association with MOVE." The FBI investigation into MOVE, for a time, was over.[23]

The police surveillance operation against MOVE, at both the federal and local level, renewed after the Guns on the Porch standoff of May 1977. In the aftermath of Life Africa's death in 1976, John Africa created two more MOVE branches in Rochester, New York, and Richmond, Virginia. His reasons were different for each new branch. The MOVE branch in Rochester would provide a safe haven for MOVE people who were wanted by the police, including John Africa. As MOVE legend has it, in June 1977, John Africa rode a bicycle over three hundred miles from Philadelphia to Rochester. There, he reunited with Mo Africa and Jerry Africa, who had arrived a few days earlier and had found a house that could be had for cheap on Flint Street, in a run-down part of the city. The three men paid $1,000 cash for the house, which had fallen into disrepair and was owned by the Department of Housing and Urban Development, and resumed their spartan MOVE lifestyle. As MOVE people understood it, Rochester provided a safe house, a sanctuary for the preservation of MOVE's leader as the System tightened its grip on the MOVE house in Philadelphia. For MOVE people who gained criminal charges as a result of the confrontations in Philadelphia, Rochester provided a hideout.[24]

The second new MOVE branch was far different from the secretive outpost in Rochester. On April 22, 1977, eight MOVE adults and ten MOVE children moved into a rented house in Richmond, Virginia. They called their new branch the Seed of Wisdom, a reference from *The Guidelines*.[25] Its purpose was twofold. First, it would provide a place for the MOVE children to live the Teachings of John Africa free from the tumult of MOVE headquarters. There, under the care of some of the MOVE women, the children could play, learn, and grow far away from the confrontations and the starvation blockades. Second, MOVE hoped that Seed of Wisdom would function as an evangelistic outpost from the group, a place open to the public where the Teachings of John Africa could be taught and practiced. Seed of Wisdom was a public place, a religious community with an outward face. It was MOVE at its most missional.[26]

For the first few days, Seed of Wisdom seemed to function well. MOVE people estimated that between fifty and a hundred people stopped by to learn about the Teachings of John Africa, to appease their curiosity, or just to gawk. When visitors stopped by, the MOVE people there gave them a tour of the house. There wasn't much to see. The whole home, like MOVE headquarters, was lit by candles. There were a few blankets strewn on the floors upstairs. The kitchen was stocked with a few pieces of cooking equipment and boxes of produce. There were a couple of telephones that they used to communicate with Philadelphia and Rochester. Five days after they moved in, they invited a reporter from the *Baltimore Afro-American* to pay them a visit. The reporter seemed charmed by the MOVE people he met there, but aghast at their living conditions. He was taken aback by the overwhelming smell of garlic as he approached the house. But MOVE people had a joke about the garlic that they used to disarm their guests: the garlic might stink, but at least they don't have to worry about vampires. As the reporter toured the house, however, he became shocked at the sight of naked children who, he learned, did not go to school. He was appalled at their diet of raw potatoes, garlic, onions, and raw eggs. Sharon Africa explained to the reporter—as she did with all of their guests—that the diet made the children "healthy" and "closer to the earth."[27]

The open-door policy at Seed of Wisdom soon backfired. The landlord threatened to evict them just days after moving in. He rented the house to Beowolf Africa with the understanding that the property would function as a single-family dwelling, but eight adults and ten children were living in the house, and dozens of curious people tramped in and out every day. The landlord told MOVE that he was "perfectly willing to renegotiate the rent to reflect the increased wear and tear on the house." To the landlord, the rise in rent only seemed fair now that the house was serving as communal housing, church, and community center. To MOVE, it seemed like extortion.[28]

The threat of eviction was just the beginning of MOVE's trouble in Richmond. On April 27, only five days after it had been established, members of the Richmond Police Department inspected Seed of Wisdom. They told the MOVE people there that they had received reports that the children "were victims of neglect" and had been "exposed to unusual behavioral patterns." They had spoken to neighbors who said the children did not wear clothes and that they had been digging for food in the ground. The MOVE people in Richmond did their best to explain that the children were healthy. The children dug food out of the ground because the adults had buried it there—it was a lesson for the children that, MOVE people explained, connected the children to their food and to Mama from whence it came. MOVE people explained to the police that the children did not wear clothes because they did not need to. They were accustomed to the elements, MOVE people argued, and were much tougher than the adults, who had to wear clothes because they were not fortunate enough to have been brought up without them. They showed the police, as they had shown the reporter, how strong the children were, how their teeth were unusually white, how their eyes were clear and bright, and how their skin was clear of blemishes. This, MOVE argued, was a testament to the Teachings of John Africa. These children were not victims of MOVE's belief. They were the beneficiaries.[29]

The police left Seed of Wisdom and, that afternoon, obtained a court order to remove the children to foster care. A large police force gathered outside Seed of Wisdom the next day to carry out the order, only to find the house barricaded. Seed of Wisdom would not allow their lawyer, who worked for the ACLU, to enter the home. The MOVE people at Seed of Wisdom understood the court order as a direct assault on their religion. Sharon Africa told reporters from the window that Seed of Wisdom was being judged "on a standard of society" that their religion was set up to oppose. She said that the children's nakedness was not neglect, but the exercise of their religion. "They don't ask a Jew to take off his skull cap or whatever it is," Sharon reasoned. "Our children wear a certain kind of outfit as dictated by their religion." After two and a half hours, the Richmond Police Department gave up and went home. The court revoked its order and dropped the neglect charges.[30]

The showdown in Richmond caught the attention of observers in Philadelphia, including George Fencl. A Philadelphia newspaper reported that a new cult espousing a "back-to-nature" philosophy had popped up in Richmond. The article noted that all of the members took the surname "Life" and ate raw food. The writer of the article learned that the group originated in Pennsylvania around 1971. Still, the article did not connect Seed of Wisdom with Philadelphia's own "back-to-nature cult." Officer Fencl was more savvy. On August 5, 1978, as the starvation blockade of MOVE's Powelton house was in its final week, Fencl, Cresci, and the Richmond Police Department, thwarted by barricades on the front door, entered the back door of the Seed of Wisdom house and arrested Gail Africa, Rhonda Africa, and Sharon Penn Africa. Their legal justification for the arrests was the bench warrant issued by Judge Fred DiBona on August 2, 1978, which gave the Philadelphia Police Department ten days to arrest all MOVE people involved in the Guns on the Porch demonstration. Of the nine adults arrested in Richmond, only Gail and Rhonda were named on that warrant. They were held in Richmond on $25,000 and $5,000 bonds, respectively. Fencl offered to release Sharon Penn Africa if she renounced John Africa. She took the deal and eventually left MOVE.[31]

In January 1980, Richmond police officers, led by Philadelphia Civil Affairs detectives, again raided Seed of Wisdom. Sharon and Valerie Africa, the only two adults left in the house, were arrested on child neglect charges. The police took custody of the fourteen MOVE children in the house and turned them over to foster care. While in foster care the children were fed cooked food and, MOVE people alleged, "subjected . . . to perversion by the other kids." They were allowed—MOVE people say forced—to watch television. MOVE people said that the MOVE children's foster parents told them that their MOVE family did not really love them, and that they tried to comb the MOVE children's natural hair, pulling it out by the roots when it resisted. MOVE people described the children's experience in foster care in nightmarish terms that are almost certainly exaggerated. But to MOVE people, the MOVE children being cared for by even the most caring foster parents amounted to the profaning of sacred beings. What made the MOVE children special within MOVE's theology was that, by living under the Law of Mama from birth, they did not inherit the distortions of the System. But that purity that MOVE had tried so hard to maintain had been destroyed. The children were no longer exempt from the System. They had been profaned.[32]

Though Seed of Wisdom discontinued operation, life for the MOVE people in Rochester continued as normal. The Rochester MOVE congregation, which had grown to nine adults and several children, was now approaching its fourth year. Over those four years, more MOVE people had arrived from Philadelphia, including Sue Africa and her son Tomaso, who made their way north after Sue was released from prison. Carlos Africa, released from prison around the same time as Sue, also moved to Rochester. MOVE gained a new convert, Teresa Africa, from Rochester.[33]

Rochester was, for a time, the religious cooperative community that MOVE people had imagined. In the late 1970s, MOVE created a document they titled "Proposal for Funding of the MOVE Organization." It was, on its face, a formal funding proposal, the kind of document that a nonprofit might use to secure a grant. But the document was also a statement of what MOVE people wanted MOVE to become; a glimpse into what the group might have looked like if they hadn't fallen on the wrong side of the law. The document imagines a near future when MOVE might continue the biweekly public meetings where the Teachings of John Africa could be shared with all who are interested. MOVE would offer classes on MOVE's natural diet, natural childbirth, community organization, physical fitness, and on "self-awareness." Through the power of the Teachings of John Africa, West Philadelphia would be rid of gangs, and the community around MOVE would overcome their addictions. Slowly, the Teachings of John Africa would transform the community and, perhaps over time, the world. The document anticipates MOVE's institutional growth as well. They would buy a garage in the city and operate their car wash out of it. MOVE would purchase and operate a small printing press so that *The Guidelines of John Africa* could find a wider audience. Most importantly, the proposal imagines a large, rural agricultural commune where MOVE people could live the Teachings of John Africa, work the land, and retreat from the hostile world. They would, however, maintain several public spaces in the city where they would hold concerts and community events, recruit new converts, and continue to offer the Teachings of John Africa.[34]

The kind of religion MOVE hoped for, the authors of the funding proposal argued, was thwarted by police intervention. For much of its early history, MOVE had been scraping by on donations, money from the car wash, moving and handyman services, and welfare checks. Much of that funding, however, had been cut off. Judges threatened to revoke bail if MOVE resumed operation of their unlicensed car wash. The police towed away the trucks and vans MOVE had used for their moving and handyman services. To make matters worse, the welfare office had stopped sending checks after public outcry. At the time the funding proposal was written, MOVE was in disarray. John Africa's congregation was split between three cities, hundreds of miles apart. Many of John Africa's most devoted converts were in prison, and the rest were fugitives from the law. The funding proposal ignores all this. Instead, its authors offered a glimpse at what MOVE might have been had the religion been allowed to develop without police surveillance and infiltration.[35]

Away from the watchful eye of the CAU and federal police, the Rochester MOVE houses functioned very much like the kind of religious community the funding proposal imagines. What began as one decrepit house on Flint Street had, by 1981, grown to seven properties and a small business. Most of the houses were previously owned by the city and abandoned. MOVE people bought them cheaply, in cash, with plans to slowly remodel them. They bought a small filling station and repaired cars there. MOVE people earned a reputation for doing good work at very reasonable prices. Mo and Conrad Africa worked full-time changing tires at a nearby Sears Roebuck. Jerry Africa drove to a produce store every Saturday, piling crates of fresh fruit and vegetables in the back of a pickup truck. John Africa spent most of his days renovating the new MOVE houses from a workshop he had built in the basement of the Flint Street house. With the exception of John and Alberta, the MOVE people in Rochester trimmed their hair to be more in line with the style. They were, for the first time in their history, fitting in.[36]

Though MOVE people made friends in Rochester, they made enemies in equal measure. Many of MOVE's neighbors appreciated the group's presence. Neighbors on Flint Street knew John Africa, whom they knew as Bill, as a gentle soul who cared for the neighborhood animals and spent most of his time fixing up the house. A woman who lived across the street said that John Africa visited her almost daily and took her dog for a walk around the block. Another neighbor said that John Africa would frequently give his children fresh fruit. He told a reporter that he loved John Africa for the kindness he showed his children. Other neighbors found MOVE people unsettling. One neighbor felt it strange that they addressed John Africa as "master" and "lord." A minister who lived across the street from the MOVE house on Flint Street had a particularly difficult time getting along with his unusual neighbors. John Africa frequently trespassed in his neighbor's backyard to feed the neighbor's dog raw meat, which John Africa believed was a more natural diet. The neighbor asked John Africa to stop feeding the meat to his dog, because the dog refused to eat kibble now that he had acquired a taste for meat. John Africa refused. Eventually, the disagreement boiled over. The neighbor caught Dennis Africa feeding the dog. He held Dennis at gunpoint until the police arrived and arrested both Dennis and John Africa on charges of disorderly conduct. John and Dennis gave the police false names to avoid detection.[37]

As MOVE's Rochester contingent successfully avoided surveillance, back in Philadelphia, a coalition of MOVE supporters, civil libertarians, religious leaders, and activists took aim at the city's pervasive surveillance operations. In the spring of 1977, the *Philadelphia Inquirer* published a series of articles exposing the shocking and endemic violence of the Philadelphia Police Department's homicide unit. The series, which won the paper a Pulitzer Prize, revealed that the Police Department routinely extracted confessions under torture, trampled constitutional rights, and exacted personal vendettas against the public, while an unconcerned district attorney's office looked the other way. The allegations were brutal: detectives stabbed men in the testicles with knives. They handcuffed suspects to a chair that was bolted to the floor, placed a phone book on the suspect's head and used a hammer to strike the phone book, causing brain and spinal injuries. Among many of the examples cited in the series was that of Larry Howard, a MOVE supporter. According to the *Inquirer*, Howard was beaten with a lead pipe, punched with brass knuckles, and kicked in the groin while being interrogated for over twenty hours. A judge ruled that the evidence gathered during Howard's interrogation was gathered illegally. Though the homicide division maintained a very high rate of confessions—87 percent of all murder cases—many of those who confessed under torture were innocent. Only 20 percent of murder cases with signed confessions led to convictions.[38]

The *Inquirer* revelations came as no surprise to MOVE people or to their allies at the American Friends Service Committee (AFSC). The Quaker activist organization had for years investigated and reported on the CAU's surveillance operations and the Philadelphia Police Department's rampant abuse and corruption. Capitalizing on the public outcry following the *Inquirer* series, the AFSC consolidated forty-five community and religious organizations already working to combat police violence and illegal surveillance under the Philadelphia Police Abuse Project. Headed out of the AFSC offices in Center City, the Police Abuse Project compiled data on police surveillance and police violence throughout the city, citing the ongoing starvation blockade of MOVE as the prime example of the Police Department's ambivalence toward civil liberties. The AFSC's Police Abuse Project also investigated the connection between the police department's CAU and federal law enforcement. The AFSC determined that George Fencl's CAU was "in close touch with the FBI," and that the FBI often stored records on area groups at the CAU because local police files were not subject to public inspection. Some of the FBI files leaked from the Media, Pennsylvania, break-in were CAU files.[39]

In response to the *Inquirer* revelations and the AFSC's Police Abuse Project, the United States Commission on Civil Rights held a series of public hearings on police abuse in Philadelphia in February 1979. Most of the witnesses from community groups and religious organizations, including several affiliated with the AFSC's Police Abuse Project, testified to widespread patterns of police violence in the city. Much of that testimony revolved around the Police Department's contentious relationship with MOVE. Two MOVE supporters, Jeanette Knighton and I. Abdul Jon, recounted five years of police violence against the group. Some of their testimony was corroborated by other witnesses. A member of the city council described the televised and photographed beating of Delbert Africa on May 20, 1978, as an "injudicious use of police restraint" and testified that the City Council appealed to the attorney general of the United States after that incident to report "a pattern" of police misconduct that "clearly infringed upon the civil rights of individuals, particularly minority individuals." Not everyone was bothered by police misconduct in the city. Representatives from the business community testified that they were very pleased with the Philadelphia Police Department's heavy-handedness. John Bunting, president of Philadelphia First Bank, argued that "you have to have a certain amount of brutality in exchange for safe streets"—a "trade-off" that the city's business community was happy to support. City officials denied that any pattern of misconduct existed. Under sworn testimony, Police Commissioner Joseph O'Neill testified, "Generally speaking, I don't think you'll find that [police brutality] in our department as an ongoing thing," and that instances of police misconduct were "miniscule." Mayor Rizzo testified that "a pattern of—police abuse absolutely does not exist in Philadelphia; it was media generated."[40]

In 1979, in response to the *Inquirer* revelations and the US Commission on Civil Rights hearings, the United States Justice Department filed suit against twenty city officials, accusing the Philadelphia Police Department of endemic corruption, violence, and lawlessness. The lawsuit was unprecedented. It was the first time the United States government appealed to federal courts to protect the constitutional rights of US citizens against their local government. It was also unusual for naming city leaders personally. Mayor Rizzo, Police Commissioner O'Neill, Prison Superintendent Edmund Lyons, and Chief Inspector Gregore Sambor (who would be named commissioner in 1984) were among the twenty city officials named. CAU head George Fencl was not. The lawsuit accused the Police Department of firebombing the home of a critic of police abuse, using unauthorized lethal force, conducting illegal arrests and surveillance, and shielding officers from prosecution. The depth of the allegations, the authors of the lawsuit wrote, "shocks the conscience." The Justice Department singled out Mayor Frank Rizzo, accusing him of having initiated many of the department's illegal tactics while he was police commissioner and abetting the corruption as mayor. Rizzo responded defiantly, calling the lawsuit "hogwash" and claiming that it was politically motivated. When asked about the threatened loss of four million dollars in federal funding in the absence of reforms, Mayor Rizzo said that he was "ready to tell them where to stick it." In October 1979, a federal judge dismissed the Justice Department's lawsuit against the city, arguing that the attorney general did not have standing to bring the suit.[41]

Their relationship with the FBI under increased scrutiny, the CAU began cooperating with another federal law enforcement agency, the Bureau of Alcohol, Tobacco, and Firearms (ATF) to build a case that, they hoped, would finish MOVE for good. Since June 1977—just two days, in fact, after John Africa left Philadelphia for Rochester—the CAU and the ATF had been building a case alleging that John Africa instructed MOVE people to stockpile explosives for use against the federal government. With the cooperation of their informant, Donald Glassey, federal prosecutors charged John Africa and ten other MOVE people with federal terrorism and weapons charges. The goal of these charges, in the words of one ATF agent, was to "get Leaphart." "If we didn't get him," the ATF agent warned, John Africa "would just go somewhere else and begin converting other people."[42]

It took four years, but the ATF eventually learned where they could find John Africa. Early in the morning of May 13, 1981, a team of sixty ATF agents and twenty Rochester Police officers met in an armory downtown to go over any final details for their planned raid on MOVE's Rochester community. The arrest was a masterpiece, the result of over six weeks of planning. Since the arrival of MOVE people in Rochester in late March, ATF agents had been surveilling them, gaining a sense of their daily habits. They determined that their best chance to arrest John Africa was to wait for him to arrive at the filling station. At 9:30 in the morning, ATF agents spotted John Africa, mulling about the gas station with several other MOVE people.[43]

Across the street from MOVE's gas station, a Rochester Police Department squad car pulled over a sedan in what appeared to be a routine traffic stop. Inside the car were four ATF agents. Meanwhile, a U-Haul truck pulled into MOVE's filling station and the driver, an undercover ATF agent, began asking for directions. As they talked, a second U-Haul truck pulled in. On cue, the rear doors of both trucks swung open and dozens of uniformed ATF agents and Rochester police officers stormed out, guns raised. The agents feigning a traffic stop ended their charade and raised weapons toward the MOVE people, too. At the same time, ATF agents raided the Flint Street house, arresting all inside. A third group of agents captured the remaining MOVE people as they jogged. MOVE people were stunned, and did not resist arrest. The raid could not have gone better for the ATF. Their main goal was to arrest John Africa. According to one agent, "if everybody but him was caught, it was a failure." The coordinated raids were a success: all nine MOVE people living in Rochester were now behind bars.[44]

Seven of the MOVE people arrested—Sue, Alberta, Conrad, Raymond, Carlos, Dennis, and Jerry Africa—were not named in the ATF indictment and were extradited to Philadelphia to face charges stemming from the Guns on the Porch standoff in 1977. On May 26, 1981, John Africa and Alphonso "Mo" Africa were arraigned at the Metropolitan Correction Facility in Manhattan. Both men faced four charges. First, the prosecution alleged that John Africa, Mo, Beawolf, Sam, Greg, Whit Africa, and Anthony Beaman, a MOVE supporter, entered into a conspiracy "to possess, to manufacture, and to not register certain firearms or destructive devices." John and Mo faced one charge for possessing bombs and another charge for possessing homemade explosives. The fourth charge was for firearms possession. Mo Africa was held on $100,000 bail. John Africa's bail was set at $750,000. Throughout the arraignment proceedings, John Africa remained silent, choosing to communicate with the court using nods and hand signals. Both men pled not guilty, and John Africa indicated that he would conduct their defense.[45]

United States v. Vincent Leaphart and Alphonso Robbins began on July 2, 1981. To the general public who followed the proceedings in the major dailies, the trial was a where-are-they-now curiosity; the epilogue to a story that had ended with the murder of Officer James Ramp in 1978. To MOVE, the trial was a religious conflict—the final showdown between the Truth of John Africa and the evil of System. As John Africa understood it, "MOVE people are being tried for our religion, our understanding of the law, the posture of true freedom, and for this we are threatened." MOVE people, to this day, refer to the trial as John Africa vs. The System.[46]

Judge Clifford Scott Green, who was Black and had been appointed to the United States District Court for the Eastern District of Pennsylvania by President Richard Nixon in 1971, presided over the trial. Over his thirty-six-year career as a district court judge (he resisted the Reagan administration's overtures to join the Third Circuit Court of Appeals), Green had built a stellar reputation for being exceedingly fair and thoroughly professional. That fairness was on display during *United States v. Leaphart*. Unlike previous MOVE trials, which often descended into chaos, *United States v. Leaphart* proceeded with congeniality and mutual respect. Media observers noted that "both the judge and Leaphart and Robbins bent over backwards to cooperate with each other."[47]

The prosecution's case revolved almost entirely around the testimony of Donald Glassey. According to Glassey, in 1976—after the death of Life Africa at the hands of police officers—John Africa abandoned his commitment to nonresistance and began stockpiling weapons in Glassey's apartment in anticipation of a final confrontation with the System. MOVE's shift away from nonviolence and the presence of illegal weapons in his apartment pushed

Glassey further away from MOVE. Out of fear, Glassey continued to cooperate with John Africa's preparations for the confrontation. In September 1976, John Africa hosted a meeting in his apartment where, Glassey alleged, he directed Glassey, MOVE supporters Gregory Howard and Sam Sanders, and MOVE member Phil Africa (father of deceased Life Africa) to fortify the MOVE house in Powelton, to stockpile ammunition, and to acquire gunpowder to make bombs.[48]

Glassey testified that, while preparations for the confrontation were underway, he, Anthony Beaman, and Gregory Howard hid bomb timing devices (non-explosive wiring mechanisms) and threatening letters in hotel rooms in Washington, DC, Boston, New York City, Chicago, and Philadelphia at the direction of John Africa. Glassey said that after they hid them, they called the hotels to tell the staff where to find the devices. The goal was to make it appear to law enforcement that there was a nationwide contingent, the Black Guard, waiting to rise up against the US government should MOVE be attacked. John Africa hoped that the illusion of a Black Guard might provide MOVE with leverage in negotiations with the city of Philadelphia.[49]

Glassey claimed that preparations for the confrontation in Philadelphia between MOVE and the System continued apace. MOVE people taught each other how to make bombs using *The Anarchist Cookbook* and continued to stockpile weapons and ammunition. In March 1977 Glassey used a fake driver's license to purchase two shotguns at a sporting goods store—a federal crime with a severe prison sentence. Glassey testified that he did not want to participate in the preparations for the confrontation. He only participated because he feared that MOVE people might kill him if he did not. The last straw for Glassey came two months later, when John Africa directed him to plant a timing device and threatening letter in a hotel in London. Glassey refused, so Anthony Beaman went instead.[50]

Glassey had finally extricated himself from the plot, but it was too late. On June 3, 1977, agents from the ATF arrested Glassey for purchasing weapons with a false identification. Facing a long prison sentence, Glassey agreed to become an informant for the ATF. In exchange, he received no jail time for the illegal gun purchase and was promised immunity from future prosecution. The ATF also gave him $1,650 for living expenses, relocation, and incidentals. Glassey testified that he was in touch with his ATF handler "three or four times a day."[51]

According to the prosecution, Donald Glassey assisted both the ATF and the CAU in foiling a MOVE plot to bomb various government buildings.

Glassey, wearing a wire, learned from MOVE supporter William "Whit" Smith that MOVE had stashed a cache of bombs in a Volkswagen bus, but that John Africa had instructed Smith to move the bombs to a safer location. At the behest of the ATF and the CAU, Glassey reinserted himself into the bomb plot. He offered to assist Smith in moving the bombs. Together, Glassey and Smith drove to three locations throughout West Philadelphia taking bombs from MOVE caches. Glassey's plan—which was really the ATF's plan—was to remove all the bombs from houses and cars and bury them in Fairmount Park. After Glassey and Smith had collected all the bombs, police officers pulled over the car, arresting Glassey (to his surprise) and Smith. Glassey was soon released to continue gathering evidence against MOVE people. On July 27, Glassey arranged for MOVE supporter Gregory Howard to purchase what he believed to be two sticks of C-4 explosives from an undercover federal agent posing as a left-wing anarchist arms dealer.[52]

The government's case was not especially strong. There was no question that MOVE people were stockpiling guns in anticipation of a confrontation. That confrontation—guns and all—took place on August 8, 1978. What was less sure was the existence of a bomb plot. The entire case rested on Glassey's testimony which was confusing and, at times, contradictory. There were obvious questions about Glassey's relationship with the ATF and the CAU, and as testimony went on, it was revealed that William "Whit" Smith and Sam Sanders had also benefitted from their testimony on behalf of the government. There was no proof that Glassey and other MOVE supporters flew around the country planting timing devices and letters. The ATF failed to locate these materials, and none of the hotels could corroborate Glassey's story. There was no proof either that a deal took place between Gregory Howard and the undercover ATF agent. The ATF said that they were pressed for time, so they did not place a sound recorder on Glassey or the agent. There was also no money exchanged between Howard and the ATF agent. The only evidence that explosives changed hands between the undercover agent and Howard was, again, the testimony of Glassey and the ATF. In short, the only people the prosecution proved possessed explosives were government informers who bought and stored those explosives at the behest of the ATF and the CAU.[53]

A lawyer might have pointed out the weakness of the prosecution's case. Instead, Mo Africa conducted most of the defense. By any objective measure, he did a poor job. Though there were plenty of holes in the prosecution's case, Mo did not spend much time refuting the prosecution's claims. As MOVE people understood it, the particulars of the case were not what was on trial. The courtroom proceedings were, to MOVE people, simply an earthly manifestation of a cosmic conflict. The particularities of the accusations—Did John Africa order MOVE people to procure explosives? Did MOVE people possess, or plan to build, explosives?—were of little importance. John Africa said during his closing arguments, "You're not really concerned with those bombs. You're concerned with putting me on trial." Instead of arguing the particulars of the case, Mo Africa attempted to prove that John Africa was a prophet and a miracle worker.[54]

Mo and John Africa's defense strategy was to call MOVE people as witnesses and have them testify to John Africa's miraculous abilities. In total, eighteen MOVE members, former members, and supporters testified in *United States v. Leaphart*, both for the prosecution and the defense. Many of them, especially those called by the defense, had little connection to the alleged bomb plot. They were there to testify to the miracles they had seen and to the divine nature of the Teachings of John Africa; to defend John Africa against the System that denied his supernatural ability. Several MOVE people testified that they had witnessed miraculous events during the August 8, 1978, confrontation. Frank Africa testified that MOVE people inside the house that day were sure that the police had come "to kill all the MOVE people." But John Africa told him that they would not be harmed. Even though he had seen countless miracles since he had begun following the Teachings of John Africa, Frank said he "couldn't accept it." He was sure they were all going to die at the hands of the police. Frank testified that he watched as police officers "fired point blank at MOVE people." But no one was killed. As Frank interpreted it, "John Africa protected us just as he always has protected us." Janine Africa echoed Frank Africa's interpretation. She recalled for the jury that she, too, was sure she and her child would die that day, and attributed their survival to "a miracle and protection of John Africa that nobody can explain."[55]

Several MOVE people testified that the Teachings of John Africa had healed their bodies. Delbert Africa testified that *The Guidelines* were "the most powerful written manuscript ever to be put on the face of the earth," and told the jury how the Teachings of John Africa helped him recover from his devastating car accident. Delbert told the jury how John Africa "explained the mystery of death to me, too. You know, the deathlessness of life, the absence of death, the fact that life is ongoing, one complete cycle." Several of the MOVE women testified that John Africa had taught them how to give birth effortlessly and without labor pains. Eddie Africa testified that "John Africa is perfect," and explained that people living in the System mistakenly believe that perfection is unattainable or "mystical." As Eddie explained, to MOVE people "perfect means doing what is right all the time . . . John Africa has done that."[56]

During MOVE's efforts to defend their prophet and their religion, Mo Africa managed to score quite a few wins for the defense. He was especially effective in questioning ATF Special Agent William McNulty—the architect of the ATF's undercover sting operations against MOVE. Mo Africa forced McNulty to admit that he saw MOVE people as "morally weak" because he did not "hold their moral values to be the same" as his own. Under questioning, McNulty admitted that all of the government's key witnesses "cooperated with the Government because they were afraid of going to jail." When Mo Africa asked McNulty if the government had influenced the testimony of their witnesses, McNulty testified that the "government influenced them, yes, quite a bit." Mo Africa's sister, who was not in MOVE, testified for the prosecution that her brother had stored bombs in her house. But when Mo Africa called her as a witness for the defense, she testified that she had not actually seen the bombs, but was told—by an ATF agent—that bombs had been removed from a footlocker in her garage. Perhaps most damaging to the prosecution, every MOVE person called by the defense directly contradicted the key claims made by Donald Glassey. They said that Glassey had overstated his early role in MOVE, and that he had not been active in the organization for years. The called Glassey "weak" and "a traitor." And they strongly insinuated that federal law enforcement had pressured him into fabricating a conspiracy against John Africa in order to destroy MOVE.[57]

John and Mo Africa's defense was designed to force the jury to understand the trial as a religious conflict. They hoped the jury would ignore the empirical evidence before them, questionable though it was, and would judge John Africa and his religion by the miracles he had performed in the lives of his followers. During closing arguments, the prosecution fought in vain to remind the jury that MOVE's religion was not on trial. The lead prosecutor reminded the jury before deliberations that they should not "convict them for their philosophy" but that they should not "be fooled by it either." The prosecutor's concerns point to the surprise success of John and Mo Africa's defense strategy: they succeeded in making *United States v. Leaphart* into John Africa versus the System. In this light, the defense that John and Mo performed was incredibly effective. They were not primarily defending themselves against the government's claims. Mo Africa's goal was for the jury to "know why MOVE people is so protective of our Guidelines, which is our Bible and why we are so protective of that man sitting over there, Vince Africa." Mo Africa and the MOVE people who testified in the trial were defending the prophetic legitimacy of John Africa, the divinity of the Teachings of John Africa, the veracity of the miracles they had witnessed, and the reality of their religious experiences.[58]

The jury deliberated for six days—a record, at the time—before acquitting John Africa and Mo Africa on all charges. A juror interviewed after rendering the verdict stated that "Glassey's testimony just didn't hold up . . . everything was based on what he said, and there were a lot of loopholes in it." The prosecutors, who had before and during the trial boasted of the strength of their case to the media, conceded, in somewhat ironic language, "that's how the system works." John Africa did not speak to the media upon his acquittal, but approached ATF agent Walt Wasyluk after the verdict, shook his hand, and said "no hard feelings." The two men, who had developed a mutual respect, made plans to meet under more cordial circumstances in the future.[59]

It is possible—and not at all out of character—that in the wake of Life Africa's death at the hands of police officers, John Africa concocted a plan to place suspicious-looking alarm clocks in hotels around the country in order to create the illusion that MOVE had the support of a nationwide, underground guerrilla operation. It is possible, even likely in my reading of the evidence, that people connected to MOVE had no qualms about using bombs to defend the MOVE house in Philadelphia against confrontations with police and may have expressed interest in acquiring C-4. It is possible that MOVE planned to use bombs to attack the System and that John Africa ordered MOVE people to acquire explosives which he planned to plant in hotels around the country, though the evidence for this claim is quite thin. All we can say with certainty is that a jury weighed the evidence for these claims and was unconvinced.

But it is also possible—and not at all out of character—that the entire plot was a fabrication of the CAU and the Bureau of Alcohol, Tobacco, and Firearms. Though the ATF records on the MOVE investigation have been heavily redacted, an internal investigation report indicates that on June 24, 1977—three weeks after Glassey was arrested by the ATF and three weeks before the ATF claims he began his undercover operation—personnel from the ATF and the CAU devised a plan to "infiltrate the MOVE organization." Their plan was to use an informant inside MOVE to gauge MOVE's interest in acquiring C-4 explosives. "Should MOVE members indicate an interest in acquiring C-4," the informant "would furnish imitation C-4 in an effort to infiltrate MOVE and prove a conspiracy violation." Two MOVE supporters—Sam Sanders and Gregory Howard—were caught in the plot. They expressed an interest in acquiring C-4, undercover agents supplied them with it, and they were convicted. But prosecuting men with only a tangential connection to MOVE was not the purpose of the ATF/CAU plot. They were, agents admitted, hoping to bring down MOVE by targeting its leader, John Africa—the same way they might destroy an organized crime syndicate.[60]

Without question, much of MOVE's history was shaped by their interaction with police. Much of that is MOVE's fault. MOVE people did break the law, routinely and often with great relish. MOVE people in the house on August 8, 1978, are responsible—directly or indirectly—for the death of Officer James Ramp. But it is also true that the police began their surveillance operations against MOVE in May 1973—years before MOVE people broke any laws. For MOVE, the result of this surveillance was that MOVE was haunted from the beginning by the specter of criminality. These associations played a critical role in categorizing MOVE, in the minds of many people outside of the group, as secular in nature rather than religious. One effect of the preemptive policing of religious groups—surveillance, infiltration, and subversion, before any crimes have been committed—is to place them outside the boundaries of true religion. Like many predominately African American religions before it, MOVE never got a chance to grow without external forces working toward its destruction. It never got to attract converts without suspecting that some of them were insincere. MOVE never got to exist as a religion without having their religion policed.[61]

Notes

1. Civil Disobedience Unit Investigation Report, "The American Christian Movement for Life (MOVE)," April 22, 1974, PSIC, Box 51, Folder 3.
2. Ibid.
3. Ibid.
4. The Philadelphia Police Department denied my multiple Freedom of Information Act (FOIA) requests on the grounds that their investigation into MOVE is still active. The Federal Bureau of Investigation redacted portions of their MOVE file, which I accessed via FOIA request, on those same grounds.

5. Katherine Gin Lum and Lerone A. Martin, "American Religion and the Rise of Internal Security," *The FBI and Religion: Faith and National Security before and after 9/11*, edited by Sylvester A. Johnson and Steven Weitzman (Berkeley: University of California Press, 2017), 31; On religion as a claim to legal belonging, see Tisa Wenger, *We Have a Religion: The 1920s Pueblo Indian Dance Controversy and American Religion Freedom* (Chapel Hill: University of North Carolina Press, 2009); On the tangled relationship between the law and the category of religion, see Winnifred Fallers Sullivan, *The Impossibility of Religious Freedom* (Princeton, NJ: Princeton University Press, 2005) and Jonathan Z. Smith, "God Save This Honourable Court: Religion and Civic Discourse," in *Relating Religion; Essays in the Study of Religion* (Chicago: University of Chicago Press, 2004), 375–390.
6. Federal Bureau of Investigation, "SAC Letter No. 55-43," June 28, 1955; Sylvester A. Johnson, "The FBI and the Moorish Science Temple of America, 1926–1960," 55–66; Karl Evanzz, "The FBI and the Nation of Islam," in *The FBI and Religion*; see also Edward E. Curtis IV, *Black Muslim Religion in the Nation of Islam, 1960–1975* (Chapel Hill: University of North Carolina Press, 2006); C. Eric Lincoln, *The Black Muslims in America* (Boston: Beacon Press, 1961), 4–5.
7. Ward Churchill and Jim Vander Wall, *The COINTELPRO Papers: Documents from the FBI's Secret Wars against Domestic Dissent* (Boston: South End Press, 1990); on the 1971 FBI Field Office break-in, see Betty Medsger, *The Burglary: The Discovery of J. Edgar Hoover's Secret FBI* (New York: Knopf, 2014); Sylvester A. Johnson, *African American Religions, 1500–2000: Colonialism, Democracy, and Freedom* (New York: Cambridge University Press, 2015) 359–360.
8. Frank Donner, *Protectors of Privilege: Red Squads and Police Repression in Urban America* (Berkeley: University of California Press, 1992); Kenneth O'Reilly, *Racial Matters: The FBI's Secret File on Black America, 1960–1972* (New York: Free Press, 1991); Hans Bennett, "The Black Panthers and the Assassination of Fred Hampton," *Journal of Pan African Studies* 3, no. 6, (2010), 215–221.
9. Dave Lieber, "George Fencl: The Cop as Folk Hero," *Today: The Inquirer Magazine*, December 2, 1979.
10. Ibid., On Frank Rizzo, see Timothy J. Lombardo, *Blue-Collar Conservatism: Frank Rizzo's Philadelphia and Populist Politics in Philadelphia* (Philadelphia: University of Pennsylvania Press, 2018).
11. Donner, *Protectors of Privilege*, 199; Lombardo, *Blue-Collar Conservatism*, 103.
12. Lombardo, *Blue-Collar Conservatism*.
13. Donner, *Protectors of Privilege*, 197–244; Karen Datko, "Intelligence Data Still Filed on So-Called 'Dissidents,'" *Philadelphia Tribune*, May 6, 1978; Pamela Smith, "Newly Released Information Indicates Widespread Police Surveillance," *Philadelphia Tribune*, June 23, 1978.
14. Donner, *Protectors of Privilege*, 207–209.
15. Ibid.; On the RAM, see Joseph Peniel, *Waiting 'Til the Midnight Hour: A Narrative History of Black Power in America* (New York: Henry Holt, 2006).
16. "MOVE History," PSIC, Box 8, Folder 5; Public Law 91-513—October 27, 1970, section 1010.

17. "MOVE History," PSIC.
18. "MOVE History," PSIC, Box 8, Folder 5; many of the details about Glassey's involvement with the CAU and ATF were revealed in *United States v. Leaphart and Robbins* (1981); MOVE, Untitled Document, Friends Peace Committee papers, 16–17.
19. FBI Director to SAC [special agent in charge], Philadelphia, "MOVE: Extremist Matter" April 7, 1975; FBI report, MOVE, June 3, 1975.
20. Director of the FBI to SAC, Philadelphia, "MOVE: EM," March 24, 1975.
21. Ibid. FBI Director to SAC [special agent in charge], Philadelphia, "MOVE: Extremist Matter" April 7, 1975.
22. Memo to SAC from SA Carl A. Turner, Subject MOVE: EM, April 28, 1975; MEMO: to SAC from Turner April 28, 1975, "Black Panther Party-Cleaver Faction: EM."
23. FBI report, MOVE, June 3, 1975; SAC to Director FBI, June 3, 1975; Director FBI to SAC Philadelphia, June 23, 1975.
24. Sue Africa, transcript of an oral history conducted in 2017 by Richard Kent Evans, MOVE Oral History Project, Special Collections and Urban Archives, Temple University, Philadelphia, PA; Mike Africa Jr., transcript of an oral history conducted in 2016 by Richard Kent Evans, MOVE Oral History Project, Special Collections and Urban Archives, Temple University, Philadelphia PA; Ashley Halsey, "Tracing the Movements of MOVE Group in Hiding," *Philadelphia Inquirer*, May 17, 1981; Mumia Abu-Jamal, "MOVE Hid in Plain Sight," *Philadelphia Tribune*, June 19, 1981.
25. The Seed of Wisdom is also a reference to the Kabbalah. In certain mystical conceptions of the divine, God is represented as having both a male component, the seed of wisdom, and a female component, often represented as a womb. The seed of wisdom is also a recurring symbol within the Theosophical tradition which is, itself, influenced by Kabbalah. See Catherine Albanese, *A Republic of Mind and Spirit: A Cultural History of American Metaphysical Religion* (New Haven, CT: Yale University Press, 2007), 143.
26. John Templeton, "Religious Cult Keeps Kids Naked, Eats Raw Food," *Afro-American*, May 14, 1977.
27. Ibid.
28. John Templeton, "Cultists Resist Try to Throw Them Out," *Afro-American*, May 21, 1977.
29. Ibid.
30. Ibid.
31. "Members of Religious Cult That Eat Raw Food Originated in Pennsylvania," *Philadelphia Tribune*, May 17, 1977; "Pennsylvania MOVE Sect Members Seized in Virginia," *Washington Post*, August 6, 1978; Laverne Sims to William H Brown III, November 9, 1985, PSIC; Pamela Smith, "MOVE Member Charges Arrests of Two Kidnapping, Says Bail Is 'Ransom,'" *Philadelphia Tribune*, August 8, 1978.
32. Hank Klibanoff, "An Insider's View of Life within MOVE," *Philadelphia Inquirer*, May 22, 1985, A1; Pamela Smith, "MOVE Calls Recent Arrests Crackdown on Group Members," *Philadelphia Tribune*, January 18, 1980.
33. Sue Africa, transcript of an oral history conducted in 2017 by Richard Kent Evans, MOVE Oral History Project, Special Collections and Urban Archives, Temple

University, Philadelphia, PA; Carlos Africa, transcript of an oral history conducted in 2017 by Richard Kent Evans, MOVE Oral History Project, Special Collections and Urban Archives, Temple University Philadelphia, PA. Teresa Africa, speech at MOVE Conference, May 6, 2017.
34. MOVE, Proposal for Funding of the MOVE organization, July 10, 1978, PSIC, Box 7.
35. Ibid.
36. Mumia Abu-Jamal, "MOVE Hid in Plain Sight," *Philadelphia Tribune*, June 19, 1981; Ashley Halsey, "Tracing the Movements of MOVE Group in Hiding," *Philadelphia Inquirer*, May 17, 1981.
37. Ibid.
38. Jonathan Neumann and William K, Marimow, "How Phila. Detectives Compel Murder 'Confessions,'" *Philadelphia Inquirer*, April 24, 1977, 1-A, 12-A; "How Police Harassed a Family," April 25, 1977, 1-A, 6-A; "A Police Beating . . . And a Decision Not to Charge Detectives," April 26, 1977, 1-A, 8-A; "Why Detectives Are Safe from Prosecution," 1-A, 8-A; Jonathan Newmann, "A Jury Doubts Police," *Philadelphia Inquirer*, May 29, 1977, 1-A, 13-A.
39. AFSC Police Abuse Project, Press Release from Coalition for a Fair Police Complaint Procedure, July 11, 1978, Box General Admin., Folder 3435, Philadelphia Police Abuse Project, Philadelphia Surveillance Program, American Friends Research Center, Philadelphia, PA; Proposal for Project to Facilitate Work against Police Abuse in Philadelphia, July 1977, Box General Admin., Folder 3436, Philadelphia Police Abuse Project, Philadelphia Surveillance Program, American Friends Research Center, Philadelphia, PA.
40. United States Commission on Civil Rights, "Hearing Before the United States Commission on Civil Rights Police Practices and Civil Rights; Hearing Held in Philadelphia, Pennsylvania, February 6, 1979, April 16–17, 1979," Volume I: Testimony (Washington, DC: U.S. Government Printing Office, 1979), 200, 245; on the US Commission on Civil Rights, see Mary Frances Berry, *And Justice for All: The United States Commission on Civil Rights and the Continuing Struggle for Freedom in America* (New York: Alfred A. Knopf, 2009).
41. *United States of America v. City of Philadelphia, et al.*; William K. Marimow, "Rizzo Denounces Police-Abuse Suit as 'Hogwash,'" *Philadelphia Inquirer*, August 14, 1979; Jan Schaffer, "U.S. Charges, Beating, Shooting, Coercion," *Philadelphia Inquirer*, August 14, 1979; Charles R. Babcock, "Justice Accuses Philadelphia of Police Abuses: Unprecedented Suit Says Rizzo Condoned Brutality, U.S. Civil Suit Charges Philadelphia with Police Abuses," *Washington Post*, August 14, 1979.
42. Ashley Halsey, "Tracing the Movements of MOVE Group in Hiding," *Philadelphia Inquirer*, May 17, 1981.
43. Ashley Halsey, "Founder of MOVE and 8 Others, Sought since '77, Arrested in N.Y." *Philadelphia Inquirer*, May 14, 1981.
44. Halsey, "Tracing the Movements of MOVE Group in Hiding."
45. Dick Cooper, "Not-Guilty Plea Is Entered for Silent MOVE Leader," *Philadelphia Inquirer*, May 27, 1981.
46. *United States v. Leaphart and Robbins.*

47. Stephen Williams, "Judge Green MOVEd Trial to 'Justice,'" *Philadelphia Tribune*, July 24, 1981.
48. Transcripts of *United States v. Leaphart and Robbins* (1981) can be found in Box 66 and 67, PSIC, Urban Archives and Special Collections, Temple University.
49. *United States v. Leaphart*.
50. Ibid.
51. Ibid.
52. Ibid.
53. Ibid.; for an overview of some of the weaknesses in the government's case, see Stephen Williams, "MOVE Trial Called a 'Farce,'" *Philadelphia Tribune*, July 21, 1981.
54. *United States v. Leaphart and Robbins*, 10.150.
55. *United States v. Leaphart and Robbins*.
56. Ibid., 5.49.
57. Ibid.
58. Closing Statement of Prosecutors in *United States v. Leaphart and Robbins* (1981), PSIC, Box 66, 10.115–10.137.
59. "Jury Acquits 2 Members of Philadelphia Cult," *New York Times*, July 23, 1981, A16; Dick Cooper, "MOVE Leader Cleared," *Philadelphia Inquirer*, July 23, 1981, 1-A, 2-A.
60. "Report of Investigation to Special Agent in Charge, ATF Philadelphia District Office," July 5, 1977, Box 66, Folder 10, PSIC; Karen Datko, "2 MOVE Supporters Found Guilty of Weapons Charges," *Philadelphia Tribune*, February 14, 1978.
61. Michael Barkun, "The FBI and American Muslims after September 11," in *The FBI and Religion*, edited by Sylvester A. Johnson and Steven Weitzman (Berkeley: University of California Press, 2017), 244–256; Donner, *Protectors of Privilege*; on Black religion and dissent, see Gayraud S. Wilmore, *Black Religion and Black Radicalism* (Garden City, NY: Anchor Press/Doubleday, 1973); Russell T. McCutcheon, *Religion and the Domestication of Dissent: Or, How to Live in a Less than Perfect Nation* (London: Equinox, 2005), especially chapter five; Edwin Gaustad, *Dissent in American Religion* (Chicago: University of Chicago Press, 1973).

6
Religion on Trial

As he sat in a federal courtroom, Frank Africa reminded himself of what John Africa had taught him. *The law is part of the System. These courts are part of the System. MOVE people answer to a higher law—the Law of Mama—a law so powerful no person could stand against it.* He knew what to say and how to hold himself. He knew he had to relax and speak slowly. Don't get angry. Trust in what is right. Let the lawyers do the talking. But Frank Africa could not help but think that he was ill-suited for this. He was shy and soft-spoken, humble and deferential. He was only twenty-one, and although he was a gifted student, he dropped out of school to commit himself fully to the Teachings of John Africa. Though he could decry the evils of the System as well as the rest of his MOVE family, belligerence and confrontation did not come naturally to Frank. He was soft-hearted. Few things bothered Frank more than the idea that someone might be mad at him. But in July 1980, he found himself standing before a District Court judge, already a convict, tasked with proving in a court of law that MOVE was a religion.[1]

The court case, *Frank Africa v. Commonwealth of Pennsylvania*, is an important event in MOVE's classification. It was one of the few times in MOVE's history where thoughtful, powerful people deliberated on the question of whether or not MOVE was a religion. On the facts, *Africa v. Commonwealth* was not at all unusual in the history of religious accommodations for prisoners. Frank Africa was a prisoner serving time in a Pennsylvania state prison. The standard prison diet did not meet the requirements of MOVE's religious diet. Frank Africa requested that the prison accommodate his religious diet, the same way they might accommodate any other prisoner with religious dietary restrictions. The prison declined his request, arguing that an abundance of fresh fruits and vegetables could be used to make contraband prison wine. Frank Africa appealed the decision, first to a district court and then to the Third Circuit Court of Appeals, and lost both times. There was, however, one unusual situation that made *Africa v. Commonwealth* a special case, both in the legal history of prison religion and in MOVE's classification: though Frank Africa's case rested on the claim that MOVE was a religion, the court was not convinced that he was correct. Therefore, what might have been a straightforward religious accommodations request, in which the court would weigh the infringement of a prisoner's religious rights against the state's interests in effective incarceration, required, instead, the court to decide whether or not MOVE was a religion.[2]

* * *

Like all MOVE people, Louise James revered her brother, John Africa. But her son, Frank, always came first. Frank Africa, Louise Africa's only son and John Africa's nephew, was born in 1959. His father was not a part of his or Louise's life. Louise raised Frank on her own in a comfortable middle-class home on Osage Avenue in West Philadelphia that she and her ex-husband had purchased when Frank was a baby. Louise worked for the Bell Telephone Company. In August 1965, when Frank was six years old, Louise took him to see Martin Luther King, Jr., speak at an open-air rally at 39th Street and Lancaster Avenue. Hundreds of people gathered in the intersection there. King spoke about segregated housing in Philadelphia and how it created a two-tiered education system. He spoke about the need for Philadelphia's Black community to work together for a better future. But what resonated most with Louise was when King spoke about Girard College.[3]

Girard College was a prep school built in 1833 with money from prominent local businessman, Stephen Girard. Per Girard's bequest, the school was surrounded by a ten-foot concrete wall and admitted "poor white orphan boys, ages six to ten." It was the kind of school Frank might have gone to if he were white. Though the school admitted boys without fathers, it refused—well into the 1960s—to accept Black boys, citing Girard's will. By the mid-twentieth century, the neighborhoods surrounding the school were predominately Black. For Philadelphia civil rights leader Cecil B. Moore, who led the fight to desegregate the school, and for King, the walled, segregated school was a perfect symbol of the rampant inequality and open segregation that plagued northern industrial cities like Philadelphia. For Louise, the walls around Girard represented her growing frustration with Frank's education. Frank was bright—maybe even brilliant. But he was stuck in an under-funded, mostly Black neighborhood school in West Philadelphia. If he could only find a school that would challenge him, he might amount to something.[4]

In 1968, Philadelphia began busing students in a push to desegregate the city's public schools. Frank rode the bus every day to a Seventh-Day

Adventist school forty-five minutes from his house in West Philadelphia. Frank had trouble adjusting to his new school. Between the pop quizzes and school dances, he struggled to fit in. Frank would come home crying. Louise hated the school. Frank was still not receiving the education he deserved, and now he had to struggle to make new friends—white friends. After King was killed, Louise began to gravitate toward the Black Panther Party. The collapse of King's coalition led Louise—and many African Americans at the time— toward the more radical voices of the Black Freedom Struggle. She followed very closely the career of Angela Davis. She wrote letters to imprisoned Black Panthers, offering her encouragement. Frank absorbed his mother's growing political consciousness. His schoolmates remember Frank being particularly insightful when it came to issues of social justice.[5]

In 1970, Louise got Frank a scholarship to attend a private preparatory school for boys in Haverford, a wealthy and predominately white suburb on Philadelphia's Main Line. Though his classmates were overwhelmingly wealthy and white, Frank fit in much better at this new school. And his political awareness was an asset among the more politically liberal environs of Haverford. Louise liked this school. She knew the school was finally giving Frank the intellectual challenge he needed. He might even go to college. In Frank's junior year at the prep school, Louise began taking seriously the writings of her brother, Vincent Leaphart. She had heard about Vincent's book in bits and pieces since 1969, when Vincent showed early chapters to their father. When their father died in 1972, Vincent skipped the funeral. Louise was hurt but not surprised. Her brother, who in the mid-1960s was one of Louise's closest friends, had become aloof and withdrawn in recent years. So she was surprised when Vincent called her shortly after their father's funeral, announcing that they were teaching his book at Philadelphia Community College. Vincent wanted Louise and her sisters Muriel and LaVerne to come to the class.[6]

Vincent's invitation came at a crucial point in Louise's life. In the summer of 1972, a twenty-four-year-old Black man named Larry Cross was driving a car with his wife, Hattie, and their young daughter through the streets of West Philadelphia, about a mile away from Louise's house, when he was pulled over by a police officer. The officer asked for Cross's license and registration, wrote him a ticket, and threw all the papers at Cross through the car window. Cross told the officer not to throw things at him. The officer demanded that Cross pick the ticket up off the floor of his car. When Cross refused, the officer and his partner pulled him out of the car. A third police officer, a Black man, arrived on the scene and implored his white colleagues to stop harassing Cross. He told Cross to get back into his car and drive to the nearest police station. When Cross and his family arrived at the police station, he was sent for booking. His wife waited in the lobby for his discharge papers to be processed and for her husband to be released. Two hours after their arrival, police officers informed Hattie that her husband had attempted suicide and was being taken to the hospital. He was pronounced dead at the hospital. Autopsies revealed that Cross had suffered serious internal injuries, including at least one serious blow to the head.[7]

When Louise heard about what happened to Larry Cross, she could not help but think of Frank. Larry Cross had the kind of life she hoped Frank would have. He was doing the right thing. He had a wife, a young daughter, a job. Still, Louise believed, as did many in Philadelphia's Black community, that Larry Cross had been murdered by the police. Incensed, Louise attended a community meeting at White Rock Baptist Church. Many of the city's Black community leaders were there, including Cecil B. Moore, Philadelphia's civil rights leader and president of the local NAACP—but Philadelphia's Black community was not. The church sanctuary, which sat several hundred people, was not even partially filled. Louise was furious. It was as if no one cared that this young Black man was dead. And worse, she heard no solutions coming from the religious leaders or the political officials there. All they offered were platitudes and rhetoric—half-hearted allusions to committees and investigations and procedures. Louise broke that night. She broke from her Black Church upbringing. She broke from her Christian faith. She broke from her hope in a political solution to racism. So when her brother called and said he had the answers, she listened.[8]

Louise and Laverne began attending Donald Glassey's class at Philadelphia Community College, where they indeed found their brother's book to be the object of study. When the semester ended, Vincent—who was now calling himself John Africa—his sisters, and a few of the students from the college class continued meeting in various people's homes. Louise continued to attend and brought Frank along with her. Frank proved to be an eager convert, and he grew very close to his uncle, the father figure he never had. Over time, Frank James became Frank Africa, John Africa's closest disciple. John Africa favored Frank both because he was his blood relative and because Frank was not as cynical as some of the other MOVE people. Louise, in particular, always had one foot outside of the group. She kept her home and her job. She was a MOVE person part-time. Frank was all in. John Africa awarded

Frank with the title of Naturalist Minister. Frank and the other young people in MOVE would routinely go throughout the neighborhood, knocking on doors, and talking to people on street corners in an attempt to gain new converts to the movement. He was arrested for the first time in June 1975 after several MOVE people formed a human chain to prevent Davita Thomas from being evicted from her home. A MOVE demonstration outside the police station after the arrests resulted in a fight between MOVE and the police and further arrests.[9]

In 1978, Frank Africa, along with John Africa and several other MOVE people, managed to leave MOVE headquarters before the blockade went into effect. While John Africa led a group to Rochester, New York, to set up a new MOVE headquarters, Frank moved back into his mother's house on Osage Avenue, about two miles west of Powelton Village. Frank was safely at Louise's house when the blockade ended with a shootout with police a year later. For the next three years, Frank managed to keep a low profile and stay out of trouble, while the other MOVE people present during the standoff were eventually arrested.

In the middle of the night, on January 14, 1980—three weeks into the MOVE 9 trial—a west Philadelphia woman called the police to report a suspected burglar trying to break into her house, which was about a mile from MOVE headquarters. When officers responded, they found Frank Africa, screwdriver in hand, trying to jimmy open a lock on the back door. The homeowner told the police she would not have called if she had known it was only Frank at the back door. He was a guest of the homeowner and was simply locked out of the house. It was a case of mistaken identity. Nevertheless, police charged Frank with criminal trespassing and attempted theft and held him on $25,000 bond.[10]

Frank was convicted on the breaking-and-entering charges and spent eighteen months at Holmesburg Prison awaiting trial for weapons and riot charges stemming from the Guns on the Porch standoff. Holmesburg was a city-run facility in the city's northeast section that had recently been embroiled in scandal after news broke that prisoners had been subjected to decades of medical experimentation as well as systemic sexual abuse. Perhaps because all eyes were on Holmesburg prison, MOVE people had a certain degree of latitude there. Prison officials at Holmesburg were accustomed to MOVE people, having housed them at various times since 1975. Frank arrived at Holmesburg in the middle of the MOVE 9 trial, and five of the MOVE 9 defendants, all of the men, were incarcerated there along with Frank. The MOVE men at Holmesburg spent their days planning their defenses, exercising, and gaining new converts. While at Holmesburg, Frank and the other MOVE men were able to follow, albeit loosely, the raw foods diet that John Africa taught. Prison officials provided them with fruits, vegetables, and raw eggs. MOVE people, like all inmates at Holmesburg, wore identification bands around their wrists that identified the prisoner's name, age, and religion. Frank's wrist band read:

Name: Africa, Frank
Age: 1
Religion: Life[11]

On July 15, 1981, Frank was sentenced to seven years in Graterford Prison, a maximum security prison run by the state of Pennsylvania, on charges stemming from his participation in the Guns on the Porch standoff. The next day, he filed an injunction in the Philadelphia Court of Common Pleas requesting that he either be permitted his religiously mandated diet at Graterford or that he be allowed to remain at Holmesburg for the duration of his sentence. On the morning of July 16, the day after Frank filed his injunction, he was transferred to Graterford, where officials refused to accommodate the MOVE diet. Later in the day, the city judge who received Frank's request ordered prison officials at Graterford to return Frank back to Holmesburg so that he could continue to receive his diet pending the court's resolution of the case. Three days elapsed before officials at Graterford complied with the court order. For those three days, Frank refused to eat. On July 20, he was sent back to Holmesburg and began preparations for a hearing in District Court a week away.[12]

At the hearing before the District Court, Ramona Africa, a new MOVE member, testified on Frank's behalf. In the late 1970s, Ramona Johnson was a pre-law major at Temple University, working toward degrees in political science and criminal justice. Her plan was to go to law school and become a lawyer or a judge. But then she met MOVE. A friend of hers, Pam Africa, who joined MOVE after the standoff on May 20, 1977, suggested that if Ramona wanted to see the American justice system up close, she should attend the trial of the MOVE 9. As she observed the trial, Ramona saw a side of the criminal justice system her coursework had not prepared her for. She witnessed what she interpreted as corrupt judges, apathetic defense lawyers, and unfair prosecutors. But she also witnessed a group of Black people standing up for themselves. Ramona began to advocate on behalf of MOVE in court, earning her a conviction for contempt of court. She served her two months alongside MOVE women. When she left prison, she was Ramona Africa, devoted follower of the Teaching of John Africa and MOVE's most capable legal advocate.[13]

Together, Ramona and Frank made the case before the District Court that MOVE was a religion and that the MOVE diet was an essential part of MOVE belief. Frank explained MOVE as a "revolutionary" group that is "absolutely opposed to all that is wrong." He gave an obfuscatory history of the group and told the Court that MOVE's purpose was "to bring about absolute peace, . . . to stop violence altogether, to put a stop to all that is corrupt." He assured the Court that, for their purposes, they could think of MOVE as a religion, but argued that, "[w]hile religion is seen as a way of life, our religion is simply THE way of LIFE, as our religion in fact is LIFE." To MOVE people, MOVE was a religion. But, as Frank explained to the Court, MOVE also transcended religion, a claim not uncommon to religious groups.[14]

Ramona testified to Frank's position in the group and to his sincerity. She told the Court that John Africa had "ordained" Frank as a "Naturalist Minister," a title John Africa bestowed onto Frank to recognize him as one of his earliest and closest disciples. Ramona told the Court that MOVE's "religion is total; it encompasses every aspect of MOVE members' lives; there is nothing that is left out." The MOVE diet was a reflection of each MOVE member's commitment to the Teaching of John Africa. Frank had proven that commitment, Ramona argued, by going without food during the three days he was at Graterford.[15]

Ramona and Frank submitted to the court a document titled "Brief to Define the Importance of MOVE's Religious Diet." That document listed the food items Frank required in order to accommodate his religiously mandated diet, which included vegetables, grains, nuts, fruits, and raw eggs, poultry, and meats. All foods had to be wild, organic, uncut, unpeeled, and unprocessed in any way in order to accommodate John Africa's teachings. It is highly unlikely that Frank received this diet at Holmesburg Prison. He received fruits, vegetables, and raw eggs, but all of the food was almost certainly the same conventionally grown food all inmates received, and it seems unlikely that prison officials fed him raw meat or poultry.[16]

In the brief, Ramona and Frank explained the religious significance of MOVE's diet. According to MOVE belief, God provided food in the form that it should be eaten. If a food could be chewed and swallowed raw, God intended it to be eaten raw. As Frank argued, "our religious diet is common and uncomplicated because our diet is provided by God and already done." The spiritual effects of deviating from the MOVE diet were severe. As Frank explained to the court, "to take away our diet is to leave me to eat nothing, for I have no choice, because when given a choice between eating poison and eating nothing, I have no choice but to eat nothing, for I can't eat other than raw. This would be suicidal and suicide is against Life's ministry." Beyond the spiritual ramifications of the diet, Frank explained the practical necessity of maintaining the diet his body was used to. MOVE people believed that eating cooked foods put them at risk of serious illness.[17]

Because Frank was sentenced to a term of seven years in prison, he could not, by law, be housed at a city-run facility. Staying at Graterford, the facility that allowed Frank to follow the MOVE diet, was out of the question. This forced the District Court to decide "the question whether MOVE may be classified as a 'religion' within the purview of the first amendment."

As luck would have it, Frank Africa's appeal landed before Judge Arlin Adams, perhaps the most preeminent theorist of religion in the American judiciary. Arlin Adams was a Philadelphian through and through: he was born in Philadelphia in 1921, earned bachelor's and master's degrees from Temple University, and attended the University of Pennsylvania Law School. Adams was a conservative. He ran Richard Nixon's presidential campaign in Pennsylvania, and President Nixon rewarded him with a nomination to the Third Circuit Court of Appeals in 1969. Nixon came quite close to naming Adams to the Supreme Court in 1971, but Attorney General John Mitchell nixed the idea (Adams had been too lenient to Christian pacifist and antiwar activist Daniel Berrigan for Mitchell's taste). In 1975, President Ford nominated John Paul Stevens to the court over Adams, who finished second. In 1987, under Reagan, Adams came excruciatingly close yet again, losing eventually to Anthony Kennedy. He stepped down after this third defeat, conceding "it wasn't going to happen." Still, throughout his nearly two decades on the Third Circuit Court of Appeals, Adams wielded tremendous influence over American law involving the religion clauses of the First Amendment. As we will see, his definition of religion was (and still is) the most influential definition of religion in American jurisprudence, and in 1990 he published a book, *A Nation Devoted to Religious Liberty*, on the religion clauses of the First Amendment.[18]

A year before he heard *Frank Africa v. Commonwealth*, Judge Arlin Adams issued a wide-ranging, precedent-setting decision that defined "religion" for the purposes of the First Amendment. In that case, 1979's *Malnak v. Yogi*, a coalition of plaintiffs including the Americans United for Separation of Church and State, various other religious liberty groups, and parents of New Jersey high school students sued the Science of Creative Intelligence (SCI) and its leader, Maharishi Mahesh Yogi, to stop the teaching of Transcendental Meditation (TM) in New Jersey public schools. The plaintiffs argued that the classes, which were offered in public schools as elective courses, violated the Establishment Clause of the First Amendment. The defense argued that SCI/TM was not a religion, that Transcendental Meditation was not a religious practice, and that the courses were more akin to philosophy courses.[19]

The Third Circuit resolved *Malnak v. Yogi* in favor of the plaintiffs, agreeing that SCI/TM was a religion masquerading as a secular philosophy. But what made *Malnak* a landmark case in religion law was the concurring opinion written by Judge Adams. Though he agreed with his colleagues that SCI/TM should be banned from public schools, Adams argued that the defendants were right about one thing: *Malnak* was the first time a court ruled a belief system to be a religion over the protestations of its adherents. The *Malnak* decision was, to Adams, a remarkable "extension of existing case law." Adams did not disagree with the Court's decision, but he wanted the Third Circuit Court of Appeals and the lower courts to understand what *Malnak* had done. In *Malnak*, the court had privileged its own definition of religion over that of representatives of religious authority and that of scholars of religion—despite how the group understood themselves. Judges had created religion where it did not previously exist.[20]

That judges could, in a sense, *create* religion alarmed Adams. In his reading of religion law, the Courts' definition of religion was expanding at an alarming rate. From the Early Republican period through the end of the nineteenth century, the Supreme Court held a largely implicit but theistic definition of religion that was drawn from Protestant Christianity. James Madison, for example, defined religion as "the duty which we owe to our creator, and the manner of discharging it."[21] The Courts, to the extent that they thought critically about the meaning of religion, found this theistic definition of religion suitable for their purposes until the 1960s, when the Warren and Burger Courts dramatically expanded what American law meant by "religion." In a 1961 decision, *Torasco v. Watkins*, the Supreme Court explicitly rejected the theistic definition of religion in use since the days of the Early Republic. In the opinion, Justice Hugo Black wrote that the First Amendment did not favor those religions that posit a belief in God against those that do not.

He included a footnote within the opinion that listed a few examples of the "religions in this country which do not teach what would generally be considered a belief in the existence of God." Included in his list were Buddhism, Taoism, Ethical Culture, and Secular Humanism. If read literally, Black's footnote suggested that even those groups that were certain they were not religions—Secular Humanism, for example—could in fact be understood as religions under the First Amendment.[22]

The Supreme Court again rejected the theistic requirement in 1965 in *United States v. Seeger* when it ruled that a belief in God was not necessary for recently drafted David Andrew Seeger to conscientiously object to fighting in Vietnam. The Court concluded that, although Seeger was unable to profess a belief in a Supreme Being, his beliefs, rooted in the Quaker Peace Testimony, "occupie[d] in the life of its possessor a place parallel to that filled by the God of those" who are typically granted conscientious objector status. And Seeger, himself, considered his pacifist beliefs to be religious in nature. The Court's definition of religion was now, convincingly, one that accommodated nontheistic religions as long as they were "based upon a power of being, or upon a faith, to which all else is subordinate or upon which all else is ultimately dependent." Five years later, the Court expanded the logic of the Seeger Decision in a case called *Welsh v. United States*. In this case, the Supreme Court granted conscientious objector status to a man who professed no religious beliefs of any kind, but opposed war on moral grounds.[23]

In the *Malnak* decision, Judge Adams decided to codify in his concurring opinion a three-part definition of religion that courts could use when deciding Free Exercise or Establishment Clause cases. He believed that he was not inventing a new definition, but rather solidifying the de facto definition already in use in American law, one that could be used in both free exercise and establishment clause cases. But Adams was not merely providing a helpful cheat sheet for future religion cases. He was attempting in his *Malnak* opinion to put the brakes on an ever-widening definition of religion. He feared that too loose a definition of religion would "create a chaotic situation, particularly in a culture in which so many entitlements and consequences attach to a determination of religious purpose or conduct." If Courts could no longer rely on a theistic definition of religion, and if professedly secular beliefs can "count" as religious beliefs for the purposes of law, what isn't a religion? To answer this question, Adams argued that American courts can recognize religion in three ways: "First, a religion addresses fundamental and ultimate questions having to do with deep and imponderable matters.

Second, a religion is comprehensive in nature; it consists of a belief-system as opposed to an isolated teaching. Third, a religion often can be recognized by the presence of certain formal and external signs." Adams's definition became the standard legal definition of religion for First Amendment cases, and it was the definition the District Court used to decide if MOVE was a religion.[24]

The District Court that heard Frank Africa's case only gestured toward Adams's definition of religion in *Malnak* in denying Frank's request for religious accommodation, calling Adams's definition of religion "inherently vague." Importantly, the Court did not reference any of Adams's three criteria individually in its decision. Rather than use Adams's three criteria as a systematic test of MOVE's beliefs and practices, the Court issued a blanket judgment that MOVE was not a religion. In the opinion of the lower court, MOVE was "merely a quasi-back-to-nature social movement of limited proportion and with an admittedly revolutionary design," a classification that was adopted by the media. The Court argued that MOVE belief was limited to ideas about natural living and health, and that this was more akin to "social philosophy" than religion. Frank may well believe that MOVE functions as a religion to him, but MOVE is, the District Court ruled, like "virtually all organizations in our society, independent of religion and with separate and distinct purposes while still respecting and abiding by external religious principles." Frank's accommodation request was denied, and officials at Holmesburg made arrangements to send him back to Graterford.[25]

Frank appealed the District Court's decision, and a week later the Third Circuit Court of Appeals agreed to take the case. Judge Arlin Adams, the architect of the definition of religion in the *Malnak* case, now had the opportunity to put his own criteria to the test. The Third Circuit Court stayed the lower court's order to send Frank back to Graterford, ordered that he be allowed his religious diet until the Third Circuit Court could rule, and appointed a lawyer to represent Frank during the appeal. Adams and two of his colleagues were set to determine, once and for all, whether or not MOVE was a religion.

As Frank's court-appointed lawyers prepared their case, the fate of the other incarcerated MOVE people worsened. While the MOVE men were housed at Holmesburg, the five MOVE women standing trial for the murder of Officer Ramp were housed at Muncy Prison, a state-run facility three hours northwest of Philadelphia. Unsurprisingly, accused cop-killers Merle, Janine, Gail, Debbie, Janet, and Sue Africa found the prison to be less than hospitable. They were kept in solitary confinement and were allowed only one hour a day outside of their cells. Prison officials at Muncy refused their requests for a raw foods diet. Like Frank, the MOVE women argued that both the diet and exercise were religious practices and that denying them adequate time out of solitary confinement amounted to religious persecution. But what really angered the MOVE women at Muncy was the prison's policy of drawing blood from prisoners to check for infectious diseases. MOVE refused to allow the blood tests, arguing that drawing blood violated their religious beliefs. Teresa Africa, one of the few MOVE people not behind bars at this point, explained to the media that MOVE people "don't give up our blood to nobody because it's against our religion."[26]

On September 10, 1981, Merle, Janine, Gail, Debbie, Janet, and Sue stopped taking food and water to protest their "religious persecution" at Muncy. They hoped that the hunger strike would force prison officials to recognize their religion, allow them to enter the prison's general population without the required medical screenings, and to grant them their raw foods diet. Officials at Muncy tried to keep news of the hunger strike from leaking. They imposed a media blackout and barred reporters from interviewing the MOVE women in person or over the phone. By mid-October, however, news had leaked. Mumia Abu-Jamal, a journalist and former NPR correspondent, invited Jeanette and Teresa Africa, who were acting as spokespeople for MOVE, to speak at an emergency meeting of Philadelphia's Association of Black Journalists (ABJ), of which Abu-Jamal was president. Abu-Jamal sympathized with Teresa and Jeanette's characterization of the hunger strike, and the ABJ passed a unanimous resolution supporting the MOVE women at Muncy in the "name of religious freedom, as guaranteed from the U.S. Constitution." Overnight, the MOVE women's hunger strike was top news.[27]

Thirty-three days into the hunger strike, prison officials confirmed that the MOVE women had each lost around thirty pounds. But officials at Muncy and at the Pennsylvania Department of Corrections also explained to the media that they had made several attempts to compromise with MOVE. They offered MOVE women the opportunity to take a saliva test instead of a blood test. MOVE declined. About three weeks into the hunger strike, Muncy officials began offering the MOVE women raw foods, per their request. Still, they refused to eat. MOVE men, housed in several facilities across the state, showed their solidarity with the women at Muncy by also refusing to take food. As an official at the Department of Corrections explained, the MOVE hunger strike had become "a crisis situation."[28]

On October 22, 1981, prison officials went to state court to received permission to force-feed the MOVE women at Muncy who had, by then, gone forty-two days without food. The judge granted prison doctors both the permission to force-feed the MOVE women and to remove the blood required to test for communicable diseases. When MOVE people outside of prison heard about the court order, they became furious. Prison officials transferred Sue Africa, the only white MOVE woman at Muncy, to an all-male prison facility over two hundred miles away. Officials at the Bureau of Corrections assumed that Sue was orchestrating the hunger strike and separated her from the other women because "it was felt she had a lot to do with the others not eating." MOVE interpreted Sue's transfer as a strategy to "divide and conquer and break the hunger confrontation."[29]

The hunger strikes loomed over the Third Circuit Court's decision. When Frank's hearing took place on September 22, 1981, the MOVE women at Muncy had gone eleven days without food. The judges realized that their decision in *Frank Africa v. Commonwealth of Pennsylvania* would have a direct effect on the hunger strike going on at Graterford. The Court's procedure was to deliberately and systematically compare Frank's understanding of MOVE belief, as recorded in the District Court transcripts, to Adams's three-part definition of religion. Adams reminded the Court that, as he stated in *Malnak*, a religion does not have to match all three criteria, but should not fail all three either. The Court should treat his three definitions as "useful indicia" of the presence of a religion.[30]

Adams's first requirement for religion was that its teachings must address "fundamental and ultimate questions having to do with deep and imponderable matters." Adams cited Protestant theological Paul Tillich as his authority. In his 1956 book *Dynamics of Faith*, Tillich offered a succinct and popular-level overview of his influential philosophical and theological writings. It is worth noting that in *Dynamics of Faith*, Tillich was working toward a liberal Christian definition of "faith," and not a definition of "religion," two concepts that Judge Adams apparently deemed interchangeable. Adams wrote that it was "difficult to conceive of a religion" that did not promote certain "underlying theories of man's nature or his place in the Universe," an assertion he borrowed from the Supreme Court decision in the 1969 case *Founding Church of Scientology v. United States*. By way of analogy, Adams pointed toward how "traditional religions" usually develop theologies around such things as "life and death, right and wrong, and good and evil." He acknowledged that religions do not have to address these exact concerns, but should consider matters of equal gravity.[31]

Frank's court-appointed legal team argued that MOVE's teaching on nature and Life fulfilled the Court's "fundamental and ultimate questions" requirement. MOVE, they argued, should be understood as a kind of pantheism in which "the entity of God is the world itself." According to this line of defense, when Frank refers to the Law of Nature, the Court should understand that as a reference to the divine, thus satisfying Adams's first criterion that religions should address "fundamental and ultimate questions." The defense team was not too far off. MOVE's conception of the divine could be categorized as panentheism. While pantheism recognizes the natural world as itself divine, MOVE understands the natural world as within—yet at times distinct from—the divine. This divinity, Mama, or Mother Nature, is not coterminous with the natural world, but is an active, creative being whose Laws govern and are evinced in the workings of nature. In MOVE theology, the evidence of God is obvious: "If you read the Bible, all the things that happen from the sea turning red, the sea parting, all the hurricanes and tornadoes and earthquake. . . . That's the force MOVE believes in." John Africa knew all of this. From birth, MOVE people believe, John Africa demonstrated a keen awareness of Mama's Natural Law. Within MOVE, John Africa was something between a prophet and a god. Like the prophets of the Old Testament, John Africa knew God's will. Unlike the Prophets, he knew it all along. His knowledge was not the result of revelation, but innate understanding—a oneness with Nature; a oneness with God.[32]

Despite Frank and Ramona's argument that MOVE did believe in God and dealt with ultimate concerns, the Court concluded that MOVE did not fulfill Adams's first criterion for religion. Importantly, Adams contended that MOVE's teachings were not "ultimate" because MOVE was not theistic—an assertion that was both counterfactual and in direct contradiction to the purposes of Adams's own first criterion. In the opinion, Adams rejected the argument that MOVE should be understood as a kind of pantheism because the Court was under the impression that MOVE did not recognize a Supreme Being or even a "transcendental or all-controlling force." For the Court's purposes, this meant that no MOVE teaching addressed "ultimate" concerns. Adams had designed this first criteria for the purpose of incorporating groups that did not acknowledge a divinity. His appeal to "ultimate concerns," instead of belief in God, was a direct response to the *Seeger* case in which the Supreme Court established that belief in a Supreme Being was not a necessary characteristic of a religion. The purpose of pointing to "ultimate concerns" instead of belief in God was to incorporate groups that did not express a belief in a transcendent being within the law's definition of religion. Even so, Adams, like Frank's lawyers, substituted the "ultimate concerns" test with a test of theism. In the opinion of the court, MOVE belief could be concerned with "ultimate matters" only to the extent that it acknowledged a personal God.[33]

Judge Arlin Adams also felt that MOVE beliefs were too involved with practical concerns such as diet, nature, and health; that they were too occupied with this world to have developed enough ideas about the next. It is true that MOVE belief is far more concerned with the natural than the supernatural. From the briefs he submitted to the Court, Adams concluded, Frank seemed to only be concerned with personal matters affecting his diet and with social concerns such as revolution. While Frank may have believed in these things very deeply, sincerity alone did not make them religious. Adams borrowed an analogy from *Wisconsin v. Yoder* to explain the difference he saw between a religious belief and a sincerely held, yet nevertheless secular belief. Frank Africa's preferred diet and his belief in John Africa's teachings regarding society were, Adams wrote, not unlike Henry David Thoreau's choice to denounce the world on Walden Pond. Thoreau, like Yoder's Old Order Amish, chose to reject the modern world and retreat into isolation. But the Amish withdrew from the world because they believed their God wanted them to. Thoreau withdrew because Thoreau wanted to. To the Supreme Court in the *Yoder* decision and to Adams, there was an obvious difference between the beliefs espoused by Thoreau and those of Yoder: the latter came from God and the former did not. Because the Court preferred to imagine MOVE as atheistic and because MOVE teaching was more concerned with practical matters than supernatural ones, Adams concluded that Frank's "mindset seems to be far more the product of a secular philosophy than of a religious orientation." MOVE failed Adams's first criterion of religion.[34]

Adams's second criterion for defining religion was that a religion must consist of a fully formed "belief-system as opposed to an isolated teaching." This criterion addressed a long-standing concern over First Amendment law. By encoding a distinction between religious belief and religious practice, this second criteria was meant to counteract the concern, expressed famously in *Reynolds v. United States* (1871), that an expanded reading of the First Amendment could make "every citizen a law unto himself," granting virtually any unlawful act immunity if it could be argued as religiously motivated.

Under this criterion, a practice must be motivated by a comprehensive belief system in order to be understood as a religious practice. For example, a Muslim fasting during Ramadan represents a religious practice because the comprehensive system (Islam) mandates the practice. Fasting is one of many religious practices that constitute Islam. What does *not* constitute a religion to Adams is a practice that is explained as a religion in itself; for example, a thief creating the Church of Grand Larceny to avoid prosecution. Adams's second criterion prevents claimants from cynically claiming religious exemptions to gain acceptance for otherwise illegal activities.[35]

Frank and Ramona told the Court that the religious diet, though a critical practice within MOVE's belief system, was not an isolated teaching imbued with religious authority but was a practice that grew out of a much broader religious system. Frank testified that the diet was just one of many religious practices MOVE people adhered to in order to follow the Teachings of John Africa. In fact, he argued, MOVE people were so devout that every activity a MOVE person engaged in constituted religious practice. Frank went so far in arguing this point that he hurt his case. Instead of pointing to other MOVE practices that, along with the MOVE diet, comprised MOVE's religious exercise, Frank testified that "[e]very time a MOVE person opens their mouth, according to the way we believe, according to the way we do things, we are holding church." The Court interpreted this as admission that the MOVE diet was not especially sacred to MOVE people. In his attempt to show that the diet was one religious practice among many, Frank inadvertently minimized its importance.[36]

The Third Circuit Court rejected Frank and Ramona's testimony that the MOVE diet was just one of many religious practices resulting from the broader Teachings of John Africa. Instead, Adams called MOVE belief a "single-faceted" ideology that did not extend past the MOVE diet. Reiterating his fear of the slippery slope, Adams emphasized the dangers facing First Amendment law if a belief system like MOVE were granted the status of religion. If MOVE belief was "comprehensive" enough to satisfy this second criterion, "it would be difficult to explain why other single-faceted ideologies—such as economic determinism, Social Darwinism, or even vegetarianism—would not qualify as religions under the first amendment." The Court determined that the MOVE diet was the totality of MOVE belief and practice; that Frank understood MOVE to be adherence to a certain diet and adherence to a certain diet to be the Teaching of John Africa. Adams determined that Frank had "shed little light upon what, if any, ethical commandments are part and parcel of the MOVE philosophy," and without some transcendent set of principles to point to, the diet could not count as a religion under his second criterion.[37]

But what most troubled the Court regarding this second criterion was the apparent lack of uniformity in adhering to MOVE's "religious diet." When Frank's case was in the lower court, the District Court Judge John Hannum and his law clerk visited Graterford Prison to investigate the feasibility of Frank's accommodation request. While at the prison, Hannum learned that Mike Africa, who was arrested after the shootout with police on August 8, 1978, and Jerry Africa, who was arrested along with John Africa and seven other MOVE people in Rochester in May 1981, were both eating standard prison food. Both the District Court and the Circuit Court found this discrepancy troubling. Hannum argued that Mike and Jerry's deviation from the diet "unequivocally establish[ed] that to comply with the MOVE proposed or preferred diet is merely a choice of personal preference." He cited court precedent siding with prisons in cases where a religious diet is not followed uniformly by all adherents and is not "required by a tenet of the organized faith to which the person belongs" to deny Frank's request in lower court.[38]

Judge Adams's third criterion stated that religions "often can be recognized by the presence of certain formal and external signs." Again, Adams explained what he meant by pointing toward "traditional religions." A religion should produce external, formal, and observable practices, institutions, and hierarchies. Any *real* religion, Adams argued, should produce a church. And that church should do what churches do: create a hierarchy of lay and clergy, build facilities, create sacred literature, try to recruit new members, celebrate festivals and holidays, and hold regular services.[39]

MOVE did, in fact, evince many of the "formal identifying characteristics" Judge Adams associated with religions. For years before the 1978 shootout with police, MOVE held biweekly teaching sessions in their house. Especially early on, MOVE actively recruited new members in a very typical, almost evangelical style. And Frank was one of the chief evangelists. Frank, Debbie, and Gail Africa would go door to door recruiting fellow teenagers to come to a MOVE meetings. MOVE's car wash, fruit stands, and moving and handyman services gave the group opportunities to spread the Truth of John Africa to anyone who would hear. They regarded their first MOVE headquarters as a sacred space, arguing that it functioned as a sort of temple. *The Guidelines* served as a scripture to MOVE people, and they often called it the "MOVE Bible." The Court was right about one thing—MOVE expressly rejected celebrating holidays or Sabbaths as arbitrary divisions of time, which itself was a profane construction of humankind. MOVE people, Frank argued, "are practicing our religious beliefs all the time."[40]

Judge Adams decided that MOVE could not evince any of the necessary "structural characteristics" of a religion. The Court looked with suspicion on the fact that "MOVE has no governing body or official hierarchy," citing the nonhierarchical nature of the group as evidence that MOVE lacked any of the usual structures of power associated with religions. Adams used Frank's assertion that MOVE consisted of only "one member," which Frank said to emphasize MOVE's egalitarian relationship with each other and to John Africa, to argue that MOVE "exists without an organizational structure." The Court also pointed out that Frank Africa failed to submit a copy of *The Guidelines* along with his accommodations request. Without this document, which MOVE people are, to this day, reluctant to share with anyone outside the group, the Court was unable to assess whether it "arguably might pass for a MOVE scripture." The Court was also concerned with MOVE's apparent lack of religious holidays, distinctly religious rituals and ceremonies, or efforts to convert new people into their organization.[41]

Adams concluded his opinion by retracing his three criteria. Frank's assertion that MOVE's belief system spoke to "ultimate" ideas struck the Court as questionable at best. There seemed to be no larger belief system mandating the practice Frank was requesting accommodation for, and MOVE evinced none of the visible external characteristics usually associated with "traditional religions." Thus, the court ruled that MOVE was "insufficiently religious," and Frank's accommodation request was denied. The Court was, however, concerned with Frank's health. The judges believed Frank when he said that MOVE people suffered health consequences from reintroducing cooked food into their diets. The Court was so impressed with this line of argument, in fact, that they suggested that Frank, Gail, and other incarcerated MOVE people could argue for their diet on the grounds that denial of their preferred diet amounted to cruel and unusual punishment under the Eighth Amendment. In his opinion, Judge Adams suggested that an Eighth Amendment claim was likely to fail, but that it was more likely to offer relief than to overturn the Court's "declaration that MOVE is not a religion."[42]

Many legal scholars have pointed out the inconsistencies in the way *Frank Africa v. Commonwealth of Pennsylvania* was decided. In their eyes, MOVE, even as it was described in the court documents, clearly functioned as a religion in Frank Africa's life and seemed to fulfill all three of Adams's requirements. Indeed, it seems that the Court reached the conclusion that MOVE was not a religion as the result of considerable logical gymnastics and, at times, the turning of quite a few blind eyes. Certainly, MOVE fit Adams's definition. Most systems of belief or practice do, in fact, meet Adams's requirement, whether they are understood as religions or not. The irony of Judge Adams's decisions, both in *Malnak v. Yogi* and in *Africa v. Commonwealth*, were that they were motivated by fear that judges, following the logic of the Warren and Burger courts, might create religion ex nihilo, thereby stretching the legal definition of "religion" so far that it might become meaningless. But "religion" was always meaningless outside of the law.

Judge Adams was right to be afraid of the power given to judges to decide so fundamental a question as what counts as religion. But that was never in question. Arlin Adams knew MOVE long before Frank Africa reached his courtroom. He knew that MOVE people caused a ruckus in dozens of functions throughout the city. They were disruptive. They killed a policeman. They made a mockery of every courtroom in Philadelphia and drew the ire of every judge they ever faced. They evidently preferred starving to death in prison to allowing officials to perform simple blood tests. And they were irrational. The Court thought MOVE people were willing to die—and let their babies die—out of a hopelessly misguided faith in an illiterate Black man. Adams and the Third Circuit Court of Appeals knew that it was unreasonable, undemocratic, and dangerous to grant a group like MOVE the legitimacy of being considered a religion. Those kinds of groups simply cannot exist as religions in a modern, secular state. So the Court worked backward. Adams contorted his own "useful indicia" to show why MOVE was not like Yoder's Old Order Amish, Seeger's commitment to nonviolence, or Maharishi Yogi's Science of Transcendental Meditation. It does not actually matter that MOVE was just as "religious" as these other groups. What mattered to the Third Circuit Court of Appeals was the fact that MOVE simply could not be considered a religion under the First Amendment. It was politically, socially, and historically impossible. MOVE had to be stopped, and imbuing the group with the social legitimacy and political utility of being legally classified as a religion was not going to help.

Notes

1. My characterization of Frank Africa's personality is gleaned from his mother's recollections, oral histories I have conducted with MOVE people, and from courtroom transcripts.
2. *Frank Africa v. Commonwealth of Pennsylvania*, 662 F.2d, 1025 (3rd Cir. 1981).
3. Louise Leaphart James, *John Africa . . . Childhood Untold until Today* (self-published, 2013), xii–x and 152–164; "Girard Wall," KYW News Footage, 13:24, Originally broadcast August 3, 1965, accessed via Civil Rights in a Northern City: Philadelphia, Temple University, http://northerncity.library.temple.edu/content/reverend-dr-martin-luther-king-7, accessed March 17, 2016.
4. Amira Rose Schroeder, "Girard College," Civil Rights in a Northern City: Philadelphia, http://northerncity.library.temple.edu/people-and-places/girard-college, accessed March 17, 2016.
5. Louise Leaphart James, *John Africa*, 152–158; Philadelphia Special Investigation Commission, Transcript of Philadelphia Special Investigation Commission Hearings, Box 8, Philadelphia Special Investigation Commission, Series 1, Special Collections Research Center, Temple University Libraries, Philadelphia, PA, 32–35.
6. Louise Leaphart James, *John Africa*, 47.
7. Joey Johnson, "Attorney Insists Man Hanged in Cell Had No 'Suicidal Tendencies,'" *Philadelphia Tribune*, August 1, 1972; "Police Claim Dead Man Tried to Hang Himself in Station House Cell," *Philadelphia Tribune*, July 25, 1972.
8. Louise Africa, "On The MOVE," *Philadelphia Tribune*, June 8, 1976; Joey Johnson, "Black Politicians Demand Justice in Larry Cross Case," *Philadelphia Tribune*, August 8, 1972; Transcript of Philadelphia Special Investigation Commission Hearings, Box 8, PSIC, 89.
9. Louise Africa, "On The MOVE," *Philadelphia Tribune*, October 14, 1975; Louise Africa, "On The MOVE," *Philadelphia Tribune*, October 28, 1975. Frank was in the MOVE house during the Guns on the Porch standoff in May 1977.
10. Dick Cooper, "MOVE Fugitive Arrested," *Philadelphia Inquirer*, January 15, 1980.
11. Allen M. Hornblum, *Acres of Skin: Human Experiments at Holmesburg Prison* (New York: Routledge, 1999), 190–192; *Africa v. Commonwealth*; Kareem Howard, transcript of an oral history conducted in 2016 by Richard Kent Evans, MOVE Oral History Project, Special Collections and Urban Archives, Temple University, Philadelphia, PA, 23.
12. *Africa v. Commonwealth*.
13. Ramona Africa, transcript of an oral history conducted in 2016 by Richard Kent Evans, MOVE Oral History Project, Special Collections and Urban Archives, Temple University, Philadelphia, PA, 23.
14. I have reformatted the Court transcripts to match the stylization of Frank Africa's submitted documents. I have changed the stylization of Frank Africa's testimony to match similar MOVE writings in an effort to present Africa's argument as it most likely appeared; *Africa v. Commonwealth*.
15. *Africa v. Commonwealth*.
16. Ibid.

17. Ibid.; Kareem Howard, transcript of oral history, 24.
18. Sam Roberts, "Arlin Adams, 94, U.S. Judge and Independent Counsel," *New York Times*, December 26, 2015.
19. Sarah Barringer Gordon, "Malnak v. Yogi," in *Law and Religion: Cases in Context*, edited by Leslie C. Griffin (New York: Aspen, 2010), 11–32.
20. *Alan B. Malnak, et al. v. Maharishi Mahesh Yogi, et al.*, 529 F.2d, 197 (3rd Cir. 1979).
21. *The Papers of James Madison*, vol. 8, *10 March 1784–28 March 1786*, edited by Robert A. Rutland and William M. E. Rachal (Chicago: The University of Chicago Press, 1973), 295–306.
22. Arlin M. Adams and Charles J. Emmerich, *A Nation Dedicated to Religious Liberty* (Philadelphia: University of Pennsylvania Press, 1990), 67–73; *Malnak v. Yogi*.
23. *United States v. Seeger*, 380 U.S. 163 (1965); Judge Arlin Adams offered his thoughts on Seeger and its legacy in Adams and Emmerich, *A Nation Dedicated to Religious Liberty*, 89–90.
24. Adams and Emmerich, *A Nation Dedicated to Religious Liberty*, 91; *Malnak v. Yogi*.
25. *Frank Africa v. The State of Pennsylvania, et al.*, 520 F. Supp. 967 (United States District Court, E. D. Pennsylvania, 1981).
26. Leon Taylor, "MOVE Members Stage Hunger Strike to Protest Prison Regs," *Daily News*, October 14, 1981.
27. Sara Schwieder, "Prison Denies Interview of Six in MOVE on Fast," *Philadelphia Inquirer*, October 16, 1981; Stephen Williams, "MOVE Hunger Strike Given ABJ Support," *Philadelphia Tribune*, October 27, 1981.
28. John F. Clancy, "6 Female MOVE Prisoners on Hunger Strike for 33 Days," *Philadelphia Inquirer*, October 14, 1981; Schwieder, "Prison Denies."
29. Stephan Salisbury, "Prison Can Force-Feed 6 in MOVE," *Philadelphia Inquirer*, October 23, 1981; Williams, "MOVE Hunger Strike Given ABJ Support."
30. *Africa v. Commonwealth*.
31. Ibid.
32. Ibid,; Ramona Africa, transcript of oral history, 11–12, 29–30.
33. *Africa v. Commonwealth*; Adams and Emmerich, *A Nation Dedicated to Religious Liberty*, 91–93.
34. The standard work on sincerity within American religion law is Charles McCrary, *Sincerely Held: American Religion, Secularism, and Belief* (Chicago: University of Chicago Press, forthcoming); *Africa v. Commonwealth*; Adams and Emmerich, *A Nation Dedicated to Religious Liberty*, 90.
35. *Africa v. Commonwealth*.
36. Ibid.
37. Ibid.; Adams and Emmerich, *A Nation Dedicated to Religious Liberty*, 92–93.
38. *Frank Africa v. The Commonwealth of Pennsylvania, et al.*, 520 F. Supp. 967 (United States District Court, E. D. Pennsylvania, 1981). Citing *Clark v. Wolf* (1972).
39. *Africa v. Commonwealth*.
40. Ibid.; Louise Africa, "On The MOVE," *Philadelphia Tribune*, September 23, 1975.
41. *Africa v. Commonwealth*.
42. Ibid.

7
Building a Cult

On July 22, 1981, John Africa walked out of the federal courthouse in Philadelphia a free man. He hugged his supporters who had gathered outside to congratulate him. He made no statement to the assembly of media members. He just smiled, accepted a box of fresh fruit from his MOVE family, got into a taxi and left. A photojournalist for the Associated Press snapped a few shots of John Africa as he left the courthouse. These are some of only a few extant photographs of John Africa during his time in MOVE. In one photograph, John Africa was hugging his court-appointed lawyer, grinning from ear to ear, as an exuberant Laverne Africa embraced him from behind. He was looking away from the camera, above the horizon. John Africa was a slight man, not much taller than his sister. The tip of his beard was gray. In his baggy T-shirt and blue jeans, he looked kind and grandfatherly. It was a hopeful image that told a certain kind of story: this is a man who is loved, who has won his freedom, and who is going to make a new start.[1]

But it was not the image that people most associated with John Africa. The image most frequently associated with John Africa was the kind of shot most photographers would leave on the cutting room floor. It was captured a few moments later, as John Africa got into the taxi to go home. John Africa's mouth was open, as if he were about to say something. His head was tilted down, but his eyes were shooting upward, directly into the camera. His brow was furrowed. His muscular hand, wrapped around the box of fruit, looked massive because of the forced perspective. This photograph told a very different kind of story: this is a menacing, controlling, and dangerous man who has managed, inexplicably, to outwit the federal government. And there was one detail in the photograph that held special significance for how people outside of MOVE were beginning to make sense of John Africa and his movement. It was a very bright day, and he had not slept well throughout the trial, so John was wearing large, dark sunglasses not unlike those favored by infamous cult leader Jim Jones.

By the early 1980s, increasing numbers of people both inside and outside of MOVE began thinking about the group as a cult. This marks an important turning point in the history of MOVE's classification. For a decade, people outside of MOVE simply did not think much about MOVE's claim that they were a religion. More often than not, the idea that MOVE was a religion struck many people as too outlandish to consider. It seemed obvious to many outside the group that MOVE was a "back-to-nature group," a "radical group," or an "extremist group,"—they were defined by their behavior, not their nature. There was simply too much distance between what MOVE was and what religion was imagined to be—too wide a gulf between how MOVE behaved and how religions were supposed to act.

But after John Africa's acquittal, this began to change. Increasingly, the idea that MOVE was a religion—albeit a bad religion—began to make sense. The Philadelphia Special Investigation Commission concluded that in the early 1980s, MOVE was evolving into a "violence-threatening cult." They suggested in their report to the city that something about the nature of the group changed in the years after John Africa was acquitted. Media coverage—especially national and international coverage—reflected this change in MOVE's classification as well. In a 1977 article written in response to the Guns on the Porch standoff, the *New York Times* classified MOVE as a "self-proclaimed revolutionary group." In a 1979 article about MOVE's apparent re-emergence, the paper classified MOVE as a "dissident group." But in a 1980 article announcing their conviction, the *New York Times* described the MOVE 9 as "cult members." To those outside the group, MOVE changed after 1981, and those changes transformed the group into a cult.[2]

Did MOVE "transform into a violence-threatening cult" in the early 1980s? To be sure, much about MOVE changed after John Africa's acquittal. The group grew more insular; they were less concerned with confronting the System than with freeing the MOVE 9. Fearing more arrests, MOVE people rarely left their houses if they could avoid it. Perhaps the biggest change was MOVE's relocation to Louise James's house on Osage Avenue, which was located in a far more conservative and middle-class neighborhood than MOVE was used to. Unbeknownst to people outside the group, the theology of the group changed significantly after John Africa's acquittal and return to Philadelphia. John Africa's prophetic career intensified. John had always claimed supernatural abilities, but in the 1970s, when supernatural events occurred, it was validation that MOVE was doing the work of God. John Africa was revered as something more than a prophet, but was still distinct from God. In the early 1980s, however, John Africa's followers began to revere him as coterminous with God. MOVE people began referring to John Africa as "the Coordinator." In *The Guidelines*, God is described as the force that "coordinates" Life: blowing the wind, directing the tides, and sprouting the seed. By the early 1980s, John Africa had grown so close to Life, that it made sense to MOVE people to call him God. There is no written record to suggest that John Africa referred to himself as God. Indeed, all documents likely produced by John Africa refer to God in the third person. In documents created for an external readership, MOVE people consistently referred to John Africa's supernatural abilities but did not reveal this theological shift. But internally, MOVE people began to refer to John Africa as a deity in the early 1980s. While these theological changes may have inspired people outside the group to think about MOVE as a cult, they were not widely known outside of MOVE.[3]

But while the changes MOVE underwent in the early 1980s may explain why MOVE never garnered the support it did in the mid-1970s, they do not account for why people began to classify MOVE as a "cult." The Special Investigation report concluded that in the 1980s, MOVE people "came to reject and place themselves above the laws, customs and social contracts of society." It says that MOVE people "saw themselves as the targets of persistent harassment by regulatory agencies, unjust treatment by the courts, and periodic violent attempts to be suppressed by the police." The Commission concluded that, in the early 1980s, MOVE became sure that a confrontation with the System was inevitable, and that MOVE people experienced an increase in "stridency and extremism." While much of what the Commission concluded is true, MOVE did not suddenly begin rejecting the primacy of laws in the 1980s. Nor did MOVE suddenly become strident or extreme. They viewed themselves as a persecuted people since the early 1970s. It is easy to overstate the changes MOVE underwent after John Africa's acquittal. Simply put, MOVE belief, practice, and lifestyle did not change all that much after the group moved to Osage.[4]

MOVE did not "transform" into a cult in the 1980s. What changed was the way Americans thought about religion. The years that MOVE was largely absent from public consciousness—1978 through 1981—coincided with a dramatic transformation in the way Americans thought about the category of religion. In the late 1970s, a new religious typology—a way of thinking about and categorizing religions—permeated American culture. In the 1970s, pseudoscientific theories about "cults," "brainwashing," and "deprogramming" filtered into the American consciousness. These new theories transformed the meaning of "cult" from a sociological classification and theological claim into a way of classifying certain kinds of religious groups. By the late 1970s, a cult, in the minds of many Americans, was a new religious movement that was especially prone to violence, which was headed by a charismatic leader who used manipulative techniques of "mind control" to coerce mentally fragile individuals into surrendering their free will. This new typology, fostered by a powerful anti-cult movement, including politicians, journalists, and academics, gave Americans a way to group together disparate organizations, beliefs, and movements they deemed threatening and to imagine the existence of patterns they had not noticed previously. Classifying MOVE as a cult allowed people inside and outside of the group to understand MOVE within an invented historical context of other religious groups including the Unification Church, the Worldwide Church of God, and the People's Temple. But it also allowed people to infer that the characteristics associated with other groups classified as "cults" applied to MOVE. The new cult typology allowed people to imagine that MOVE people suffered from mental illness, that MOVE was especially prone to violence, and that John Africa had brainwashed his followers. But the cult typology also gave people a way of thinking about MOVE *as a religion*.[5]

Despite his victory over federal prosecutors, John Africa's religion was in shambles. Three years had passed since the August 8th confrontation with police, and most MOVE people in the group then were now behind bars. The MOVE 9 had been convicted of murder in the third degree the previous summer, and were awaiting what they assumed would be life sentences. The nine MOVE people, including John Africa, who fled to Rochester had all been arrested. Only John Africa and Alphonso Africa managed to evade prosecution. The other seven were convicted on various crimes. The new MOVE people who had joined after the 1978 shootout, including Ramona Africa, Michael Jones Africa, Theresa Brooks Africa, and Jeanette Knighton Africa, were in and out of jail on contempt of court charges stemming from their behavior at other MOVE trials.[6]

For John Africa, the disaster of the previous three years was personal. His nephew Frank's imprisonment caused a rift between John and his sister Louise, Frank's mother. But Frank, in prison on conspiracy to riot charges, would soon be released. John's sister Laverne, one of John's earliest disciples, now wanted nothing to do with her brother. All five of her children had followed her into MOVE. Now, Chuckie and Debbie were convicted murderers awaiting sentencing. Law enforcement officials in Virginia wanted her daughter Gail Africa on charges of child abuse and for absconding with the MOVE children. Though Chuckie and Debbie knew their imprisonment was a part of John Africa's plan, and that their leader would soon have them freed, Laverne and Sharon began to question the wisdom of the Coordinator.[7]

After his acquittal, there was only one place for John Africa to turn—Louise James's house on Osage Avenue in West Philadelphia. Though it was only two miles from where the first MOVE house once stood, the Cobbs Creek neighborhood was a world away. Powelton Village, where the first MOVE house was located, was a neighborhood defined by social experimentation and a live-and-let-live attitude. It was a hotbed of New Left radicalism, a multiracial enclave consisting of college students, professors, and longtime Black residents struggling against gentrification. It was the kind of neighborhood that would, as they did in 1977, instinctively side with a group like MOVE over the police. The Cobb's Creek neighborhood where Louise lived, however, was a very different neighborhood. It was the kind of neighborhood that valued respectability. It was a neighborhood consisting of upwardly mobile African Americans, most of whom had only recently risen out of the working class and who were enjoying middle-class stability for the first time. As one observer put it, Cobbs Creek consisted of "those uppity Black people that have advanced from the ghettoes of North Philadelphia."[8]

After he settled into the Osage house, John began to rebuild his congregation. Ramona Johnson, now a fully coordinated MOVE member called Ramona Africa, moved into the Osage house. Larry Howard, who was now calling himself Kareem Howard, stayed there periodically as he adjusted to life outside of prison. Sharon and Gail, who left Philadelphia after the 1978 shootout to start the Seed of Wisdom in Richmond, made a harrowing return to Philadelphia weeks earlier. Faced with impending child endangerment charges, they smuggled the eleven children living with them onto a U-Haul truck in the middle of the night and drove 250 miles north back to Philadelphia. Sharon, Gail, and the children moved into a house on Reno Street, across town. Other MOVE people moved in with Jeanette Knighton—now Jeanette Africa—at her home on Osage Avenue, just a half a block away from the now vacant lot upon which MOVE's original house used to stand. Within a few months of John Africa's acquittal, MOVE had established three houses in Philadelphia.[9]

Life inside the Osage house, like before, was ascetic. Soon almost every room in the house was emptied. Louise James, unwilling to live MOVE's spartan lifestyle, resigned herself to her bedroom. John Africa also lived upstairs and rarely came down, especially when non-MOVE members dropped by. Kareem Howard never met John Africa face to face, but he felt (and continues to feel) John Africa's presence. One day, John Africa received word that Kareem had a lovely singing voice. Calling down from upstairs, he asked Kareem to stand at the base of the stairs and sing him a song. After he had finished singing, John relayed a message through Frank, "Tell Kareem his voice sounds like sunshine." John Africa's response to his singing stunned Kareem. "How would [he] know what sunshine sounds like?" To Kareem, John Africa's message to him was validation that John Africa was a superhuman being who was "very close to nature, extremely close."[10]

Despite the troubles facing MOVE people in prison, MOVE people went to work endearing themselves to their neighbors. In an interview with a journalist from the *Inquirer*, MOVE's neighbors on Osage Avenue reported that MOVE people were model neighbors. They washed an elderly neighbor's clothes when she became too ill to perform her chores. They helped a pregnant woman do her shopping. They were, according to one neighbor, "very, very nice." The MOVE contingent on Osage Avenue shoveled the sidewalks after snowfalls, refusing pay for their service. According to one of the neighbors, MOVE got along with everyone on Osage for at least two years.[11]

But not everyone was happy about MOVE's new environs. Louise James, John Africa's sister and Frank Africa's mother, did not appreciate MOVE living in her house. For years, Louise went by Louise Africa, just like any other MOVE person. But she made it clear to her brother when MOVE began that she had no interest in living the MOVE lifestyle. She had no interest in asceticism and resented sharing a home with animals. She had no intention of getting beaten by the police or in getting arrested. Her contributions to MOVE were the money she made through her job at the telephone company and her talent as a writer. In 1974, Louise began publishing a column titled "On the MOVE" in the *Philadelphia Tribune*. In the column, she kept the public up to date on MOVE's public engagements, their frequent run-ins with law enforcement, and the ways the Teachings of John Africa could improve the lives Philadelphia's Black community. She stopped writing in August 1976, after Frank was arrested for contempt of court.[12]

For the next five years, Louise maintained a comfortable distance from MOVE. She believed in the Teachings of John Africa as her source of religious inspiration, but Louise's relationship with MOVE and with her brother, John Africa—which had always been complicated—began to deteriorate after the group set up its new headquarters in her home. She never wavered in supporting MOVE financially, emotionally, and legally. But she felt conflicted over the very serious legal trouble her son, her nieces, and her nephews found themselves in. It was bad enough that Frank never finished high school; now he had a criminal record. Both Louise and Laverne visited their imprisoned children as often as they could. Belonging to MOVE meant going to jail. But two of Laverne's children might be going to prison for the rest of their lives. This was a different matter altogether. It was a test of faith.[13]

Lee Sing Africa also grew frustrated with MOVE. Ever since moving from the Seed of Wisdom back to Philadelphia, Lee Sing, a Jewish woman named Sharon Penn, had begun to doubt the Teachings of John Africa. Her legal troubles in Virginia had followed her to Pennsylvania. A judge in Virginia reinstated the child neglect charges, and warrants were issued for both Lee Sing and Fox Africa for abducting the MOVE children to Philadelphia. After moving into the Osage house, Lee Sing was once again subject to MOVE's rigid discipline. She began to worry that her two children, who were three and seven at the time, would be socially crippled because of their lack of formal education. And she didn't want them to have to grow up in such an ascetic lifestyle. In the middle of the night in April 1981, Lee Sing woke up her children, buckled them into Louise's car, and left MOVE.[14]

After leaving the group, Sharon Penn (formerly Lee Sing Africa) viewed her experience in MOVE through the cult typology. In an interview with a reporter, Penn suggested that she was only attracted to MOVE because she was "very vulnerable" and "downright gullible." She fell in love with Donald Glassey, the father of her first child, in 1972 and joined MOVE shortly thereafter. She lived in Glassey's house, not the MOVE house in Powelton. Still, she understood John Africa as a charismatic leader with supernatural abilities. In the interview, she described John Africa as "extraordinary" and "magical." John Africa had the ability to communicate "with Life itself," and was so wise that it seemed as if "he'd lived everybody's life before." Though she believed MOVE to be a nonviolent group while she was a part of it, now that she had left the group, she could see "precursors of violence." She pointed to John Africa's teaching that technology should only be used to destroy technology. According to *The Guidelines*, "If you have to use the airplane to blow up the airplane factory then use it." While she was in MOVE, the idea that someone might actually blow up an airplane factory seemed like a harmless trope. Now, however, it seemed clear that John Africa was preaching violence. Penn ended her interview by reassuring the readers that she was no longer brainwashed, but was now "free and clear of MOVE."[15]

While some in his congregation began to stray, John Africa did his best to tend to his imprisoned flock. In a letter to Conrad Africa, who was arrested on conspiracy charges in Rochester, John acknowledged that MOVE was at a low point. Still, he encouraged Conrad to stay faithful. MOVE people were not actually imprisoned, according to John Africa, because MOVE people "don't believe in prisons just like we don't believe in Christianity." Those outside of MOVE, those who were beholden to the System, were the ones who were truly in prison. John believed that the incarceration of so many MOVE people provided them an opportunity to point out the hypocrisy in the American judicial system. He reminded Conrad that this was all part of a larger strategy. MOVE people believed that convicting all nine MOVE people accused of killing Officer Ramp was against the law. In their minds, it was impossible for nine people to be responsible for the murder of one police officer unless all nine people pulled the trigger together. MOVE people knew that Judge Malmed would convict. That is why they declined a jury trial. But John Africa hoped that the conviction of nine people for the murder of one person would be so obviously contradictory to the law that the conviction of the MOVE 9 would draw further attention to the hypocrisy of the System.[16]

John Africa also hoped that the incarceration of so many MOVE people would lead to more converts. He urged Conrad to explain MOVE beliefs to anyone who was interested and to relish the opportunity to debate fellow prisoners, writing "we of MOVE is [sic] secure that our religion is right, and because we know that our religion is right, we welcome anybody to prove our religion wrong." Converting people to MOVE, John argued, was not a complicated endeavor. The Truth of John Africa was self-evident. John told Conrad that MOVE people "don't have to hide our religion behind the excuse of blind faith, when asked to explain our religion all MOVE asks is that you listen to our explanation." But for most of the forty-five-page letter, John Africa wrote as a minister to his imprisoned followers. He encouraged Conrad and the other incarcerated MOVE people to take comfort knowing that they were "doing the work of God." But he warned Conrad of what lie ahead for MOVE people. "The things you will have to face," John Africa prophesied, "will bring horror to your very soul."[17]

The horror John Africa prophesied came to pass on December 2, 1981. Merle, Janine, Gail, Debbie, Janet, and Sue Africa, who were incarcerated at Muncy Prison, crowded into a cell there and refused to come out. When prison guards went in to remove them, a fight broke out, and the MOVE women took the brunt of it. The MOVE men housed at Holmesburg heard a local radio station report that MOVE women had been beaten by the prison guards. According to prison officials, one of those MOVE men grabbed a guard's keys and retreated into a cell. Inside the cell, all seven MOVE men at Holmesburg—Delbert, Chuckie, Mike, Phil, Eddie, Dennis, and Carlos Africa—and three MOVE supporters waited for the prison guards to attack.[18]

One of those MOVE supporters was Larry Howard. In the early 1970s, Howard joined the Black Unity Council, an offshoot of the Black Panther Party. He considered himself a revolutionary. In 1972, he was convicted of attempted murder after shooting a police officer while trying to break Russell Shoats, the founder of the Black Unity Council, out of Holmesburg Prison. While in prison on those charges in 1975, he saw a news documentary on MOVE. In the documentary, MOVE people explained why they objected to zoos and dug up the sidewalk in front of their home. Their beliefs made sense to Howard, and MOVE's unafraid defiance held a certain allure for him.[19]

He watched in awe the news broadcasts of May 1977 and saw MOVE people—men and women—dressed in military fatigues and armed with rifles, facing down Rizzo's police force. Attracted to MOVE's "revolutionary fervor," Howard began corresponding with MOVE people from prison. From his cell in solitary confinement, Howard watched the live television coverage of the city's starvation blockade and the eventual shootout in 1978. After 1978, Howard was transferred to Holmesburg where the men of the MOVE 9 awaited trial, where he learned more about MOVE under the tutelage of Phil Africa. Howard grew to trust MOVE, but as he sheltered in the cell waiting for an impending melee with prison guards, he admitted that he could not see the wisdom in their plan. "I was scared to death, because I saw no end."[20]

Hours after the MOVE men locked themselves in the cell, the prison went on lockdown, and the guards donned their riot gear. They used a firehose to flood the cell with water. It was difficult to walk around in the 11' x 17' cell, especially as the water began to rise. Because the cell door was so narrow, only one prison guard at a time could enter the cell. As they entered, the MOVE men attacked. Prison officials say that the MOVE men were armed with sharpened sticks, mop handles, and bricks and that they were using mattresses as shields, though it is unclear how they would have gotten their hands on such dangerous objects. Larry Howard claims that a prison guard stabbed him in the back with an icepick and that the other guards were carrying baseball bats. It also seems unlikely that the prison guards were armed with these objects. What we know for sure is that all ten MOVE men were sent to the hospital with injuries ranging from broken limbs to lacerations.

Some of their injuries required extensive hospital stays. Seventeen guards were sent to the hospital for what prison officials described as "minor injuries." They were all discharged the same day.[21]

To people outside of MOVE, the prison skirmishes confirmed a sneaking suspicion: even prison could not cure MOVE people from their delusional devotion to John Africa. Media coverage from this time evinces a growing fascination with John Africa's purported supernatural abilities. On August 31, 1981, Judge James McDermott, the same judge who had Sue Africa committed to Byberry Mental Hospital four years earlier, sentenced Sue to a minimum of six years in prison for riot and assault. At her sentencing Sue Africa spoke at length about her devotion to John Africa, his miraculous abilities, and the strength she drew from her religion. Rarely were MOVE people allowed such time to discuss their beliefs. But, for Sue, being one of MOVE's few white members carried certain privileges. She told the judge that John Africa had cured her of her headaches and her colitis, and had healed her addition to drugs and cigarettes. Before MOVE, Sue "didn't know the meaning of love, of family, of home." The media, always fascinated with Sue, was growing more interested in MOVE's religious claims.[22]

Media coverage of the sentencing of the MOVE 9 evinced the same fascination with MOVE's religious beliefs. It was fitting that, after the longest and most expensive trial in the history of the state, sentencing the MOVE 9 was an exhausting experience. One by one, the MOVE 9 were led into the courtroom, where Judge Malmed delivered his sentence: one hundred years in prison, eligible for parole after thirty. After almost a decade of media coverage of MOVE's sensational courtroom appearances, the MOVE trial report had become something of a genre in Philadelphia newspapers. Reporters always enjoyed reporting on MOVE's profanity, their poor hygiene, and haggard appearance. But the media coverage of the sentencing of the MOVE 9 was quite different. The MOVE 9 almost seemed joyful that they were being sentenced. (And indeed they were, because they believed that their incarceration was a turning point in John Africa's religious revolution). As usual, MOVE people threatened Judge Malmed during sentencing. But to the reporters covering the sentencing, these threats seemed more pointed, more eerie, and more supernatural. More like prophecies than harangues. One of the MOVE 9 warned Judge Malmed that John Africa was going to "make your heart jump right out of your chest." Another cautioned the judge that "John Africa is God, and you are fighting God." The news media, both local and national, had always classified MOVE in secular terms. But that classification made little sense against MOVE's increasingly religious public pronouncements. It seemed that MOVE had become a "radical religious cult."[23]

The idea that MOVE was a cult gained further credence in the minds of people outside the group when a bit player in MOVE's history found himself the most famous death-row inmate in the world. Mumia Abu-Jamal, the former president of the Association of Black Journalists who had forced Philadelphia's white media establishment to pay attention to MOVE's hunger strikes in prison just two months before, was driving a taxi cab the night of December 9, 1981, when he came upon his brother, William Cook, in a physical altercation with Philadelphia police officer Daniel Faulkner. What happened next is disputed. According to prosecutors, Abu-Jamal grabbed a gun he had stowed beneath his seat, got out of his taxi, and rushed Officer Faulkner. He shot Daniel Faulkner once in the back, and while Faulkner lay wounded, Abu-Jamal stood over him and fired a single shot into his head. When police backup arrived on the scene, they found Abu-Jamal wounded from a single gunshot wound to the chest. Police officers transported Abu-Jamal to the hospital. By the time he arrived at the emergency room, he had been severely beaten in the head, face, and neck. Officer Daniel Faulkner was dead at the scene. When the *New York Times* reported on the shooting, they described Abu-Jamal as a "close supporter" of the "radical group called MOVE."[24]

Abu-Jamal's involvement with MOVE months earlier had left him deeply impressed. After working to bring attention to MOVE's prison hunger strikes, he turned his attention to the John Africa trial. He attended every session and published news accounts of the proceedings. When John Africa won his acquittal, Abu-Jamal was shocked. By the time of his arrest, Abu-Jamal was a MOVE supporter—someone who understood and accepted the Teachings of John Africa, but who did not do so exclusively. Many MOVE supporters came into MOVE from other religious traditions. Eddie Africa was in the Nation of Islam before converting to MOVE. Sharon Penn was Jewish. Several MOVE people came to MOVE from Christianity. For them, joining MOVE was a conversion. They no longer belonged to the faiths they used to have and now followed the Teachings of John Africa as their sole religious guidance. Believing the Teachings of John Africa exclusively was what it meant to be a MOVE member. John Africa welcomed those who could not fully convert to his teachings, but not as MOVE members. Those MOVE people, like Abu-Jamal, Larry Howard, and many others, who could not convert fully to MOVE were welcomed into the MOVE family as "MOVE supporters."[25]

Mumia Abu-Jamal was a Rastafarian, and he understood MOVE as analogous to Rastafari beliefs. When MOVE people referred to the System, he recognized the Rastafari concept of Babylon. John Africa's teaching on food was familiar to Abu-Jamal as well. But there were other aspects of MOVE belief to which Abu-Jamal did not subscribe. For example, Abu-Jamal was an advocate of marijuana—something John Africa strictly forbade for his followers. Abu-Jamal's relationship to MOVE was one of syncretism. He even received validation for his syncretism when he once interviewed Bob Marley. After Abu-Jamal explained MOVE belief to him, Bob Marley exclaimed, "MOVE *is* Rasta!" He understood the Teachings of John Africa within a long tradition of Black liberation. To Abu-Jamal, John Africa was in the same lineage as Edward Blyden, Marcus Garvey, Martin Luther King Jr., and Malcolm X—visionary and prophetic. To MOVE members, John Africa was one of a kind.[26]

Six days after his arrest, the court appointed attorney Anthony Jackson to represent Mumia Abu-Jamal. Unhappy with Jackson's representation during pre-trial hearings, Abu-Jamal requested and received permission to represent himself in court. The judge presiding over pre-trial hearings agreed under the condition that Jackson stayed on as backup counsel. Both Abu-Jamal and Jackson protested this decision. Jackson wanted nothing to do with the case. He testified that he was "unprepared" to handle the case and that he "abandoned all efforts at trial preparation" before the trial began. The court did not supply Mumia or his defense team enough funds to hire investigators, pathologists, ballistics experts, or a second attorney (which was typical in murder cases). Thus, Mumia and Jackson had no way of challenging the testimony of the over one hundred prosecution witnesses.[27]

The trial began on June 7, 1982, under Judge Albert Sabo. Prior to becoming a judge, Sabo had been second in command of the Philadelphia County Sheriff's Office. He was a member or former member of almost every law enforcement association in the region. He presided over more death penalty cases than any other judge in the United States, sentencing thirty-one defendants to death. All but two of those he condemned were racial minorities. Sabo was not well respected in Philadelphia's legal community. A 1983 poll of the Philadelphia Bar association found that over one-third of lawyers thought Sabo was unqualified to be a judge. During jury selection, the prosecution used eleven of its fifteen peremptory strikes against African Americans in the jury selection pool. As a result, only two African Americans served on the sixteen-person jury pool, far below what would have been proportional representation, considering that 40 percent of Philadelphians were Black. One of those Black jurors was dismissed during the trial and was replaced by an alternate juror who admitted during jury selection that he did not "think he could be fair to both sides." Abu-Jamal's defense lawyer requested that this juror be removed for cause, but Judge Sabo denied the request. On the third day of jury selection, Sabo reversed his decision to allow Abu-Jamal to represent himself and installed Jackson as the lead defense attorney at the request of the prosecution. Jackson protested the decision and requested that he be removed from the case, telling Sabo that he was not prepared to defend Abu-Jamal. Sabo rejected Jackson's request and threatened him with jail time if he would not represent his client.[28]

The prosecution's case rested on the testimony of witnesses of questionable credibility. The prosecution produced two witnesses, a hospital security guard and a police officer, who testified to hearing Abu-Jamal shout, "I shot the motherfucker, and I hope the motherfucker dies," while in the hospital the night of the shooting. Both witnesses did not report hearing Abu-Jamal's confession until two months after the night of the shooting—and only after being interviewed by Internal Affairs officers. The doctors who treated Abu-Jamal reported that he was drifting in and out of consciousness and made no comments while in the hospital. Several other police officers on duty guarding Abu-Jamal in the hospital also made no mention of any comments, let alone a confession. When Jackson tried to locate one of these officers, the officer was on vacation, despite orders to be available to testify. Judge Sabo rejected Jackson's request to delay the trial until this witness could be located, telling Abu-Jamal, "your attorney and you goofed."[29]

The prosecution also called three eyewitnesses who testified that they saw Abu-Jamal shoot Faulkner once in the back and once in the head. The first witness, Cynthia White, was a sex worker who testified that she was working the area the night of the shooting. Her testimony changed slightly from initial interview to trial, but she corroborated the prosecution's understanding of the events. However, it seems as if White benefited from her testimony. At the time of the trial, she was awaiting arraignment on three separate charges for prostitution. She was never prosecuted as a result of those arrests. The defense countered White's testimony with an eyewitness named Veronica Jones. She testified that she was also working the area the night of the shooting. Jones testified that she saw two unidentified men running away from the scene of Officer Faulkner's shooting. She also testified that police officers asked her to corroborate White's testimony. If Jones identified Abu-Jamal as the shooter, the police would allow her to "work the area" without arrest. Unfortunately for the defense, Judge Sabo ordered the jury to leave the courtroom before Jones delivered her testimony. He then ruled Jones's testimony inadmissible.[30]

The star witness for the prosecution convinced the jury of Abu-Jamal's guilt because he linked him with MOVE. The night of the shooting, Robert Chobert testified that he was writing on his logbook in his taxi, which was parked behind Faulkner's police cruiser. He heard gunshots and looked up to see "a Black MOVE member" shoot Faulkner and then run away. Prosecutors asked Chobert how he knew the perpetrator was a MOVE member, and he responded that the shooter had dreadlocks. Judge Shabo refused to allow Jackson to introduce evidence about Chobert's checkered past, including convictions for driving under the influence and setting fire to a school. Jackson was also forbidden from informing the jury that Chobert's driver's license was suspended the night of the shooting.[31]

But what bothered Mumia Abu-Jamal the most about his trial was that Judge Sabo barred John Africa from the defense table. At the beginning of the trial, Abu-Jamal attempted to have John Africa serve as his attorney. This was not allowed under Pennsylvania law because John Africa was not a licensed attorney and had not passed the Pennsylvania bar exam. Sabo even went to the Supreme Court of Pennsylvania to receive confirmation that John Africa could not serve as Abu-Jamal's attorney. Abu-Jamal then requested that John Africa be present at his defense table. In this arrangement, Abu-Jamal would serve as his own attorney and John Africa would assist in an unofficial capacity.[32]

Abu-Jamal's request to have John Africa serve as an advisor was permissible under Pennsylvania law and was not an uncommon tactic in murder cases. Judge Sabo, however, denied the request, continuing to cite the prior Pennsylvania Supreme Court ruling. Abu-Jamal, assured that Sabo's ruling on this would be of interest to the appellate court, took every opportunity to remind the court that he was being poorly represented by Jackson and that he was being denied the right to have John Africa at his defense table. Reporters covering the case understood Abu-Jamal's repeated references to John Africa as evidence that brainwashed Abu-Jamal was evoking the spirit of his cult leader against his enemies. One writer mistook Abu-Jamal's repeated reminders that he was denied John Africa's counsel to be "attempts to worship God in the spirit of John Africa, and to have the spirit of John Africa aid in his defense." To the journalist, Abu-Jamal invoking the name of John Africa cast an "eerie atmosphere" over the courtroom.[33]

To people outside of MOVE, Mumia Abu-Jamal was a victim of the MOVE cult. An editorial in the *Philadelphia Tribune* shows how the Mumia trial allowed MOVE's critics to understand the group using the cult typology. Abu-Jamal was once a "top notch minority reporter and commentator" whose "calm, even, [and] soft voice," made him an effective community leader on issues of racial and social justice. Tragically, and "ominously," Abu-Jamal's passion for social justice led him to MOVE, and "his defense of MOVE's civil rights and his claims that they're helpless victims of religious and racial persecution gradually switched to defending MOVE's religious claims." The article, written by a white Quaker activist named Richard Kanegis, gives the impression that Abu-Jamal got too close to MOVE, and that he became brainwashed as a result. Mumia Abu-Jamel was "destroyed by the MOVE cult and in his place stands Mumia Africa," and "unless Jamal's mother hires a good deprogrammer," Mumia was going to die as a sacrifice to John Africa.[34]

Mumia Abu-Jamal was not the only person thought to be "brainwashed" by John Africa's charismatic leadership. Kanegis's article also mentions Jeanette Knighton, who, like Abu-Jamal, tragically succumbed to MOVE's dangerous allure. She was now Jeanette Africa, a "foul-mouthed religious fanatic." The writer believed John Africa was using Jeanette Knighton and Mumia Abu-Jamal for his own insidious plan, and, worse, that MOVE had claimed its two new victims from among the best and the brightest of Philadelphia's Black community. Though both Abu-Jamal and Knighton sincerely believed that Abu-Jamal was framed, in reality, "the MOVE cult is setting themselves up on a lot of phony charges, seeking to serve them in prison where they can better recruit for God." This was all a part of John Africa's plan, the writer alleged. Once behind bars, Mumia Abu-Jamal and the other incarcerated MOVE people could "appear to be helpless victims of persecution and thus prove that civilization is evil."[35]

Kanegis's op-ed after Mumia Abu-Jamal's conviction is significant because it makes full use of the cult typology to make sense of MOVE. Interestingly, the author had no qualms about recognizing the religious character of the group. He noted that the MOVE people in jail "expound on the glories of John Africa and of God Almighty when they're not being beaten by the guards or serving in solitary confinement." It seemed clear to the writer that

MOVE shared many characteristics with groups like the Unification Church and The Way International—groups that had emerged, the writer argued, because President Ronald Reagan's cuts to social programs made people "susceptible to cult influences." The author also felt the need to qualify his stance on MOVE. His willingness to recognize MOVE as a religion—as a cult—should not be taken as an endorsement of the havoc "that the new religious cults" were wreaking throughout America.[36]

A week after the op-ed was published, Jeanette Africa and a small group of MOVE members and supporters arrived at the offices of the *Tribune* looking for a fight. When Richard Kanegis emerged from the building, a group of MOVE people were waiting to argue with him about the op-ed. MOVE people began to push Kanegis, and the argument escalated into a brawl. Abu-Jamal also took issue with Kanegis's piece. In a response published in the *Tribune*, Abu-Jamal argued that it was inappropriate for Kanegis, a white man, to position himself as an authority on the issues facing African Americans. He also questioned why Kanegis, who had only sat in on one day of deliberation, wrote as if he had witnessed much of the trial. But interestingly, Abu-Jamal made no attempt to counter Kanegis's representation of MOVE as a cult. Rather, Abu-Jamal reminded the Quaker activist that he too belonged to a religious group that was once persecuted for unorthodox religious beliefs. Indeed, Abu-Jamal argued, anyone who claims to be a Christian belongs to a group that was once considered a radical cult.[37]

Around the time of Abu-Jamal's conviction, MOVE began to attract the attention of the anti-cult movement. One local anti-cult group, the Personal Freedom Association, began writing letters to the mayor, warning him of the dangers of MOVE. The Personal Freedom Association consisted of about one hundred members, most of whom had children or other relatives who had joined cults. They met monthly at Trinity Church in a suburb of Philadelphia. The group sometimes hired deprogrammers to abscond with their children and attempt to return them to more traditional religious beliefs. They also stayed abreast of the most recent anti-cult literature. They recommended that the mayor read Flo Conway and Jim Siegelman's *Snapping: America's Epidemic of Sudden Personality Change* as well as Ted Patrick's *Let Our Children Go!*—two wildly popular anti-cult books.[38] (Ted Patrick was notorious for kidnapping people whose parents objected to their religious or political opinions—a career he called "deprogramming.") To the Personal Freedom Association, letting MOVE exist was courting danger. MOVE could lead to a "Jonestown-type incident."[39]

The growing tendency to characterize MOVE as a cult was not lost on those within the group. Despite John Africa's prophecy that MOVE people would be released from prison, more MOVE people were being sent to prison all the time. In December 1982, Carlos Africa, who was arrested along with John Africa in Rochester, was sentenced to between six and twelve years in prison on the same charges for which John Africa was acquitted. Alberta Africa, John Africa's wife, received a sentence of twenty-two months to seven years. Dennis Africa, Laverne's son and John Africa's nephew, received a sentence of thirty-eight months to twelve years. Desperate and in need of a new strategy, John Africa turned to a tactic dreamt up in the imaginations of the ATF.[40]

John Africa used the cult typology—especially the association with violence—to MOVE's advantage. As they built their conspiracy case against John Africa, federal law enforcement agents revived a theory proffered by the FBI years earlier: the existence of a massive underground network of MOVE supporters who would commit acts of terrorism at John Africa's command. John Africa realized that by insinuating that this underground was real, he could play into the ATF's paranoia to free his incarcerated followers. On November 10, 1982, ten judges received threatening letters from a group that called itself M-1, the "MOVE Underground." Some of the letters were delivered to the judges' offices. Others were delivered to the judges' homes. All of the letters were hand-delivered. John Africa also directed several of his followers to inform federal law enforcement officials of the threat posed by M-1. On January 25, 1983, Jerry, Frank, Ramona, Conrad, and Mo Africa met with Agent Wasyluk, another agent from the ATF, and an agent from the United States Marshall Service at the ATF field office in Philadelphia. Officers from Philadelphia's Civil Affairs Unit listened in on a secret recording device. Over the course of three hours, Jerry and the other MOVE people explained that M-1 was only loosely affiliated with MOVE. MOVE people were nonviolent but M-1 was not. M-1 was prepared to commit acts of violence, which could be averted, Jerry said, if the governor of Pennsylvania agreed to meet with MOVE, if the MOVE 9 were freed, and if the ATF delivered a letter from MOVE to President Reagan.[41]

The next morning, agents from the ATF, the Pennsylvania State Police, and the Civil Affairs Unit (CAU) met again at the ATF field office to devise a response to the threat posed by M-1. While the meeting was underway, Jerry Africa called Agent Wasyluk with a second set of demands. This time, he told Wasyluk that M-1 would be appeased if all of the male MOVE prisoners were transferred to the state prison in Dallas, Pennsylvania, if all female MOVE prisoners were transferred to the state prison in Muncy, and if all of them were housed with the general population. Jerry Africa still insisted that a letter be delivered to the president, but informed Agent Wasyluk that it had not yet been written. Shortly after the conversation, Dick Thornburgh, the governor of Pennsylvania, received his own threatening letter from M-1, demanding the release of the MOVE 9 and the end to the religious persecution of MOVE. The agents from the ATF, CAU, and the state police decided to inform more federal agencies of the M-1 threat. By January 27, agents from the Secret Service and the FBI had been dispatched to Philadelphia to coordinate with the ATF, CAU, and the State Police on how best to respond to M-1.[42]

While MOVE people frequently boasted about a MOVE underground, there was no cabal of MOVE foot soldiers living undercover across global capitals as MOVE claimed. M-1 was a defensive strategy meant to give MOVE leverage in their attempt to free the MOVE 9. And it worked. By January 1983, the CAU and the Major Investigations Squad of the Philadelphia Police Department, the ATF, the FBI, the Secret Service, the US Marshals Service, and the Pennsylvania State Police were all investigating MOVE. But the M-1 strategy was also an example of John Africa's increasing desperation. His prophecies were not coming true. There was no sign that the MOVE 9 would be released any time soon, especially after Judge Malmed denied a retrial of the case. Their legal options exhausted, John Africa realized that the only hope for the release of the MOVE 9 was a miracle. (MOVE people have assured me that a "MOVE underground" indeed exists, but they prefer not to discuss the MOVE underground or its activities.)

MOVE people took out their growing frustrations on their lapsed members. Ishongo Africa had not seen another MOVE member since he escaped the starvation blockade in 1978, but he was still identifying as Ishongo Africa, which was not his legal name. On April 16, 1983, Frank and Conrad Africa found Ishongo selling fruit from a roadside stand just a few blocks from the Osage house. They confronted Ishongo for his lack of faith, and the confrontation soon esclatated to violence. As Frank and Conrad punched and kicked Ishongo, leaving his face bloody and bruised, they bemoaned that he "no longer lived by the God line" and had "back-slided." To MOVE people, Ishongo had become "stagnated and was violating" the Law of Life. Agents from the ATF interviewed Ishongo three days later. They were hoping he might serve as an informant for federal law enforcement. Ishongo told them that, while John Africa was no longer "first" in his life, he had no interest in serving as an informant or filing a criminal complaint against Frank and Conrad.[43]

Louise James also took the brunt of John Africa's growing frustration. In October 1983, Louise checked the mail and found a letter addressed to her from Sue Africa, who was incarcerated at Muncy Prison. Louise knew what was in this letter before she opened it. The MOVE women at Muncy learned about Louise's growing defiance, and Sue had written to berate Louise back into the fold. Louise tried to stuff the letter in her pocket, but Frank saw her. He took the letter from Louise and gave it to John Africa. John Africa gathered everyone in the living room and asked Louise to read Sue's letter out loud. After reading a few paragraphs, in which Sue hurled obscenities at Louise and cursed her disloyalty, Louise decided she'd had enough. She told John Africa she was done reading the letter. John Africa ordered Frank to attack Louise. Frank beat his mother until she vomited. Then, Frank grabbed a pillow and began to smother Louise. As she suffocated, Frank asked John Africa if he wanted Louise killed. The Coordinator responded, "Not at this time." A few days later, Louise received permission from John Africa to spend a week in Atlantic City. She packed a few clothes in some garbage bags and left MOVE.[44]

By December 1983, it was clear to John Africa that the threat of M-1 alone was not enough to free the MOVE 9. So, he devised a new plan. Like MOVE had done in 1977, they would instigate another armed standoff with police. He began his confrontation on Christmas morning, 1983. At dawn, MOVE people turned on a loudspeaker for the first time at the Osage house. MOVE people warned that any police officers who attempt to enter the house to serve warrants would be shot. MOVE people took turns on the loudspeaker, threatening their neighbors, the president, the mayor, judges, and the police. But their plan did not work this time. Remarkably, there were no outstanding warrants against MOVE, and the Philadelphia Police Department knew better than to be drawn into another blockade situation. Weeks passed and John Africa's confrontation never came to fruition.[45]

The imprisoned MOVE people, however, were under the impression that John Africa's confrontation was well underway. In January 1984, several imprisoned MOVE people wrote letters to their respective prison officials gloating about the ongoing armed confrontation between MOVE and the city of Philadelphia. And they were still confident that the confrontation would result in their release. Delbert Africa boasted that "John Africa has told you people that he gon' bring his family home and it will be done . . . 'cause you've seen the power of John Africa exhibited before." Carlos Africa warned that MOVE prisoners would participate in the confrontation as well. In the letters, the MOVE prisoners complained that the media had instituted a blackout in order to prevent support for John Africa's religious revolution. But the "armed confrontation" was not in the news because it didn't exist. While behind the scenes, federal, state, and local law enforcement officials took MOVE's M-1 threat very seriously, MOVE people haranguing their neighbors on the loudspeaker had elicited little reaction.[46]

Though law enforcement officials largely ignored MOVE's loudspeaker confrontation, MOVE's neighbors did not have that luxury. As was the case in Powelton, the neighbors' initial complaints were relatively minor. In September 1983, some of MOVE's neighbors on Osage Avenue complained to the police about a fence MOVE constructed behind their house which blocked neighbors' access to the shared rear alley. They complained that a large sack of bird food left outside attracted rats. John Africa tried to initiate a final confrontation between MOVE and the System, but succeeded only in irritating his neighbors.[47]

By 1984, people outside of MOVE and people who had left MOVE were convinced that the group was a cult. On the afternoon of February 20, 1984, Louise James, her sister Laverne Sims, and Laverne's daughter Sharon Sims met with Officer Delores Thompson in a hotel room downtown. Unbeknownst to Louise, Laverne, and Sharon, four other police officers from CAU and from the Organized Crime Unit listened in from the adjacent room. The three women told officer Thompson that they had left MOVE. Though they still believed in the Teachings of John Africa, the group had changed since John Africa moved into Louise's house on Osage. The Coordinator had become more controlling. Sharon told Officer Thompson that her sister Gail Sims left the group after John Africa tried to arrange a marriage between her and Jerry Africa. Gail refused and complained to her mother, Laverne. Laverne called John Africa and the two argued over his insistence that Gail marry Jerry. John Africa was enraged that his sister would defy his wishes. The Leaphart family was supposed to be the most loyal of all. After the phone call, John Africa ordered Frank to go to his aunt's room and assault her as other MOVE people watched.[48]

Of Laverne's five children, three (Dennis, Debbie, and Chuckie) were in prison and two (Gail and Sharon) had left the group. Laverne had a stack of letters from her children, from other MOVE people in prison, and from MOVE supporters which were filled with hateful and threatening rhetoric.

MOVE people also harassed Laverne through the phone. The phone calls came at all hours of the day and night—as many as sixty per twenty-four hours. Collect calls from her children in prison were very expensive, and the conversations were hurtful. She eventually disconnected her phone. To MOVE people, Louise, Laverne, Gail, and Sharon had fallen back into the System. They believed the lie. They were both traitors and victims. But these former MOVE members were left deeply hurt by the abuse they suffered at the hands of their family and their former religion.[49]

After she left the group, Louise James continued to pay the bills at the Osage house. She even bought MOVE a van. And when that van accumulated parking tickets, she paid those too. Louise told Officer Thompson that she continued to support MOVE because she was concerned about her son. Her friends in the neighborhood reported that he looked sickly. She believed Frank had been "brainwashed." He could not leave the house without John Africa's permission. When Frank did go to the grocery store, he had to stop at every pay phone along the way and check in with the Coordinator. To MOVE people, this was a necessary response to the frequent arrest of MOVE people. But to Louise, it was evidence that John Africa had become a tyrannical cult leader and was "legally insane." MOVE, she believed, had become a cult.[50]

There is, to be clear, no such thing as a cult. The category "cult," like a number of other religious categories (fundamentalism, sect, superstition), does not reflect an empirical reality. There are no charges that can be leveled at "cults" that cannot also be leveled at things we call "religions." The category "cult" is what Robert Orsi calls a "nomenclature of containment"—it is an implicit argument about what the observer imagines "true religion" to be. It is a way of policing the boundaries of the category of religion, of deciding which beliefs and practices are legitimate and which are not. We call groups "cults" if they seem to be too controlling—as if real religions are defined by individual autonomy and free agency. We call groups "cults" if they strike us as especially dangerous—as if real religions do not engage in violent or threatening behavior. We call groups "cults" if their teachings seem outlandish—as if real religions are true. The cult typology served an important social function for Americans in the late 1970s and early 1980s. It allowed Americans to believe that their own religious beliefs were fundamentally rational, while the beliefs of those who joined the new religions were irrational. It allowed Americans to imagine that their own religious beliefs had nothing at all to do with their emotional fragility. And it allowed them to believe that their own religions were incapable of violence.[51]

Contrary to the findings of the MOVE Commission, MOVE did not "evolve into a violence-threatening cult" after John Africa's acquittal. John Africa did not suddenly become a "charismatic leader" who "brainwashed" his followers. But people inside and outside the group did begin to classify MOVE as a cult during these years. MOVE's critics, supporters, and members, newly educated about the dangers of cults, mind control, brainwashing, programming, and religious violence, increasingly used this new typology to make sense of the group. This allowed them to imagine that MOVE was more sinister than they were before, that MOVE people were mentally ill, and that John Africa brainwashed his followers with his supernatural abilities. The allure of the cult typology was powerful, even to those within the group. MOVE people used the cult typology in an attempt to gain leverage over the System. People who left MOVE used the cult typology to make sense of their experience in the group. But most importantly, understanding MOVE as a cult allowed Americans to protect what they imagined true religion to be.[52]

Notes

1. The photo I have described ran on page two of the *Philadelphia Inquirer* and was taken by William F. Steinmetz. See Dick Cooper, "MOVE Leader Cleared," *Philadelphia Inquirer*, July 23, 1981, 2.
2. James F. Clarity, "Armed Group Defies Police in Philadelphia," *New York Times*, June 16, 1977; "'Move' Group Emerges Again in Philadelphia," *New York Times*, February 20, 1979; "Murder Trial Nearing for MOVE Cultists," *Atlanta Daily World*, December 13, 1979; Ben A. Franklin, "9 Cult Members Found Guilty in Death of a Policeman: 100-Year Sentences Possible, Judge Difficult to Hear," *New York Times*, May 9, 1980; "Cultists Guilty in Police Killing," *Globe and Mail*, May 9, 1980.
3. The latest extant document authored by John Africa seem to be letters he wrote to the MOVE 9, shortly after their conviction, but before their sentencing. The letters John Africa sent to the MOVE 9 are undated. However, the letters mention that Jimmy Carter is president of the United States and anticipate an upcoming Reagan administration. Therefore, the letters were most likely composed in November or December 1980; John Africa to Conrad Africa, Box 5, Folder "MOVE Writings," Philadelphia Special Investigation (MOVE) Commission Records, Urban Archives, Temple University, Philadelphia, PA.
4. Philadelphia Special Investigation Commission, "The Findings, Conclusions, and Recommendations of the Philadelphia Special Investigation Commission," March 6, 1986, Box 2, PSIC; "'Move' Group Emerges Again in Philadelphia," *New York Times*, February 20, 1979.

5. David G. Bromley and Anson D. Shupe, *Strange Gods: The Great American Cult Scare* (Boston: Beacon Press, 1981); J. Gordon Melton and Robert L. Moore, *The Cult Experience: Responding to the New Religious Pluralism* (New York: Pilgrim Press, 1982); Lowell D. Streiker, *Mind-Bending: Brainwashing, Cults, and Deprogramming in the '80s* (Garden City, NY: Doubleday, 1984); Sean McCloud, *Making the American Religious Fringe: Exotics, Subversives, and Journalists, 1955–1993* (Chapel Hill: University of North Carolina Press, 2004).
6. "Four in MOVE Curse Judge, Are Ousted," *Baltimore Afro-American*, January 26, 1980; "3 in Move Group Convicted," *New York Times*, December 24, 1981; Kendall Wilson, "MOVE Fought Stacked Deck, Say Backers," *Philadelphia Tribune*, December 25, 1981.
7. Laverne Sims to William H. Brown III, November 9, 1985, Box 7, Folder 20-1, Philadelphia Special Investigation (MOVE) Commission Records, Urban Archives, Temple University, Philadelphia, PA; Sharon Sims, "My Life in MOVE," *Philadelphia Magazine*, September 1985.
8. American Friends Service Committee, "Voices from the Community: Everyday Thinking People Share Their Views on the Philadelphia-MOVE Confrontation and Reflect on Its Meaning for Their Communities," Box 26, Folder 4, Father Paul Washington Papers, Charles L. Blockson Afro-American Collection, Temple University, Philadelphia, PA.
9. Mike Africa Jr., transcript of an oral history conducted in 2016 by Richard Kent Evans, MOVE Oral History Project, Special Collections and Urban Archives, Temple University, Philadelphia, PA.
10. Kareem Howard, transcript of an oral history conducted in 2016 by Richard Kent Evans, MOVE Oral History Project, Special Collections and Urban Archives, Temple University, Philadelphia, PA.
11. Jan Pogue, "MOVE Comes Back to Pearl Street," *Philadelphia Inquirer*, August 6, 1981.
12. Louise Leaphart James was forthcoming about her tension with MOVE before the MOVE Bombing. See Testimony of Cassandra Carter before the Philadelphia Special Investigation (MOVE) Commission, Box 7, PSIC; Civil Affairs Unit, Investigation Report, Box 51, Folder 3, PSIC; Testimony of Louise James before the Philadelphia Special Investigation (MOVE) Commission, Box 7, PSIC. Since, she has been reluctant to speak about her relationship to MOVE during these years. See Louise Leaphart James, *John Africa . . . Childhood Untold until Today* (self-published, 2014), 141–143.
13. Civil Affairs Unit, Investigation Report, Box 51, Folder 3, PSIC; Testimony of Louise James before the Philadelphia Special Investigation (MOVE) Commission, Box 7, PSIC.
14. Hank Klibanoff, "An Insider's View of Life within Move," *Philadelphia Inquirer*, May 22, 1985.
15. Ibid.; Steve Stecklow and Mary Jane Fine, "Group Members Had Set up Homes in Other States," *Philadelphia Inquirer*, May 16, 1985.
16. John Africa to Conrad Africa, Box 5, Folder "MOVE Writings," PSIC. See note 4.
17. Ibid., 20–22.

18. Philadelphia Police Department, "Prison Incident Involving M.O.V.E. Members on December 1, 1981," December 18, 1981, PSIC; Mike Freeman, "MOVE Battle Injures 27 at Prison," Philadelphia Daily News, December 4, 1981; Mike Leary, "Latest in Nearly a Decade of MOVE Confrontations," *Philadelphia Inquirer*, December 4, 1981; Ashley Halsey, "27 Hurt in Holmesburg Melee," *Philadelphia Inquirer*, December 4, 1981.
19. Kareem Howard, transcript of an oral history conducted in 2016 by Richard Kent Evans, MOVE Oral History Project, Special Collections and Urban Archives, Temple University, Philadelphia, PA.
20. Ibid.
21. Ashley Halsey, "27 Hurt in Holmesburg Melee," *Philadelphia Inquirer*, December 4, 1981; "Holmesburg Incident Involving M.O.V.E. Members," December 3, 1981, PSIC.
22. Joyce Gemperlein. "Member Extolls MOVE, Is Sentenced," *Philadelphia Inquirer*, September 1, 1981.
23. Ibid.; Jan Pogue, "MOVE Comes Back to Pearl Street." *Philadelphia Inquirer*, August 6, 1981.
24. "Policeman's Death Stirs Race Tension," *New York Times*, December 13, 1981; Amnesty International, "A Life in the Balance: The Case of Mumia Abu-Jamal," 2000, 6–7.
25. Mumia Abu-Jamal, "Ultimate in Caricature," *Philadelphia Tribune*, February 8, 1980; Mumia Abu-Jamal, "Will Steel Pulse Fill Void Left by Marley," *Philadelphia Tribune*, June 12, 1981; Mumia Abu-Jamal, "MOVE Hid in Plain Sight," *Philadelphia Tribune*, June 19, 1981; Mumia Abu-Jamal, "The Man They Call John Africa," *Philadelphia Tribune*, June 19, 1981.
26. Carole D. Yawney, "Only Visitors Here: Representing Rastafari into the 21st Century," in *Religion, Diaspora, and Cultural Identity: A Reader in the Anglophone Caribbean*, edited by John W. Pullis (Amsterdam: Gordon and Breach Publishers, 1999), 172.
27. Amnesty International, "A Life in the Balance: The Case of Mumia Abu-Jamal," 8–12.
28. Ibid.
29. Ibid.
30. Norris West, "Unanswered Questions Cloud Jamal's Trial," *Philadelphia Tribune*, July 2, 1982.
31. Amnesty International, "A Life in the Balance."
32. *Commonwealth v. Mumia Abu-Jamal, aka Wesley Cook*; Amnesty International, "A Life in the Balance"; Mumia Abu-Jamal, "Abu-Jamal Blames Justice System, Not MOVE for Conviction," *Philadelphia Tribune*, August 31, 1982.
33. Norris West, "Unanswered Questions Cloud Jamal's Trial," *Philadelphia Tribune*, July 2, 1982; Richard Kanegis, "Is Abu-Jamal Being Destroyed by MOVE Cult?" *Philadelphia Tribune*, August 17, 1982.
34. Kanegis, "Is Abu-Jamal Being Destroyed by MOVE Cult?"
35. Ibid.
36. Ibid.
37. Mumia Abu-Jamal, "John Africa," *Philadelphia Tribune*, September 7, 1982; "Our Opinion: MOVE Has Its Rights, but Others Have Rights Too," *Philadelphia Tribune*, August 27, 1982.

38. Unfortunately, it may very well be the case that Flo Conway and Jim Siegelman shaped how Americans thought about religion in the 1980s more than any scholar of religion. *Snapping* (1987) taught Americans why they ought to fear religious groups deemed "cults," just as their "muckraking exposé" *Holy Terror* (1982) "attempted to demonstrate that fundamentalists all over the globe are engaged in systematic campaigns against freedom, justice, progress, and democracy." See David Harrington Watt, *Antifundamentalism in Modern America* (Ithaca, NY: Cornell University Press, 2017), 126, 135–137.
39. Personal Freedom Association to City of Philadelphia, Box 7, Folder 3, PSIC; David Zucchino, "Mother Abducts Daughter for Activism," *Boca Raton News*, July 21, 1980; David Morrison to Emerson Moran, January 9, 1986, Box 7, Folder 2, PSIC.
40. Dave Racher and Maria Gallagher. "Judge Ignores Threats, Give MOVE Man 38 Months in Jail," *Philadelphia Daily News*, December 11, 1982; Joyce Gemperlein, "3 MOVE Members Convicted in '77 Incident," *Philadelphia Inquirer*, December 23, 1981.
41. Philadelphia Police Department, "Letters Written by MOVE Member Inmates to Pennsylvania State Prison Officials," January 16, 1984, PSIC; Philadelphia Police Department, "Information Report," undated, Box 51, Folder 3, PSIC; Philadelphia Police Department, "Information on Threats by Phone Made by MOVE Members," April 21, 1983, Box 51, Folder 3, PSIC.
42. Major Investigation Division, Philadelphia Police Department, "Chronology of Meetings Attended by Major Investigations Division Intelligence Regarding MOVE," May 23, 1985, Box 51, PSIC.
43. Major Investigation Division, Philadelphia Police Department, "Information Report Regarding Assault on Ishongo Africa on Highway, 60th and Ludlow Streets," April 19, 1983, Box 51, PSIC.
44. Civil Affairs Unit, Philadelphia Police Department, "Information Report, RE: Meeting with MOVE Members," February 21, 1984, Box 51, Folder 3, PSIC.
45. James J. Creaturo, transcript of interview with Herbert Kirk for the Philadelphia Special Investigation Commission, September 11, 1985, Box 51, PSIC.
46. Janet Hollaway to Corrections Commissioner Jeffes, January 11, 1984, Box 51, PSIC; Carlos Africa to Superintendent Ryan, SCI Dallas, Box 51, PSIC; Delbert Africa to Supt. Ryan; MOVE women at Muncy to Commissioner Jeffes, January 23, 1984, Box 51, PSIC.
47. Testimony of Philadelphia Department of License and Inspections Officers Pergolli and Paliaga before the Philadelphia Special Investigation Commission, Box 7, PSIC.
48. Civil Affairs Unit, Philadelphia Police Department, "Information Report RE: Telephone Conversation with Louise James of MOVE," July 26, 1984, Box 51, Folder 3, PSIC.
49. Ibid.
50. Philadelphia Police Department, "Information Report RE: Telephone Conversation with Louise James of MOVE," July 26, 1984, Box 7, PSIC.
51. Robert A. Orsi, *Between Heaven and Earth* (Princeton, NJ: Princeton University Press, 2005), 187. On the utility of religious categories for creating a threatening

other, see David Harrington Watt, *Antifundamentalism in Modern America* (Ithaca, NY: Cornell University Press, 2017).

52. Philadelphia Special Investigation Commission, "The Findings, Conclusions, and Recommendations of the Philadelphia Special Investigation Commission," March 6, 1986, Box 2, PSIC.

8

Innocence

Five months after the MOVE Bombing, the boy who used to be Birdie Africa sat before a video camera in the office of his lawyer. He wore a red, white, and blue striped polo shirt, slacks, and loafers. His hair was cut short. His face was scarred from the burns, though it could pass for an acute case of teenage acne. He was a skinny boy and small for his age, but he had a belly now, the result of weeks of acclimating himself to a typical American diet. Birdie now went by the name Michael Ward, which was also not his legal name. Birdie's parents, long before MOVE, had named him Oyewolffe Momer Puim Ward. But now, his father decided, it was time for a new name. Birdie's father brought him a Bible, and together they chose the name Michael after the archangel described in the Book of Daniel as "the great prince who standeth for the children." Michael's father, Andino Ward, sat to Michael's left. Michael had just recently gotten to know his father. His mother, Rhonda Africa, had separated from Andino Ward when Michael was two years old. She brought Michael with her into MOVE two years after that. As far as Michael knew, Frank Africa was his father. Michael Ward met Andino Ward two days after the bombing as he lay in the hospital. Andino Ward was a stoic man—a Vietnam vet who now worked in finance—though he seemed agitated that his son had to relive these memories yet again.[1]

This was the sixth time Michael had told his story of the MOVE Bombing. Two and a half hours after he escaped the fire, as he lay in the hospital with second-degree burns over much of his body, detectives from the Major Investigation Division visited him. There, without anyone else present, the detectives asked Birdie to confirm their suspicions. How many snipers had MOVE positioned in the house? How many weapons and bombs had MOVE stockpiled? Had Ramona poured gasoline on the roof to encourage a fire? Could he corroborate the threats and obscenities MOVE broadcasted over the loudspeaker that morning? Who was in the house? Birdie, who was covered in bandages and breathing through an oxygen mask, told the detectives that after the bomb, Theresa, Ramona, and his mother Rhonda Africa were lying in the basement "dying." The other children, Phil, Melisa, Tree, Netta, and Tomaso, were there too. Birdie told the detectives that Frank and Conrad were in the house as well, and that he had not seen John Africa since he was a baby. Police and Fire Department investigators interviewed Birdie three more times within two days of the bombing. The transcripts that resulted from those interviews are suspicious. At times, Birdie speaks an awful lot like a grizzled homicide detective, providing unusually lucid physical descriptions of the other MOVE people in the house—complete with heights and weights, clothing colors, and aliases. He even uses police lingo.[2]

This time, in his lawyer's office, with his father by his side, Michael told his story one more time, from beginning to end, in his own words. On video, he was shy and withdrawn. His interviewer, William Brown III, a Philadelphia lawyer and former head of the Federal Equal Employment Opportunity Commission, tried to loosen him up in the beginning by asking him about swimming, playing in the park, and who in MOVE he loved the most. At times throughout the interview, Michael grew sullen and inattentive. Several times Brown asked him questions that struck Michael as stupid, like when he asked Michael if he knew what an explosion was or if he had ever seen a gun. Each time, a flash of teenage sarcasm flashed across his face. But each time he quickly reverted to his polite, soft-spoken answers. His face also contorted whenever the topic of his mother came up. He called her "Rhonda." It felt strange to think of his mother as a woman named Rhonda. And it hurt to think about her now that she was dead. Over the course of an hour and a half, Michael created a confusing, incomplete, and at times contradictory picture of how he experienced the MOVE bombing. The confusion wasn't entirely his fault. Brown asked him questions that were out of sequence. Sequence was important for Michael; he could not tell time. The answers Brown managed to elicit from Michael were short and mumbled. Brown had to ask Michael to repeat himself often, and to verbally say "yes" or "no" instead of shaking his head. Over the course of an hour and a half, Michael told William Brown, the rest of the MOVE Commission, and the tens of thousands of people watching at home, about the day the System attacked the MOVE house with military rifles, machine guns, and bombs. He told them how the police dropped one of those bombs from a helicopter onto the roof, about how the bomb started a fire, and about how the police shot at them as they tried to escape the flames.[3]

When Michael Ward finished telling his story, his lawyer, David Shrager, addressed the camera. For the most part, Shrager said, Michael's testimony spoke for itself. But what was most important to Shrager was how his client was being categorized. Shrager told the MOVE Commission and the audience watching the testimony from their homes that they should consider Michael an innocent victim of this tragedy. They should keep in mind that Michael was just a child. He was not like the MOVE adults who were at least partly responsible for their own deaths. He did not convert to this cult willingly. His mother brought him into the group when he was a toddler. For these reasons, the Commission should be careful not to describe his client as a "MOVE member," Shrager argued. Michael Ward "was no more a member of MOVE than a child of Republican or Democratic parents would be styled by a particular party label." As far as Shrager was concerned, being a "MOVE member"—belonging to MOVE—was a choice, one that Michael Ward never made.[4]

Shrager's comment belies a common, and fundamental, cultural assumption about the nature of true religion. True religion, it is often thought, comes as the result of careful deliberation over a set of truth-claims. It is a freely made decision; the result of an agentive human being exercising his or her free will. Religious adherence, in order for it to be authentic, must not be forced upon anyone. Rather, people must decide their religions for themselves. They must be free to adopt a new belief system whenever they see fit. And, of course, people are free in our modern world to choose *not* to believe in the transcendent, all without interference from societies or governments. We are—we must be, in order for our belief to be authentic—religious free agents. This assumption about the nature of true religion—which we might call the assumption of agentive assent—is the assumption that, for religious adherence to be legitimate, it should be "the exercise of one's freedom in private." At first blush, the assumption of agentive assent seems entirely reasonable. It fits our modern worldview: we are beings with free will and agency who make our way through the world by making one calculated decision after another that is, we think, within our best interest.[5]

The idea that religion must be freely chosen is nearly as old as the category of religion itself. In *A Letter Concerning Toleration*, which was translated into English in 1689, John Locke described a religion as "a voluntary Society of Men, joining themselves together of their own accord." To him, choosing a religion was not unlike entering into a contract: it is an agentive decision, one that must be made by a cognizant, consenting adult. Indeed, Locke wrote that "no body is born a member of any Church . . . No man by nature is bound unto any particular Church or Sect, but everyone joins himself voluntarily to that society." Locke reasoned that if "the religion of parents would descend unto children," then religion would be inherited much like "temporal estates, and every one would hold his faith by the same tenure he does his lands." To Locke, "nothing can be more absurd." In the over four centuries since Locke's treatise, the concept of agentive assent has become foundational to the way many Westerners think about religion. Religion is thought of as something that is assented to after an act of careful deliberation over one or several competing truth claims. And religious adherence arrived at by any other means does not count. Agentive assent is so integral to the way we think about the category of religion because, like the category of religion generally, it is so thoroughly Protestant. Agentive assent is, after all, a logical byproduct of thinking about religion primarily as a set of beliefs, as opposed to practices.[6]

Although it is difficult to conceive of the practice of "true religion" without agentive assent, if we view religious belonging as a voluntary, agentive arrangement, not unlike entering into a contractual agreement, we must invalidate the membership of all those who are incapable of entering into such an agreement. After all, if true religion is the exercise of one's freedom in private, what are we to make of the religious lives of those who, by definition, have neither freedom nor privacy? Children are incapable of deliberating over a set of truth claims, of assessing their veracity, and deciding one belief system which seems to them to be the most rational choice among others. This is why children usually do not enter into contracts without the guidance of a cognizant adult acting on their behalf. For this reason, according to the logic of the assumption of agentive assent, children cannot be fully religious people. This is the logic that informs the Protestant doctrine of believer's baptism, the belief that the rite of baptism ought to be reserved for those who have reached the age of accountability (i.e., when a person is old enough to be responsible for his or her own sins). It is a distinctly Protestant way of thinking about religious belonging. And yet, few Protestants would argue that their children are not Protestants until they have been baptized. Even fewer would say that their children are not religious at all. But this is precisely what happened to the MOVE children. The belief that some people's religions do not count and that they are in need of rescue is a recurring theme in American religious history. Frequently, those who require saving are women and children.[7]

John Africa taught that the MOVE children were sacred beings because they were free from the corruption of the System. Those who converted to MOVE as adults could never live a life fully exempt from the distortions caused by the System. Only the children, who grew up outside of the System, could live in full accord with the Law of Mama. That is why the children did not participate in distortion days and did not eat meat: they didn't have to oblige the addictions of the System. They were pure. They were the first generation of MOVE people to live the Teachings of John Africa without pollution; the first to dwell in the sacred without having tasted the profane. For this reason, they had to be protected above all else. They had to be kept "sacred."

John Africa's theology of the sacredness of the MOVE children manifested at times as threats to commit redemptive sacrificial violence. He taught that it was better for the children to die than to fall victim to the System. The sacredness of the MOVE children necessitated, as a last resort, sacrificing their lives. It is probably not coincidental that MOVE's theology of redemptive sacrifice emerged in the spring of 1976, shortly after the infant Life Africa was killed while MOVE people fought with the police. John Africa spent a lot of time counseling Phil and Janine Africa after Life died. It is possible that this particular theology emerged out of those conversations. MOVE first threatened sacrificial violence in an interview with the *Philadelphia Inquirer* in April 1976. Sue Africa told the reporter, who was investigating the death of Life Africa, that MOVE "won't let our children fall into their hands. They'll just see how committed we are to our religion." Alberta Africa was less ambiguous: "If they violate the sanctity of our home, we will cycle our children before we let them take the children away." The message was clear. MOVE thought it was better for the children to die than fall victim to the System.[8]

People outside of MOVE, however, were reluctant to think about MOVE children as religious people. Rather, they viewed the MOVE children not as *MOVE* children at all, but as unwilling hostages to MOVE's ideology. Critics of MOVE who understood the group as a secular organization rejected the idea that there could be such a thing as a "MOVE child." David Shrager is a good example of this. To him, joining MOVE was a political affiliation—not unlike joining the Democratic Party. It was a decision that children were unable to make. Schrager's argument—that children cannot purposefully participate in party politics—is not unreasonable. But this argument gets considerably more complicated when it is applied to religious affiliation. Those critics of MOVE who had, by the early 1980s, begun to think about MOVE as a cult reached a conclusion not dissimilar to Schrager's. They argued that the MOVE children were victims of their parents' religion. Though the adults may have chosen to join the MOVE cult, the children did not. Whether their critics thought MOVE was religious or secular, their assumption was the same: membership in MOVE was a decision made by a free-thinking, agentive adult. The children never chose to join MOVE and, thus, it made no sense to think of them as religious people. MOVE's claims over them were invalid. Using the cult typology, they argued that MOVE children could not be "religious" in any meaningful sense. They were hostages.

The assumption that the MOVE children were victims of MOVE—captives to a belief system rather than adherents—was one reason why federal and local law enforcement officials began planning the raid that eventuated in the MOVE Bombing. On May 30, 1984—nearly a year before the MOVE Bombing—John Hogan, the head of the FBI field office in Philadelphia, Secret Service head Kevin Tucker, and representatives from the Justice Department met with Mayor Wilson Goode, District Attorney Ed Rendell, City Manager Leo Brooks, State Police Commissioner Robert Armstrong, and City Solicitor Barbara Mather to discuss legal grounds for raiding the house. They found none. The Secret Service had investigated MOVE's threats against President Reagan and found them to be too vague to prosecute. Neither the FBI nor the Justice Department could think of a justifiable reason to storm the house or to remove the children. There were no outstanding federal or state warrants. If the confrontation that John Africa prophesied was going to happen, MOVE would have to start it. And they all agreed that August 8, 1984—the sixth anniversary of the 1978 shootout—was a likely date for MOVE to commit a large-scale act of violence, either against themselves or others.[9]

Despite having no legal reason to raid the house, after that meeting, Police Commissioner Gregore Sambor began drawing up plans for an offensive against the occupants of the MOVE house on Osage Avenue. In May, Sambor hand-selected a group of six officers from across the Police Department to plan the raid. The group, which court documents refer to as the "A Certified personnel" were privy to top-secret evidence gathered by the FBI, the Secret Service, the ATF, and the Chester Police Department, as well as the Major Investigations Division and Civil Affairs Unit (CAU) of the Philadelphia Police Department. They reported directly to Sambor. The group was headed by Sergeant Herbert Kirk, a former stakeout unit member who was now lead instructor at the Philadelphia Police Academy. Sambor chose Kirk because he had attended the FBI academy and was familiar with FBI tactics. Joining Kirk was an officer from the Stakeout Unit, two detectives from the Major Investigation Division, Captain James Shanahan from CAU, and Lieutenant Frank Powell, a member of the Bomb Squad. The first recorded meeting of this group was on May 30, 1984. They met at least seven times before putting the plan into place on August 8, 1984. Commissioner Sambor attended some of these meetings.[10]

The plan they devised went like this. The Police and Fire Departments would surround the house early in the morning, to preserve the "element of surprise." Like they had done in 1978, Fire Department personnel would use deluge guns to blow open the windows and flood the house. Unlike 1978, the Police Department planned to use bombs to blow holes in the walls and the roof of the MOVE house. They hoped the holes would allow them to fill the house with tear gas. Frank Powell fashioned a device that would allow the Police Department to pump the maximum amount of tear gas into the house in the minimum amount of time. If the water and the tear gas did not flush MOVE out, another bomb would be used to blow off the front door, allowing a seven-man assault team to storm the house. If MOVE tried to escape out the back, they would be met by another assault team. Four stakeout units— snipers, presumably— would be stationed on the roofs of nearby houses.[11]

Throughout the summer, the police planners rehearsed the raid at the Police Academy. Frank Powell built prototypes of the bombs he planned to use. The bombs were made from PETN (a powerful explosive, one of the benefits of which is that it is unlikely to combust and, if it does, that it burns slowly) pressed into a Tupperware container which was filled with water. Powell even donned a bomb-proof suit and tested the strength of his bombs by standing near the explosion. Lieutenant Kirk took several reconnaissance flights in a helicopter over the MOVE house to ensure the tactical viability of the plan. The team employed a graphic artist to create renderings of the MOVE house and the surrounding neighborhood. It was planned down to the last detail. Several months after the MOVE Bombing, Lieutenant Kirk told an investigator that one of the reasons for the aggressiveness of the plan was that they feared MOVE might use the "children in the MOVE compound as human shields."[12]

As Sambor's team rehearsed the raid, MOVE tried to salvage their relationship with their neighbors. On May 13, 1984, MOVE invited their neighbors to an open forum outside the Osage house. Around two hundred people showed up. MOVE allowed their neighbors—supporters and critics—to air their grievances on MOVE's bullhorn. Some of the neighbors commended MOVE for refraining from using the bullhorn, which the group had not used since Christmas Eve 1983. But other neighbors complained about the wooden fence behind the MOVE house which blocked the shared rear driveway. And they wished MOVE would not put out raw meat to feed the neighborhood pets, as it smelled and attracted rats. Conrad Africa felt that the neighbors were missing the point. "We ain't talking about no damn fence or feeding the animals," he said. "We're talking about blood. We're talking about revolution. The System is rotten." As more neighbors approached the bullhorn to communicate their grievances, MOVE people grew more resolute in their rebuttals. They argued that the neighbors should direct their anger at the government for incarcerating the MOVE 9. When a neighbor complained that MOVE's guns made her nervous, a MOVE person asked, "What about the government who got guns? The government got atomic bombs." Some of the neighbors present at the meeting felt that MOVE was dismissive of their complaints, telling reporters that the meeting was "supposed to allow residents to air their minds" but devolved into "screaming, yelling, and cursing." MOVE called another forum a week later, but drew little interest.[13]

MOVE was also preparing for the final confrontation with the System that John Africa had prophesied. On May 3, 1984, a television news reporter interviewed Jerry Africa at the Osage house. During the taping of the interview, news cameras panned up to the roof to show Frank Africa wearing a hooded rain poncho and holding a rifle. The camera operator called the police, and soon over forty officers responded. The police shut down the roads and watched as Frank stood silently on the roof. He never put his finger on the trigger and never pointed the gun at anyone, so police had no reason to arrest him. The police packed up and left, and Frank climbed down from the roof. Police sources told reporters that a MOVE "gunman" had been menacingly prowling the roof wearing an "executioner's mask." This confrontation was the last straw for many of MOVE's Osage Avenue neighbors, who feared that MOVE was growing even more violent. Jerry Africa, in a later interview, said that MOVE was making it clear to the police that they were, in fact, armed should they try to raid the house.[14]

On May 20, 1984—eighty days before Sambor's planned raid was to go into effect—MOVE turned on the bullhorn again. They demanded the release of the MOVE 9 and an end to religious persecution. They threatened, in a skillfully vague and thus not illegal way, the lives of politicians, judges, and police officers. When this failed to produce a showdown with police, they tried again two days later. This time, they said that they would be on the loudspeaker every day until the confrontation began and that they would kill any police officer who attempted to enter the house. Undercover Civil Affairs officers observed MOVE people unloading sandbags from trucks into the Osage house. MOVE was trying their best to provoke a confrontation, but the police would not take the bait.[15]

On the morning of August 8, 1984, three hundred Philadelphia Police officers and firefighters surrounded the MOVE house on Osage to carry out the raid Sambor's team had planned. They brought with them fifteen paddy wagons, two armored cars, the bomb squad, and several firetrucks and ambulances. Most of the neighbors had evacuated the night before, per police orders. The police officers manned their guns and waited. But nothing ever happened. Nobody inside the house said a word. No one came out onto the porch. Hours went by. At 12:15 p.m., a police officer threw a cherry bomb onto the porch hoping to provoke a response. It disturbed the dogs, but there was still no response from MOVE people. The afternoon dragged on into night. Dozens of officers took a break that evening to watch the Phillies game in a nearby hotel lobby. By six the next morning, they packed up and left. When curious reporters asked the police commissioner why his department had surrounded the house, he told them they were there "to make sure nothing happens."[16]

There were several problems with the attempted raid of August 8, 1984. First of all, there was no legal reason for staging it. The Police Department had no legal grounds for entering the house, and no one seemed to have bothered to look for one. This is probably why they tried to provoke MOVE to initiate the fighting. Only then would they have legal grounds to enter the house. Second, the police had lost the "element of surprise." The day before, a radio talk show host announced the police raid and explained the plan in great detail. Anyone who was listening—and it was a predominately Black radio station—knew that the police planned to storm the house with deluge guns, tear gas, and bombs. Still, Sambor decided to press on with the raid. On the morning of the raid, because of the radio show the day before, numerous onlookers had gathered around the MOVE house hoping to watch the raid unfold. The raid had become too risky for both the police and the bystanders. According to Lieutenant Kirk, City Manager Leo Brooks "was running around all upset" before he called off the attack.[17]

Over the next nine months, law enforcement and city leaders grew increasingly worried that MOVE people might harm themselves or their children. Their fears were based on reports of child abuse coming from both MOVE's critics and former MOVE people. On July 24, 1984, Louise James and Laverne Sims met with the city's managing director and informed him that they had heard rumors that some of the MOVE children were in poor health. The next day, Louise phoned her police contact, officer Dolores Thompson, and told the detective that some of the neighbors had informed her that they heard thirteen-year-old Tree Africa screaming at all hours of the night. In her testimony before the MOVE Commission, Louise James denied that this telephone conversation ever happened. Rumors of child abuse from MOVE's critics mounted as well. Mostly, criticism of MOVE focused on the children's dress, diet, and lack of education. Arguing that MOVE "people were disobeying the law and neglecting and in their own way abusing their children," one external critic of MOVE believed that the children should be taken away from MOVE. "If I don't send my child to school, my child was taken away from me." Why, this critic wondered, should MOVE not be subject to the same parenting standard as everyone else?[18]

In January 1985, Laverne Sims brought her nine-year-old granddaughter, one of the MOVE children, to the hospital for medical treatment. The hospital staff summoned a social worker from the city's Department of Human Services to speak with Sims and the child. The social worker asked Sims why the girl was not in school and inquired as to her living conditions. Sims informed the social worker that MOVE children do not attend school and that her granddaughter resided, at various times, at many different MOVE houses, including the primary MOVE house on Osage. When the social worker asked to visit Laverne Sims's home on Reno Street, where many of the MOVE children lived, Sims declined. Worried that social workers might try to take the children away from MOVE, Laverne Sims phoned a detective from CAU and warned that there "will be a major confrontation if an attempt is made by the city to interfere with the MOVE children." Sims told the detective that, while the adult MOVE members are used to being targeted by the police, the MOVE children were held "sacred" and that MOVE could not allow them to fall victim to the System.[19]

Rumors of child abuse are not uncommon in and around religious groups that people associate with the cult typology. James T. Richardson, a prominent scholar of new religious movements, called allegations of child abuse the "ultimate weapon" against emergent religious groups. Often, Richardson points out, claims of child abuse usually fall within four categories: concerns over the efficacy of religious homeschooling, fears of corporal punishment, allegations of substandard living conditions, and accusations of sexual abuse. It is important to point out MOVE's critics did not accuse MOVE people of physically or sexually abusing their children. Birdie Africa was asked directly in his videotaped deposition if anyone had ever hit him, and he said no. When Michael Ward revisited his memories of MOVE in 2007 for a team of researchers working on a documentary, he painted a grimmer picture of life in the group. He recalled John Africa telling him not to speak with his mother anymore. Ward told the researchers that in the summer of 1984, he and the other children hatched a plan to run away. They found a pair of scissors and cut their hair so that they would blend in, and when the adults were busy, they made a run for it. They made it halfway down the block before the adults caught them and returned them to the MOVE house. John Africa called a meeting to discuss the children. Frank, the man Birdie thought was his father, grew so angry that he punched Birdie in the face, knocking him unconscious. When it comes to allegations of abuse in MOVE, it is hard to draw a clear distinction between falsification and the effects of memory. Michael Ward and Birdie Africa had little in common. Michael Ward was deeply troubled by his childhood in MOVE and cut off all his relationships with the group after 1985. He was certainly not sympathetic toward MOVE in 2007, and had many reasons to harbor a deep resentment toward MOVE people. But thirteen-year-old Birdie Africa also had little reason to lie to investigators when he said that he had never even been spanked. When William Brown III asked him whether he enjoyed his life in MOVE, Birdie equivocated. He was curious about the outside world, desperate to know what it was like not to be sacred, but to be a normal child. There were lots of other children living in the neighborhood, and they would sometimes bring Birdie toys, comic books, and candy. They would talk about what it was like to go to school. Birdie envied their lives, and he desired a normal childhood. But he told Brown that he loved his MOVE family—especially John Africa, Conrad Africa, and his mother, Rhonda Africa. He seemed genuinely confused when Brown asked him if he had ever seen any of the MOVE children get hit. He replied that MOVE people "don't believe in spanking."[20]

The mounting rumors of child abuse were only one sign that John Africa's religion was crumbling. The MOVE 9 were still in prison, though he had prophesied that they would be freed long ago. His own sisters, Louise James and Laverne Sims, had fallen back to the System. Even his brother, Alphonso Leaphart, was openly blaspheming him. Alphonso Leaphart had never joined MOVE, though he told his brother that he agreed with the Teachings of John Africa in principle. After Louise and Laverne left the group, Alphonso's relationship with MOVE grew hostile. In July 1984, Leaphart allowed MOVE to borrow his car, which they were using to haul supplies they used to reinforce the house. When he went to the MOVE house to pick up the car, Frank Africa told him that they intended to keep it for another month. Leaphart and Frank Africa began arguing. Leaphart told Frank, "You did your mother wrong and

I am here to get her home back if I have to kill all of you." Theresa and Ramona Africa, as well as Kareem Howard, joined Frank on the porch, and Leaphart told them, "You're all fools and you need to be in jail with the rest." Frank Africa objected to Leaphart's blasphemy and told him that "John AFRICA is God and if it don't be for him, you would be dead." Leaphart responded, "To hell with John Africa. My brother is not here." Theresa, Ramona, Frank, and Kareem Howard told Alphonso Leaphart to go home because he was "crazy." Leaphart did go home, but returned the next day. Undercover CAU officers watched as John Africa's brother drove up and down Osage Avenue, honking his horn, trying to rally the neighbors to help him evict MOVE from the house. No one wanted to get involved. Leaphart parked in front of the MOVE house and began arguing with Frank Africa again. This time, Frank was holding an axe. The CAU officers arrested Leaphart, ostensibly for inciting a riot, to prevent the situation from escalating.[21]

The city's fear that MOVE might devolve into Jonestown-style sacrificial violence added further urgency to their planning. After the aborted August 8, 1984, raid, Commissioner Sambor's elite group of planners met infrequently. Records of MOVE-related meetings kept by the Major Investigation Division show that their detectives did not attend any meetings on MOVE for six months. Lieutenant Kirk, who led Sambor's planning unit, retired in February 1985, around the same time the other members of the group began meeting again. When investigators asked Kirk if he had any involvement in revising the assault plans after his retirement, he smiled coyly and said, "I'd rather not answer that." Major Investigation Division detectives attended thirteen meetings between February 1985 and May 13, 1985. They met every day from May 2 to May 11.[22]

As the second attempt to raid the MOVE house grew near, the city investigated the possibility of rescuing the children from MOVE. Police Commissioner Gregore Sambor phoned Irene Pernsley, the city's Commissioner of Human Services, and requested that her department take custody of the children. Sambor knew that MOVE adults took the MOVE children to the park every morning to play, exercise, and bathe. Perhaps Pernsley's agency could take the children into custody while they were playing in the park. Sambor suggested the morning of May 13. Pernsley informed Sambor that Human Services could not rescue the children, as they had received no complaints or reports of neglect or abuse of the MOVE children. There were simply no legal grounds for removing them. After Sambor was rebuffed, the City Solicitor's office went to family court and requested that Pernsley's department be granted the authority to apprehend the children. They received an "extraordinary temporary restraining order" from a Family Court judge, which allowed Pernsley's Department of Human Services to seize the MOVE children on the morning of May 13 and hold them for up to 72 hours. However, Pernsley was never informed of this court order and was never told to take custody of the children.[23]

In the weeks before the raid, authorities interviewed MOVE supporters who might have some insight into the group's plans. They asked a MOVE supporter, Tony Crumpler, if he thought "MOVE members were suicidal or that they wished any harm to come to the children." Crumpler told authorities that he did not take MOVE's threats of sacrificial violence literally, but that "they were like anybody else when they're angry. They say a lot of things they don't always mean." On May 11, an unnamed neighbor told police she had heard Ramona Africa say, "If they [the police] try to come in, then we will kill these children," over the bullhorn. Wilson Goode, the mayor of Philadelphia, grew increasingly worried about the prospect of sacrificial violence as well. Days before the raid, he met with Fareed Ahmed, the director of a community group who was trying to negotiate a peaceful surrender. Ahmed relayed to the mayor that he thought MOVE would not leave the house until "those imprisoned brothers and sisters were released from prison." Ahmed urged the mayor to "make a special effort to save the children" because he "believed the MOVE members were to use themselves as a sacrificial lamb." The mayor told Ahmed that he had every intention of ending the confrontation without harm to any MOVE members, "especially the children." The mayor left the meeting under the impression that "nothing would remove [MOVE people] from the house" and that they were willing to sacrifice themselves and their children.[24]

Meanwhile, some of MOVE's other neighbors had reached a breaking point. On February 22, 1985, Conrad Africa was unloading stacks of burned wood from a truck into the MOVE house while, next door, a man was washing his truck. The man—whose father was a detective in the Philadelphia Police Department—complained that the ashes from the wood were blowing onto the truck he was trying to wash. An argument ensued, which led to pushing. Conrad Africa punched the neighbor in the face before other MOVE people broke up the fight. The neighbor declined to press charges. Around the same time, MOVE constructed a walkway suspended over the rear driveway to connect the main level of the house with the backyard. The walkway blocked the neighbors' full access to the driveway. Neighbors continued to contact the CAU with complaints that MOVE people were putting raw meat outside to feed the neighborhood animals, attracting rats. In October 1984, MOVE built a wooden structure on the roof, a small shed that one or two people could fit inside. It had slats at the top at eye-level, which could plausibly be used for firing weapons. The police called this structure a bunker. The neighbors complained to city leaders that they were "tired of having to live in the shadow of the MOVE fortress," that they were sick of "being forced to live in MOVE filth," and that they were being played as "sacrificial lambs for both sides." If the city did not "stop 'saving face' and deal with this problem directly," one neighbor warned in a letter to police, "uncontrolled warfare will be a direct consequence."[25]

MOVE's neighbors began to suspect that the city government and the Police Department were unwilling or unable to solve their problem. Undercover CAU detectives, surveilling meetings of angry neighbors, overheard threats to burn down the MOVE house and take up arms against MOVE people. On May 1, a group of MOVE's neighbors held a press conference, which was picked up by the Associated Press, announcing that city officials had proven incapable of doing anything "about the general state of fear we are forced to live under by the MOVE organization." The neighbors said that MOVE was a "clear and present danger to the health and safety of our entire block." They announced that they had written to the governor asking for him to send in state police to evict MOVE from their house.[26]

His authority challenged, Mayor Wilson Goode held his own press conference on May 1, 1985—just a few hours after the neighbors'—informing the public that neither the city, the state, nor the federal government had any legal reason to evict MOVE from their house. No one living in the house had committed any crimes. There were no outstanding warrants. There were no official complaints about the children's welfare. The only reason anyone could think of to intervene legally was through the process of eviction. Louise James owned the house and MOVE people were living there despite her objections. There were also likely housing code violations, though no one could be sure because there was no way to get inspectors safely in the home. Though he understood the neighbors' frustrations, the mayor reminded them that he could not, "in order to protect the rights of a group of people, violate the rights of a single person." The neighbors' press conference and Mayor Goode's ineffectual response prompted a barrage of news stories and editorials excoriating the city to do something about MOVE. An editorial in the *Philadelphia Inquirer* declared that "a small group of malcontents and nonconformists cannot be allowed to continue to intimidate and hold an entire neighborhood, and in effect the city government, hostage." Another editorial in that same paper mocked MOVE with a tongue-in-cheek announcement that a new "back-to-the-city cult" had been created called HALT. All "HALT Members" take the surname Suburbia to honor their "spiritual leader, Ozzie Nelson Suburbia." They promised to construct a sound system outside their "split-level ranch house" in the suburbs to blast muzak all day—"until a neighbor complains."[27]

Four days after the neighbors' press conference, city authorities found the legal cover they needed to storm the house. On May 5, Sambor's planning squad met with District Attorney Ed Rendell to find a legal basis for the raid. After that meeting, Rendell issued warrants for the arrest of Frank, Conrad, Ramona, and Theresa Africa on various charges including parole violations, making terroristic threats, contempt of court, and firearms violations. Federal law enforcement officials from the Secret Service, the FBI, and the ATF investigated threats against public officials in the fall of 1984 and found that MOVE had not broken the law because their threats were too vague. If, for example, MOVE had said, "We are going to kill President Reagan," they might have faced charges. However, MOVE's threats over the loudspeaker were usually more general. They threatened to go down to the White House and show them a thing or two, but knew better than to detail plans to assassinate public figures. MOVE's threats may have been reprehensible, but they were not illegal. If MOVE issued illegal threats over the loudspeaker—as Ed Rendell alleged—they must have done so on April 29, 1985, when they turned on the loudspeaker for the first time since the previous fall. Civil Affairs detectives overheard MOVE threaten to shoot the mayor in the head, and they saw men carrying rifles into the house. Now that MOVE's threats had become prosecutable in the eyes of the district attorney, the police had a legal basis for entering the MOVE house.[28]

The raid did not catch MOVE by surprise. Though they did not know the exact date and time, they knew that the System was closing in on them. The constant anticipation took a toll on MOVE people. The children were having nightmares that they were being visited by demons. On May 7, 1985, John Africa called a meeting—the last one he would lead—to teach MOVE about the demonic realm and what the children's dreams portended. To him, it was a sign that the System was closing in. He issued his last prophecy. He told his followers that the police would soon surround the house and kill them all. They would drop a bomb from a helicopter.

MOVE people took to the bullhorn to request negotiations with the city. They provided a list of four people who could represent MOVE: Jerry Africa, two journalists: Barbara Grant and Harvey Clark, and a radio personality named Irv Homer. MOVE suggested that they had backed the city into a corner, and that "y'all are going to want to stop this confrontation." Officers from the CAU recorded the names, but never contacted the people on the list.[29]

Early in the morning on May 12, 1985, the Philadelphia Police Department began going door to door, ordering residents who lived near the MOVE house to evacuate their homes. Theresa Africa sat on the front stoop with a friend, Novella Williams, who was an old schoolmate of Frank Africa's. Theresa told Williams that MOVE knew what was about to happen. As helicopters circled overhead, Theresa said that the police were coming to kill them. MOVE knew, Theresa said, that the police were "going to drop something from the helicopter on our roof and then come in through the back door." Williams assured Theresa that the police would do no such thing, that they would never risk the lives of the children, and that they just wanted everyone to surrender safely. Theresa Africa scoffed at the idea. "They comin' to kill us," Novella Williams remembered her saying. "They don't want any of us left alive." The children spent the evening on lookout duty until it got late. Birdie slept uneasily that night, dreaming of demons.[30]

MOVE people awoke before dawn on the morning of May 13, 1985, to the sound of an army outside, just as they had nine months earlier. Police Commissioner Gregore Sambor announced over the bullhorn, "Attention, MOVE. This is America. You have to follow the laws of the United States." He listed the warrants and told the MOVE people inside that they had fifteen minutes to evacuate the house before the police would move in. The adults, who had slept in the same room as the children that night in anticipation of the attack, hurried the children down two stories to the basement. Ramona took to the bullhorn and told Sambor to go fuck himself. The children descended the wooden stairs to the basement, and water began to pour in through the street level window. MOVE people had prepared the basement well for the siege and had been choreographing their response to the city's offensive for months. They had blankets soaking in buckets of water to protect the children from the tear gas. They carved a hole into the wall separating the basement, which was toward the front of the house facing Osage Avenue, from the garage facing the rear of the house. The children each grabbed a wet blanket and climbed through the hole into the garage, which was fortified by railroad ties. The adults said that they would be safe in there, even from bombs. Ramona, Theresa, and Rhonda Africa joined the children in the basement, and Conrad pushed a heavy latch over the hole. The children piled on each other to keep safe from the tear gas as the MOVE women tried to comfort them, and the dogs whined and paced around the garage. The children were terrified, so Rhonda told them to chant "Long Live John Africa," for bravery.[31]

Upstairs, Raymond Africa, Frank Africa, and John Africa took up arms against the police outside. Armed with a .22 caliber rifle, a shotgun, and two pistols, the men began shooting. (There is some evidence to suggest that the police shot first.)[32] The police responded by firing more than ten thousand rounds into the MOVE house with Uzi submachine guns, shotguns, Thompson submachine guns, sniper rifles, and M-16s—weapons that they had acquired from the FBI and the ATF for the purposes of the raid. For ninety minutes, hundreds of police officers fired into the house. When they ran out of bullets, they went to get more. At 7:30 a.m., two "insertion teams" entered the houses adjacent to the MOVE house and began using explosives to blow holes in the firewall. The women and children could hear the police yelling through the walls. Through a drain pipe, the police in the adjacent house could hear the children crying. When they finally opened up a large enough hole, the insertion teams threw tear gas canisters into the basement and the garage. Periodically, one of the MOVE men upstairs would descend to the garage to update the women. On one of these trips down, Conrad told the women and children that the police "had some mean bombs." John and Frank stayed upstairs, returning fire.[33]

At around 8:30 in the morning, police officers outside began throwing bundles of C-4 explosive at the MOVE house. In January 1985, an agent out of the Philadelphia field office of the FBI delivered thirty-eight pounds of C-4 to the Philadelphia Police Department to use the next time they attempted the raid. Unlike Tovex, C-4 is highly flammable. Tovex is designed to move obstacles (such as rock walls in mines) as safely as possible, but C-4 is designed to inflict maximum damage. The first bundle, one and a half pounds of Tovex, combined with at least two pounds of C-4, blew a hole into the front porch. Unsatisfied with the results, the police tried again. At 10:40, a second bomb blew the front wall off of the MOVE house and damaged three neighboring houses. The blast destroyed the stairs leading to the basement, separating John, Frank, and Raymond Africa upstairs from Ramona, Theresa, Rhonda, Conrad, and the MOVE children in the garage.

Outside, police officers saw the decapitated body of John Africa lying in the rubble. After John Africa died, the MOVE house fell silent. There was no more shooting, no more taunts from the bullhorn. At noon, many of the police officers took a lunch break, driving to nearby fast food restaurants or to the cafeteria of a nearby hospital which was serving as a mobile command post. At four in the afternoon, a community mediator was permitted through the barrier to attempt to persuade MOVE to surrender. There was no answer from inside the house.[34]

At 3:30 p.m., as an eerie silence emanated from the MOVE house and anxious police officers paced around outside, Mayor Wilson Goode gave a press conference from his home where he was monitoring the attack on a television in his kitchen. He told the press corps that "the members of the group are barricaded inside," and that he and his team were "assessing the situation at this time and trying to determine what steps to take next." Goode affirmed that the police would not withdraw until MOVE had been evicted from the house, and promised to "take control of the house by any means necessary." He warned, however, that MOVE was "bent on violent confrontation." He concluded his press conference by saying, "I pray to Almighty God the children will not be hurt."[35]

As Goode assessed the situation from his kitchen, Police Commissioner Sambor decided to move forward with the final frontal assault phase of the Kirk plan. This phase of the plan, which had been in place since the summer of 1984, involved blowing off the front door with a bomb, which would allow an assault team to enter. Entering the front door was no longer an issue—the whole front wall of the house had been blown off by the second bomb. The problem was the shed on the roof. MOVE built the shed after the August 8, 1984, raid. Sambor and Brooks—both military men—knew that the shed proved a challenge to the assault team. If there were any MOVE people inside the shed, they had the high ground, a decent firing angle at the assault team, and plenty of cover from return fire. It would have been foolish to assault the house from the front with that shed intact. So, Brooks, Sambor, and Frank Powell—the member of the Philadelphia Police Department's Bomb Squad who was a member of Sambor's planning team—began to brainstorm how to get a bomb onto the roof. They weighed dropping the bomb from a construction crane, but it would take days to get one tall enough. They could get a shorter one within hours, but the operator would be in the direct line of fire if anyone was in the shed.[36]

At 4:30, Sambor, Brooks, and Powell decided to drop the bomb from a helicopter instead. Fifteen minutes after they decided to drop the bomb, Brooks phoned Mayor Goode and informed him that all efforts at a peaceful resolution had been exhausted and encouraged him to approve a plan to use explosives to dislodge the shed on the roof. At 5 p.m., Goode gave Brooks permission to move forward with the plan. There is some discrepancy as to what Brooks told Goode during this phone call. Goode testified that he was not told about a new bomb or that it would be dropped from a helicopter. Sambor and Brooks testified that the mayor had known all along that explosives were a part of the plan. As Goode and Brooks talked on the phone, the two large fire engines positioned outside the MOVE house trained their deluge guns on the roof so that MOVE people in the house or on the roof could not see to shoot at the helicopter overhead. At 5:20, Frank Powell dropped a third bomb—nearly four pounds of C-4 mixed with two pounds of Tovex, onto the roof of the MOVE house. This final act illustrated the degree of coordination between city, state, and federal governments in the MOVE raid. Powell, a member of the Philadelphia Police Department, dropped the bomb that he had acquired from the FBI from a Commonwealth of Pennsylvania Police helicopter. Reporters sequestered blocks away felt the explosion rock through the neighborhood.[37]

The bomb created a fireball that reached over seven thousand degrees Fahrenheit and caused a concussion felt blocks away. What was left of the roof burst into flames immediately. The Fire Department turned off the deluge guns. Within minutes, the fire began to spread throughout the MOVE house and across the roof to the adjacent houses. As the fire grew, Sambor and Fire Commissioner William Richmond discussed what to do about it. Sambor decided to "let the fire burn." He could use the fire as a tactical weapon. If the water, tear gas, bombs, and gunfire could not drive MOVE out of the house, perhaps fire could. Richmond did not object to this plan. His main concern was to keep his firefighters out of harm's way. They were not police officers, Richmond reasoned, and should not be near the MOVE house if there was still a risk of gunfire.[38]

As the fire spread above them, the MOVE people inside the house decided to surrender. According to Birdie Africa's testimony, the water in the basement that MOVE people had been wading in all day began to grow hot. Conrad lit a match to try to find out what was going on. They realized that the haze in the air wasn't tear gas anymore, but smoke. The house was on fire.

The heat grew more and more intense. Conrad used a monkey wrench to unlatch the door to the rear of the house and announced that the children were coming out. His announcement was answered with a volley of gunfire. He waited for the shooting to die down and tried again. Conrad, Ramona, and Rhonda repeatedly tried to tell the police that they were sending the children out, but each time they tried to step out of the garage, the police opened fire.[39]

At around seven in the evening, the adults decided that they had to get everyone out immediately, regardless of the gunfire. They lined up the children. Birdie was in the back of the line. The youngest, Sue Africa's nine-year-old son Tomaso, was in front. Conrad grabbed Tomaso around his waist and carried him through the hatch to the back alley. As soon as he and Tomaso emerged, they were both struck by buckshot from a police shotgun. Conrad carried Tomaso back inside and gave him to Theresa. Birdie remembers Tomaso crying. The basement grew hotter and the smoke dense. The adults told the children that it was going to be okay, that it was time to cycle. What was left of the structure of the house—that which had not yet been destroyed by bombs, water cannons, and machine gun fire—began collapsing around them. Everyone laid down, covered their heads and waited to die. Birdie watched as Phil's skin began to melt. Birdie heard Tomaso crying even louder. He was lying face down on Theresa's lap as she tapped on his back trying to comfort him. A few moments passed and Tomaso stopped crying. He stopped moving. Theresa kept trying to resuscitate him. She was crying too.[40]

Ramona, Conrad, Rhonda, and the five MOVE children were trapped in the basement for a half an hour before Ramona decided she couldn't take the pain anymore. Conrad opened the latch again and Ramona ran out, testing the waters. She was not shot, so she yelled for Conrad to send the rest of the children out. According to Birdie Africa, Tree was the first child to run out to Ramona. Phil followed, then Birdie. Birdie watched as Ramona helped Tree and Phil climb up on the makeshift bridge that MOVE had built over the driveway, which was suspended about five feet in the air. Tree and Phil made it up and began running down the alley toward the police. But Birdie had trouble getting up on the walkway. Ramona climbed down and helped Birdie up. Ramona then stumbled into the rear alley and collapsed, her body severely burned. Birdie made it to the bridge and began crawling across. He lost his balance and fell from the walkway, cracking his head on the rear driveway. A burning branch from a tree fell on top of him. He lay in puddles unconscious until police officer James Berghaier decided he could not watch as this child burned to death. His partner told him not to go, as Birdie was certainly a trap. He went anyway, risking getting shot. He swept up Birdie and ran him to an awaiting police van. Ramona was arrested in the back alley on charges of inciting a riot. She was taken to the hospital for her burns but refused treatment. Birdie did not remember anything after he bolted through the flames out of the house, but a press photographer captured a picture of him sitting in the back of the police van. He was naked, gasping for air, and burned over much of his body.[41]

At 9:00 p.m., as the fire burned, Mayor Goode held a press conference in City Hall and offered the first official account of the MOVE Bombing. Appearing devastated and disheveled, Goode announced that Ramona Africa and Birdie Africa had been taken to the hospital. He also told reporters, mistakenly, that three armed MOVE adults had escaped from the fire and were engaged in a protracted gun battle with police in the back alley. The ongoing gun battle, the mayor said, was preventing the Fire Department from combating the blaze. The mayor described the police operation as "a difficult attack" and likened it to war. Goode told the assembled reporters that the city knew attacking the house would lead to "war," and that, because MOVE "intended to have a violent confrontation," "there's no way that you could avoid . . . the loss of some life." At a second press conference after midnight, Goode admitted that the attack on the MOVE house was "a disaster." And, for the first time, he suggested publicly that children might have died. "Anytime there is the possibility that a child's life is lost you have to be doubly sad. I feel nothing but sadness deep down inside me."[42]

The day after the bombing, the nation awoke to confusing and bewildering reports coming out of Philadelphia—mostly based on Goode's initial press conference. In a typical article, the *Chicago Tribune* reported that MOVE and the police had been involved in a protracted gun battle which lasted all day and into the night, and that the battle culminated in police dropping a bomb onto the MOVE house, causing a fire. The *Tribune* reported that "at least four members of the radical group, which calls itself MOVE, emerged from the inferno" and continued firing upon police officers. The shootout, combined with "a severe lack of water pressure," prevented the Fire Department from extinguishing the fire before it was too late. The report in the *Chicago Tribune* was typical of one line of storytelling to emerge from the MOVE Bombing: MOVE had been heavily armed and shooting at the police nearly all day. The police used an explosive device to dislodge a bunker on the roof, causing an unexpected fire. The fire forced at least some of the MOVE people outside, where they continued their gun battle with police, preventing firefighters from extinguishing the flames. However, as early as the morning of the 14th, a second account of events began to emerge—one based on at-the-scene interviews rather than Goode's press conference. The *New York Times*, for example, reported that the police responded to shooting at around six in the morning, and that MOVE and the police traded gunfire for ninety minutes. Most of the day, they reported, there was no activity at the MOVE house at all—at least nothing that the bystanders and press members observed from several blocks away.[43]

While reporters struggled to determine the series of events, city officials offered a narrative for framing the MOVE Bombing that positioned MOVE as the perpetrators and the neighbors as the victims. On May 14, 1985, Mayor Goode, Police Commissioner Gregore Sambor, and Fire Commissioner William Richmond gave a joint press conference. This time, Goode read a prepared statement meant to "put the tragic events of the past two days in perspective." Goode told his citizens that MOVE was "a group dedicated to the destruction of our way of life." He reminded them that MOVE killed a police officer in 1978. Goode's message to the press was that the neighbors whose homes burned were the victims of the MOVE Bombing—not MOVE, not even the MOVE children. The police commissioner explained that the bomb dropped from the helicopter was a two-pound bundle of Tovex explosive and explained that "there would never have been any fire unless it was assisted by some inflammatory material." He was alleging that Ramona Africa had poured gasoline onto the roof of the house in anticipation of the bomb—something she had threatened to do over the bullhorn. Sambor insisted that the "plan was a good one." He explained that MOVE had heavily fortified their row home. Aside from the "bunker" on the roof, they had brought in large tree trunks to reinforce the walls. He also speculated that MOVE people had dug a system of tunnels beneath the house which they could have used to escape into the neighborhood. Perhaps most importantly, the officials reiterated their belief that MOVE people "were prepared to die, to go on a suicide mission." Even so, Sambor insisted, "As far as we're concerned" the planned raid presented "no possible danger to the children."[44]

Goode's reframing of the MOVE Bombing as an unavoidable tragedy, with the neighbors as the victims, proved influential. In the days after the bombing, a few newspapers ran the photograph of Birdie Africa in the police van. Others ran photographs of Ramona Africa surrendering to police. But the majority of news accounts of the MOVE Bombing ran several photographs taken by news helicopters which showed the entire 6200 block of Osage Avenue—sixty-four houses in all—decimated by fire. Both the *New York Times* and *Time* magazine ran photos of the burned-out block on their covers. For the time being, the neighbors whose homes had been destroyed provided sympathetic victims. If the public could not mourn for MOVE people, they could sympathize with the neighbors whose houses burned.[45]

Within a few days, news trickled out that bodies had been discovered in the rubble. City officials used cranes to knock down the remaining walls so that they would not collapse on investigators. But this piled yet another layer of rubble onto the bodies they were trying to recover. Investigators brought in large claw machines to clear the debris, which only further destroyed the bodies—many of which were already charred beyond recognition. Once it cooled, federal and local forensics teams sifted through the rubble, separated human bones from dog bones, and pieced together fragments of burned bodies. The process took weeks, but they eventually found the remains of eleven people. John Africa had died early in the day, probably from the second bomb blast. Examiners were unable to provide a positive identification, as only a burned torso remained. Frank Africa and Raymond Africa died either from the same bomb or from police gunfire shortly thereafter. There was no smoke or ash in the remains of their lungs, indicating that they were dead before the fire. Conrad Africa, Rhonda Africa, and Theresa Africa died sometime after the final bomb, either from gunshot wounds, smoke inhalation, or the flames. The children—Sue Africa's nine-year-old son Tomaso, Consuella Africa's two daughters Zanetta and Tree, thirteen and fourteen, Janine and Phil Africa's ten-year-old son Phil, and Delbert and Janet Africa's twelve-year-old daughter Delisha—died in the basement. Remains from one of the children—examiners were unable to determine who, though it was likely Tomaso—contained buckshot pellets from a police shotgun. According to police records, 500 rounds of buckshot were brought to the scene, and zero were used. (Somehow, even though Birdie saw Tree and Phil run toward the police, their charred remains were found in what was left of the garage of the MOVE house. This discrepancy is one of the enduring mysteries of the MOVE Bombing. Were Tree and Phil turned away by police gunfire, forced to return to the burning house? Did they never leave the basement? Were their bodies placed in the fire to cover up whatever forensic evidence they may contain?)

Once it became clear that several of the victims of the MOVE Bombing had been children, journalists, activists, and religious leaders began to construct a new narrative of the MOVE Bombing—one that contrasted the complicity of the MOVE adults with the innocence of the MOVE children.

Responding to the deaths of the MOVE children, Gregory Williams, a child psychiatrist, wrote an essay in which he pondered a broader lack of empathy toward children within American culture. He wrote about how he was raised "a Baptist Protestant Christian," but had lost his faith as he "wondered, with great philosophical concern and anxiety," whether God would have damned him to hell merely for being born into the wrong religion—something that he had no control over. Williams, like the MOVE children, had been "indoctrinated with views" that he never chose. Like the children of MOVE, he and the countless other children that were taught God had damned them to hell were "innocent victims" to their parents' ideologies. Who could believe in a God, Williams wondered, who would "wantonly cause the death and suffering of what I considered innocent children?" But, to Williams, society was as cruel as this false god. Clearly, he reasoned, "we do not unambivalently love children." If we did, the state would have removed the MOVE children years ago. According to Williams, "the adult members of MOVE have been labeled by us as being pathologically dangerous or emotionally ill," and "to shackle one's children with an archaic system of magical beliefs of superiority and omnipotence hardly prepares them for a future world." For those reasons, it was "our responsibilities as citizens in a democracy" to remove the MOVE children from MOVE long before their lives were ever put at risk.[46]

Many people in Philadelphia and around the country echoed Williams's sentiment. In the weeks that followed the bombing, the American Friends Service Committee (AFSC) devised a series of projects that shaped the way the broader public understood the MOVE Bombing. Their first major undertaking, begun four months after the MOVE Bombing, was the Philadelphia Perspectives Project, in which AFSC staffers conducted in-depth one-on-one interviews with people living in and around Philadelphia to gauge their reactions to the MOVE Bombing. To find their respondents, staff members at the AFSC cold-called Philadelphians and asked them a series of questions ranking their knowledge of MOVE and the MOVE Bombing, the strength of their opinions, and their willingness to conduct an interview. AFSC staffers conducted interviews with those who ranked highly on the phone questionnaire, either at the AFSC offices downtown or at the respondents' homes. The Philadelphia Perspectives Project gathered audiotapes and produced transcripts from interviews with forty-five people. Though the Philadelphia Perspectives Project made no pretensions of being a scientific poll, the respondents were a relatively close sampling of the Philadelphia community. They interviewed twenty-four African Americans and thirteen whites.

Five respondents identified as Hispanic, and three as Asian. Twenty-six of the respondents were female. Many of the respondents requested anonymity, and some asked to review the transcripts to make sure there was no identifying information. The interviews were generalized into a report called "Voices from the Community," which the AFSC made available to the press.[47]

Though the AFSC claimed the Philadelphia Perspectives Project had gathered an "extraordinary diversity of views," the original transcripts evince a remarkable consensus. Almost all of the respondents felt that the MOVE Bombing was a bungled operation—a foolish way to solve an admittedly intractable problem. Though most agreed that the bombing was the wrong thing to do, they agreed that something had to be done and that violence was unavoidable. Almost everyone agreed that MOVE wanted a violent confrontation and that they had provoked it through years of bad behavior. Most people believed that Mayor Wilson Goode was not primarily to blame, though a few believed that he deserved criticism for overseeing the police commissioner and the city manager. The respondents were divided on how to characterize MOVE. Many thought they were a cult, and a few compared MOVE with the Symbionese Liberation Army and the People's Temple. Others used secular categories such as "political group" or "radical group." Only one thought MOVE was a religion.[48]

The respondents to the Philadelphia Perspectives Project agreed on three other points that demonstrate how deeply ingrained the assumption of agentive assent was to their conception of true religion. Almost all of the respondents believed that the MOVE adults in the house were culpable in—or even welcomed—their own deaths. A forty-eight-year-old African American man who worked as a mail carrier placed "ninety-nine and nine tenths of the blame on MOVE." He believed it was "disgraceful how they carried on" and suggested that he "might have punched a few of them" if he'd had the chance. He told the interviewer that he was not surprised when he learned of the MOVE Bombing "for the simple reason, anyone who would go to any length to force their ideas and their way of living on someone else" invites violent conflict. "This is what they wanted. Total destruction . . . they were just a form of a cult, a form of terror." A Black man in his late sixties—a retired staffer at the Cardinal's Commission on Human Relations—was reticent to say conclusively that MOVE intended to die on May 13th, but that suicidal behavior was not out of character for groups who were "willing to die for their cause." Tellingly, he used the cult typology to reach this conclusion. "People, more recently in Jonestown come to my mind."[49]

A second point on which most of the respondents agreed was that the children were not MOVE people, but innocent victims held captive to MOVE. A middle-aged white man who worked as a chef and lived in West Philadelphia told his interviewer that "one thing I could never conceive of is . . . adults keeping their children, you know, forcing them into staying and living that type of life." Another respondent agreed that the MOVE children should not be thought of in the same category as the adults. "As an adult you have options. You choose how you want to live. You choose what your beliefs and your creeds are. The children don't." Another respondent lamented that the MOVE children "didn't have the say whether they should stay with these people." A couple of respondents dissented from the view that the children were not authentically religious people. A white housewife in her late thirties rejected her interviewer's suggestion that the children were "hostages" to MOVE. "That's totally alien to me," she said. "Whatever I am, my children are. I'm of a different religious persuasion. My children were reared in this religious persuasion also. I was questioned very often about this by the community. "Why do your children do so and so?" And then I would say, "Well, don't your children follow your ways? Why is it that my children shouldn't follow mine?" To this respondent, MOVE was "their own little community. The children need the parents and the parents need the children."[50]

A third point on which most of the respondents agreed was that the MOVE adults sacrificed the MOVE children as martyrs and that they, not the government, were ultimately responsible for the deaths of the children. A white schoolteacher in her early thirties said that she "felt the city's hopelessness." MOVE, she thought "were willing to sacrifice children, they weren't going to even let the children out of the house. And that, to me—I'm a child advocate, and that was the very horrendous, not even pathetic—it was just a horrendous thing to do." She agreed with many of the respondents that MOVE adults wanted "to be a martyr," but that, as a decent human being, you "don't take the children with you." The forty-eight-year-old mail carrier voiced a common theme. "Who would board their wives and children inside a building . . . would have open warfare with police," he asked. "They have no respect for children. So as far as their children getting killed or their way of life to be a martyr, it didn't surprise me." Another respondent believed that the children "were a sacrificial lamb," that "they just happened to be caught in the middle," and that "they were victims. Victims of a cause."[51]

The construction of this narrative of the MOVE Bombing, in which the MOVE children were hostages caught in the crossfire of an unavoidable conflict, shifted some of the blame for their deaths away from political leaders. But by no means were city leaders spared from criticism. New York City Mayor Ed Koch made national news when he excoriated Philadelphia officials for their handling of the raid, saying that he would fire a police commissioner on the spot if he presented such a "stupid" idea. City politicians and community leaders began calling for resignations. City Manager Leo Brooks announced his resignation on June 3, effective at the end of the month. He attempted to distance himself from the decision to drop the bomb by telling reporters that he was out of town visiting his parents in Virginia the week before the raid. Police Commissioner Gregore Sambor resigned on November 13 in a tearful speech at the Police Academy. He complained to reporters on his way out of office that Mayor Goode had forced him to resign, a claim that Goode denied. Fire Commissioner William Richmond had been considering leaving the Fire Department prior to the MOVE Bombing. At the urging of the mayor and his family, he chose to stay on until his retirement in 1988.[52]

Wilson Goode received much less criticism than either Sambor or Brooks. *Time* magazine polled Philadelphians weeks after the bombing and found that 71 percent thought the mayor "had done a good or excellent job handling the MOVE confrontation." Partly, Goode's initial support was due to the loyalty of Philadelphia's African Americans, who supported the city's first Black mayor at levels approaching unanimity. Though the MOVE Commission report placed the blame for the MOVE Bombing squarely on the mayor's shoulders as the city's chief executive, Goode was reelected to a second term as mayor in 1987, fighting off District Attorney Ed Rendell in the primary and defeating Frank Rizzo in the general election. James Berghaier, the police officer who rescued Birdie after he collapsed in the rear alleyway, left the Police Department after he was subjected to harassment for what he had done. In one instance, his colleagues wrote "nigger lover" on his locker.[53]

Though I have argued that an impulse to rescue the MOVE children was one of the main reasons the City of Philadelphia and federal law enforcement groups planned and carried out the MOVE Bombing, I want to be very clear that I do not suggest that any agents of the state set out to kill the children on May 13, 1985. In fact, I would not feel comfortable saying for sure that agents of the state set out to kill anyone that day. But there are a few firm details that give me pause. The plan to attack the MOVE house was in place since the summer of 1984—long before there was any legal reason to attack the house. Those in charge of the MOVE operation knew the children were in the house. They had ample opportunity to take the children into custody before May 13th and chose not to. They attacked the house with a ferocity so out of balance with MOVE's show of force that it bordered on the absurd. The bomb squad personnel who built the bombs supplemented the already incommensurate tactical explosives with C-4, an explosive not meant for tactical purposes, but to inflict maximum damage. Police Commissioner Gregore Sambor decided to use fire as a tactical weapon against all who were inside. And the police shot at those who tried to escape the fire, striking at least one of the children. These are difficult details to think about. These details make it difficult to arrive at the conclusion that the MOVE Bombing was simply a comedy of errors, a bungled operation by inept city officials who wanted to play army. Instead, these details lend themselves to an interpretation of the MOVE Bombing in which the state killed the children in order to save them from MOVE.

But that is not the story that is usually told about the MOVE Bombing. The story that is often told is one in which the MOVE children are innocent victims. In this narrative of the MOVE Bombing, the children were hostages caught in a crossfire of a conflict they had no stakes in. It is a way of naturalizing their deaths, of shifting blame away from the state and onto MOVE. With the children as innocent victims, instead of as religious people killed for their religion, one could say that the city was negligent in its duties to protect them from harm. But, in this interpretation of the MOVE Bombing, ultimately it was MOVE's fault for holding the children there in the first place. These stories have become popular in collective memory because they provide a degree of comfort; they dispel the ambiguity that follows a complicated story made even more tangled by memory, trauma, and self-interest. But the primary reason these stories are the ones we tell about the MOVE Bombing is because they allow us to imagine that the MOVE Bombing was an aberration, an inexplicable but rare incident that was confined to a particular place and time. The debate over whether or not the MOVE children could be authentically religious was central to the decision to attack the MOVE house. The MOVE Bombing was the culmination of over a decade of debating over MOVE's classification. If MOVE were a true religion—if MOVE behaved the way we like our religions to behave—there would have been no question as to whether the children were authentically religious. If MOVE were a true religion, in the eyes of those with power to decide these sorts of things, it is hard to imagine such a violent act taking place.

The belief that Birdie Africa had been a victim to his mother's religion followed him throughout his life. A few months after the bombing, a journalist from the *Wall Street Journal* paid Michael and Andino Ward a visit.

Andino Ward told the reporter that he and his new wife were doing all they could for Michael, but that he would probably always be a victim of MOVE. He was struggling in school, despite the intensive tutoring he received in his special education program. He was beginning to recognize letters, words, and numbers, but arithmetic and reading still eluded him. He once put a pair of his underwear and a T-shirt on a stuffed bear and brought it to school with him. His father and Michael's psychologist thought these episodes were Michael regressing—a way of dealing with his traumatic childhood. But maybe Michael was learning that it was wrong to be naked. The psychologist said that Michael suffered from "cognitive deprivation." As a result of growing up in MOVE, he was not provided with "sufficient experiences to stimulate the mind," and that he probably would not be a fully functioning adult until he was forty years old. Michael's father and stepmother told the reporter that they were doing their best to provide him with the experiences he lacked. He enjoyed watching television. His favorite show was Miami Vice. But Birdie's parents, psychologists, and teachers worried that he was not processing his emotions properly. He was having nightmares "that the whole world was on fire," but they were happening less and less. Andino Ward told the reporter that when Michael woke up in the night with these nightmares, he would remind him that "it's very normal to have that feeling of guilt."[54]

Andino Ward told the journalist that he had recently asked Michael a question. If he'd had a choice, would he have chosen to live in MOVE, or would he have chosen life in the normal world? Andino Ward told the reporter that Michael "very clearly said 'I'd choose to be out here.'" His father had presented him with a series of truth claims about the nature of his existence and invited him to weigh them against other options. This time, Ward believed, Michael had been given an authentic choice over his life, and he chose the normal world.

This time, it counted.[55]

Notes

1. Video of Testimony of Michael Ward, Philadelphia Special Investigation Commission, Series 1, Special Collections Research Center, Temple University Libraries, Philadelphia; Transcript of Testimony of Michael Ward, Box 20, Folder 1, Philadelphia Special Investigation Commission, Series 1, Special Collections Research Center, Temple University Libraries, Philadelphia, PA.

2. Philadelphia Police Department Homicide Division, Investigation Interview Record, May 14, 1985, Box 63, Folder 9, PSIC; Philadelphia Police Department Homicide Division, Investigation Review Record, May 18, 1985, Box 63, Folder 9, PSIC; Ralph Teti to William Lyton, July 9, 1985, Box 63, Folder 7, PSIC [enclosure]; Philadelphia Police Department Civil Affairs Unit, Confidential Police Report, May 15, 1985, Box 63, Folder 9, PSIC; Philadelphia Police Department Juvenile Aid Division, Interview of Birdie Africa, undated, Box 63, Folder 9, PSIC.
3. Video of Testimony of Michael Ward, PSIC.
4. Statement by David Shrager, On Behalf of Michael Moses Ward, Box 7, Folder 5, PSIC.
5. John Modern, *Secularism in Antebellum America* (Chicago: University of Chicago Press, 2011), 5; Robert A. Orsi, *Between Heaven and Earth: The Religious Worlds People Make and the Scholars Who Study Them* (Princeton, NJ: Princeton University Press, 2005), 187–189; Russell T. McCutcheon, *Religion and the Domestication of Dissent: Or, How to Live in a Less than Perfect Nation* (London: Equinox, 2005), 1–15; William E. Arnal and Russell T. McCutcheon, *The Sacred Is the Profane: The Political Nature of "Religion"* (New York: Oxford University Press, 2013), 114–133.
6. John Locke, *A Letter Concerning Toleration* (Huddersfield, UK: J. Brook, 1796), 14. Locke's treatise was originally written in Latin. Locke used the words "ecclesia" (church) and "religionum" (religion) interchangeably. For example, Locke uses "ecclesia" in a comparative-religious sense when equating Christian sects and the religion/culture of the "Turks." On the evolution of the word "religion" and its synonyms, see Brent Nongbri, *Before Religion: A History of a Modern Concept* (New Haven, CT: Yale University Press, 2015); Orsi, *Between Heaven and Earth*, 1–18.
7. See Patrick Q. Mason, *The Mormon Menace: Violence and Anti-Mormonism in the Postbellum South* (New York: Oxford University Press, 2011); Katie Oxx, *The Nativist Movement in America: Religious Conflict in the 19th Century* (New York; London: Routledge, 2013); James D. Tabor and Eugene V. Gallagher, *Why Waco?: Cults and the Battle for Religious Freedom in America* (Berkeley: University of California Press, 1997); David Chidester, "Saving the Children by Killing Them: Redemptive Sacrifice in the Ideologies of Jim Jones and Ronald Reagan," *Religion and American Culture: A Journal of Interpretation* 1, no. 2 (1991): 177–201.
8. Sharon Sims Cox, "My Life in MOVE," *Philadelphia Magazine* (September 1985) 171; Philadelphia Police Department Civil Affairs Unit, Information Report, January 11, 1985, Box 63, Folder 2, PSIC; Charles Layton, "Body of Baby Seen at MOVE Commune," *Philadelphia Inquirer*, April 10, 1976.
9. United States Attorney Edward S. G. Dennis to William H. Brown III, January 3, 1986, Box 7, Folder 2, PSIC; Emerson Moran to Bill Brown, January 9, 1986, Box 7, Folder 2, PSIC; Philadelphia Police Department Chronology of Meetings Attended by Major Investigation Division Intelligence Regarding MOVE, May 23, 1985, Box 51, PSIC.
10. Philadelphia Special Investigation Commission, Interview with Police Officer Herbert Kirk, September 11, 1985, PSIC; Chronology of Meetings, PSIC.
11. Herbert Kirk Interview, PSIC; Chronology of Meetings, PSIC.
12. Herbert Kirk Interview, PSIC; On the use of PETN, see Global Security, "PETH [Pentaerythritol tetranitrate]" http://www.globalsecurity.org/military/systems/munitions/explosives-nitrate-petn.htm. Accessed June 19, 2017.

13. Philadelphia Police Department Civil Affairs Unit, MEMO to Police Commissioner from Chief Inspector, Civil Affairs Bureau Subj: Community Meeting—Sunday, May 13, 1984, at 6221 Osage Avenue, Box 51, Folder 3, PSIC; Alexander Reid, "Move Meets Their Neighborhood," *Philadelphia Daily News*, May 14, 1984; Tony Haye, "MOVE Talk No Help to Neighbors," *Philadelphia Tribune*, May 15, 1984; Tony Haye, "Neighbors Fear MOVE," *Afro-American*, May 19, 1984; Linn Washington, "Move Showing Contempt for Its Black Neighbors," *Philadelphia Daily News*, May 22, 1984; Chronology of Meetings, PSIC.
14. SCRC, Part 1, page 8; Joe O'Dowd, Leon Taylor, and Maria Gallagher, "Police Surround Move Gunman," *Philadelphia Daily News*, May 3, 1984; Philadelphia Police Department Major Investigation Division, MOVE Incident of Thursday, May 3rd, 1984, at 6221 Osage Avenue, May 3, 1984, Box 51, Folder 3, PSIC.
15. "Move Showing Contempt for Its Black Neighbors," *Philadelphia Daily News*, May 22, 1984.
16. Kirk Interview, PSIC; Vince Kasper, "New Names, New Dates, Same Story," *Philadelphia Daily News*, August 9, 1984; Leon Taylor, "Giant Move Stakeout Becomes Vigil," *Philadelphia Daily News*, August 9, 1984; Leon Taylor, "Giant Stakeout Ends at Move," *Philadelphia Daily News*, August 9, 1984; Robert J. Terry and Michael E. Ruane, "Police Out in Force at Move House," *Philadelphia Inquirer*, August 9, 1984; Thomas Gibbons and Robert J. Terry, "Police Scale Back Move Stakeout," *Philadelphia Inquirer*, August 10, 1984, sec; Christopher Hepp, "Move, City Now at Standoff," *Philadelphia Daily News*, August 10, 1984; "MOVE Staked out on 6th Anniversary: Police, Firefighters Respond to Threats on Goode's Life. Siege Ends with No Violence," *Philadelphia Tribune*, August 10, 1984.
17. Kirk Interview, PSIC.
18. Louise James Testimony; Civil Affairs Unit, Investigation Report, Box 51, Folder 3, PSIC.
19. "Memo to Philadelphia Special Investigation Commission" SCRC Box 7, Folder 3.
20. The 2007 interview with Michael Moses Ward can be found in the second epilogue to Michael Boyette and Randi Boyette, *Let It Burn: MOVE, The Philadelphia Police Department, and the Confrontation That Changed a City*, 2nd edition (San Diego: Quadrant Books, 2015), 301–315; James T. Richardson, "Social Control of New Religions: From 'Brainwashing' Claims to Child Sex Abuse Accusations," *Children in New Religions*, edited by Susan J. Palmer and Charlotte E. Hardman (New Brunswick, NJ: Rutgers University Press, 1999), 172; Video of Testimony of Michael Ward, PSIC.
21. Philadelphia Police Department Civil Affairs Unit, Internal Incident Report, July 1984, Box 6, PSIC; Testimony of James C. Pryor, PSIC.
22. Chronology of Meetings, PSIC; Kirk Interview, PSIC.
23. Testimony of Irene Pernsley, PSIC; Testimony of Ralph Teti, PSIC; The CAU kept meticulous records of MOVE's day-to-day activities, recording that the children routinely visited Cobb's Creek, Philadelphia Police Department, Information Report, undated, Box 51, Folder 3, PSIC; Testimony of Richard Gold, Divisional Deputy City Solicitor.
24. Interview with Tony Crumpler, PSIC, Box 8, Folder 2; Interview with Fareed Ahmed, PSIC, Box 8, Folder 2.

25. Civil Affairs Unit report, "Information Regarding Assault by MOVE Member, Conrad Africa," Box 63, Folder 2, PSIC; Philadelphia Police Department Civil Affairs Unit, Additional Information Regarding MOVE House 6221 Osage Avenue, October 3, 1984, PSIC; Leon Taylor, "Move's Afoot: We've Had It, Neighbors Warn," *Philadelphia Daily News*, May 2, 1985; Testimony of Officers Cresci and Draper, PSIC; Associated Press, "Unhappy Neighbors Want MOVE to Move," *Morning Call*, May 3, 1985.
26. "The Scene: In Philadelphia and Its Suburbs," *Philadelphia Inquirer*, May 3, 1985; Irv Randolph, "Make MOVE Move, Neighbors Plead," *Philadelphia Tribune*, May 3, 1985.
27. Ibid.; "What Should Be Done about MOVE?," *Philadelphia Tribune*, May 7, 1985; Steven A. Marquez, "Move's Afoot: Our Hands Tied, Officials Say," *Philadelphia Daily News*, May 2, 1985; Edward S. G. Dennis, Jr., United States Attorney to William H. Brown III, Esq., January 3, 1986, Box 7, Folder 2, PSIC; United States Attorney Edward S. G. Dennis to William H. Brown III, January 3, 1986, Box 7, Folder 2, PSIC.
28. Chronology of Meetings, PSIC; Philadelphia Police Department Major Investigation Division, Attempted Placement of Listening Devices Inside 6221 Osage Avenue, May 18, 1985, Box 51, folder 7, PSIC; Testimony of Officers Cresci and Draper, PSIC.
29. Transcript of *Commonwealth v. Ramona Johnson, A/K/A Ramona Africa*, Court of Common Pleas of Philadelphia County, First Judicial District of Pennsylvania, Criminal Trial Division, PSIC, Box 5.
30. Interview with Novella Williams of Citizens for Progress, Box 63, Folder 9, PSIC; Boyette and Boyette, *Let It Burn*, 301–315.
31. Michael Ward Testimony, PSIC; Philadelphia Police Department Homicide Division, Investigation Interview Record, May 14, 1985, Box 63, Folder 9, PSIC; Philadelphia Police Department Homicide Division, Investigation Review Record, May 18, 1985, Box 63, Folder 9, PSIC; Ralph Teti to William Lyton, July 9, 1985, Box 63, Folder 7, PSIC [enclosure]; Philadelphia Police Department Civil Affairs Unit, Confidential Police Report, May 15, 1985, Box 63, Folder 9, PSIC; Philadelphia Police Department Juvenile Aid Division, Interview of Birdie Africa, undated, Box 63, Folder 9, PSIC.
32. William Lyton to Emerson D. Moran, September 9, 1985, Box 8, Folder 1, PSIC.
33. Michael Ward Testimony; Philadelphia Police Department Homicide Division, Investigation Interview Record, May 14, 1985, Box 63, Folder 9, PSIC; Philadelphia Police Department Homicide Division, Investigation Review Record, May 18, 1985, Box 63, Folder 9, PSIC; Ralph Teti to William Lyton, July 9, 1985, Box 63, Folder 7, PSIC [enclosure]; Philadelphia Police Department Civil Affairs Unit, Confidential Police Report, May 15, 1985, Box 63, Folder 9, PSIC; Philadelphia Police Department Juvenile Aid Division, Interview of Birdie Africa, undated, Box 63, Folder 9, PSIC.
34. Philadelphia Special Investigation Commission, The Findings, Conclusions, and Recommendations of the Philadelphia Special Investigation Commission, PSIC.
35. Randy Whitestone, "Fire Nearly Destroys Radicals' House; Blaze Started after Daylong Police Siege," *Boston Globe*, May 14, 1985.
36. Testimony of Leo Brooks, PSIC; Testimony of William Richmond, PSIC; Testimony of Gregore Sambor, PSIC; Philadelphia Special Investigation Commission, The Findings, Conclusions, and Recommendations of the Philadelphia Special

Investigation Commission, PSIC; 1. Vernon Loeb, "Sambor Says Bomb Was 'Tactical Necessity,'" *Philadelphia Inquirer*, May 16, 1985; Russell Cooke, "Brooks Discloses Plan to Resign: Notified the Mayor Weeks Ago," *Philadelphia Inquirer*, May 22, 1985; Philip Lentz, "Fire Commissioner Challenges Police Chief in MOVE Inquiry," *Chicago Tribune*, October 31, 1985; Associated Press, "MOVE Bomb 'Wrong Thing,'" *Morning Call*, November 2, 1985; Lindsey Gruson, "Expert Disputes Decision on Bomb: Pathologist Says 5 Children in Move House Should Be Termed Murder Victims," *New York Times*, November 6, 1985.

37. Philadelphia Special Investigation Commission, The Findings, Conclusions, and Recommendations of the Philadelphia Special Investigation Commission, PSIC.
38. Testimony of William Richmond, PSIC; Testimony of Gregore Sambor, PSIC.
39. Michael Ward Testimony, PSIC; Philadelphia Police Department Homicide Division, Investigation Interview Record, May 14, 1985, Box 63, Folder 9, PSIC; Philadelphia Police Department Homicide Division, Investigation Review Record, May 18, 1985, Box 63, Folder 9, PSIC; Ralph Teti to William Lyton, July 9, 1985, Box 63, Folder 7, PSIC [enclosure]; Philadelphia Police Department Civil Affairs Unit, Confidential Police Report, May 15, 1985, Box 63, Folder 9, PSIC; Philadelphia Police Department Juvenile Aid Division, Interview of Birdie Africa, undated, Box 63, Folder 9, PSIC.
40. Ramona Africa Testimony in *Ramona Africa v. City of Philadelphia*; Michael Ward Testimony; Philadelphia Police Department Homicide Division, Investigation Interview Record, May 14, 1985, Box 63, Folder 9, PSIC; Philadelphia Police Department Homicide Division, Investigation Review Record, May 18, 1985, Box 63, Folder 9, PSIC; Ralph Teti to William Lyton, July 9, 1985, Box 63, Folder 7, PSIC [enclosure]; Philadelphia Police Department Civil Affairs Unit, Confidential Police Report, May 15, 1985, Box 63, Folder 9, PSIC; Philadelphia Police Department Juvenile Aid Division, Interview of Birdie Africa, undated, Box 63, Folder 9, PSIC.
41. Michael Ward Testimony; Philadelphia Police Department Homicide Division, Investigation Interview Record, May 14, 1985, Box 63, Folder 9, PSIC; Philadelphia Police Department Homicide Division, Investigation Review Record, May 18, 1985, Box 63, Folder 9, PSIC; Ralph Teti to William Lyton, July 9, 1985, Box 63, Folder 7, PSIC [enclosure]; Philadelphia Police Department Civil Affairs Unit, Confidential Police Report, May 15, 1985, Box 63, Folder 9, PSIC; Philadelphia Police Department Juvenile Aid Division, Interview of Birdie Africa, undated, Box 63, Folder 9, PSIC; Testimony of James Berghaier, PSIC.
42. Vernon Loeb and Russell Cooke, "Goode Says He's 'Fully Accountable' for Siege," *Philadelphia Inquirer*, May 14, 1985; "The Move Siege: Chronology of Events," *Philadelphia Inquirer*, May 14, 1985.
43. "Philadelphia Inferno: Cop Attack on Radicals Backfires Inferno," *Chicago Tribune*, May 14, 1985; William K. Stevens, "Police Drop Bomb on Radicals' Home in Philadelphia," *New York Times*, May 14, 1985.
44. May Lee and John J. Goldman, "6 Bodies in Rubble of Bombed House Goode Vows to Rebuild Neighborhood as He Defends Raid on Radical Cult," *Los Angeles Times*, May 15, 1985; "Goode: The Right Decision, Despite the Consequences," *Philadelphia Inquirer*, May 15, 1985.

45. Frank Trippett, Kenneth W. Banta, and Joseph N. Boyce, "'It Looks Just like a War Zone': A Police Raid in Philadelphia Turns to Tragedy," *Time* 125, no. 21 (May 27, 1985): 16; Lindsey Gruson, "Search for Bodies, and for Reason, in Smoky Ruins," *New York Times*, May 15, 1985.
46. Associated Press, "Pathologist: 5 MOVE Children Homicide Victims, Fire Could Have Been Extinguished, Expert Says," *Morning Call*, November 6, 1985; Gregory Williams, "And What of the Children?," Father Paul Washington Papers, Box 26, Folder 4, Charles L. Blockson Afro-American Collection, Philadelphia, PA.
47. I have chosen to honor these original requests for anonymity. This is why I am not using respondents' names and using general references to the collection as a whole. However, I have included some information about the respondents, including race, gender, employment, and—in one instance—former organizational affiliation because I deem this information relevant.
48. American Friends Service Committee, "Voices from the Community," 1986, American Friends Service Committee Archives, Philadelphia, PA; Philadelphia Perspectives Project, American Friends Service Committee Archive, Philadelphia, PA.
49. Philadelphia Perspectives Project, AFSC.
50. Ibid.
51. Ibid.
52. Russell Cooke, "Brooks Discloses Plan to Resign: Notified the Mayor Weeks Ago," *Philadelphia Inquirer*, May 22, 1985; Tommie Hill, "Brooks Resigns," *Philadelphia Tribune*, June 4, 1985; Lee Linder, "Sambor Resigns in Phila.: Police Chief Steps Down 6 Months after MOVE," *Morning Call*, November 14, 1985; Ann Moore, "Sambor Says Goode Forced Him to Quit," *Philadelphia Inquirer*, February 9, 1986; Howard Schneider, "Goode: Did Not Coerce Sambor," *Philadelphia Daily News*, February 11, 1986; Robin Clark, Robert J. Terry, and William K. Marimow, "Sambor Expected to Quit Today: Deputy Seen as Successor," *Philadelphia Inquirer*, November 13, 1985; Joseph R. Daughen, Joe O'Dowd, and Kit Konolige, "Sambor Resigns as City's Top Cop," *Philadelphia Daily News*, November 13, 1985.
53. Frank Trippett, Kenneth W. Banta, and Joseph N. Boyce, "'It Looks Just like a War Zone': A Police Raid in Philadelphia Turns to Tragedy," *Time 125*, no. 21 (May 27, 1985): 22; Craig R. McCoy, "Ex-Officer Bares His Torment to Move Jury: James P. Berghaier Was There to Take Birdie Africa's Hand When He Fled the Burning House. Berghaier Remains Emotionally Scarred," *Philadelphia Inquirer*, May 31, 1996.
54. Francine Schwadel, "In Philadelphia, a Child of 'Move' Begins a New Life," *Wall Street Journal*, November 1, 1985, 1.
55. Ibid.

9
Unthinkable

For years, activist groups, MOVE's international community of supporters, and historical preservationists have petitioned the city of Philadelphia and the state of Pennsylvania to place a historical marker on Osage Avenue in West Philadelphia, the site of the MOVE Bombing. In 2016, a team headed by a historic preservationist began the process of formally petitioning the Pennsylvania Historical and Museum Commission to erect a historical marker and asked me to help. This was a fraught undertaking; one that, admittedly, I was not looking forward to. The Pennsylvania Historical and Museum Commission usually only erects markers for history that sheds a "positive light" on the state. Even more difficult, there are still basic facts about the MOVE Bombing that are unsettled—not because the evidence is unclear, but because that evidence points to conclusions that are too horrendous for many to accept. How does one explain—in less than fifty words and in a way that is acceptable to all the parties involved—what happened on Osage Avenue on May 13, 1985?[1]

Unbeknownst to our team of preservationists and historians, we were beaten to the punch by a group of fifth graders from the Jubilee School in southwest Philadelphia, who successfully petitioned the Pennsylvania Historical and Museum Commission to install a commemorative marker on Osage Avenue. The students began researching the MOVE Bombing after Freddie Gray, a twenty-five-year-old Black man from Baltimore, was killed while in police custody. Eager to learn about past instances of police violence against African Americans, the students dug into historical newspaper accounts of MOVE and the MOVE Bombing and spoke to witnesses, including Ramona Africa. When they had completed their study, the students asked the Pennsylvania Historical and Museum Commission to place a historical marker on Osage Avenue. The children pulled no punches in their petition. They wrote that the MOVE Bombing was "one of the most extreme cases of police violence and government abuses of power" in American history. They argued that "because there were no consequences to the police and city officials for their actions, it paved the way for government assistance to, and

MOVE. Richard Kent Evans, Oxford University Press (2020). © Oxford University Press.
DOI: 10.1093/oso/9780190058777.001.0001

tolerance of, police brutality." The students hoped a marker could "spread awareness of a troubled history which has been buried for so many years."[2]

The schoolchildren's petition reflected some of the tensions within this history. On one hand, there has been a desire since May 13, 1985, to contextualize the MOVE Bombing: to place it within its history and to assign it to a broader national narrative. This is an admirable impulse. It is, after all, what historians do. But doing so runs against the other tension within this history that the schoolchildren picked up on: the MOVE Bombing is remarkable in that it has been so thoroughly forgotten.

The MOVE Bombing has indeed largely been forgotten, but it has not been buried. It has been forgotten because it is unthinkable. Governments are not, we like to believe, supposed to attack their own citizens. In those cases where they must, they are not supposed to behave with such unchecked brutality or with such a thin legal pretext. Agents of the state, who exist as such for our protection, are not supposed to watch as children burn. They are not supposed to shoot at people trying to escape a burning building. The state is not supposed to act like that.

The MOVE Bombing was unthinkable for MOVE people as well. By the early 1980s, John Africa was a fully divine figure whom MOVE people believed "would never die and will live on forever." To MOVE people, the death of John Africa was the death of a god. It wasn't supposed to happen. In the months that followed his death, the few surviving MOVE people tried to disentangle the death of John Africa from the death of Vincent Leaphart; as if the two were separate beings; one mortal, the other immortal. Since 1985, MOVE people have struggled to articulate the relationship between John Africa and Vincent Leaphart. It is an internal theological debate that resembles, in some respects, Christological debates, and continues to this day. The theological confusion surrounding the relationship between John Africa and Vincent Leaphart stems from the fact that, for MOVE people and for many who know this history, the MOVE Bombing simply wasn't supposed to happen. That it has been forgotten is not the fault of memory, but of history.[3]

What happened on May 13, 1985? And how do we tell a story that is, for many, unthinkable? The first serious attempt to answer these questions was the Philadelphia Special Investigation Commission, commonly referred to as the MOVE Commission, which was founded by the mayor's office in the days following the MOVE Bombing. The MOVE Commission was a ritual of storytelling, trauma, and power. It was a way of coming to grips with an act of violence that many found unthinkable. But the MOVE Commission was also a simulacrum of the relationship between power and the production of history. Like all interrogations into the past, the MOVE Commission looked backwards selectively. Some stories it crafted, others it silenced. The result of this ritual was the creation of a single narrative: a story that made the MOVE Bombing an aberration, a story that made the conceivable inconceivable, a story whose incongruence facilitated its forgetting.[4]

The MOVE Commission first met, albeit in an unofficial capacity, on May 28, 1985—just two weeks after the bombing. On June 19, 1985, Mayor Wilson Goode issued an executive order formally establishing the Philadelphia Special Investigation Commission. The mayor instructed the commission to "find facts and prepare a report for the Mayor and the Citizens of Philadelphia concerning the operation of City government as it relates to the events giving rise to the incident of May 13, 1985." The Commission had some subpoena power, emanating from the mayor's office, but it could not recommend the firing or prosecution of any city officials. Rather, the commission was asked to "make suggestions for future handling of similar situations."[5]

The MOVE Commission consisted of eleven members, all of whom volunteered their time. Six of the commission members—William Brown, Charles Bowser, Bruce Kauffman, Charisse Lillie, Henry Ruth, and Neil Welch—were experts in law. Kauffman was a former justice of the Pennsylvania Supreme Court. Lillie was a professor of law at Villanova University and an Assistant US Attorney. Henry Ruth was Special Prosecutor in the US Justice Department during Watergate. Two of the commission members—M. Todd Cooke, vice chairman of a bank, and Julia Chinn, president of the town watch for the neighborhood where the MOVE house was located—represented the community at large. The remaining three Commission members were religious leaders. Rev. Paul Washington, who mediated between MOVE and the police during the 1978 standoff, served on the commission alongside Rev. Msgr. Edward Cullen, director of Catholic Social Services for the Archdiocese of Philadelphia, and Rev. Audrey Bronson, founder and pastor of a predominately African American Protestant church in West Philadelphia.

The Commission's work was supported by a staff of sixteen lawyers, researchers, and investigators. One of those lawyers was William Lytton, a methodical, even-tempered former Assistant US Attorney who led the proceedings and performed most of the questioning. He was assisted by H. Graham McDonald, a former prosecutor and lawyer, and Carl Singley, dean of the law school at Temple University. A team of seven investigators decoded the forensics evidence for the Commission members. The lead investigator, Neil Shanahan, was a former supervisor at the FBI who investigated the bombing of the 16th Street Baptist Church in Birmingham and the break-in at the FBI field office in Media, Pennsylvania, which had exposed the bureau's illegal COINTELPRO programs. The other six investigators were all career law enforcement professionals at the local and federal levels.

The MOVE Commission encountered obstacles from the very beginning of their investigation. The first was a suspicious public who feared that some of the members of the Commission, whom Mayor Goode had handpicked, were trying to "whitewash" the investigation to protect city officials. The professionalism and fairness with which the Commission conducted its investigation soon put any concerns about whitewashing to rest. The second and more formidable obstacle was the Fraternal Order of the Police. The organization told Philadelphia police officers not to cooperate with the MOVE Commission and challenged the Commission's legal authority in court. Some members of the Philadelphia Police Department, emboldened by the FOP, refused to turn over documents and lied to investigators. Throughout the proceedings, members of the Philadelphia Bomb Squad submitted false testimony, changed their stories when they were caught, and attempted to intimidate the members of the Commission. The MOVE Commission subpoenaed MOVE-related documents from thirty-six government agencies. Some of those requests were unsuccessful. Several agencies, including the Philadelphia Police Department, the FBI, and the ATF, stonewalled the commission, turned over inadequate documentation, and submitted newly created documents meant to replace documents relating to events that took place years prior that they said were lost.[6]

Despite these challenges, the MOVE Commission proved itself up to the task at hand. Over the course of six months, the Commission conducted over 900 interviews with people they believed to be either "major participants" in, or witnesses to, the MOVE Bombing. The Commission viewed or listened to dozens of hours of audio and video evidence, and they read reams of forensics reports, affidavits, and interview transcripts.

Most of the work done by the Commission took place behind closed doors, but on October 8 to November 6, 1985, the MOVE Commission conducted public hearings. The most important witnesses—Mayor Wilson Goode, Managing Director Leo Brooks, Police Commissioner Gregore Sambor, Fire Commissioner William Richmond, and dozens of others, submitted their depositions to public scrutiny. The hearings took place in a television studio at the local public television station and were broadcast over television and radio. The public hearings captivated Philadelphia. They were inescapable: the video played on every television; the audio feed on every radio. People tuned in to the hearings for different reasons. Some were curious. Others were seething with anger. One person told a reporter, "I keep hoping that if I listen long enough I'll hear a good reason for why it happened." Another man told reporters he had been clipping articles out of the papers for his children and grandchildren, sure that the MOVE Bombing had been a "historic event." The proceedings of the MOVE Commission aroused national interest as well. The *New York Times*, the *Washington Post*, and *Time Magazine* provided regular updates to their readers.[7]

The first witnesses to testify publicly before the MOVE Commission were Officers Cresse and Draper of the Civil Affairs Unit (CAU). (George Fencl, longtime head of the CAU, had retired in 1983). Cresse and Draper spent the first day of testimony detailing the CAU's long history with MOVE. They told the Commission that the CAU had been investigating MOVE since 1973, and that they intensified their surveillance operations in 1976. They testified that the Guns on the Porch standoff on May 20, 1977, was the first time they had ever seen MOVE with guns, and that no one other than Chuckie Africa had committed a crime that day. In their second day of testimony, the officers told the MOVE Commission about the threats MOVE people had made against three presidents (Ford, Carter, and Reagan) and three mayors (Rizzo, Green, and Goode). They listed the people involved in physical altercations with MOVE people since the early 1970s, and they offered statistics on the hundreds of arrests and dozens of trials MOVE people had accrued. It was a thorough accounting of the crimes MOVE people had committed. In the face of those statistics, one could be forgiven for thinking MOVE had more in common with a criminal syndicate than a religious group.[8]

On the second day of testimony, MOVE's Osage Avenue neighbors testified before the Commission. Most of the neighbors blamed Mayor Goode for promising, but failing, to solve the MOVE problem peacefully. A few neighbors testified that MOVE had been a positive presence in the neighborhood before about 1983, when the group grew insular and paranoid. The highlight of the neighbors' testimony was that of Cassandra Carter, who testified that she had seen Frank Africa chase Louise James down the street, axe in hand. (MOVE people strongly reject this claim. They argue that it would have been physically impossible for Louise James, who was a middle-aged woman, to outrun her son, who was in peak physical condition. It is worth pointing out that Frank Africa did threaten someone with an axe once before.) The only MOVE people to testify before the Commission were Louise James and Laverne Sims, who no longer identified as MOVE members, and Birdie Africa, who submitted prerecorded testimony. Nearly everyone else who might have testified on behalf of MOVE was in prison or dead.[9]

The highlight of the public hearings was the testimony of the men the media dubbed the "Big Four"—Mayor Wilson Goode, Police Commissioner Gregore Sambor, Fire Commissioner William Richmond, and City Manager Leo Brooks. The testimony of the Big Four did little to inspire confidence in their competence or decency. Each man pointed the finger at the others. Leo Brooks testified that Mayor Wilson Goode was briefed on the plan to drop a bomb at least twice, and that the mayor gave his approval for the tactic over the phone a half hour before Frank Powell dropped the bomb. But Brooks told the Commission that he had been out of the state during the final stages of planning, and thus bore no responsibility for the decision to drop the final bomb. Goode denied knowing much of anything about the plan, and characterized Sambor, Richmond, and Brooks as insubordinate rogues. Sambor was defiant. Astoundingly, he characterized the raid as "the most conservative, controlled, disciplined and safe operation which we could devise." A scathing editorial in the *Philadelphia Inquirer* summarized the testimony of the Big Four this way:

> The people of Philadelphia have been able to look deeply into an incredible debacle. They have seen a police commissioner pleading ignorance so deep that—if he is telling the truth—such ignorance alone should be grounds for dismissal; seen a fire commissioner who agreed to let a fire grow out of control; seen a managing director who may better have remained on vacation. They saw a mayor, too, who did not say "no" to dropping a bomb; a mayor who opted for the sidelines as police confronted MOVE and a neighborhood was consumed.[10]

The testimony of the Big Four was embarrassing, but it shielded the men from even the slightest repercussions. Their testimony helped to create a false narrative of the MOVE Bombing that has prevailed ever since—what might be called the bumbling-officials narrative. The story goes like this: the police showed up outside the Osage house on May 13th to apprehend those MOVE people inside wanted on arrest warrants. Importantly, in this narrative, the police intended to perform an ordinary police function, hoping to avoid any loss of life. Things got out of control when MOVE people started shooting at police. In the haste and confusion, city officials began making a series of decisions that were poorly informed at best, idiotic at worst. Chief among those decisions was the decision, made impromptu, to drop a bomb from a helicopter with hopes of dislodging the "bunker" on top of the house. When, much to their surprise, that bomb caused a fire, the officials made the decision—again, on the spot and with little consideration of possible ramifications—to let the fire burn. Their hope was that the fire might succeed where the water, tear gas, bullets, and other explosives had failed, and finally force MOVE people to surrender. In this story, which is more fiction than fact, no one intended to hurt anybody, MOVE people were culpable for their own deaths, and the MOVE Bombing was all an unfortunate series of accidents. The bumbling-officials narrative worked because it relied on a story which many people are predisposed to believe: that government leaders can be astoundingly inept. It was, and is, the most comforting of the limited options available for making sense of such an unthinkable act of violence.[11]

The bumbling-officials narrative has been influential, but it is, I think, hard to reconcile with the evidence. It ignores the fact that the raid had been in the works for over a year, and that the raid had been attempted once before. This narrative ignores the fact that the MOVE Bombing was a collaborative assault planned by the Philadelphia Police Department, the ATF, and the FBI, and that several bombs had been used that day prior to the one dropped from the helicopter. Indeed, it is difficult to avoid reaching the conclusion that the United States government, at all three levels, had simply grown tired of MOVE and sought to eradicate them. With thin legal pretext, an army of police officers, with the blessing of federal law enforcement, attacked MOVE with explosives, heavy artillery, and fire, understanding that all those inside—men, women, and children—would likely die as the result.

The Philadelphia Special Investigation Commission published its report on March 6, 1986. The Commission concluded that MOVE "used threats, abuse, and intimidation to terrify their neighbors and to bring about confrontation with City government." This problem was exacerbated by Mayor Goode, whose "policy toward MOVE was one of appeasement, non-confrontation, and avoidance." Attempts to appease MOVE were clearly failing, and by 1984, the group was operating under the impression that they were "above the law." The MOVE Commission agreed that Sambor had conducted most of the planning that went into the raid and that the planning was done "hastily and without sufficient information or intelligence." The report made clear that both Sambor and Brooks knew days in advance that children were in the house and called both men "grossly negligent" for having "clearly risked the lives of the children by failing to take effective steps to detain them" before the operation.[12]

The MOVE Commission called the MOVE Bombing "reckless, ill-conceived," and "unconscionable," and suggested that any competent city official should have rejected it out of hand. The report noted that the police fired over 10,000 rounds of ammunition into the MOVE house within ninety minutes—a figure the Commission called "clearly excessive and unreasonable." The report called the use of explosives "excessive and life-threatening," and accused the members of the Bomb Disposal Unit of being unqualified to use them. It also noted that the FBI had provided "substantial quantities of C-4" that went into the making of those bombs, and that the transaction was not recorded by either the FBI or the PPD as it should have been. The report denounced Richmond, Sambor, and Brooks for using fire "as a tactical weapon." Most damningly, the MOVE Commission concluded that police officers positioned in the back alley had fired upon MOVE people as they tried to escape the burning house, and called the deaths of the five MOVE children "unjustified homicides which should be investigated by a grand jury." The Commission agreed on sixty-eight findings. Sixty-six were unanimous. Bruce Kauffman, the former Justice of the Supreme Court of Pennsylvania, dissented on two points: he disagreed that the 10,000 rounds of ammunition were excessive and was not convinced that police gunfire prevented MOVE people from escaping the house.[13]

The MOVE Commission report told the truth about the MOVE Bombing in a way that few documents since have done. However, like any interrogation into the past, the MOVE Commission asked some questions that precluded the asking of others. In its desire to produce a cohesive, understandable, and actionable explanation of events, it privileged some stories and silenced others. In many ways, the narrative of the MOVE Bombing created by the MOVE Commission ensured that the MOVE Bombing would fade from public memory.[14]

The MOVE Commission facilitated the forgetting of this history because it did not seriously investigate what MOVE was. Again, this was structural. Very few MOVE people participated in the Commission's investigations. It is unlikely that a more thorough investigation into what MOVE was would have altered the Commission's findings at all, but in the dearth of information, the

Commission relied on characterizations of MOVE produced by the CAU. The CAU was, indeed, an informed source of empirical knowledge about MOVE. But Officers Draper and Cresce were police officers, not ethnographers. They classified MOVE as a criminal operation, not as a religion. This is why the MOVE Commission resorted to empty signifiers to describe MOVE. To the Commission, MOVE was "a group of radicals," "a violence-threatening cult," and "a small group of self-styled back-to-nature, anti-technology, anti-social advocates." These words tell us almost nothing about what MOVE meant to MOVE people, how the group might be classified, and what MOVE people believed and practiced. They serve only to devalue the humanity of the people to whom they are applied; to make their concerns and their experiences seem invalid. These empty signifiers have followed MOVE ever since.[15]

The MOVE Commission also seriously downplayed the role of federal law enforcement in the planning and implementation of the MOVE Bombing. Because the MOVE Commission was tasked with investigating "the operation of City government as it relate[d] to the events giving rise to the incident of May 13, 1985," it was largely unconcerned with the role federal law enforcement had played in the design and orchestration of the MOVE Bombing. Again, this was structural: the Commission's power, such as it was, originated in the mayor's office. They had no legal authority over federal law enforcement agencies involved (the FBI and the ATF, especially) and some of those agencies were not forthcoming. For this reason, the MOVE Bombing has been remembered as a local event—a Philadelphia story. It was not. We know more now about the federal government's relationship to MOVE than before. For example, we know that the FBI had been working closely with the CAU Unit, which began investigating MOVE in 1973; that the FBI, the ATF, and other federal law enforcement agencies had been watching MOVE closely since the mid-1970s; and that the PPD had acquired the C-4 and Tovex explosives and a large cache of military grade weapons from the FBI in the months and weeks leading up to the raid. We know that the FBI was integral to the planning and implementation of the MOVE Bombing, but, in the absence of the full FBI file, we can say little else. Hopefully, these files will one day be made available and the history of the federal government's involvement with MOVE and the MOVE Bombing will need to be rewritten.[16]

But the primary historical question that went unasked, the one that most facilitated the MOVE Bombing's forgetting, was this: where does the MOVE Bombing sit within American history? To the MOVE Commission, the MOVE Bombing was outside of history. It was unprecedented; disconnected from a broader national narrative of state-sanctioned racial and religious violence. In the early months of the investigation, William Lyton asked a research assistant to find historical precedents for the MOVE Bombing. He asked, specifically, for examples of police killing "activist groups" and for instances when police used deadly force that endangered the lives of children. The researcher returned with a list containing three historical precedents matching Lyton's questions. The first was the misnamed Tulsa "Race Riot" of 1921, when white mobs, working with the police and the National Guard, violently rampaged Tulsa's Black population, murdering three hundred and displacing thousands. Like in the MOVE Bombing, Tulsa city police used airplanes to drop turpentine bombs onto the city's Black business district, and National Guardsmen used machine guns to fire into crowds. The second historical precedent the researcher proposed was the sensational and short career of the Symbionese Liberation Army. The third historical precedent for the MOVE Bombing was the American common law tradition of *posse comitatus*. The MOVE Commission did not use the researcher's work in their deliberations or conclusions. Despite this early research, the MOVE Commission made no effort to connect the MOVE Bombing to any broader historical context.[17]

From my perspective, the tragedy of the MOVE Bombing is that it is perfectly ordinary. The United States government kills its citizens all the time (to say nothing of all the non-citizens it kills). And it has killed Black people with prolificacy. When MOVE people talk about the MOVE Bombing as a historical event, they place it within a historical context beginning with Nat Turner's revolt. They are not wrong to do so. There are certainly parallels between him and John Africa. Nat Turner was a Black man—a slave—who believed himself a prophet. Acting, he believed, on behalf of God, Nat Turner led a slave revolt that killed around sixty white men, women, and children. White authorities killed Turner and his accomplices, then murdered hundreds of slaves—men, women, and children, many of whom had nothing to do with the revolt—in revenge.

But one does not have to go back to the 1830s to find a historical context for the MOVE Bombing. We see antecedents for the MOVE Bombing in the Attica Prison Uprising of 1971, when state police wantonly put down a prisoner revolt during peaceful negotiations, killing thirty-nine people, both hostages and prisoners. We see the context for the MOVE Bombing in the 1963 16th Street Bombing, when four Ku Klux Klan members bombed a predominately African American church, killing four children, then evaded justice with the help of a complicit legal system. We see antecedents for the MOVE Bombing when, in 1968, Chicago's Police Department, working in concert with the FBI, murdered Fred Hampton as he slept in his bed. We see antecedents for the MOVE Bombing in the hundreds of "race riots" in twentieth-century America, and in the thousands of Black men and women lynched by white mobs while local law enforcement looked the other way or participated. And we see the legacies of this history when unarmed Black men, women, and children are killed by the police. The MOVE Bombing was not unprecedented. It was not unusual. It is only unthinkable if one prefers not to think about it.[18]

After the MOVE Commission published its report, the Philadelphia district attorney impaneled a grand jury to consider whether charges should be filed against city officials for their role in the MOVE Bombing. The grand jury investigation lasted nearly three years, and mirrored the MOVE Commission investigation. On May 3, 1988, the district attorney announced that the grand jury had voted sixteen to one against pressing charges against city officials. In their report, the grand jury noted that they did "not exonerate the men responsible for this disaster." "Rather than a vindication of those officials, this report should stand as a permanent record of their morally reprehensible behavior." Still, the grand jury did not recommend charges, because they were unconvinced that Gregore Sambor, William Richmond, Leo Brooks, or Wilson Goode *intended* to kill MOVE people that day. Instead, the grand jury relied upon the bumbling-officials narrative crafted by the MOVE Commission. The report called the MOVE Bombing "an epic of governmental incompetence," and placed the blame on the poor decision-making of the Big Four. The district attorney, explaining why no one would face charges for the MOVE Bombing, told reporters that "our society cannot condone prosecutions motivated solely by grief or rage."[19]

The grand jury report also moderated many of the findings of the MOVE Commission. The grand jury was not convinced that police officers were shooting at MOVE people as they escaped. Both William H. Brown, the chairman of the MOVE Commission, and David Shrager, Birdie Africa's lawyer, objected to the grand jury's attempt to cast doubt on these findings. Both men pointed out that forensics evidence proved that at least one of the children had been shot, and it strained credulity to suggest that MOVE people ran back inside a building that was engulfed in flames for no reason. The jury chose to believe that police officers would not do something so heinous as to shoot at children trying to escape a burning building. They chose, instead, to believe that the MOVE Bombing had been an accidental tragedy—the work of bumbling officials whose incompetence, not hate, had motivated their actions. This was the story the district attorney provided them. It was a flimsy story, but the alternative was unthinkable.

In the end, only one person went to jail because of the MOVE Bombing: Ramona Africa. Ramona was taken into police custody on May 13, 1985, and was taken to a hospital. She suffered severe burns from the fire, the scars from which she still bears today. She refused medical treatment on May 13, citing her religious beliefs, and was taken to jail. She faced nine charges: three counts of aggravated assault, three counts of recklessly endangering another person, inciting a riot, conspiracy, and resisting arrest. Ramona was charged with aggravated assault and recklessly endangering another person because three police officers alleged that they had been struck, or nearly struck, by bullets on May 13. One police officer said a bullet struck his helmet and grazed the back of his neck. Another police officer said he was shot in the back, but that the bullet was stopped by his bulletproof vest. A third officer alleged that he was nearly shot. The judge set Ramona Africa's bail at $2.5 million.[20]

Ramona acted as her own legal counsel throughout her trial. She was, without a doubt, MOVE's most capable legal advocate. She had studied law at Temple University and had worked for a year as a paralegal. She represented Frank Africa in *Africa v. Commonwealth* with great skill but little success. In pretrial proceedings, she impressed reporters, the judge, and even the prosecutor with her legal mind, and, even in the wake of tragedy, her pleasant demeanor. The prosecutor, Assistant District Attorney Joseph McGill, told reporters that Ramona Africa had "many skills" and that he found it "much more difficult to prosecute a case against a defendant than the most skilled defense attorney." Reporters remarked that, unlike previous MOVE trials, Ramona was professional and polite. One reporter observed an "informal conference" between Ramona and Judge Michael Stiles that "ended with her jokingly tapping Stiles' elbow and softly laughing. Africa walked back to the defense table grinning; the judge was smiling as he returned to the bench."[21]

The trial, *Commonwealth of Pennsylvania v. Ramona Johnson*, began on January 14, 1986. Because she could not afford her bail, Ramona was brought into the courtroom every morning in handcuffs. She had a team of supporters doing the legwork for her, and coordinated her defense from behind bars. These were not ideal conditions for conducting a legal defense, but Ramona and her supporters were convinced that the truth was on her side. "The presence of truth is the power of God," Ramona told the jury in her opening statement. "And that's what I rely on."

The prosecution's strategy was to limit the scope of the proceedings to the events immediately preceding the raid of May 13 and the "first eight hours" of the confrontation. That is, the prosecution did not want to discuss the third bomb, the city's decision to let the fire burn, the shooting in the back alley, or the eleven dead MOVE people. The prosecution's strategy was to prove that Ramona was part of a conspiracy that resulted in three police officers being shot at. In making his case, however, Assistant District Attorney Joseph McGill classified MOVE as a dangerous, insurrectionist "cult" that was "rigid in its resolve to a philosophy which they, in their own words, call revolution." He reminded jurors that MOVE had built a bunker on the roof of the MOVE house which he characterized as a "fortress which by itself shouts resistance." McGill called to the witness stand two of MOVE's neighbors, Cassandra Carter and Milton Williams (who also testified at the MOVE Commission hearings) who related that MOVE had made their lives "hell." Carter testified that Ramona had said MOVE would "take the block with" them if the police attacked. Williams testified that Conrad Africa had threatened to "kick my door in, rape my wife, and kill all my mother fucking children."[22]

Where the prosecution wanted to limit discussion as much as possible, Ramona Africa's defense was to establish a long-term, "conscious, deliberate conspiracy on the part of the System officials to stop the MOVE organization." Ramona did not deny that MOVE people shot at police on May 13, but she hoped to convince the jury that MOVE people acted in self-defense. This argument required convincing the jury that the police did not intend to conduct a normal arrest on May 13, but, in fact, set out to kill MOVE people inside the house.

For most of the trial, Ramona conducted an impressive, even convincing defense. On the second day of the proceedings, the prosecution called Lieutenant Dominic Marandola, who was in charge of the police officers on the ground on May 13 and who reported directly to Police Commission Sambor. Marandola testified that "officers were allowed to fire only after requesting permission from a supervisor who would, in turn, clear" the request through Marandola—unless, of course, the officer faced a "life-threatening situation." Marandola told McGill that he knew of no situations in which an officer fired without orders. That was a crucial mistake. On cross-examination, Ramona pressed Marandola on this apparent discrepancy. The prosecution's case revolved around three police officers who were shot at, yet it seemed that no police officers had faced "life-threatening" situations which would allow them to return fire. Ramona asked Marandola if it "would be safe to assume from that that no officer was in a life-and-death situation." The prosecution objected, and the court sustained. (I am not alleging that anyone lied under oath, but Marandola's testimony makes more sense if he were interested in deflecting attention from the fact that police officers shot at MOVE people as they tried to escape the burning house.)[23]

Ramona also scored points with the jury during her cross-examination of Officer Draper, a detective with the CAU who also testified at the MOVE Commission hearings. Draper testified that MOVE people had asked for negotiations on May 13, and had provided a list of community activists and journalists who could negotiate on MOVE's behalf to end the standoff peacefully. Draper told the jury that none of the people on the list had been contacted. Ramona asked Draper if "there was a possibility of negotiation." Draper testified that there was, but that he "didn't do anything about it." This admission shocked the jury, some of whom were observed shaking their heads in disgust, sighing, and scratching their heads.[24]

For two weeks, Ramona defended herself ably, but on January 28, the stress got the best of her. She had been polite to the previous witnesses—even Mayor Goode—but Ramona could not muster the same professionalism for now-former Police Commissioner Gregore Sambor. She could not hide her anger toward Sambor, and drew the rebuke of the prosecution and the judge. Sambor, for his part, kept his emotions in check for most of his testimony. He raised his voice once in disgust at Ramona's accusation that he did not consider the lives of the MOVE children of much importance. Toward the end of Sambor's testimony, Ramona asked him a question of critical importance: "How long did you plan to drop a bomb on MOVE people?" The prosecution objected to the phrasing, and after several attempts to reword the question, Ramona lost her temper: "I just want to point out on the record that Mr. McGill, or nobody else in this courtroom is going to intimidate me at all," she said. "I'm fighting for my freedom." When the prosecution requested that the judge remind Ramona to follow the rules of the court, she replied that "I abide by the rules of God." Eventually, Ramona asked the question in a way that satisfied the judge. Sambor testified, falsely, that "the planning relative to the explosive device was formulated on May thirteenth."[25]

As the trial stretched into its third week, Ramona grew increasingly frustrated. Much of her frustration stemmed from the fact that an important witnesses, Lieutenant Frank Powell, pled the Fifth and refused to take the witness stand. Powell was a member of the Bomb Squad who had been a member of the "A Certified personnel" who had been planning the attack a year before the MOVE Bombing. His Bomb Squad added the C-4 to the Tovex explosive, and he personally dropped the bomb from the helicopter. He was, to Ramona, the key to persuading the jury that the MOVE Bombing was not an arrest-gone-wrong, but a calculated attack. On February 5, Ramona asked the judge if she could call Mayor Goode and Police Commissioner Sambor back to the witness stand. The judge refused and urged Ramona to rest her defense. Instead, she stormed out of the courtroom in the middle of proceedings. Her court-appointed backup counsel convinced her to return the next day, where she finally delivered a closing statement.[26]

As the jury deliberated, Rev. Paul Washington led a large demonstration outside, calling for Ramona Africa's release. Instead, on February 9, 1986, a jury convicted Ramona of two charges, riot and conspiracy, but acquitted her on four others. The jury "wanted to make a statement" with the split verdict: "MOVE was wrong. The police were wrong. . . . It could have been handled a lot better." The prosecutor announced after the trial that the verdict was a "compromise." Ramona told the court that she had been convicted "because I'm a MOVE member and I survived." She pointed out, correctly, that "not one single official has been brought into a court, tried, and convicted of anything." She was sentenced to prison for a term of sixteen months to seven years. It was a relatively lenient sentence. District Attorney Ronald Castille pushed the court to sentence Ramona to the maximum of fourteen years and considered appealing the sentencing. Given credit for time served, Ramona was eligible for parole after five months in prison, on the condition that she sever all ties to MOVE. She refused, served all seven years of her sentence, and returned to MOVE upon her release on May 13, 1992. She is to this day the only person to have gone to jail for the MOVE Bombing.[27]

In 1996, MOVE people again tried to hold public officials responsible for the MOVE Bombing. In 1996, Louise James, acting as administrator of her son Frank Africa's estate, Alphonso Leaphart, administrator of his brother John Africa's estate, and Ramona Africa independently sued the city of Philadelphia, Police Commissioner Gregore Sambor, and Fire Commissioner William Richmond. The District Court consolidated those lawsuits for trial, which began in April 1996. The plaintiffs—Louise James and the estates of John and Frank Africa—alleged that the events of May 13, 1985, constituted an "unreasonable seizure" under the Fourth Amendment. Lawyers for Ramona Africa argued that Ramona suffered "severe physical and emotional injuries" that day, and the estates of John and Frank Africa argued that the actions of the city, generally, and Sambor and Richmond, specifically, "caused the deaths of the decedents." The jury sided with Ramona Africa and the Leapharts, awarding the three plaintiffs $500,000 each. The jury also found Sambor and Richmond personally responsible, and awarded the two men to pay each plaintiff one dollar a week for eleven years. It was, of course, a largely symbolic award. The significance of the jury's decision was that Sambor and Richmond could not evade responsibility under official immunity.[28]

Both parties filed post-trial motions. The city argued that the bomb and ensuing fire were used to destroy the bunker, not to *seize* anybody. Thus, the city reasoned, no illegal seizure could have taken place. The District Court found this argument "not persuasive." The city also argued that John Africa was not a victim of an illegal seizure because he was not named on the arrest warrant that the police used as a legal pretense to raid the house. The District Court again found this argument wanting. They noted that, although Sambor did indeed have arrest warrants for four MOVE people in the house, he had ordered "all occupants of the house to peaceably evacuate the premises and surrender"—apparently, Sambor testified, the result of some last-minute revision. The city asked the District Court to overrule the jury's decision in favor of MOVE. The court refused to do so, but did throw out the jury's decision to hold Sambor and Richmond personally responsible, ruling instead that both men could claim official immunity.

As the MOVE Bombing turned from event to history, certain details faded from public memory. Perhaps the most damning detail to emerge from the MOVE Commission investigation—that police shot at MOVE people as they tried to escape the fire—dissolved from fact to question to rumor. One of the best, most widely read accounts of the MOVE Bombing was co-written by a journalist who served on the grand jury that declined to press charges against city officials in 1986. When the book, *Let It Burn*, was first published in 1989, the authors were "confident"—contradicting the findings of the MOVE Commission investigation—"that there was no evidence of police gunfire in the back alley that prevented the kids and others from escaping." The authors believed that "there were too many witnesses and too much evidence to cover up." When the authors revised the book for a second edition, which was published in 2013, they were "less confident, though still not convinced that there was a shooting." The second edition of that book served as the basis for a remarkable documentary, *Let the Fire Burn*, which was also released in

2013. Like the book, the documentary is ambivalent about whether police shot at MOVE people as they tried to escape the fire.

* * *

What happened on May 13, 1985? We can say with a high degree of confidence that the events we call the MOVE Bombing are these: On May 13, 1985, the Philadelphia Police Department, using military grade firearms and explosives they borrowed from the FBI, raided the MOVE house on Osage Avenue, ostensibly to serve arrest warrants on four MOVE people inside. MOVE people inside the house fired at police. The police responded by firing over 10,000 rounds of ammunition into the house over the course of ninety minutes. They used explosives to blow holes into walls, which they used to fill the MOVE house with tear gas. One of those bombs killed John Africa by removing his head from his body. The Fire Department used water cannons to flood the basement. These tactics did not force the surrender of MOVE people inside, and several hours passed without any confrontation as the MOVE children sheltered in the flooded garage and Frank, Raymond, and John Africa lay dead upstairs. At around five in the afternoon, a member of the Philadelphia Police Department's Bomb Disposal Unit, using a Commonwealth of Pennsylvania helicopter, dropped a bundle of highly flammable C-4 explosives and Tovex onto the roof of the MOVE house on Osage Avenue. The decision to drop a bomb on the house was not improvised, but had been planned for over a year. The bomb created a massive explosion and fire, which officials used to their tactical advantage. The fire forced the surviving MOVE people—four adults and six children—to flee the basement into the back alleyway. Once outside, members of the Philadelphia Police Department opened fire, shooting Conrad Africa and Tomaso Africa, and forcing the others back into the flames, where all but two died.

* * *

On June 24, 2017, MOVE people hosted a small ceremony to unveil the new historical marker commemorating the MOVE Bombing. Around two hundred people attended. The poet Ursula Rucker spoke briefly about her memories of the MOVE Bombing and its precarious place in Philadelphia's public memory. Ramona Africa spoke about the importance of what the schoolchildren had achieved. Sonia Sanchez, a longtime MOVE supporter, congratulated the schoolchildren for their successful petition, despite the fact that the city "does not want a discussion about this." The marker was unveiled, but it was not installed. When the ceremony was over, the marker was placed in a van and driven away.[29]

The teacher from the Jubilee School who had overseen the students' petition had heard that the "neighbors were not happy about having it on the parkway." The block captain representing Osage Avenue residents told reporters that the marker was "not our priority right now." A City Council member who supported the marker admitted that the MOVE Bombing was "a sensitive issue," and that she would ensure that everyone's concerns were heard.[30]

Two months later, the marker was installed in secret, presumably to ward off controversy. Its installation caught even MOVE people by surprise. The marker read:

> On May 13, 1985, at 6221 Osage Avenue, an armed conflict occurred between the Phila. Police Dept. and MOVE members. A Pa. State Police helicopter dropped a bomb on MOVE's house. An uncontrolled fire killed eleven MOVE members, including five children, and destroyed 61 homes.

The marker bespeaks an unthinkable event. The passive voice deflects attention away from the incongruities. "An armed conflict occurred. . . ."; "A helicopter dropped a bomb"; "An uncontrolled fire killed. . . ." One could read that sign and believe that the MOVE Bombing had been an act of nature. The marker does not speak the truth, except to say that something happened here that people aren't quite ready to deal with. Something happened here that is unthinkable.

Notes

1. Bobbi Booker, "Historic Marker for '85 MOVE Bomb Site," *The Philadelphia Tribune*, March 31, 2017.
2. Ibid.
3. My thoughts on the unthinkable nature of the MOVE Bombing originate in Michel-Rolph Trouillot, *Silencing the Past: Power and the Production of History* (Boston: Beacon Press, 1995), 70–107; Interview with Gerald Africa, Box 8, Folder 1, PSIC.
4. Philadelphia Special Investigation Commission, "The Findings, Conclusions, and Recommendations of the Philadelphia Special Investigation Commission," Box 4, PSIC.

5. Ibid.
6. William H. Brown III, "Foreword to the Report of the Philadelphia Special Investigation Commission," *Temple Law Quarterly* 267, no. 302 (1986): 271.
7. David O'Reilly and Terry E. Johnson, "The City Tunes in to MOVE," *Philadelphia Inquirer*, October 30, 1985.
8. Philadelphia Special Investigation Commission, Examination of Officers Cresse and Draper of Civil Affairs, October 8, 1985, Box 19, PSIC.
9. Philadelphia Special Investigation Commission, Testimony of Cassandra Carter before the Philadelphia Special Investigation (MOVE) Commission, October 9, 1985, Box 7, PSIC.
10. Larry Eichel, "MOVE Hearings: Quietly Momentous: Assembling a Chain of Spectacular Failures," *Philadelphia Inquirer*, November 8, 1985, 1.
11. Bill Peterson, "Goode's Account of Assault against MOVE Disputed," *Washington Post*, October 17, 1985.
12. "The Findings," 9–10.
13. Ibid., 10.
14. Trouillot, *Silencing the Past*, 31–69.
15. "The Findings," 9–10.
16. The Pulitzer Prize–winning historian Heather Ann Thompson is currently writing a book on the MOVE Bombing which will undoubtedly shed new light on this history.
17. William Lyton to Sue Ranieri, Box 5, PSIC.
18. Heather Ann Thompson, *Blood in the Water: The Attica Prison Uprising of 1971 and Its Legacy* (New York: Pantheon, 2016).
19. William K. Stevens, "Grand Jury Clears Everyone in Fatal Philadelphia Siege," *New York Times*, May 4, 1988, 18.
20. For an in-depth account of the Ramona Africa trial written by two people who attended the proceedings, see John Anderson and Hilary Hevenor, *Burning Down the House: MOVE and the Tragedy of Philadelphia* (New York: W. W. Norton, 1987), part II; Maida Odom, "Africa Adjusts to System to Mount Her Own Defense," *Inquirer*, January 12, 1986.
21. Cynthia Burton, "Not by the Books," *Philadelphia Daily News*, January 8, 1986; Maida Odom, "Africa Adjusts to System to Mount Her Own Defense," *Philadelphia Inquirer*, January 12, 1986.
22. Maida Odom, "Osage Resident Tells Africa Trial of 'MOVE Heat,'" *Philadelphia Inquirer*, January 15, 1986, 5; Cynthia Burton, "Ramona, Neighbors Trade Snarls," *Philadelphia Daily News*, January 15, 1986.
23. *Commonwealth v. Johnson*; Maida Odom, "Africa Seeks Testimony That MOVE Did Not Threaten Lives of Police," *Philadelphia Inquirer*, January 17, 1986.
24. *Commonwealth v. Johnson*; Maida Odom, "Africa Seeks Testimony That MOVE Did Not Threaten Lives of Police," *Philadelphia Inquirer*, January 17, 1986.
25. As has been demonstrated, the plan to raid the MOVE house with bombs was initiated on May 30, 1984.
26. *Commonwealth v. Johnson*; Cynthia Burton, "Ramona Walks Out of Her Trial," *Philadelphia Daily News*, February 6, 1986.

27. Ramona Africa Trial; "The Ramona Africa Verdict," *Philadelphia Inquirer*, February 11, 1986; "The Ramona Africa Sentence," *Philadelphia Inquirer*, April 16, 1986; Jim Quinn, "Move v. the City of Philadelphia," *Nation* 242, no. 12 (March 29, 1986): 441–458; *Commonwealth v. Johnson*; Kitty Caparella and Cynthia Burton, "The Verdict: 'Nobody Was Right,'" *Philadelphia Daily News*, February 28, 1986; Maida Odom, "Ramona Africa Given Jail Term for Siege Role," *Philadelphia Inquirer*, April 15, 1986.
28. *Opinion In Re City of Philadelphia Litigation; Ramona Africa v. City of Philadelphia, et al.; Louise James, Administratrix of the Estate of Frank James v. City of Philadelphia et al.; Alfonso Leaphart, Administrator of the Estate of Vincent Leaphart v. City of Philadelphia, et al.* 938 F. Supp. 1278 *1281; 1996 U.S. dist. LEXIS 12682, p. 7.
29. Alicia Victoria Lozano, "32 Years Later, Philadelphia Commemorates MOVE Bombing," *NBC Philadelphia*, June 24, 2017, https://www.nbcphiladelphia.com/news/local/Philadelphia-Commemorates-MOVE-Bombing-430588023.html.
30. Cherri Gregg, "Efforts Stalled in Placing Permanent MOVE Bombing Historical Marker," *CBSPhilly*, June 22, 2017, http://philadelphia.cbslocal.com/2017/06/22/efforts-stalled-in-placing-permanent-move-bombing-historical-marker/.

Conclusion

John Africa's Body

For six months the bodies of the MOVE people killed in the MOVE Bombing decomposed in a city morgue. Their bodies had been left out in the rubble at Osage Avenue for days, and the remains were not carefully removed. Large excavating machines lifted the bodies out, along with the other debris. Machine operators crushed bones and mangled skeletons. When the excavated remains finally reached the office of the medical examiner, the bones of the dead had to be separated from dog bones, and dismembered bodies had to be reassembled. Two of the bodies were cremated and buried immediately, so the medical examiners working for the MOVE Commission had to exhume them to rescue what little evidence they contained. The other nine bodies were stored for two months in a city morgue that did not have adequate refrigeration, and the bodies rapidly decomposed in the summer heat. When an outside medical examiner took over the investigation on behalf of the MOVE Commission, he found them covered in multicolored mold. He had the bodies transferred to another facility, but the stench made his work almost unbearable. The medical examiner described John Africa's remains as a "headless, armless body" that was "partly flesh covered . . . badly decomposed," and "burned." The exposed bones had been "charred" in the fire which raged hours after John Africa had been decapitated. The tissue had grown "rigid, hardened as the consistency of leather" and covered in fungus.[1]

To MOVE people, John Africa's body, once dead, was not special. Like all living things, it was a collection of carbon that would, over time, decompose, then recompose into new Life—all part of God's cycle of existence. But the life that had once inhabited that body had been special. That life had transcended the mundane. It had escaped the System. The life that once inhabited that body could rightly be called God. So the death of that man, John Africa, was both ordinary and unimaginable. His death was the death of a god.

As John Africa's body lay decomposing in the city morgue, a fight raged in a Philadelphia courtroom over what should become of it. Once the medical examiners had done their work, John Africa's body had been given to his next-of-kin, Vincent Leaphart's wife Dorothy Clark. She and Vincent

Leaphart had never formally divorced, so she—not John Africa's sisters or any surviving MOVE people—took possession of the remains. Dorothy Clark contacted the funeral director who buried or cremated the other MOVE people who died in the bombing and arranged for John Africa's remains to be cremated in a private ceremony. John Africa's sisters, Laverne Sims and Louise James—both former MOVE people themselves—read about Dorothy's plan to cremate John Africa's body in the paper. They knew that John Africa viewed cremation as "diametrically opposed to . . . his religion," and objected to the fact that Dorothy Clark, who had not seen Vincent Leaphart in eighteen years and had, so to speak, never met John Africa, had reappeared to claim the body. James and Sims petitioned a court to stop the transfer of the body from the city morgue to the funeral director Clark had hired.[2]

The dispute landed on the desk of Judge Edmund Pawelec of Philadelphia's Orphan Court. Dorothy Clark argued that, in situations such as this one, the law was clear: Dorothy Clark and Vincent Leaphart may have been estranged, but they were still married. She was the next of kin. The body belonged to her. But to Louise James and Laverne Sims, it also seemed clear that this was no ordinary body. The remains in question did not belong to "Vincent Leaphart," but to John Africa. And John Africa viewed cremation as "sacrilegious." MOVE's religious teachings prohibited the use of coffins, caskets, or embalming. "When a person died," the sisters explained to Judge Pawelec, "they are still free, and should be allowed to maintain that freedom."[3]

The court fight over John Africa's body was the history of MOVE's classification writ small. As had happened many times before, MOVE people found themselves in front of an agent of the state, advocating for their religion. Like before, they insisted their beliefs and practices were real and warranted respect—even when they conflicted with the law of the land. In this context, the immediate question facing Judge Pawelec was whether John Africa's religious beliefs ought to take precedence over a clear chain of custody. But on a broader scale, the question facing the court was the question that defined MOVE's history from the very beginning: was MOVE a religion?

On November 22, 1985, Judge Edmund Pawelec ruled that John Africa's body should be turned over to his sisters, Louise James and Laverne Sims, for burial according to MOVE's religious practices. In his decision, Pawelec wrote that "Vincent Leaphart's beliefs preclude a ritualistic burial and instead mandate the allowance of the body to return to its natural state." It was clear to Judge Pawelec that John Africa's religious beliefs were sincerely held and that his sisters were willing and capable of carrying out his wishes. And it was clear to the judge that Dorothy Clark did not intend to respect John Africa's religious preferences with her preferred method of cremation. Finally, after so many failures, MOVE had been recognized as a religion in a court of law.[4]

On the morning of December 5, 1985, Laverne Sims and Louise James met at the morgue to claim the bodies of their dead loved ones. They brought with them blankets they had taken from their beds. Laverne wrapped the burned and decayed torso of her brother, John Africa, in her blanket. Louise wrapped the skeletal remains of her son, Frank Africa. They lifted the remains and placed them on a gurney which conveyed them to a hearse waiting outside. The hearse drove the bodies to a funeral home which served as a meeting place for anyone who wanted to follow the hearse to the burial site.[5]

John Africa and Frank Africa's funeral was well attended—especially by representatives of religious communities. The service was informal. Louise and Laverne said a few words, but emotions got the best of them. As Louise James lowered the body of her son into the grave, a photographer from the *Philadelphia Daily News* captured a photograph of her grief. She is bent over, wailing in despair as she places her hands one last time on the blanket covering her son. She is flanked by a young Black man, a member of the Nation of Islam's paramilitary unit, the Fruit of Islam. A Catholic nun has placed both of her hands on Louise's shoulders in an attempt to console her. In the background stands Jesse Jackson, looking on in sorrow. The photograph is symbolic of much of MOVE's history. For years, MOVE people fought for their religion to be recognized. That image of Louise James surrounded by representatives of three different religious communities captures a fleeting moment in time, and one that turned out to be ephemeral. It captures a moment when MOVE attained—after so much suffering and bought with so much death—the religious legitimacy they so desired.[6]

Much has changed about MOVE in the past thirty-five years. Since her release from prison in 1997, Ramona Africa has been the engine of the group. It is inappropriate to call her MOVE's leader—John Africa is MOVE's leader—but her talent for organization and advocacy is stunning to watch. She is tireless. She has made MOVE into a very different organization than it was when she first found it. MOVE maintains an international network of supporters—numbering, I would estimate, in the thousands. Many of these supporters advocate for the release of the MOVE 9 and of Mumia Abu-Jamal, whose writings on John Africa, MOVE, and his own experience as the world's most famous death-row inmate have brought MOVE's story to a wider audience.

Ramona Africa is impressive, but she is growing weak. In the summer of 2018, she was admitted to a hospital. Media reports state that she is suffering consequences from post-traumatic stress disorder. MOVE people have told me she suffered a stroke, and that she has cancer. I have been unable to contact her directly since she was admitted to the hospital.

Ramona's work on behalf of the MOVE 9 is finally beginning to pay off. When I first began writing this book, I was confident that the MOVE 9 would spend the rest of their lives in prison. For two of them—Merle Africa and Phil Africa—that turned out to be true. Merle died in prison in 1998, and Phil died in 2015. The MOVE 9 have been eligible for parole since 2008. The MOVE 9 have been model prisoners. They had no disciplinary issues in prison, and participated in mentoring programs. Some of the incarcerated MOVE women trained service dogs. Still, the parole board denied every request. One of the sticking points for the parole board was their insistence that paroled MOVE people disassociate with other MOVE people—a request that would be patently unconstitutional if MOVE were a religion.

Then, in June 2018, Debbie Africa was granted parole. The board's sudden change of heart caught everyone by surprise. In October, her husband, Mike Africa, was also granted parole. The couple—who have not seen each other since 1978—have begun rebuilding their lives. Their son, Mike Africa, Jr., is able to sit with his parents together in the same room for the first time in his life, and Mike and Debbie are getting to know their grandchildren. It has been gratifying to watch this family reunite.

In May 2019, Janet Africa and Janine Africa were granted parole as well. Janine lost two children to police violence, Life Africa and Phil Africa, Jr. Upon her release, she explained to a reporter that "there are times when I think about Life and my son Phil, but I don't keep those thoughts in my mind long because they hurt. The murder of my children, my family, will always affect me, but not in a bad way. When I think about what this system has done to me and my family, it makes me even more committed to my belief." In June 2019, Eddie Africa was paroled, and in January 2020, Delbert Africa was finally released. As of writing, only Chuckie Africa remains in a Pennsylvania state prison for the murder of Officer James Ramp.[7]

Mike, Debbie, Janet, Janine, Eddie, and Delbert Africa are returning to a MOVE that is stronger than it has ever been. There are, I estimate, one hundred MOVE people today. Many of them are the children and grandchildren of the original converts. A group of young MOVE people have formed a hip-hop group, and their lyrics are inspired by *The Guidelines of John Africa*. They frequently perform at public MOVE events.

MOVE's focus today is on freeing Chuckie Africa and Mumia Abu-Jamal. MOVE people maintain a headquarters near Clark Park in Philadelphia in a pair of homes they bought using funds they won from their lawsuit against the city. The behavior that irritated MOVE's neighbors in decades past—the abundance of dogs, the composting—are no longer an issue. MOVE people today—and I can attest to this personally—are model neighbors. Many of the countercultural behaviors that earned MOVE so much ire in the 1970s and 1980s—their hairstyle, their diet, even their burial practices—have become mainstream. MOVE people enjoy pointing out to me that John Africa prophesied this would be so.

We began this story by asking how all this could have happened. And I was circumspect about my ability to answer this question. I do, however, feel confident that Laverne Sims was correct when she argued that one cannot understand the MOVE Bombing—let alone MOVE's entire history—without understanding MOVE *as a religion*. That is what I have tried to do in this book.

Is MOVE a religion? Here is what we can say for sure: MOVE people thought they were a religion. They still think that. MOVE matches any definition of religion we can apply to it. Scholars working in religious studies are generally reluctant to offer a definition of religion—I have successfully avoided doing so in this book—but the kinds of groups, beliefs, and practices we usually teach and write about tend to look like MOVE. MOVE has a sacred text that attends to ultimate concerns—life and death, good and evil, being and transcending. MOVE people revere a prophetic leader. They maintain a set of practices—bodily discipline, aesthetics, diet—that they understand as religious in nature. In light of this evidence, it is tempting to conclude that MOVE was, in fact, a religion.

But MOVE was not a religion; or, more precisely, MOVE was not allowed to be a religion. There are many people who believe that this is MOVE's fault. Chief among their complaints is that MOVE is responsible—either directly or indirectly—for the death of Officer James Ramp. (MOVE people, it should be noted, deny any responsibility for the death of Officer James Ramp.) Others connect MOVE to Mumia Abu-Jamal and, thus, the murder of Officer Daniel Faulkner. They are not wrong to do so. MOVE fully supports Mumia Abu-Jamal, and Abu-Jamal still considers himself a MOVE supporter. To many Philadelphians, MOVE people are cop killers. But the criticisms of MOVE have always been broader than this. MOVE's critics have found them to be obnoxious, even hateful, toward people with whom they disagree. Critics often point out MOVE's hypocrisy. Nearly every article or book written about MOVE points out that John Africa would go out of his way to avoid stepping on a bug but had no problem shooting at police officers. These critics wonder, not unfairly, how MOVE claims to respect the sanctity of life while behaving so violently. These are the same criticisms MOVE has received all their history. These are the criticisms that kept MOVE from the religious legitimacy they desired. And these criticisms are entirely fair.

This is the defining irony within the history of MOVE. It would be easy to say, as MOVE's critics did, that groups like MOVE are not religions because of how they behaved. It is easy to point out that people threw away promising futures, left their families, and broke their marriages to follow religious teachings that proved to be destructive. It would be easy to say that groups like MOVE are scapegoats upon which we project all our anxieties, and that these bad religions are "othered" because they allow us to define what it is we imagine ourselves to be. But what we see when we look at the history of MOVE is not the inversion of "true religion." We see, in MOVE, acts of violence amidst proclamations of peace. We see in MOVE hypocrisy and irrational superstition. We see a group that refuses to acknowledge the harm it has wrought. We see abuse masquerading as spiritual discipline. We see a history that has hurt many people. And we also see a religious system that gave meaning to the lives of dozens of people. We see, in MOVE, people striving toward what they believed was a better world and grappling with what it means to be authentically human. We see the voiceless and the marginalized believing in their own agency. All of this—the pain and the joy, hypocrisy and commitment, violence and peace, despair and hope, life-giving and death-bringing—is precisely what religion is.

Notes

1. Medical Report of Ali Z. Hameli, M.D., P.A., to William B. Lytton, November 4, 1985, Box 5, Folder "Medical," PSIC.
2. Louise Leaphart James, *John Africa . . . Childhood Untold until Today* (self-published, 2013), 118–121.
3. Cynthia Burton, "Judge: Sisters Can Claim MOVE Leader's Remains." *Philadelphia Inquirer*, November 23, 2985.
4. Cynthia Burton, "Judge: Sisters Can Claim MOVE Leader's Remains."

5. James, *John Africa*, 123–126.
6. The photograph I have described ran in the December 6, 1985, edition of the *Philadelphia Inquirer*, and is reproduced in James, *John Africa*, 128.
7. Ed Pilkington, "Move 9 Women Freed after 40 Years in Jail over Philadelphia Police Siege," *The Guardian*, May 25, 2019, https://www.theguardian.com/us-news/2019/may/25/move-9-black-radicals-women-freed-philadelphia.

Works Cited

Adams, Arlin M., and Charles J. Emmerich. *A Nation Dedicated to Religious Liberty.* Philadelphia: University of Pennsylvania Press, 1990.
Albanese, Catherine. *A Republic of Mind and Spirit: A Cultural History of American Metaphysical Religion.* New Haven, CT: Yale University Press, 2008.
Alvarez, Elizabeth Hayes, ed. *Religion in Philadelphia.* Philadelphia: Temple University Press, 2016.
Anderson, John, and Hilary Hevenor. *Burning Down the House: MOVE and the Tragedy of Philadelphia.* New York: W.W. Norton, 1987.
Arnal, William E., and Russell T. McCutcheon. *The Sacred Is the Profane: The Political Nature of "Religion."* New York: Oxford University Press, 2013.
Asad, Talal. *Formations of the Secular: Christianity, Islam, Modernity.* Stanford, CA: Stanford University Press, 2003.
Asad, Talal. *Genealogies of Religion: Discipline and Reasons of Power in Christianity.* Baltimore, MD: Johns Hopkins University Press, 1993.
Assefa, Hizkias, and Paul Wahrhaftig. *The MOVE Crisis in Philadelphia: Extremist Groups and Conflict Resolution.* Pittsburgh: University of Pittsburgh Press, 1990.
Baker, Kelly J. *The Gospel According to the Klan: The KKK's Appeal to Protestant America, 1915–1930.* Lawrence: University of Kansas Press, 2011.
Bender, Courtney, and Ann Taves. *What Matters? Ethnographies of Value in a Not So Secular Age.* New York: Columbia University Press, 2012.
Bennett, Hans. "The Black Panthers and the Assassination of Fred Hampton." *Journal of Pan African Studies* 3, no. 6 (2010): 215–221.
Berry, Mary Frances. *And Justice for All: The United States Commission on Civil Rights and the Continuing Struggle for Freedom in America.* New York: Alfred A. Knopf, 2009.
Best, Wallace D. *Passionately Human, No Less Divine: Religion and Culture in Black Chicago, 1915–1952.* Princeton, NJ: Princeton University Press, 2004.
Biernacki, Loriliai, and Philip Clayton, eds. *Panentheism across the World's Traditions.* New York: Oxford University Press, 2014.
Bisson, Terry. *On a Move: The Story of Mumia Abu-Jamal.* New York: Litmus Books, 2001.
Bowler, Peter J. *The Eclipse of Darwin: Anti-Darwinian Evolution Theories in the Decades around 1900.* Baltimore, MD: Johns Hopkins University Press, 1992.
Bowser, Charles W. *Let the Bunker Burn: The Final Battle with MOVE.* Philadelphia: Camino Books, 1989.
Boyette, Michael, and Randi Boyette. *Let It Burn: MOVE, the Philadelphia Police Department, and the Confrontation That Changed a City.* San Diego: Quadrant Books, 2013.
Bromley, David G., and Anson D. Shupe. *Strange Gods: The Great American Cult Scare.* Boston: Beacon Press, 1981.
Campbell, Bruce F. *Ancient Wisdom Revived: A History of the Theosophical Movement.* Berkeley: University of California Press, 1980.

Chevannes, Barry. *Rastafari: Roots and Ideology.* Syracuse, NY: Syracuse University Press, 1994.

Chidester, David. "Saving the Children by Killing Them: Redemptive Sacrifice in the Ideologies of Jim Jones and Ronald Reagan." *Religion and American Culture: A Journal of Interpretation* 1, no. 2 (1991): 177–201.

Churchill, Ward, and Jim Vander Wall. *The COINTELPRO Papers: Documents from the FBI's Secret Wars against Domestic Dissent.* Boston: South End Press, 1990.

Countryman, Matthew J. *Up South: Civil Rights and Black Power in Philadelphia.* Philadelphia: University of Pennsylvania Press, 2005.

Curtis, Edward E., IV. *Black Muslim Religion in the Nation of Islam, 1960–1975.* Chapel Hill: University of North Carolina Press, 2006.

Curtis, Finbarr. *The Production of American Religious Freedom.* New York: New York University Press, 2016.

Donner, Frank. *Protectors of Privilege: Red Squads and Police Repression in Urban America.* Berkeley: University of California Press, 1992.

Dubler, Joshua. *Down in the Chapel: Religious Life in an American Prison.* New York: Farrar, Straus, and Giroux, 2013.

Eichler-Levine, Jodi. *Suffer the Little Children: Uses of the Past in Jewish and African American Children's Literature.* New York: New York University Press, 2013.

Evans, Curtis J. *The Burden of Black Religion.* New York: Oxford University Press, 2008.

Evans, Richard Kent. "World Religions." In *Religion in Philadelphia*, edited by Elizabeth Hayes Alvarez, 35–42. Philadelphia: Temple University Press, 2016.

Evans, Richard Kent. "MOVE." In *Religion in Philadelphia*, edited by Elizabeth Hayes Alvarez, 254–261. Philadelphia: Temple University Press, 2016.

Farber, David. *The Age of Great Dreams: America in the 1960s.* New York: Hill and Wang, 1994.

Fessenden, Tracy. *Culture and Redemption: Religion, the Secular, and American Literature.* Princeton, NJ: Princeton University Press, 2007.

Fiscella, Anthony T. "Removing MOVE: A Case Study of Intersectional Invisibility within Religious and Legal Studies." *International Journal for the Study of New Religions* 7 (2016): 3–41.

Fiscella, Anthony T. "Universal Burdens: Stories of (Un)Freedom from the Unitarian Universality Association, the MOVE Organization, and Taqwacore." PhD diss. Lund University, 2015.

Flake, Kathleen. *The Politics of American Religious Identity: The Seating of Senator Reed Smoot, Mormon Apostle.* Chapel Hill: University of North Carolina Press, 2004.

Floyd-Thomas, J. M. "The Burning of Rebellious Thoughts: MOVE as Revolutionary Black Humanism." *The Black Scholar* 32 (2002): 11–21.

Gaustad, Edwin. *Dissent in American Religion.* Chicago: University of Chicago Press, 1973.

Geertz, Clifford. "Religion as a Cultural Symbol." In Geertz, *The Interpretation of Cultures: Selected Essays.* Waukegan, IL: Fontana Press, 1993, 87–125.

Gitlin, Todd. *The Sixties: Years of Hope, Days of Rage.* New York: Bantam Books, 1987.

Goode, W. Wilson, and Joann Stevens. *In Goode Faith: Philadelphia's First Black Mayor Tells His Story.* Valley Forge, PA: Judson Press, 1992.

Gordon, Sarah Barringer. "Malnak v. Yogi." In *Law and Religion: Cases in Context*, edited by Leslie C. Griffin, 11–32. New York: Aspen, 2010.

Gregory, James N. *Southern Diaspora: How the Great Migrations of Black and White Southerners Transformed America.* Chapel Hill: University of North Carolina Press, 2005.

Hamburger, Philip. *Separation of Church and State.* Cambridge, MA: Harvard University Press, 2002.

Harry, Margot. *"Attention, MOVE! This Is America!"* Chicago: Banner Press, 1987.

Hornblum, Allen M. *Acres of Skin: Human Experiments at Holmesburg Prison.* New York: Routledge, 1999.

Hucks, Tracey E., and Charles H. Long. *Yoruba Traditions and African American Religious Nationalism.* Albuquerque: University of New Mexico Press, 2012.

Hurd, Elizabeth Shakman. *The Politics of Secularism in International Relations.* Princeton, NJ: Princeton University Press, 2008.

James, Louise Leaphart. *John Africa . . . Childhood Untold until Today.* Self-published, 2013.

Johnson, Sylvester A. *African American Religions, 1500–2000: Colonialism, Democracy, and Freedom.* Cambridge; New York: Cambridge University Press, 2015.

Johnson, Sylvester A., and Steven Weitzman. *The FBI and Religion: Faith and National Security before and after 9/11.* Berkeley: University of California Press, 2016.

Joseph, Peniel E. *Waiting 'til the Midnight Hour: A Narrative History of Black Power in America.* New York: Henry Holt, 2006.

Keats, Jonathan. *You Belong to the Universe: Buckminster Fuller and the Future.* New York: Oxford University Press, 2016.

Levitt, Laura. *Afterlives of Objects: Holocaust Evidence and Criminal Archives.* University Park: Penn State University Press, 2020.

Lincoln, Eric, and Lawrence Mamiya. *The Black Church in the African American Experience.* Durham, NC: Duke University Press, 1990.

Linenthal, Edward T. *The Unfinished Bombing: Oklahoma City in American Memory.* New York: Oxford University Press, 2001.

Lloyd, Vincent W. *Black Natural Law.* New York: Oxford University Press, 2016.

Lofton, Kathryn. *Consuming Religion.* Chicago: University of Chicago Press, 2017.

Lombardo, Timothy J. *Blue-Collar Conservatism: Frank Rizzo's Philadelphia and Populist Politics in Philadelphia.* Philadelphia: University of Pennsylvania Press, 2018.

Lum, Kathryn Gin, and Paul Harvey, eds. *The Oxford Handbook of Religion and Race in American History.* New York: Oxford University Press, 2018.

Maffly-Kipp, Laurie F. *Setting Down the Sacred Past: African American Race Histories.* Cambridge, MA: Harvard University Press, 2010.

Mahmood, Saba. *Religious Difference in a Secular Age: A Minority Report.* Princeton, NJ: Princeton University Press, 2016.

Mason, Patrick Q. *The Mormon Menace: Violence and Anti-Mormonism in the Postbellum South.* New York: Oxford University Press, 2011.

McCloud, Sean. *Making the American Religious Fringe: Exotics, Subversives, and Journalists, 1955–1993.* Chapel Hill: University of North Carolina Press, 2004.

McCrary, Charles. *American Religion, Secularism, and Belief.* Chicago: University of Chicago Press, forthcoming.

McCutcheon, Russell T. *Religion and the Domestication of Dissent: Or, How to Live in a Less than Perfect Nation.* London: Routledge, 2005.

Medsger, Betty. *The Burglary: The Discover of J. Edgar Hoover's Secret FBI.* New York: Alfred A. Knopf, 2014.

Melton, J. Gordon. *The Encyclopedia of American Religions,* Volume II. Wilmington, NC: McGrath, 1978.

Melton, J. Gordon, and Robert L. Moore. *The Cult Experience: Responding to the New Religious Pluralism.* New York: Pilgrim Press, 1982.

Modern, John Lardas. *Secularism in Antebellum America: With Reference to Ghosts, Protestant Subcultures, Machines, and Their Metaphors; Featuring Discussion of Mass Media, Moby-Dick, Spirituality, Phrenology, Anthropology, Sing Sing State Penitentiary, and Sex with the New Motive Power.* Chicago: University of Chicago Press, 2011.

Moore, R. Laurence. *Religious Outsiders and the Making of Americans.* New York: Oxford University Press, 1986.

Morgan, Letisha Yvonne. "Representing Blackness: MOVE, the Media, and the City of Philadelphia." PhD diss., University of Warwick, 2004.

Moyn, Samuel. *The Last Utopia: Human Rights in History.* Cambridge, MA: Belknap Press of Harvard University Press, 2010.

Nongbri, Brent. *Before Religion: A History of a Modern Concept.* New Haven, CT: Yale University Press, 2012.

O'Reilly, Kenneth. *Racial Matters: The FBI's Secret File on Black America, 1960–1972.* New York: Free Press, 1991.

Orsi, Robert A. *Between Heaven and Earth: The Religious Worlds People Make and the Scholars Who Study Them.* Princeton, NJ: Princeton University Press, 2005.

Orsi, Robert A. *History and Presence.* Cambridge, MA: Belknap Press of Harvard University Press, 2016.

Orsi, Robert, ed. *Gods of the City: Religion and the American Urban Landscape.* Bloomington: Indiana University Press, 1999.

Oxx, Katie. *The Nativist Movement in America: Religious Conflict in the 19th Century.* New York; London: Routledge, 2013.

Pérez, Elizabeth. *Religion in the Kitchen: Cooking, Talking, and the Making of Black Atlantic Traditions.* New York: New York University Press, 2016.

Porterfield, Amanda. *Healing in the History of Christianity.* New York: Oxford University Press, 2005.

Primiano, Leonard Norman. "When 'God in a Body' Lived in Philadelphia." In *Religion in Philadelphia*, edited by Elizabeth Hayes Alvarez, 247–253. Philadelphia: Temple University Press, 2016.

Rey, Terry. *The Priest and the Prophetess: Abbé Ouvière, Romaine Rivière, and the Revolutionary Atlantic World.* New York: Oxford University Press, 2017.

Rey, Terry, and Ariella Werden-Greenfield. "African Spirits in the Holy Experiment: Philadelphia's Botanicas and the Odunde Festival." In *Religion in Philadelphia*, edited by Elizabeth Hayes Alvarez, 271–278. Philadelphia: Temple University Press, 2016.

Richardson, James T. "Social Control of New Religions: From "Brainwashing" Claims to Child Sex Abuse Accusations." In *Children in New Religions*, edited by Susan J. Palmer and Charlotte E. Hardman. New Brunswick, NJ: Rutgers University Press, 1999.

Rossinow, Doug. *The Politics of Authenticity: Liberalism, Christianity, and the New Left in America.* New York: Columbia University Press, 1998.

Roy, Ralph Lord. *Apostles of Discord: A Study of Organized Bigotry and Disruption on the Fringes of Protestantism.* Boston: The Beacon Press, 1953.

Savage, Barbara Dianne. *Your Spirit Walks Beside Us: The Politics of Black Religion.* Cambridge, MA: Belknap Press of Harvard University Press, 2008.

Scherer, Matthew. *Beyond Church and State: Democracy, Secularism, and Conversion.* New York: Cambridge University Press, 2013.

Schmidt, Leigh Eric. *Restless Souls: The Making of American Spirituality from Emerson to Oprah.* New York: HarperCollins, 2005.

Schmidt, Leigh Eric. *Hearing Things: Religion, Illusions, and the American Enlightenment.* Cambridge, MA: Harvard University Press, 2000.

Sehat, David. *The Myth of American Religious Freedom.* New York: Oxford University Press, 2011.

Smith, Jonathan Z. *Relating Religion: Essays in the Study of Religion.* Chicago: University of Chicago Press, 2004.

Sorett, Josef. *Spirit in the Dark: A Religious History of Racial Aesthetics.* New York: Oxford University Press, 2016.

Streiker, Lowell D. *Mind-Bending: Brainwashing, Cults, and Deprogramming in the '80s.* Garden City, NY: Doubleday, 1984.

Sullivan, Winnifred Fallers. *The Impossibility of Religious Freedom.* Princeton, NJ: Princeton University Press, 2005.

Sullivan, Winnifred Fallers. *Prison Religion: Faith-Based Reform and the Constitution.* Princeton, NJ: Princeton University Press, 2009.

Sullivan, Winnifred Fallers, and Lori G. Beaman, eds. *Varieties of Religious Establishment.* Farnham, UK: Ashgate, 2013.

Tabor, James D., and Eugene V. Gallagher. *Why Waco?: Cults and the Battle for Religious Freedom in America.* Berkeley: University of California Press, 1995.

Taylor, Charles. *A Secular Age.* Cambridge, MA: Belknap Press of Harvard University Press, 2007.

Taylor, Clarence. *Black Religious Intellectuals: The Fight for Equality from Jim Crow to the Twenty-first Century.* New York: Routledge, 2002.

Thompson, Heather Ann. *Blood in the Water: The Attica Prison Uprising of 1971 and Its Legacy.* New York: Pantheon, 2016.

Tolnay, Stewart E., and E. M. Beck. *A Festival of Violence: An Analysis of Southern Lynchings, 1882–1930.* Urbana-Champagne: University of Illinois Press, 1995.

Truillot, Michel-Rolph. *Silencing the Past: Power and the Production of History.* Boston: Beacon Press, 1995.

Tweed, Thomas A. *Crossing and Dwelling: A Theory of Religion.* Cambridge, MA: Harvard University Press, 2006.

Ulett, Mark A. "Making the Case for Orthogenesis: The Popularization of Definitively Directed Evolution, 1890–1926." *Studies in History and Philosophy of Biological and Biomedical Sciences* 45 (2014): 124–132.

Wagner, Peter. *Progress: A Reconstruction.* Cambridge, UK: Polity Press, 2016.

Wagner-Pacifici, Robin. *Discourse and Destruction: The City of Philadelphia versus MOVE.* Chicago: University of Chicago Press, 1994.

Washington, Father Paul M., with David McInnes Gracie. *"Other Sheep I Have": The Autobiography of Father Paul M. Washington.* Philadelphia: Temple University Press, 1994.

Washington, Linn. "MOVE: A Double Standard of Justice?" *Yale Journal of Law and Liberation* 1 (1989): 67–82.

Watt, David Harrington. *Antifundamentalism in Modern America.* Ithaca, NY: Cornell University Press, 2017.

Watts, Jill. *God, Harlem U.S.A.: The Father Divine Story.* Berkeley: University of California Press, 1992.

Weiner, Isaac. *Religion Out Loud: Religious Sound, Public Space, and American Pluralism.* New York: New York University Press, 2013.

Weisenfeld, Judith. *New World A-Coming: Black Religion and Racial Identity during the Great Migration.* New York: New York University Press, 2017.

Wenger, Tisa. *Religious Freedom: The Contested History of an American Ideal.* Chapel Hill: University of North Carolina Press, 2017.

Wenger, Tisa. *We Have a Religion: The 1920s Pueblo Indian Dance Controversy and American Religious Freedom.* Chapel Hill: University of North Carolina Press, 2009.

Wideman, John Edgar. *Philadelphia Fire.* New York: Vintage Books, 1991.

Williams, Jakobi. *From the Bullet to the Ballot: The Illinois Chapter of the Black Panther Party and Racial Coalition Politics in Chicago.* Chapel Hill: University of North Carolina Press, 2013.

Wilmore, Gayraud S. *Black Religion and Black Radicalism.* Garden City, NY: Anchor Press/Doubleday, 1973.

Yawney, Carole D. "Only Visitors Here: Representing Rastafari into the 21st Century." In *Religion, Diaspora, and Cultural Identity: A Reader in the Anglophone Caribbean*, edited by John W. Pullis. Amsterdam: Gordon and Breach, 1999.

Index

For the benefit of digital users, indexed terms that span two pages (e.g., 52–53) may, on occasion, appear on only one of those pages.

abortion, 53
Abu-Jamal, Mumia
   1981 incident of, 185, 259–60
   arrest and trial of, 186–89
   call for release of, 257–58
   claims of MOVE's brainwashing of, 188–89
   on MOVE's hunger strike, 71
   religious faith of, 185–86
ACLU (American Civil Liberties Union), 77–78, 105, 135
Adams, Arlin, 160–71
Africa, Alberta, 79, 137–38, 141–42, 191, 205
Africa, Alphonso. *See* Africa, Mo; Leaphart, Alphonso
Africa, Beowolf, 131–32, 134
Africa, Birdie
   experience in MOVE Bombing, 1–4, 11, 215–21
   MOVE Commission testimony by, 210–11, 239–40
   nightmares of, 1, 215, 216, 228–29
   See also Ward, Michael
Africa, Carlos, 108–9, 136, 141–42, 182–84, 193–94
Africa, Chuckie
   arrests of, 73–74, 95
   charges of Ramp's murder against, 116, 178–79
   incarceration of, 258
   introduction to MOVE, 27–28, 31–32
   police brutality against, 84–85
   prison melee of, 182–84
   See also Sims, Charles "Chuckie"
Africa, Conrad
   arrests of, 73–74, 101, 141–42
   courtroom tactics of, 81–82
   death of, 11, 223
   experience in MOVE Bombing, 1–2, 3–4, 201–2, 216–21
   FBI surveillance of, 131
   fight with neighbor by, 213–14
   incarceration of, 82–83, 111–12, 182
   M-1 demands by, 191–92
   police brutality against, 80–81, 84–85
   prison hunger strike of, 74–75, 76–77
   work of, 137–38
Africa, Consuella, 74–75, 76–77, 131, 223
Africa, Debbie
   arrests of, 79–80
   charges of Ramp's murder against, 116, 178–79
   incarceration of, 82–83, 163–65, 182–83
   introduction to MOVE, 27–28, 31–32
   parole of, 258
   See also Sims, Debbie
Africa, Delbert
   on armed self-defense policy, 106–7
   arrests of, 72–74
   in "Black Guard," 131–32
   charges of Ramp's murder against, 116
   conversion to MOVE of, 24, 27–28, 31
   Courtney's boarding homes and, 38–40
   in defense of John Africa, 145–46, 193–94
   DNC convention and, 24–26
   incarceration of, 79–80, 258
   as Minister of Confrontation, 94–95
   police brutality against, 84–85, 117, 139–40
   prison hunger strike of, 74–75, 76–77
   prison melee of, 182–84
   at school board demonstrations, 70–71
   speaking to the Quakers by, 46–47
   See also Orr, Delbert
Africa, Delisha, 1–2, 11, 223

Africa, Dennis
  arrests of, 138, 141–42, 191
  introduction to MOVE, 27–28
  prison melee of, 182–84
  See also Sims, Dennis
Africa, Donald
  arrest of, 72–73, 80, 81
  incarceration of, 82–83
  on MOVE's global activities, 94
  purchase of firearms by, 94–95
  role as MOVE supporter, 27–28, 71–72
  See also Glassey, Donald; Grossman, Donald
Africa, Eddie
  charges of Ramp's murder against, 116
  in defense of John Africa, 145–46
  incarceration of, 258
  prison hunger strike of, 74–75, 76–77
  prison melee of, 182–84
  trial of, 73–74
Africa, Fox, 74–75, 76–77, 181
Africa, Frank
  arrests of, 78, 156–57
  assaults by, 193, 194, 210–11
  burial of, 255–57
  death of, 2–3, 11, 223
  in defense of John Africa, 145
  early life and MOVE teachings of, 27–28, 154–55, 156–57
  experience in MOVE Bombing, 201–2, 216–21
  Frank Africa v. Commonwealth of Pennsylvania, 9, 153–54, 163–71, 246
  incarceration of, 157–58
  M-1 demands by, 191–92
  testimony on threat by, 239–40
Africa, Gail
  arranged marriage and, 194
  arrests of, 79–80, 135
  incarceration of, 163–65, 182–83
  introduction to MOVE, 27–28
  prison hunger strike of, 74–75
  at Reno Street house, 179
  warrants for, 178–79
  See also Sims, Gail
Africa, Greg, 84–85
Africa, Hampton, 131–32

Africa, Ishongo, 104, 192–93
Africa, Israel, 32–33
Africa, Janet
  charges of Ramp's murder against, 116
  incarceration of, 163–65, 182–83
  introduction to MOVE, 30–31
  parole of, 258
  See also Hollaway, Janet
Africa, Janine
  charges of Ramp's murder against, 116
  death of children and, 84–85, 89, 258
  in defense of John Africa, 145
  incarceration of, 163–65, 182–83
  parole of, 258
Africa, Jeanette Knighton, 107, 139–40, 178, 179, 189
Africa, Jerry
  arrest of, 73–74, 141–42
  in defense of MOVE, 216
  incarceration of, 82–83, 111–12, 169
  introduction to MOVE, 27–28
  M-1 demands by, 191–92
  police brutality against, 84–85
  prison hunger strike of, 74–75, 76–77, 78
  probation sentences of, 79–80
  in Rochester branch, 133, 137–38
Africa, John
  arrest of, 141–42
  birth of Israel Africa and, 32–33
  burial of, 255–57
  on children's nightmares, 1, 215
  courtroom strategy of, 82–84
  death of, 2, 11, 218, 223, 236, 255
  decomposed body of, 255
  on Delbert's conversion, 24
  descriptions of, 37, 138
  Dick Gregory and, 24–26
  early life as Vincent Leaphart, 4, 15–22
  experience in MOVE Bombing, 2, 216–18
  Fuller and, 61–62
  origin of name of, 54
  United States v. Vincent Leaphart and Alphonso Robbins, 141–48, 175
  wife and child of, 79, 191, 205
  See also The Guidelines of John Africa (Africa); MOVE

INDEX

Africa, Laverne
  incarceration of, 82–83
  as MOVE person, 27–28, 178–79
  prison hunger strike of, 74–75
  See also Leaphart, Laverne; Sims, Laverne
Africa, Lee Sing, 32–33, 181. *See also* Penn, Sharon
Africa, Life
  death of, 4, 84–85, 89
  neighborhood introduction of, 91–92
  presentation of the body of, 93–94
Africa, Melisa, 201–2
Africa, Merle
  charges of Ramp's murder against, 116
  FBI surveillance of, 131
  incarceration of, 79–80, 82–83, 163–65, 182–83, 258
Africa, Michael, Sr.
  charges of Ramp's murder against, 116
  incarceration of, 169
  introduction to MOVE, 31–32
  parole of, 258
  prison melee of, 182–84
Africa, Michael Jones, 178
Africa, Mo, 133, 137–38, 141–42, 144–47, 191–92. *See also* Robbins, Alphonso
Africa, Muriel, 27–28, 155
Africa, Netta. *See* Africa, Zanetta
Africa, Phil, Jr.
  death of, 11, 223, 258
  experience in MOVE Bombing, 1–2, 3–4, 201–2, 215–21
Africa, Phil, Sr.
  arrest and trial of, 112–13, 142–43
  charges of Ramp's murder against, 116
  incarceration of, 258
  Life Africa's death and, 89
  police brutality against, 84–85
Africa, Ramona
  arrests of, 178, 246
  Commonwealth of Pennsylvania v. Ramona Johnson, 246–49
  in defense of Frank Africa, 158, 246
  experience in MOVE Bombing, 2, 3–4, 11, 201–2, 216–21
  health of, 257–58
  incarceration of, 249
  M-1 demands by, 191–92
  as MOVE person, 179, 257–58
  Ramona Africa v. City of Philadelphia, et al., 249–50
  understanding of her body, 52. *See also* Johnson, Ramona
Africa, Raymond
  arrest of, 79–80, 141–42
  death of, 11, 223, 251
  experience in MOVE Bombing, 2–3, 216–21
Africa, Rhonda
  arrests of, 78–80, 135
  death of, 11, 202, 223
  experience in MOVE Bombing, 1, 3, 201–2, 216–21
Africa, Robert
  arrests of, 101
  on education, 69
  incarceration of, 111–12
  on MOVE's theology, 77
  presentation of Life Africa's body by, 92–94
  on wife's incarceration, 75–76
Africa, Sam, 73–74, 141–42
Africa, Sharon, 27–28, 136, 179. *See also* Sims, Sharon
Africa, Steve, 79–80
Africa, Sue
  arrest and trial of, 100, 112–13, 141–42
  on burial of Life Africa, 89
  in defense of MOVE, 184
  FBI surveillance of, 131
  incarceration of, 163–65, 182–83
  prison hunger strike of, 74–77
  in Rochester, 136
  on sacrificial violence, 205
Africa, Ted, 70–71, 76–77, 82–83
Africa, Theresa
  arrests of, 178
  death of, 223
  experience in MOVE Bombing, 3, 201–2, 216–21
  on pending police raid, 216
  on prison hunger strike, 163–64

Africa, Tomaso
  birth of, 79–80
  death of, 11, 223
  experience in MOVE Bombing, 1–2, 3, 201–2, 215–20
  in Rochester, 136
Africa, Tree
  death of, 11, 223
  experience of MOVE Bombing, 1–2, 3–4, 201–2, 215–20
  night screaming of, 209–10
Africa, Valerie, 79–80, 136
Africa, Zanetta, 1–2, 11, 201–2, 223
African American Islam. See Nation of Islam
Afro-Protestantism, 18
agentive assent, 203–4, 205–6
Ahmed, Fareed, 213
alcohol, 51
Alfonso Leaphart, Administrator of the Estate of Vincent Leaphart v. City of Philadelphia, et al., 249–50
American Friends Service Committee (AFSC)
  in defense of MOVE, 90
  on neighborhood blockade, 98, 105–8
  Philadelphia Perspectives Project by, 223–26
  Police Abuse Project by, 105, 138–39
  See also Quakers
American Indian Movement, 64–65
American progress. See progress
Americans United for Separation of Church and State, 160–61
American Veterinary Medical Association, 67
The Anarchist Cookbook, 143
animals, MOVE's theology on, 66–67, 96, 112–13. See also dogs
anti-cult movement, 190. See also cults
armed self-defense, MOVE's policy on, 90, 94–95, 106–7, 181. See also nonviolence, MOVE's philosophy on
Armstrong, Robert, 206
Asad, Talal, 7–8
asceticism, 21–22, 29, 179–80, 181
Association of Black Journalists (ABJ), 71, 185

ATF. See US Bureau of Alcohol, Tobacco, and Firearms (ATF)
Attica Prison Uprising (1971), 244–45
Austin, Merle, 27–28. See also Africa, Merle
Austin, Muriel, 27–28. See also Africa, Muriel
Aytch, Louise, 76

Baltimore Afro-American, 133–34
Baptist Church, 17–18
Beaman, Anthony, 143
Berghaier, James, 220–21, 227
Berrigan, Daniel, 160
Birmingham church bombing (1963), 237–38, 244–45
birth control, 53
Black, Hugo, 161–62
Black Church, 17–18, 40
Black Guard (MOVE), 131–32, 143
Black Guard (RAM), 129
Black Panthers, 22–23, 24, 40–41, 105–6, 154–55
Black religions, history of persecution against, 124–26, 148
Black Unity Council, 183
Blackwell, Lucien, 81–82, 92
Blavatsky, Helena, 44
blockades against MOVE
  (1977) observation blockade, 98–99
  starvation blockade, 9, 90, 99–100, 102–3
blood draws, 163–64
Blyden, Edward, 186
bomb plot, charges of, 141–48
Bonhoeffer, Dietrich, 40–41
Bowser, Charles, 237
Bronson, Audrey, 237
Brooks, Leo
  grand jury's review of, 245
  involvement in MOVE Bombing, 206, 209, 218–19
  MOVE Commission testimony by, 238–39, 240–41
  resignation of, 226–27
Brown, William, III, 202, 237, 245–46
Buddhism, 44–45
Bunting, John, 139–40
burial practices, 255–57

C-4 explosives
  PPD's use of in MOVE Bombing, 217, 219, 227–28, 242, 243, 248–49, 251
  supposed acquisition by MOVE of, 143–44, 147–48
Candomblé, 18
Carter, Cassandra, 239–40, 247
Carter, Jimmy, 98–99, 106–7
car wash operation, 50, 137
Castille, Ronald, 249
Catholic Church, 103, 111, 257
Catholic Social Services for the Archdiocese of Philadelphia, 237
CAU. *See* Civil Affairs Unit (CAU)
Chavez, Cesar, 65
Chicago Police Department, 22, 125–26
Chicago Tribune, 221–22
Chicano movement, 65
childbirth, 29, 145–46
children
  charges of abduction of, 178–79, 181
  charges of abuse and neglect of, 134–35, 136, 178–79, 209–11
  custody seizure orders of, 212–13
  diet of, 133–34, 209–10
  examples of state violence against, 127, 243–44
  in foster care, 136
  human rights violations and, 108
  MOVE's theology on childrearing, 52–53
  MOVE's theology on sacredness of, 49–50, 69, 204–5, 210
  police gunfire against, 219–21, 223, 242, 250–51
  religious choice and, 202–4, 205–6, 223–24, 226
  runaway attempt by, 210–11
  starvation blockade and, 102–3, 107–8, 110
Chinn, Julia, 237
Chobert, Robert, 188
Chomsky, Noam, 98–99
Christian existentialism, 40–41
Christianity, 185–86
Christian Science, 41–42
circuses, 66–67

Citywide Black Coalition for Human Rights (CWBCHR), 105, 106, 109. *See also* Washington, Paul
Civil Affairs Unit (CAU)
  classification of MOVE by, 242–43
  court testimony of members of, 248
  establishment of, 126–27
  FBI coordination of, 129, 139, 243
  Fencl's strategy with, 128
  Glassey as informant of, 130
  M-1 threat and, 191–92
  MOVE Commission testimonies of, 239
  Police Abuse Project against, 105, 139
  See also FBI (Federal Bureau of Investigation)
Clark, Dorothy, 21, 255–57
Clark, Harvey, 216
Clark, Joseph, 63–64
Clark, Mark, 22
Cobbs Creek, Philadelphia, 179
COINTELPRO, 125–26. *See also* FBI (Federal Bureau of Investigation)
Coleman, Joseph, 92
commemorative marker of the MOVE Bombing, 235–36, 251–52
Commonwealth of Pennsylvania v. Africa, 80–84
Commonwealth of Pennsylvania v. Ramona Johnson, 246–49
Concerned Citizens to Insure Justice, 107
conscientious objection, 162
consent. *See* agentive assent
Continental Congress bicentennial celebration (1974), 57–58, 72–73
conversions of first MOVE people, 27–28
  of Delbert Africa, 23–24
  of Janet Africa, 30–31
  of John Africa, 16
Cooke, M. Todd, 237
Cornelsen, Rufus, 103–4, 105, 108–9
Courtney, Edward, 38–40
Coxe, Spencer, 77–78, 105
Cross, Larry, 155–56
Crumpler, Tony, 213
Cullen, Edward, 237

cults
  anti-cult movement, 190
  as category, 9–10, 177–78, 195
  child abuse charges and, 210–11
  classification of MOVE as, 175–77, 188–90, 194, 195, 196, 247
  See also religion

Davis, Adele, 123
Davis, Andrew Jackson, 60–61
Davis, Angela, 154–55
Davis, Michael, 31–32. *See also* Africa, Michael, Sr.
death, MOVE's theology on, 205, 255–57
Democratic National Convention (1968), 15–16
Democratic National Convention (1972), 24–26
Devlin, Charles, 103–5, 108–9, 110–12, 114–16
DiBona, Fred, 103–4, 107–8, 110, 112–13, 115, 135
diet, 133–34
  lectures on, 29
  Lee Sing on, 32–33
  MOVE's theology on, 50, 159–60, 168–69
  in prison, 9, 153–54, 159
divorce
  MOVE's theology on, 53
  of Vincent Leaphart, 4, 15, 21, 255–56
  See also marriage
dogs
  exercise of, 50
  experience in MOVE Bombing, 216–17, 255
  The Guidelines on, 66
  in MOVE family, 28–29, 50
  SPCA's involvement with, 102, 111–13
  training of service, 258
domestic violence, 21
drug use policy, 51, 186
Dynamics of Faith (Tillich), 165–66

East Powelton Concerned Residents, 130
Eddy, Mary Baker, 41–42, 60–61
Eden narrative, 40–41, 54

education
  of Frank Africa, 153, 154–55, 180–81
  legal cases involving, 160–61
  of Michael Ward, 228–29
  MOVE's school board demonstrations on, 70–71, 72
  MOVE's theology on, 69, 133–34, 209–10
  of Vincent Leaphart, 15, 19
Ellsberg, Daniel, 64
Episcopal Church of the Advocate, 95–96
Episcopal Diocese of Pennsylvania, 76, 90, 110–11
evil, *The Guidelines* on, 38
explosives. *See* C-4 explosives; Tovex explosives

family, MOVE's theology on, 52–54
Farmer, Clarence, 76
Father Divine, 18
Fattah, Falakah, 105–9
Faulkner, Daniel, 185, 259–60
FBI (Federal Bureau of Investigation)
  on Black Panthers, 22
  case on MOVE by, 130–33
  CAU coordination with, 129, 139, 243
  COINTELPRO, 125–26
  coordination in MOVE Bombing, 9, 219
  mission of, 124
  on Philadelphia Field Office's MOVE investigation, 131, 132–33
  response to MOVE Commission by, 238
  See also Civil Affairs Unit (CAU)
The FBI and Religion, 124
Fencl, George
  CAU establishment of, 126–27, 128
  in *Commonwealth of Pennsylvania v. Africa* trial, 81–82
  on FBI's MOVE investigation, 132–33
  on MOVE raid, 114
  Seed of Wisdom and, 135
  See also Civil Affairs Unit (CAU)
Fifty Ninth Street Baptist Church, 17–18
First Amendment, religious clause, 160–71
Fonda, Jane, 64

Ford, Gerald (president), 57, 160
Ford, Jerry (MOVE person), 27–28
Founding Church of Scientology v. United States, 165–66
Frank Africa v. Commonwealth of Pennsylvania, 9, 153–54, 163–71, 246
Frankford Quakers, 45–48
Fraternal Order of Police (FOP), 71, 238
free will, 202–4, 205–6
Friendly Presence (organization), 105–6
Fuller, Buckminster, 60–64
funerary rituals, 255–57. *See also* death, MOVE's theology on

gang violence, 31
Garvey, Marcus, 186
Gaskins, Oscar, 112–13
Geertz, Clifford, 47–48
Geist, Charles, 117
Georgia, 16–17
Gibbons, Thomas, 126
Girard College, 154
Glassey, Donald, 129–30, 140–41, 142–44. *See also* Africa, Donald; Grossman, Donald
God
  John Africa as, 176–77, 255
  John Africa on, 42–44
Goode, Wilson
  bombing orders by, 219
  court testimony of, 248
  grand jury's review of, 245
  MOVE Commission testimony by, 238–39, 240–41
  on MOVE eviction, 214–15, 218
  planning of MOVE raid by, 206
  public support of, 227
  report of MOVE Bombing by, 221
  on sacrificial violence, 213
Gracie, David, 76
Grant, Barbara, 216
Graterford Prison, 158, 163–65
Gray, Freddie, 235–36
Great Depression, 17–18
Great Migration, 16–17, 18
Green, Clifford Scott, 142
Gregory, Dick, 24–26, 123

Grossman, Donald
  as college professor using *The Guidelines,* 27–28
  on MOVE's underground support, 94
  school board demonstration by, 72
  See also Africa, Donald; Glassey, Donald
The Guidelines of John Africa (Africa)
  on animals, 66–67
  Democratic National Convention and, 24–25
  FBI's copy of, 131
  Grossman's college course on, 27
  hip-hop group and, 258–59
  on illness and addiction, 41–42
  on Jesus as God, 42–44
  on living in harmony, 42–43, 50
  on the origin of the System, 40–41
  on profanity, 68–69
  on progress, 58–60, 63–64
  on religious embodiment, 48–50
  on supernaturalism, 43–44, 46–47
  on the System, 38–39
  on time, 62–63
  writing of, 37–38
  See also Africa, John; MOVE
Guns on the Porch standoff (1977)
  arrests and charges due to, 101, 141–42, 157, 158
  CAU testimony on, 239
  FBI surveillance due to, 133
  as response to death of Life Africa, 90
  Washington and, 106

Hampton, Fred, 22, 125–26, 244–45
Hayden, Tom, 64
Hegel, Georg Wilhelm Friedrich, 38, 54
hip-hop music, 258–59
Hogan, John, 206
Hollaway, Janet, 30–31. *See also* Africa, Janet
Holmesburg Prison, 157–58, 182–84
Homer, Irv, 216
homosexuality, 53, 65–66
Hoover, J. Edgar, 22, 125. *See also* FBI (Federal Bureau of Investigation)
horse-racing, 67

Howard, Gregory, 142–43, 144, 147–48
Howard, Kareem, 179–80
Howard, Larry, 138–39, 179, 183–84
Hughes, John, 106, 112
humanism, 43–44
human rights
   AFSC on violation of, 98
   Philadelphia's religious community on violation of, 90–91
   political use of concept, 98–99
hunger strikes
   (1975), 74–77, 78
   (1981), 163–65
hygiene, 51, 52, 184–85

"illegitimate violence," 10. *See also* state violence, overview
illness and addiction, 41–42. *See also* alcohol; drug use policy
International Druidic Society (IDS), 45
International Women's Day celebration (1974), 65–66
Islam, 125. *See also* Nation of Islam

Jackson, Anthony, 186–89
Jackson, Jesse, 257
James, Frank, 27–28, 154–57. *See also* Africa, Frank
James, Louise Leaphart
   beating of, 193
   on child abuse and neglect, 209–11
   childrearing of Frank by, 154–57
   early life and family of, 17, 19
   FBI surveillance of, 131
   introduction to *The Guidelines*, 27–28
   on John Africa's control and brainwashing, 194, 195
   on law, 73
   Louise James, Administratrix of the Estate of Frank James v. City of Philadelphia et al, 249–50
   MOVE Commission testimony by, 239–40
   as MOVE person, 27–28, 180
   on nonviolent demonstrations, 69
   "On the MOVE" column by, 91–92, 94, 180
   testimony on Frank's threat to, 239–40
   See also Africa, Louise

Jamison, Judith, 77–78
Jeffers, Joseph, 21, 21n.13
Jesus of Nazareth, 42–43
Jim Jones, 175
John Africa vs. The System. *See United States v. Vincent Leaphart and Alphonso Robbins*
Johnson, Lyndon, 15–16. *See also* Vietnam War
Johnson, Ramona, 158
   Commonwealth of Pennsylvania v. Ramona Johnson, 246–49
   See also Africa, Ramona
Johnson, Sylvester A., 125
Jon, I. Abdul, 139–40
Jones, Veronica, 187–88
Jubilee School children, 235–36, 251–52
Judaism, 185–86

Kanegis, Richard, 189–90
Kauffman, Bruce, 237, 242
Kelly, Clarence, 131
Kennedy, Robert, 15–16
Kierkegaard, Søren, 40–41
King, Martin Luther, Jr., 15–16, 24–25, 154, 186
Kingdom of Yahweh, 21
Kirk, Herbert, 206, 207, 212
Knighton, Jeanette. *See* Africa, Jeanette Knighton
Koch, Ed, 226–27
Korean War, 19–21
Kubacki, Stanley L., 117
Ku Klux Klan, 16–17, 237–38, 244–45

Laird, James, 47
law, MOVE's theology on, 73–74
Law of Equal Distribution, 64–65
Leaphart, Alphonso, 211–12, 249–50. *See also* Africa, Mo
Leaphart, Dennis, 19–20
Leaphart, Fonnie, 15–16, 17, 19–20
Leaphart, Frederick, Jr., 17, 18–19
Leaphart, Frederick, Sr., 16–17, 18–19
Leaphart, Laverne, 27–28, 155, 156–57. *See also* Africa, Laverne; Sims, Laverne
Leaphart, Lennie, 16–17, 18–19
Leaphart, Lillian, 17

Leaphart, Louise. *See* James, Louise Leaphart
Leaphart, Marv, 19–20
Leaphart, Muriel, 155. *See also* Africa, Muriel
Leaphart, Vincent, 4, 15–22, 236
   United States v. Vincent Leaphart and Alphonso Robbins, 141–48, 175
   See also Africa, John
Leaphart, Wayne, 19–20
"legitimate violence." *See* state violence, overview
Let It Burn (Boyette), 250–51
Let Our Children Go! (Patrick), 190
A Letter Concerning Toleration (Locke), 203–4
Let the Fire Burn (film), 250–51
Lillie, Charisse, 237
Lloyd, Vincent W., 73
Locke, John, 203–4
Lombardo, Timothy, 127–28
Louise James, Administratrix of the Estate of Frank James v. City of Philadelphia et al., 249–50
Lubitz, Ken, 38–39
lynchings, 16–17, 244–45
Lyons, Edmund, 140
Lyton, William, 237–38, 243–44

M-1 (MOVE Underground), 191–92, 193–94
MacArthur, Douglas, 20
MacDonald, H. Graham, 237–38
Madison, James, 161–62
Maharishi Mahesh Yogi, 45, 160–61. *See also Malnak v. Yogi*
Malcolm X, 186
Malmed, Edwin, 116–17, 184–85
Malnak v. Yogi, 160–61, 162–63, 165, 171
Marandola, Dominic, 247–48
marijuana, 51, 129–30, 186
marriage, 52–53. *See also* divorce; family, MOVE's theology on
Marvin (chimpanzee), 67–68
Marx, Karl, 22, 24, 38, 54
Mather, Barbara, 206
McDermott, James, 100–1, 184
McGill, Joseph, 246, 247, 248
McGovern, George, 24–25

McNulty, William, 146
Means, Russell, 64–65
meditation, 45, 160–61
Mike Douglas Show, 67–68
military service, 19–20, 31–32
Mitchell, John, 160
mixed-race families, 53–54
Mondale, Walter, 64
Moore, Cecil B., 154, 156
Moorish Science Temple, 125
Mount Sinai Holy Church of America, 18
MOVE
   overview of religious system, 5–11, 48, 54, 95, 166–67, 259–60
   on animals, 66–67, 96, 112–13
   armed self-defense policy of, 90, 94–95, 106–7, 181
   asceticism of, 21–22, 29, 179–80, 181
   (1984) attempted police raid of, 206–7, 209
   car wash operation of, 50, 137
   charges of bomb plot against, 141–48
   charges of child abuse and neglect by, 134–35, 136, 178–79, 209–11
   child custody orders against, 212–13
   on childrearing, 52–53
   Clark Park homes of, 259
   classification as a criminal operation, 242–43
   classification as a cult, 175–77, 188–90, 194, 195, 196, 247
   on Continental Congress, 57–58, 72–73
   current organization of, 257–59
   on death of John Africa, 236, 255–57
   dialogue with Fuller, 61–64
   on diet, 50, 133–34, 159–60, 168–69
   on drug use, 51, 186
   early religious conversions to, 16, 23–24, 27–28, 30–31
   on education, 69, 133–34, 209–10
   emergence of, 4
   on family, 52–54
   on gender, 65–66
   Glassey's claims against, 142–44
   hunger strikes by, 74–77, 163–65
   inter-religious dialogue of, 7, 43–48
   legal determination of religious categorization of, 9, 153–54, 163–71
   (1976) melee of, 84–85, 91–92

MOVE (*cont.*)
   as name, 33, 123–24
   on natural law, 73–74
   nonviolent demonstrations of (*see* MOVE nonviolent demonstrations)
   nonviolent policy of, 108, 130–31, 181
   (1977) observation blockade of, 98–99
   "On the MOVE" newspaper column, 91–92, 94, 180
   Osage Ave home of, 176–77, 213–15
   as panentheism, 43, 166
   Powelton house of, 28–29
   on profanity, 68–69, 74, 80–81, 83–84
   on progress, 58–66, 69
   "Proposal for Funding of the MOVE Organization," 136–37
   (1978) raid of, 113–15
   on religious embodiment, 48–52
   Richmond Seed of Wisdom branch, 133–36
   Rochester branch of, 113, 133, 136–38, 141–42
   on sacredness of children, 49–50, 69, 204–5, 210
   (1978) starvation blockade of, 9, 90, 99–100
   surveillance of, 123
   on understanding death, 205, 255–57
   use of "Africa" in names, 54
   on work, 50
   See also *The Guidelines of John Africa* (Africa); religion; *specific names of members*
MOVE 9. See *names of specific persons*
MOVE Bombing (May 13, 1985)
   1996 trial on, 249–50
   AFSC's Philadelphia Perspectives Project on, 223–26
   commemorative marker for, 235–36, 251–52
   Commonwealth v. Johnson on, 246–49
   description of events, 1–4, 11, 216–21, 251
   differing conclusions of, 226–28, 241
   grand jury's report on responsibility in, 245–46
   media reports on, 221–23
   MOVE's defensive preparations for, 207–8, 213–14, 215–16
   official statements on, 221, 222
   planning operations of, 206–8, 212–13, 243, 248
   publications on, 5
   summary of loss of life during, 223
   See also MOVE
MOVE Commission
   establishment of, 236–38
   interviews of, 202–3, 238–41
   on MOVE as cult, 196
   obstacles of, 238
   report and conclusions by, 4–5, 241–44
   See also MOVE Bombing (May 13, 1985)
MOVE nonviolent demonstrations
   against 1974 Continental Congress, 57–58, 72–73
   city injunction against, 71, 72–73, 74
   FBI surveillance at, 131
   against juvenile sentences, 72–73
   on May 20, 1977, 95–98
   against mistreatment of animals, 67–68
   gainst MOVE person's eviction, 78, 156–57
   prison hunger strike, 78
   prison hunger strikes, 74–77, 78, 163–65
   at school board meetings, 70–71, 72
   See also MOVE; nonviolence, MOVE's philosophy on
MOVE Underground (M-1), 191–92. See also MOVE
Moyn, Samuel, 98–99
Mulvihill, Terrence, 117
Muncy Prison, 163–65, 182–83

A Nation Devoted to Religious Liberty (Adams), 160
Nation of Islam, 18, 125, 185–86, 257
Native Americans, 64–65
natural law, 73–74
New York branch of MOVE. See Rochester MOVE branch
New York City School Board, 70, 71
New York Times, 20, 176, 185, 221–23, 238–39
Nix, Robert, 92, 107–8
Nixon, Richard, 24–25, 57–58, 129–30, 142, 160
nonviolence, MOVE's philosophy on, 108, 130–31, 181. *See also* armed self-defense, MOVE's policy on; MOVE nonviolent demonstrations

North Korea, 20–21

observation blockade against MOVE (1977), 98–99
Ogilby, Lyman, 110–11
O'Neill, Jerome, 72–73, 96–97, 139–40
Orr, Delbert, 22–24. *See also* Africa, Delbert
Orsi, Robert, 195
orthogenesis, 19, 19n.8

panentheism, 43, 166
pantheism, 43, 166
Pawelec, Edmund, 256–57
peace, 63–64
Peace Mission Movement, 18
Penn, Sharon
  arrest of, 135
  introduction to MOVE, 32
  prison hunger strike of, 74–75, 76–77
  on religious persecution, 135
  renouncement of MOVE by, 135, 181
  See also Africa, Lee Sing
Pennsylvania Historical and Museum Commission, 235–36
Pennsylvania State Police, 9, 191–92, 214, 219, 252. *See also* Philadelphia Police Department
Pentecostal Church, 18
Perez, Elva and Pedro, 108–9
Pernsley, Irene, 212–13
Personal Freedom Association, 190
Philadelphia Daily News, 77, 102–3, 257
Philadelphia Inquirer, 60, 78–79, 95–96, 138–39, 214–15, 240
Philadelphia Perspectives Project (AFSC), 223–26
Philadelphia Police Abuse Project (AFSC), 105, 139–40
Philadelphia Police Department
  1984 attempted MOVE raid by, 206–7, 209
  AFSC's Police Abuse Project on, 105, 139–40
  CAU establishment in, 126–27
  federal charges against, 140
  media reports on abuse and brutality by, 95–96, 138–39
  public support of, 95–96
  response to MOVE Commission by, 238
  use of explosives by, 217, 219, 227–28, 242, 243, 248–49, 251
  See also MOVE Bombing (May 13, 1985); Pennsylvania State Police; state violence, overview
Philadelphia Revolutionary Action Movement (RAM), 129
Philadelphia School Board demonstrations, 70–71
Philadelphia Special Investigation Commission. *See* MOVE Commission
Philadelphia Tribune, 39–40, 180, 189–90
police brutality
  AFSC's Police Abuse Project on, 105, 139–40
  against Conrad Africa, 79–81
  against Delbert Africa, 84–85, 117, 139–40
  in March 1976 melee, 84–85, 91–92
  media reports on, 95–96, 138–39
  against Rhonda Africa, 78–79
  by Rizzo, 127
  See also Philadelphia Police Department; state violence, overview
posse comitatus, 243–44
Powell, Frank, 206–7, 218–19, 248–49
Powelton Emergency Human Rights Coalition (PEHRC), 98–100
Powelton Village, Philadelphia, 28–29, 98–99
Principle of Caring, 52–53
Principle of Sharing, 52–53
prison hunger strikes, 74–77, 163–65
profanity, 68–69, 74, 80–81, 83–84
progress, 57–66, 69
"Proposal for Funding of the MOVE Organization," 136–37

Quakers
  MOVE's inter-religious dialogue with, 7, 45–47
  response to MOVE blockade, 105–9
  See also American Friends Service Committee (AFSC)

race, John Africa on, 53–54
RAM (Revolutionary Action Movement), 129

Ramona Africa v. City of Philadelphia, et al., 249–50
Ramp, James, 4, 90, 114–16, 259–60
Rastafarianism, 186
red squads, 22, 125–26
religion
   Adams on legal definition of, 160–63, 165–71
   assumption of agentive assent and, 202–4, 205–6
   burial practices and classification of MOVE as, 255–57
   categorization of, 7–8, 10–11, 123–24, 260
   children and choice in, 202–4, 205–6, 223–24, 226
   cults and, 195
   Devlin on MOVE and, 115–16, 117–18
   during Great Migration, 17–18
   MOVE's interreligious dialogue, 43–48
   summary of MOVE as a, 5–11, 48, 54, 95, 166–67, 259–60
   Washington on behavior and, 97, 117–18
   See also cults
religion in prison. *See Frank Africa v. Commonwealth of Pennsylvania*; prison hunger strikes
religious conversions. *See* conversions of first MOVE people
religious diet. *See* diet; prison hunger strikes
religious liberty *vs.* human rights, 90–91, 104–6, 108–9
religious persecution
   history of Black religions of, 124–26, 148
   Laverne Sims on, 5–6, 259
   MOVE people's interpretation of, 71, 74, 77–79, 106–7
   MOVE support by Philadelphia's religious community and, 90–91, 104–6, 108–9
   prison hunger strike on, 74–77
   Sharon Africa on, 135
   Sue Africa on, 100–1
   See also religion

Rendell, Ed, 99–100, 206, 215
Reynolds v. United States, 167–68
Richardson, James T., 210–11
Richmond, William
   1996 legal case against, 249–50
   grand jury's review of, 245
   involvement in MOVE Bombing, 113–14, 219
   MOVE Commission testimony by, 238–39, 240–41
   report on MOVE Bombing by, 222
   retirement of, 226–27
Richmond MOVE branch (Seed of Wisdom), 133–36
Rizzo, Frank
   on accusations of corruption and police brutality, 139–40
   description of and brutality by, 127–28
   Fencl and CAU collaboration with, 126–27
   food and water offer by, 110
   MOVE's plea for apology from, 106–7
   PEHRC and, 99
   public support of, 95–96
   starvation blockade by, 9, 102–3
Robbins, Alphonso
   United States v. Vincent Leaphart and Alphonso Robbins, 141–48
   See also Africa, Mo
Roberts, Samuel, 83
Robinson, Ida B., 18
Rochester MOVE branch, 136–38
   establishment of, 133
   John Africa residing at, 113
   raid and mass arrest of, 141–42
Roman Catholicism, 18
Rucker, Ursula, 251–52
Rush, Bobby, 22
Ruth, Henry, 237

Sabo, Albert, 186–89
sacred text. See *The Guidelines of John Africa* (Africa)
sacrificial violence, 205, 212, 213, 225–26
Sambor, Gregor
   grand jury's review of, 245
   involvement in MOVE Bombing, 1, 206, 216–17, 218–19

lawsuits against, 140, 249–50
MOVE Commission testimony by, 238–39, 240–41
resignation of, 226–27
Sanchez, Sonia, 251–52
Sanders, Sam, 142–43, 144, 147–48
Santería, 18
school board demonstrations, 70–71, 72
Science of Creative Intelligence, 45, 160–61
Seed of Wisdom. *See* Richmond MOVE branch (Seed of Wisdom)
Seeger, David Andrew, 162
sex, 53
Shabazz, Ali, 105
Shanahan, James, 206
Shanahan, Neil, 237–38
Shrager, David, 202–3, 205–6, 245–46
Siegel, Bernard, 101
Sims, Charles "Chuckie," 27–28, 31–32. *See also* Africa, Chuckie
Sims, Debbie, 27–28, 31–32. *See also* Africa, Debbie
Sims, Dennis, 27–28, 31–32. *See also* Africa, Dennis
Sims, Gail, 27–28, 194. *See also* Africa, Gail
Sims, Laverne
  on child abuse and neglect, 209–10
  introduction to *The Guidelines,* 27–28
  MOVE Commission testimony by, 239–40
  as MOVE person, 31
  on MOVE's religious persecution, 5–6
  See also Africa, Laverne; Leaphart, Laverne
Sims, Sharon, 27–28, 31–32, 194. *See also* Africa, Sharon
Singley, Carl, 237–38
Sixteenth Street Baptist Church bombing (Birmingham, 1963), 237–38, 244–45
Smith, Joseph, 60–61
Smith, William "Whit," 143–44
smoking, 51
Snapping (Conway and Siegelman), 190, 190n.38
Society for the Prevention of Cruelty to Animals (SPCA), 102, 111–13

Society of Friends. *See* Quakers
South Korea, 20–21
starvation blockade (1978), 9, 99–100, 102–3, 107–12
state violence, overview, 10, 235–36, 243–45. *See also* MOVE Bombing (May 13, 1985); Philadelphia Police Department; police brutality
Stevens, John Paul, 160
Stiles, Michael, 246
Student Nonviolent Coordinating Committee (SNCC), 40–41, 129
Students for a Democratic Society, 40–41
supernaturalism, 43–44
surveillance. *See* Civil Affairs Unit (CAU); FBI (Federal Bureau of Investigation); US Bureau of Alcohol, Tobacco, and Firearms (ATF)
Symbionese Liberation Army, 243–44
the System, *The Guidelines* on, 38–39, 40–41

Theosophical Society, 44
Thomas, Davita, 78
Thompson, Delores, 194
Thornburgh, Dick, 191–92
Tillich, Paul, 40–41, 165–66
time, 62–63
Time (publication), 222–23, 227, 238–39
Torasco v. Watkins, 161–62
Tovex explosives, 217, 219, 222, 243, 248–49, 251
Transcendental Meditation, 45, 160–61
Truman, Harry, 20–21
Tucker, Kevin, 206
Tulsa "Race Riot" (1921), 243–44
Turner, Carl, 131–32
Turner, John, 45
Turner, Nat, 243–44
Tylor, E. B., 19n.8

United Farm Workers, 65–66
United States Commission on Civil Rights, 139–40
United States v. Seeger, 162, 166–67
United States v. Vincent Leaphart and Alphonso Robbins, 141–48, 175

US Bureau of Alcohol, Tobacco, and
    Firearms (ATF)
  M-1 threat and, 191–92
  response to MOVE Commission by, 238
  surveillance and raid by, 9, 140–44
US Constitution. *See* First Amendment,
    religious clause
US Secret Service, 9, 191–92, 206, 215

Vietnam War
  conscientious objection to, 162
  service members in, 19–20, 22, 31–32
  Tet Offensive, 15–16
violence. *See* MOVE Bombing (May 13,
    1985); police brutality; sacrificial
    violence; state violence, overview
Vodoun, 18

Wagner, Peter, 58, 62–63
Ward, Andino, 201, 228–29
Ward, Michael
  on childhood in MOVE, 210–11
  on MOVE Bombing, 201–3
  post-bombing life of, 228–29
  See also Africa, Birdie
Washington, Christine, 96
Washington, Paul
  conflict intervention by, 95–98
  in defense of MOVE, 90, 105, 106, 249
  on MOVE Commission, 237
  on prison hunger strike, 76
  religious authority of, 108–9, 112,
    117–18
  on starvation blockade, 108–9, 110–11
  See also Citywide Black Coalition for
    Human Rights (CWBCHR)
Washington Post, 238–39
Wasyluk, Walt, 147, 191–92
Weisenfeld, Judith, 18
Welch, Neil, 237
Welsh v. United States, 162
White, Cynthia, 187–88
Williams, Gregory, 223–24
Williams, John H., 17–18
Williams, Milton, 247
Williams, Novella, 216
Wisconsin v. Yoder, 167
women's movement, 65–66
work, MOVE's theology on, 50
World War II, 19–20
wrongful convictions, 138–39

YMCA, 40–41
Yost, Charles Woodruff, 63–64
Young, Andrew, 100–1

Zagame, Joseph, 117
zoos, 66–67